THE **PENGUIN RAY** LIBRARY

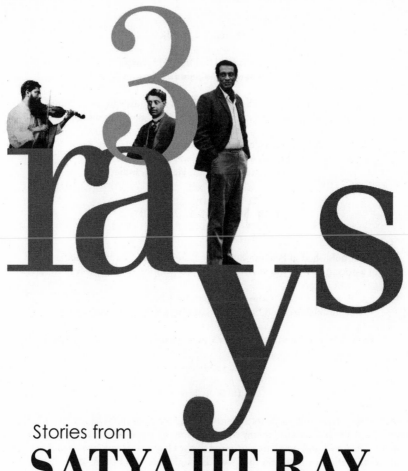

3 rays

Stories from
SATYAJIT RAY

Edited by Sandip Ray

Co-edited by Riddhi Goswami
Layout and design by Pinaki De

THE **PENGUIN RAY** LIBRARY

PENGUIN BOOKS

An imprint of Penguin Random House

PENGUIN BOOKS

USA | Canada | UK | Ireland | Australia
New Zealand | India | South Africa | China

Penguin Books is part of the Penguin Random House group of companies
whose addresses can be found at global.penguinrandomhouse.com

Published by Penguin Random House India Pvt. Ltd
4th Floor, Capital Tower 1, MG Road,
Gurugram 122 002, Haryana, India

First published in Penguin Books by Penguin Random House India 2021
In association with the Society for the Preservation of Satyajit Ray Archives

Copyright © Sandip Ray 2021
'Upendrakishore' and 'Sukumar' copyright © Indrani Majumdar 2021

Vector illustration of Satyajit Ray's portrait on half-title page by Pinaki De

ISBN 9780143448983

Typeset in Minion Pro
Printed at Thomson Press India Ltd, New Delhi

www.penguin.co.in

CONTENTS

SATYAJIT TRANSLATES SATYAJIT

SATYAJIT'S ORIGINAL STORIES IN ENGLISH

FOREWORD

My earliest memories of my grandfather's (Sukumar Ray) nonsense rhymes and great-grandfather's (Upendrakishore Ray Chowdhury) folk tales go back to my childhood days—even before I started reading—listening to them from my grandmother every day before she put me to sleep. Later on I became aware of their other contributions in printing, typography, songs and illustrations—primarily through the children's magazine *Sandesh* founded by Upendrakishore in 1913 and later edited by Sukumar and then my father, Satyajit Ray. While Upendrakishore was a gifted illustrator and painter, Sukumar illustrated his inimitable nonsense rhymes with his unique sense of imagination. Baba, too, started his writing career in *Sandesh*, when he revived the magazine in 1961 after a long gap. Soon he became an extremely popular writer for young people, writing detective fiction, science fantasy and other stories bordering on supernatural. Baba took up translation of Sukumar's and Upendrakishore's literary works in his leisure time; usually in between shooting of films. It stemmed mainly from his desire to present them to a wider readership. Both Sukumar and Upendrakishore—although being immensely popular in Bengali literature—have not been translated much, and hence practically were little known outside Bengal. It is an interesting fact to note that Baba started translating Sukumar's nonsense rhymes quite unexpectedly, while waiting at an airport lounge due to a long flight delay. Then there were occasional requests from English

periodicals for stories and that is how Heshoram Hoshiar and the folk tales by Upendrakishore got translated. During the post-recovery period from his heart ailment, Baba turned to translation once again because he was stuck for original story ideas, and thus there was a phase where he translated quite a few of his own stories at one stretch.

The present volume is a compilation of some of Sukumar's and Upendrakishore's writings translated by Satyajit Ray, along with translations of his own stories. It brings together the diverse literary creations by the three Rays—ranging from simple, innocent folk tales to quirky humour of nonsense rhymes, culminating in the modern world of crime, fantasy and macabre. It also includes Baba's only two original English stories written during his art apprenticeship days in Shantiniketan in the early forties. During the filming of *Goopy Gyne Bagha Byne* from his grandfather's story, Baba made a film version of the story as a prequel to the actual scenario. This previously unpublished piece has been unearthed from his film notebooks along with his sketches and doodles. A few unpublished translations of his own stories have also been recently discovered.

I am grateful to Penguin Random House India for their unstinted support in this endeavour. I especially want to thank Premanka Goswami, executive editor, Penguin Random House India, for his vision to conceptualize 'The Penguin Ray Library' and his belief in our project in these trying times.

I sincerely hope that the readers—particularly the present generation non-aficionados of these literary geniuses—will enjoy these timeless classics and go on to discover their original body of work. This book is a rare compilation of three generations of cultural heritage; Satyajit Ray paying homage to his father's and grandfather's literary legacy and telling his own stories as well—a fitting tribute on his birth centenary.

1/1 BISHOP LEFROY ROAD   **SANDIP RAY**
KOLKATA
2021

Portrait of Upendrakishore drawn by Satyajit Ray.
The longhand calligraphy—'Upendrakishore Ray Chowdhury' by Ray has been taken from his notebook.

SATYAJIT *translates*
UPENDRAKISHORE

Ray's illustration of his ancestral house at 100 Garpar Road, Kolkata (*Jokhon Choto Chilam*, Ananda Publishers, 1982)

UPENDRAKISHORE

The original Bengali essay, written and read by Satyajit Ray at Mahabodhi Society Hall, Kolkata, during the centenary celebration of Upendrakishore, was first published in *Prabandha*, Puja Annual, 1963. It was translated into English by Indrani Majumdar. The illustrations in the essay are by Satyajit Ray, originally drawn for the book *Upendrakishore* by Leela Majumder (New Script, 1963). The endpiece illustration is a decorative woodblock bought by Satyajit Ray from Banaras.

I have no personal memory of Upendrakishore; and it's not possible to have any because he passed away six years before my birth.

The house which he had built on 100 Garpar Road and the same house where he died was also the house where I was born. My childhood was spent in this house and quite a bit of my growing up years were occupied in one particular portion of the building, within which was housed the U. Ray & Sons printing press.

What work was being done in that press, how it was being done, how exactly this press was different from the other such presses—I still wasn't old enough to

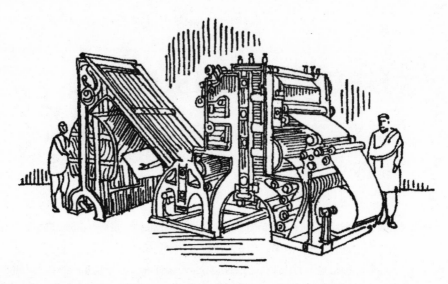

understand such logistics. Six years after this business had folded up I left Garpar and went to live in Bhawanipore in a completely different milieu. The only link with U. Ray & Sons that remained was through a few books written by him, a few bound volumes of *Sandesh*, some of his own drawings and the prints of his paintings.

As I had not had the fortune to meet Upendrakishore and know him personally, perhaps that was why I tried to discover him through his writings and drawings time and again. This quest for discovery is still on. Thanks to the revival of the *Sandesh* magazine in the recent past, I have had the opportunity to go through the writings and paintings

published during his association with *Sandesh*, once again in detail. While studying his works repeatedly I realized that in the way Upendrakishore had captured the spirit of juvenile literature, he remains matchless even today. And the persona that appears through these paintings and writings, is that of a calm yet vivacious, level-headed and dynamic person who is indeed a rare personality.

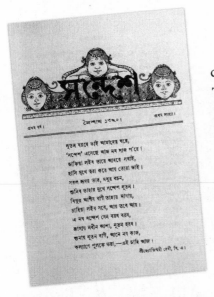

If one judges, it can be easily said that in the world of children's literature there's none to equal Upendrakishore. The essence of literature along with his charming language that's found in *Tuntunir Boi* (The Tailorbird Book), *Chheleder Mahabharat* (Mahabharata for Young Boys), *Chhotoder Ramayan* (Ramayana for Children) or in the numerous articles, poems, or stories which have appeared in *Sandesh*, despite belonging to a genre of literature meant for all, without doubt, every child can enjoy the true spirit of these writings. In Bengal there's a significant body of children's writings whose true spirit can perhaps be appreciated only by the adult reader. This holds true in the case of children's works by writers like Rabindranath, Abanindranath, and even in case of writings by Sukumar Ray and Lila Majumdar. The flavour which you discover reading *Ha-ja-ba-ra-la* (A Topsy-Turvy Tale) or *Buro-Angla* (The Big Adventures of a Little Hero) is certainly not the same flavour you enjoy when you read *Tuntunir Boi*. To appreciate *Tuntunir Boi* at a mature age you need to awaken the child hidden in your heart.

The magic of Upendrakishore's writings is the ease with which it stimulates and rouses the innocence of a child's mind. For how many writers of children's literature can you say the same?

The two most amazing qualities of Upendrakishore as an artist are his multifacetedness—his versatility, and a successful synthesis of eastern and western art in his talent. He has chiefly produced two kinds of art. One was his favourite oil paintings, the majority of which were landscapes and the other were his illustrations. There is no doubt that his real expertise lay in the oil paintings. I've personally seen many of these—the Sal forest of Giridih, the Usri River, the hills of Darjeeling, or the sea of Puri. The most noticeable feature of these drawings is that the nature's unique beauty, disposition or mood seemed to have left an indelible impression on him—and that was the quality of profound serenity. This tranquil moment touches on a note of mystical ecstasy in his

personality. The technique used in these paintings doesn't reveal any garish manipulation nor is there any overtone of colours. It almost seems as if the artist's message is—'Here my role is non-existent; it is nature that is omnipresent. Nature is beautiful, nature is serene; hence my picture is beautiful and serene, too.' The presence of this element of devout worship comes out as the most distinguished element in all his paintings.

Both content and method mark his oil paintings, but the exact opposite is observed in his illustrations. The poets of East and West spoke of harmony—this comes out alive in all his illustrations. Even if his technique leaned towards the West, the illustrations he used for the Indian stories, did not bear the evidence of western or mixed in influences. And being a scientist himself, even while dismissing anatomy he did not adopt the so-called Oriental style of over imposed embellishments in his drawings. Yet, within this boundary of naturalism, he produced a marvellous range of styles. On the one hand there was the influence of the English academic art, the Japanese woodcut, Rajput and

Mughal miniatures, even the use of Bengal folk elements and on the other, the use of extraordinary power of personal observation—in all what Upendrakishore created was discernible a style that was essentially his own. With the result, every time one came across his work one never mistook it as someone else's. In the first three volumes of his *Sandesh*, during the last phase of his output, and in the illustrations done for the book *Hindustani Upokotha* (Folk Tales of Hindustan) compiled by Sita Devi and Shanta Devi, one sees the finest examples of his creativity.

The indispensable relationship which the form and the language share is something that is beautifully reflected in Upendrakishore's writings. Those who have missed out on reading his articles and essays on science written for children would never get to know how such a difficult subject can be addressed with such lucidity.

This simplicity perhaps highlights all of Upendrakishore's creative activities. Only

after putting in serious efforts, imagination, thoughts, thorough research and intense hard work, can one arrive at this level of effortlessness. Those who are real artists have the capacity to unravel the mysteries of all creative acts. While living in Calcutta, improving on the concept of half-tone block printing, or writing such an exemplary children's book

such as *Tuntunir Boi*, or composing a song like *Jago Purobasi / Bhagavata Prem Piyasi* (*Awake citizens / those who desire the love of God*), it was Upendrakishore who alone was capable of producing such an amazing range of work all by himself.

MAJANTALI SARKAR

First published in the book *Tuntunir Boi* (U. Ray & Sons, 1910)—a collection of East Bengal (now Bangladesh) folk tales retold by Upendrakishore. Some of the ideas were previously published in articles written by Upendrakishore in the magazines *Mukul* and *Sakha* as 'Biraler Jaat' (January 1899) and 'Biral' (February 1889), respectively. The English translation by Satyajit Ray was published in *Target* (March 1984). The illustrations in the story are by Upendrakishore Ray Chowdhury. The endpiece illustration is a decorative woodblock bought by Satyajit Ray from Banaras.

In a village there lived two cats. One lived in the milkman's cottage. He had cream and butter and cheese to eat. The other lived in the fisherman's cottage. All he ever got was kicks and blows on his head. The milkman's cat was fat and went about with his head held high. The fisherman's cat was nothing but skin and bones. He stumbled when he walked and wondered how he could ever become as fat as the milkman's cat.

One day the fisherman's cat said to the milkman's cat, 'Brother, you must come and dine with me tonight.'

He was only pretending, of course. How could he ask anyone to dinner when he had nothing to eat himself? But he asked him all the same because he thought: 'If that fat cat comes to our place and is beaten and killed, then I can go and take his place in milkman's cottage.' It worked out just as he had thought. As soon as the milkman's cat came to the fisherman's place, the fisherman shouted. 'There! It's that pampered butterfed cat from the milkman come after our fish!'

He gave the cat such a thrashing that the poor creature finally died. The lean cat knew this would happen, so he lost no time in making his way to the milkman's. There he stuffed himself with cream and cheese and butter and soon grew fat. He stopped talking to the other cats, and if anybody asked him who he was, he would draw himself up and say, 'My name is Majantali Sarkar.'

One day Majantali took a pen and a notebook and went for a walk. Strolling in the forest, he came upon three tiger cubs romping about in a clearing. He gave three whoops at them and said, 'Ho there—pay up your taxes!' The tiger cubs got very scared at his shouting, and at the sight of pen and paper. They ran up to their mother and said, 'Mummy, come and look, somebody's here and is trying to tell us something.'

The tigress came out and saw Majantali. 'Who are you, my boy?' she asked. 'Where are you from? What do you want?'

Majantali said, 'I'm the king's manager. My name is Majantali Sarkar. You live in the king's country. What about taxes? Come on, pay up!'

The tigress said, 'We don't even know what taxes are. We only live in the forest and eat what comes our way. Why don't you wait a while; my husband will be back soon.'

So Majantali sat down below a tall tree and peered around. Soon he spotted the tiger coming.

He quickly put his notebook down and clambered up to the topmost branch of the tree.

When the tiger came home, the tigress told him everything. This greatly annoyed him. He gave a nasty growl and said. 'Where's that little devil? I'll catch him and twist his neck.'

Majantali shouted down from the top of the tree. 'Ho there, Tiger-boy. What about your taxes? Come on out and pay up!'

At this the tiger roared and gnashed his teeth and in mighty leaps was up on a high branch of the tree. But he was still nowhere within reach of Majantali. Being small and light, the cat could sit on the thin top branches, while the tiger couldn't climb beyond the stout branches lower down. When the tiger found he couldn't reach the cat, he became wild with rage, gave a leap, lost his footing, and slipped. Plummeting down, his head got caught between two branches, and in no time, he was dead of a broken neck.

When Majantali saw what had happened, he climbed down and drew three scratches on the dead tiger's nose with his claws. Then he called the tigress and said. 'Look what I've done to him for being so haughty.'

This scared the life out of the tigress. She trembled and said, 'Please, Mr Majantali, sir, I beg you to spare our lives. We'll be your slaves for as long as we live.'

'All right,' said Majantali, 'I'll spare you. But you must work hard and do your chores and feed me well.'

So Majantali lived in the tiger's den as a guest. He stuffed himself with the best food and rode around on the backs of the cubs. The cubs always lived in fear of him, and thought he must be somebody very big and strong.

One day the tigress folded her palms and said to Majantali. 'Mr Majantali, sir, the animals in this forest are so small they seldom make a square meal for you. There's a big forest across the river with big animals in it. Why don't we all go and settle there?'

Majantali said. 'Very well, let's go to the other forest.'

Now it took the tigers no time to swim across the river; but what about Majantali? Ma Tiger and the cubs looked all around for him, and at last spotted him in the middle of the river, flapping his arms about and gasping for breath.

Majantali had been swept away by the strong current, and had nearly lost his life fighting the waves. He could see that a few more waves like that and he would be a dead cat. Just in time one of the tiger cubs swam up and dragged him off to the shore, saving him from certain death.

But Majantali had no wish to admit that he had been in trouble. As soon as he scrambled to his feet on the shore, he rolled his eyes and cursed and made a gesture as if to slap the tiger cub. 'You stupid fool,' he shouted, 'now look what you've done! You dragged me out of the water before I'd finished my wonderful calculations. I was working out how much water there was in the river, and how many waves and how many fish, and you had to come like an idiot and spoil everything. Well, His Majesty will surely get to know about this, and then you'll see what happens.'

The tigress bowed her head in shame and said, 'Mr Majantali, sir, please forgive him this time. It's only because he never went to school that he made such a foolish blunder.'

'All right,' said Majantali, looking around for a patch of sunlight in which to dry himself. 'I forgive him this time. But I warn you—this must never happen again.' Sunlight seldom reached the ground in those thick forests. To find it one had to go to the top of a tree.

Majantali climbed up a very tall tree. When he looked around from his high perch, he spotted a dead buffalo king in the middle of a clearing. He quickly climbed down, ran up to the dead beast and drew some scratches on it with his claws. Then he strode up to the tigress and said, 'I've just killed a buffalo. Run along and fetch it.'

The tigress and the cubs went straight off to look, and sure enough, there was the big buffalo lying dead. The four of them puffed and panted while they dragged the dead beast home. 'How strong Mr Majantali is!' they all thought.

One day they said to the cat, 'Mr Majantali, sir, there are big rhinos and elephants in the forest. Let's go and hunt them some time.'

'Very good,' said Majantali. 'Rhinos and elephants are what we should be hunting. Let's go today.'

So, they all set out to hunt the rhinos and the elephants. On the way the tigress said to Majantali, 'Mr Majantali, sir, which would you rather be—a Pouncer or a Bouncer?'

Now, a pouncer is one who waits for the prey to appear, and then pounces on it; while a bouncer is one who bounces around the prey and drives to a clearing where it can be killed by the pouncer. Majantali thought: 'I don't think I could ever get a big animal to budge by my bouncing.' So, he said. 'Of course, I could be a bouncer and drive all the big game your way, but I doubt if you'd be able to kill them. So, I'd rather you did the bouncing and I did the pouncing.'

So, the tigress and her three cubs went off into the forest and started to chase the animals with a lot of shouting and jumping about. When Majantali heard the roar of all those animals, he went and sat cowering under a tree and shivered. Soon a porcupine came scampering his way. Majantali screamed at the sight and hid behind a thick root. Just then an elephant came lumbering up. One of its feet landed on the root and all but squashed the life out of poor Majantali.

After bouncing about for a long time, the tigers thought, 'Mr Majantali must have killed a lot of animals by now. Let's go and find out.' When they found Majantali in the state he was in, they shook their heads and said, 'Alas! How did such a thing ever happen, Mr Majantali?'

Majantali said, 'It's very simple. It's all those animals you sent scurrying my way. When I saw how small they were, I split my sides laughing.' With these words, Majantali breathed his last.

THE TOONY BIRD

First published in the book *Tuntunir Boi* (U. Ray & Sons, 1910) as *Tuntuni aar Rajar Katha*. The English translation by Satyajit Ray was published in *Target* (April 1984). The illustrations in the story are by Upendrakishore Ray Chowdhury. The endpiece illustration is a decorative woodblock bought by Satyajit Ray from Banaras.

The Toony-bird's nest was in a corner of the king's garden. One day, some coins from the king's treasury had been put out in the garden for an airing. When they were taken back in the evening, one of them got left behind by mistake.

Toony found the shiny coin, took it up in her beak and put it in her nest. 'How rich I've become!' she thought. 'I've got the same thing in my nest as the king has got in his treasure chest.' The thought ran in her mind, and she sang:

> What the king has in his chest
> Toony too has in her nest.

When the king heard the song, he said, 'What does the bird mean by that?'

The men of the court folded their palms and said, 'Your Majesty, the Toony-bird says she's got something in her nest which makes her as rich as Your Majesty.'

This amused the king very much. He said, 'Go and find out what she's got.'

So they found out and came back to say, 'Your Majesty, there's a silver coin in the Toony-bird's nest.'

'But that must be my silver,' said the king. 'Go and fetch it.'

The king's men went and brought the silver back. Sadly, the Toony-bird sang:

The king must be very needy
If my silver makes him greedy.

This made the king chuckle again. 'That's a cheeky bird, the Toony,' he said. 'Go and give her back the silver.'

Toony was happy to get her silver back. This time she sang:

The king is scared of me, I see,
To send my silver back to me.

The king asked his men, 'What is that bird saying now?'

'She says Your Majesty got scared,' they said, 'and that is why the silver was sent back to her.'

At this the king flew into a rage and said, 'Is that so? Well, catch that bird and bring her to me.'

Poor Toony was caught in no time and fetched. The king clutched the bird in his hand and went straight into the palace to his seven queens. 'Have the bird roasted nicely for my dinner,' he told them.

When the king left, the seven queens took a good look at the bird. One of them said, 'What a dainty little thing! Please let me hold it.' When she took it in her hand, another queen wanted to hold it too. While being passed from one queen to another, Toony suddenly managed to wriggle out and fly away.

'Oh, what a misfortune!' thought the queens. What were they to do now? If the king found out, there would be real trouble.

While they stood moping and worrying, a big toad went hopping by close to them. When the seven queens saw it, they all swooped down upon it and caught it. Then they whispered. 'Shush—no one must know about this. We'll have this toad roasted instead of the bird. The king will never know the difference.'

So, they skinned the toad and roasted it, and when the king ate it, he found it delicious.

Next day, just as the king was about to sit on the throne, thinking, 'I've taught that bumptious bird a good lesson,' Toony sang out—

Who's the winner? I'm the winner!
The king has had a toad for dinner.

When the king heard this, he fairly leapt out of the throne. Then he spat, and he choked, and he washed his mouth and gargled, and at the end of it all he punished his queens. 'Have their noses chopped off!' he ordered.

The order was obeyed and the seven queens all lost their noses. Toony came to know about this and sang—

When clever Toony so disposes
Seven queens lose seven noses.

The king heard this and said, 'Fetch that bird again, I'll swallow her alive. Let's see how she gets out of it this time.'

So poor Toony was caught and fetched.

'Bring me some water,' ordered the king.

When the water came, the king filled his mouth with it, tossed the bird in, and gulped.

Everyone said, 'That's the end of the wily bird.'

But in a little while the men of the court were startled by the sound of a mighty belch which came out of the king's throat. And with the belch, out came the Toony bird flapping her wings.

'There she goes! Grab her, grab her!' shouted the king, and the poor bird was caught again.

Once again, the king filled his mouth with water, while a sentry stood by with a bared sword to bring it down on the bird if she should come flying out again.

This time the king kept his hand pressed over his mouth after swallowing the bird.

Poor Toony wriggled and fluttered about in the king's stomach.

The king bore it for a while. Then, all of a sudden, he screwed up his face, made a noise like 'Wack!' and was sick. And once again Toony came out flapping her wings.

The men of the court set up a great hue and cry. 'Kill the bird, sentry! Kill the bird!' they shouted. 'Don't let her get away!'

The sentry, muddled by all the shouting, swung his sword wildly and, instead of hacking the bird in two, hacked off the king's nose.

The king let out a wild yell, and with him yelled all the courtiers. Then the doctor came and bandaged the king's nose and managed to bring him round. Toony saw all this and sang:

The king is in a sorry plight
He's lost his nose; it serves him right.

With this song, little Toony flew far and high away to another land.

NARAHARI DASS

First published in the magazine *Mukul* (July 1899). This was later revised and
expanded when published in *Tuntunir Boi* (U. Ray & Sons, 1910). The English translation
by Satyajit Ray was published in *Target* (May 1984). The illustrations in the story are
by Upendrakishore Ray Chowdhury. The endpiece illustration is a decorative woodblock
bought by Satyajit Ray from Banaras.

On the edge of a big forest which lay at the foot of a mountain there was a meadow. In that meadow there was a hole in which lived a baby goat. He was so small that he wasn't allowed to go out at all. If he wanted to, his mother would say, 'No, you mustn't go out. If you do, a bear might catch you, or a tiger snatch you, or a lion eat you up.' This scared the baby goat, and he stayed in without a murmur.

When the baby goat grew up a little, he became a bit bolder, so that when his mother was out, he would put his head out of the hole and peer around. At last, one day, he was bold enough to come out of the hole.

Nearby stood a big ox eating grass. The goat had never seen such a huge animal before. But when he saw the ox's horns he thought, 'He must be a goat grown big and strong because he eats good food.' He went up to the ox and said, 'Please, sir, tell me what you eat.'

The ox said, 'I eat grass.'

The goat said, 'My mother eats grass too. Why isn't she as big as you?'

The ox said, 'I eat more and better grass than your mother does.'

'Where do you get such grass?' asked the goat.

'Over there, in that forest,' said the ox.

'I wish you would take me there,' said the goat.

So, the ox took the young goat to the forest. The grass in the forest was indeed delicious, and the goat ate as much of it as he could. At the end of the meal his stomach was so full that he could barely move.

As dusk fell the ox said, 'Let's go home now.'

But the goat couldn't walk; how was he to go back? So, he said, 'You carry on. I'll go back tomorrow.'

The ox went away. The goat found a hole and crawled into it.

Now, that hole happened to be the home of a jackal. The jackal was out dining at Uncle Tiger's. He came back late in the evening and found that his hole had been taken over by a strange creature. Since the goat was black and it was dark inside the hole, the jackal couldn't see very clearly. He thought the creature must be some kind of a monster. So, his voice shook a little when he asked, 'Who's that in there?' The young goat was very clever. He said—

> My long beard
> Is by all feared
> I'm the lion's big brother,
> Narahari Dass.
> I dine on fifty tigers,
> While others eat grass.

When the jackal heard this, he gave a yell and bolted. He stopped running only when he reached Uncle Tiger's house.

The tiger was very surprised to see the jackal. 'Why, nephew,' he said, 'you left only a little while ago; what brings you back so soon? And why do you look so flustered?'

The jackal replied panting. 'Oh, Uncle, we're done for. There's a Narahari Dass in the hole where I live. He says he eats fifty tigers for dinner.'

The tiger got very angry at this. 'What cheek!' he said. 'Come along. We shall see how he eats fifty tigers.'

The jackal said, 'I'm not going back. If he was charging at us, you'll run away for sure. But I cannot run as fast as you, so I'll be the one to be gobbled up.'

The tiger said, 'Don't be silly. How can you ever think I'll leave you behind?'

'Then tie me to your tail,' said the jackal.

So, the tiger tied the jackal's tail to his own, and the jackal thought, 'Now Uncle Tiger can't run away without me.'

The two of them set out for the jackal's hole. The young goat spotted them from a distance and shouted—

> *You good-for-nothing,*
> *See what you've done,*
> *I paid for ten tigers*
> *And you've brought only one.*

At this the tiger's heart stopped beating. He thought the jackal must have led him there to be eaten up by Narahari Dass. So, he swung round and was off with a leap that took him ten yards. Then he broke into a run with the jackal still tied to his tail.

The poor jackal was up in the air one moment, and dashed to the ground the next. He got scratched all over from thorny bushes, and his head kept bumping against trees. And the more he

yelled, the more the tiger felt sure that Narahari Dass was about to catch up wit[h]
which made him run all the more.

Thus, they ran all through the night.

Next morning, the young goat found his way back home.

The jackal, of course, had learnt his lesson. He was so angry with the tiger that h[e]
never spoke to him again.

THE BENT OLD WOMAN

First published in the book *Tuntunir Boi* (U. Ray & Sons, 1910) as *Knujo Burir Katha*. The English translation by Satyajit Ray was published in *Target* (October 1985). The illustrations in the story are by Upendrakishore Ray Chowdhury. The endpiece illustration is a decorative woodblock bought by Satyajit Ray from Banaras.

There was once an old woman who was quite bent with age. She could only walk with the aid of a stick. When she walked, her legs wobbled, and with her legs, her head wobbled too. She had two pet dogs called Ronga and Bonga.

The old woman was about to go visiting her granddaughter. So, she called her two dogs and said, 'Stay at home and keep watch while I'm away.'

Ronga and Bonga said, 'Very well.'

Then the old woman set off, rapping her stick on the ground. While she walked, her legs wobbled, and with her legs her head wobbled too.

She had gone some way when a jackal saw her. 'There goes the old hag,' said the jackal. 'Old hag, I'm going to eat you up.'

The old woman said, 'Wait till I come back from my granddaughter's. She'll feed me well and I'll grow fat. I'm only skin-and-bones now.'

The jackal went away saying, 'All right, I'll come back and eat you when you're fat.'

The old woman wobbled on, and her head wobbled too.

When she had gone some way further, a tiger saw her and said, 'There goes that old hag. Old hag, I'm going to eat you up.'

The old woman said, 'I'm off to my granddaughter's to grow fat. Eat me when I come back. I'm only skin-and-bones now.'

'All right,' said the tiger. 'I'll wait till you come back fat.'

The old woman wobbled on, and her head wobbled too.

Further on, she met a bear. The bear said, 'Old hag, I'm going to eat you up.'

'I'm off to my granddaughter's to grow fat,' said the old woman. 'Eat me when I come back. I'm only skin-and-bones now.'

The bear said, 'Very well, I'll wait for you to grow fat.'

The bear went off.

Soon the old woman reached her granddaughter's place. There she grew so fat on curd and cream that if she had grown any fatter she would have burst like a balloon.

One day the old woman said to her granddaughter, 'It's time for me to go back home. But I'm so fat that I can't walk. I'll have to go back rolling like a ball. The trouble is—the jackal, the tiger and the bear are all waiting for me. They'll surely not spare me this time, so tell me what I should do.'

The granddaughter said, 'Don't worry. I'll put you inside an empty pumpkin and send you rolling. No one will know you're inside, so you'll reach home safe.'

So, the granddaughter put the old woman inside an empty pumpkin, gave her some rice and pickles to eat on the way, and set the pumpkin rolling with a big push.

The pumpkin rolled on, while the old woman sang:

Pumpkin, pumpkin, roll along,
Keep on rolling all the way,
Eat your pickles, sing your song—
Skin-and-bones is miles away.

The bear stood in the middle of the road, waiting to eat up the old woman. But there was no old woman to be seen. All he saw was a pumpkin come rolling down. He stopped the pumpkin, sniffed it, and felt it with his paws. Then he decided that it was neither the old woman nor anything worth eating. What's more, a voice from inside the pumpkin kept saying 'skin-and-bones is miles away', so he thought the old woman must have gone. Grunting, he gave the pumpkin a kick which sent it rolling again like a carriage on wheels.

The pumpkin rolled on, and the woman sang—

Pumpkin, pumpkin, roll along,
Keep on rolling all the way,
Eat your pickles, sing your song,
Skin-and-bones is miles away.

Now there was the tiger waiting to eat up the old woman. He saw something coming down, but it was not the old woman, only a rolling pumpkin. He stopped it and pawed it, and heard a voice from inside saying, 'skin-and-bones is miles away'. So, he thought the old woman must have gone. Growling, he gave the pumpkin a push which sent it rolling.

A little further on, in the middle of the road, sat the jackal. He took one look at the pumpkin and said, 'H'm . . . whoever heard of a singing pumpkin? I must find out what's inside the shell.' He gave the shell a hefty blow which split it open, and there was the old woman curled up inside. 'Well, old hag,' said the jackal, 'I'm going to eat you up now.'

The old woman said, 'Of course! That's what I'm here for. But won't you let me sing you a song first?'

The jackal said, 'That's not a bad idea. I'm something of a singer myself.'

The old woman said, 'Very well, then. Let's get on top of that mound and sing.'

So, they climbed the mound, and the old woman sang out: 'Come, Ronga, come, Bonga—come, come!'

And the two dogs came bounding from her house. One grabbed the jackal's neck and the other his waist. One pulled one way and the other pulled the other way. And they pulled and pulled and pulled till all the jackal's bones were broken and his tongue hung out and he was quite dead.

THE ANT, THE ELEPHANT AND THE BRAHMIN'S SERVANT

First published in the book *Tuntunir Boi* (U. Ray & Sons, 1910) as *Pipre, Hati Aar Bamuner Chakor*. The English translation by Satyajit Ray, hitherto unpublished, has been transcribed from Ray's literary notebook. The translation remains incomplete. The illustrations in the story are by Upendrakishore Ray Chowdhury. The endpiece illustration is a decorative woodblock bought by Satyajit Ray from Banaras.

Mr and Mrs Ant loved each other very much. One day Mrs Ant said to Mr Ant: 'If I should die before you, I'd like you to cast my body into the Holy river. Will you promise to do that, Mr Ant?'

Mr Ant said, 'Yes, Mrs Ant, I certainly will. And if I should die before you, you must promise to cast my body into the Holy river, won't you?'

Mrs Ant said, 'That goes without saying. I certainly will.'

Soon after this, Mrs Ant died. Mr Ant sat and wept for a long time. Then he thought: 'Now I must take Mrs Ant to the Holy river.'

So Mr Ant took the dead Mrs Ant on his back and set out. The Holy river was a long way away, and it took many days to reach it. Mr Ant walked the whole day with Mrs Ant on his back. When dusk fell, he found himself in a stable where the king's elephants were kept. As Mr Ant was very tired, he put Mrs Ant down on the ground thinking he would take a rest. A large elephant stood chained nearby. It happened to be the favourite of the king. It stood swinging its trunk, and with every breath that came out of its nostrils, Mr Ant found himself blown further and further away. This made Mr Ant so angry that he shouted, 'Hey there! Stop!' But the elephant heard nothing. Soon, another breath of air came out and blew Mr Ant even further away. This time Mr Ant grew even more angry. 'Ho there, I warn you!' he screamed. 'This is going to mean trouble for you!'

The elephant thought, 'That's funny! I'm sure I heard a thin voice shouting at me, but I don't see anyone around.' Then he raised his foot to stamp it down on the ground where he thought the voice had come from.

Mr Ant was in real trouble now. He thought, 'Dear me, I'm going to be crushed now.' But luckily this didn't happen. Just in time Mr Ant was able to drag himself and Mrs Ant down into a tiny pit on the ground below the elephant's foot.

Mr Ant was very happy now. He sat in the pit and started to eat into the elephant's flesh through the sole of his foot. He kept eating and eating and burrowing and burrowing while dragging Mrs Ant upwards with him. At last, one day, he reached right inside the elephant's brain.

Now, this caused the elephant to fall very sick. He started to shake his head and stamp about wildly. Everyone said, 'Poor dear, whatever is the matter with him?' Nobody could guess that there was a live ant lodged in his brain. If they could, they'd have rubbed some sugar on the sole of his foot, and the smell of it would have brought the ant climbing down the tunnel and out of it. But because they didn't know, they sent for the doctor, who gave the elephant some medicine. Soon after this, the elephant died.

The same night the king had a dream in which the elephant came up to him and said, 'Your Majesty, I've served you long and faithfully. Please have my body cast into the Holy river.'

Next morning, the king gave orders for the elephant's body to be taken to the Holy river. Thick ropes were tied to the dead elephant's legs, and three hundred strongmen set about hauling it to the Holy river. It being a huge animal, the task was not an easy one. The men grew tired, and every now and then they had to stop and take rest.

A Brahmin and his servant were passing by. When the servant saw the king's men sitting and panting, he said, 'An elephant no bigger than a mouse, and all those men have to sweat and fume to drag it. Why, I could have done it all by myself.'

The king's men heard the servant's boast and jumped up. 'Oh, is that so?' they said, 'You think you can do single-handed what even three hundred of us together can't do properly? Well, we must get this matter settled before we get on with our task. Let's take him to our king, and then we shall see how strong he is.'

The servant said, 'All right, let's go. You'll see I'm not an ordinary strongman.'

So they left the elephant on the road and went back to the king. 'Your Majesty,' they said, 'it's taking three hundred of us to haul that elephant, and this man comes along and says he can do it all by himself. We should like to have this matter settled before we go back to our task.'

The king called the servant up to him and said, 'Well, do you really think you can tug that elephant alone?'

The servant said, 'I can, if Your Majesty so wishes. But before I do it, I must have a good meal.'

The king ordered, 'Give this man a seer of rice and some cooked vegetables. Let him have a meal first, then he'll tackle the elephant.'

The servant burst out laughing. 'Your Majesty,' he said, 'it's only the sweepers who take a seer of rice. How can it do for one who must haul an elephant?'

'How much do you want?' asked the king.

'I'll be modest,' said the servant. 'Let me have a *maund* or two of rice, the meat of two whole goats, and a maund of curd.'

The king said, 'That's what you'll get. But you must finish off everything.'

'At your service, Your Majesty,' said the servant.

The Brahmin's servant finished off all the rice and meat and curd. Then he went and had a nap. On waking up, he took a piece of cloth and tied the elephant up into a bundle with it. Then he tied the bundle at the end of a stick, took the stick on his shoulder, put a dozen paans into his mouth, and set off humming towards the Holy river.

The king's mouth fell open at the sight, and so did the mouths of all his men, who ran about telling everybody what they had seen.

In the meantime, the servant had gone a long way towards the river. The sun was up high and shone fiercely. The servant had gone quite far when he suddenly stopped and said, 'How hot is the sun today! My throat is all dried up. I wish I could have a drink of water.'

Just then he spotted a pond nearby. Beside the pond, in the shade of a tree, stood a farmer's cottage. The servant put down his bundle by the pond and went up to the cottage. He found a little girl sitting there.

He said to the girl, 'I'm very thirsty. Please give me some water to drink.'

The girl said, 'There's only one jar of water in the house. If I gave it to you, there'd be nothing left for my father when he comes back from his farming.'

The servant got very angry at this. 'So you refuse to give water to a thirsty man?' he said. 'Well, I'll see where you get your drinking water from now on.'

The servant now went back to the pond, went down into the water and started to drink it up. In no time he had finished off all the water of the pond. While he drank, his stomach first grew as big as a drum, then it grew as big as an elephant, then at the end it was as big as a mountain.

The servant now found it very hard to hold the water in his stomach. So he quickly swallowed a banyan tree. The tree stuck in his throat and stopped the water from gushing out.

This pleased the servant very much, and he went off to sleep on the bank of the pond. His stomach rose higher than a coconut tree, and looked just like a mountain.

The little girl's father was working in the field. Then he saw the mountain-like stomach, he thought, 'My goodness, what on earth is that?' and came running back home.

As soon as he came into his cottage, his daughter said, 'Father, see how wicked that man is! He came and asked me for a drink of water. When I told him that there would be nothing left for you, he went and drank up all the water of our pond.'

The two had walked up to the servant sleeping by the pond. The little girl now wrinkled up her nose and said, 'What a horrid smell! Look, Father, he's got a rotten mouse or something wrapped up in that bundle.'

The farmer now gathered all his strength and gave a mighty kick in the servant's stomach. It was a kick the like of which one had never seen before. It brought the banyan tree shooting out of the servant's mouth, and all the water in his stomach gushing out in a great flood which swept away the farmer's cottage and all his belongings and his daughter as well. The only things left were the farmer himself and the Brahmin's servant. These two now hugged each other warmly. The farmer said, 'Brother, I've never met anyone mightier than you. To think that you could drink up all that water in the pond!'

'Brother,' said the Brahmin's servant, 'you are the mightiest of all. To think that with one kick you made me feel so much lighter!'

The two now started arguing, each saying the other was the mightier of the two. Who was to decide who was right?

After much arguing they decided to go to some marketplace and have a wrestling match. Whoever won would prove to be the mightier.

So they set out to look for a market place. On the way they met a fishwife who was on her way to the market with a basket of fish on her head. She said to them, 'Where are you off to, my lads?'

They said, 'To the market place, to have a wrestling match.'

The fishwife said, 'You'll never make it to the market place; it's too far away. Why don't you have your wrestling match in my fish basket! When the basket tips on one side, I'll know the loser is on that side.'

This made the two men very happy. 'Splendid!' they said, 'We can have our wrestling match, and we don't have to walk further.'

So they got into the fish basket and started to wrestle, while the fishwife walked on to the market place.

In that country there lived a monstrous kite who fed on cows, buffaloes, horses, elephants or any other animals that came his way. Only the fishwife he could never get the better of. Whenever he went for the fish in her basket, she gave him such a scolding that he didn't know what to do. Of course, this made him all the more angry, and he thought he must find a way to get at that basket.

The kite was out on a hunt now, and one could hear the swish of its great wings from far away.

A cowherd had taken his seven hundred buffaloes to graze in a meadow. When he heard the swish of the kite's wings, he thought, 'My God! There comes that devil of a kite. He'll surely eat up my buffaloes. What am I to do now?'

What he did was stuff the buffaloes in his pocket and go whizzing back home.

His people asked him, 'What's the matter? Why did you come back in such a hurry?'

He said, 'What d'you think? That monster kite is out on a hunt again. He'd have swallowed up all my buffaloes.'

'And where did you leave the buffaloes?' they asked.

'Leave them?' he said. 'I've brought them all back with me.'

'And where are they?' they asked.

'Here they are,' he said. He turned his pocket out and all the seven hundred buffaloes dropped out of it.

His people were very pleased at this and said, 'It was clever of you to put them in your pocket, or they'd surely have been swallowed up by now.'

THE TIGER IN THE CAGE

First published in the book *Tuntunir Boi* (U. Ray & Sons, 1910) as *Dushtu Bagh*.

The English translation by Satyajit Ray, hitherto unpublished, has been transcribed from

Ray's literary notebook. The illustrations in the story are by Upendrakishore Ray Chowdhury.

The endpiece illustration is a decorative woodblock bought by Satyajit Ray from Banaras.

Next to the gate of the King's palace there was a big cage, and in that cage was kept a huge tiger. Many people passed by the palace gate, and to every one of them the tiger would fold his palms and say, 'Kind brother, please open the cage door for me.' To this everyone replied, 'Why do that—only for you to come out and break our necks!'

One day there was a big feast in the palace to which many people were invited. Among them were some learned Brahmins. One of these Brahmins looked like a simple, kindly man. The tiger saw him and kept folding his palms and bowing to him again and again. The Brahmin saw the tiger and said, 'Poor creature, you look such a nice tiger. What do you want?'

The tiger folded his palms again and said, 'Please, sir, open the cage door for me, I beg of you.'

The Brahmin being a really kind-hearted person quickly opened the door for the tiger.

The tiger came out grinning and said, 'Well, sir, I must eat you up now!'

Anyone else would have run away at this, but the learned Brahmin had never learnt to run. He got very upset and said, 'I've never heard such words in my life. I've done you such a good turn, and yet you say you want to eat me up. How can anyone even think of doing such a wicked thing?'

The tiger said, 'Everyone does it, sir. People are always doing things like that.'

The Brahmin said, 'I don't believe it. Let's go and find three witnesses and ask them.'

'All right,' said the tiger. 'If those three witnesses agree with you, I'll let you off. But if they say I'm right and you're wrong, then I'll eat you up.'

So the two of them went out into the field. Now, between the two ploughed fields there was a raised path which was called the *aal*. The Brahmin pointed to the aal and said, 'That's my first witness.'

The tiger said, 'Very well, let's see what he has to say.'

The Brahmin said to the aal, 'Well, Mr Aal, if you did somebody a good turn, would he turn round and do you a bad one?'

The aal said, 'But that's what they all do. Look at me how I lie high between two fields, which is such a blessing for the farmers. I guard the two fields from each other, and don't let the water from one run into the other. And yet one farmer hacks me down with this plough just to make his own field bigger than the other's.'

The tiger said, 'Well, sir, you heard how a good deed is paid back with a bad one.'

The Brahmin said, 'Wait a minute; I have two more witnesses.'

'All right,' said the tiger. 'Let's go to them.'

In the middle of the field stood a banyan tree. The Brahmin now pointed to the tree and said, 'That's my second witness.'

'Very good,' said the tiger. 'Ask him what he has to say.'

The Brahmin turned to the banyan tree and said, 'Mr Banyan, sir, you're an ancient person. You've seen much and heard much. Tell me now, if you did somebody a good turn, should he turn round and do you a bad one?'

Banyan said, 'That's what they usually do. Look at those men. They sat here resting in my shade, but that didn't stop them from digging into my bark for gum and tearing off my leaves to put the gum in. And you can see they've broken off one of my branches too.'

The tiger said, 'Well, sir, you heard what he said.'

The Brahmin was in a fix now, and didn't know what to answer. Just then he saw a fox walking by in the distance. He pointed to the fox and said, 'That's my third witness.'

Then he called out to the fox and said, 'Stop a moment Mr Fox, you're my witness.'

The fox stopped, but came no nearer. He raised his voice from where he stood and said, 'What d'you mean? How can I be your witness?'

The Brahmin said, 'Tell me, Mr Fox, if someone did you a good turn, would you do him a bad one in return?'

The fox said, 'Before I answer that, I must know who did whom what good turn, and who did whom what bad one.'

The Brahmin said, 'You see, this tiger was in the cage and I was passing by when—'

'That's very complicated,' said the fox cutting him short. 'I must see the cage first, and I must see which way you passed before I can say anything.'

So the three of them went back to the cage. For a long time, the fox just circled around it. Then he said, 'All right. I know about the cage now, and I know how the street lies. Now tell me the rest.'

The Brahmin said, 'The tiger was inside the cage and I, the Brahmin, was walking on the street outside, and—'

'Don't go so fast,' said the fox. 'Let me get that bit right first. You said the tiger was a Brahmin, and the street was inside the cage walking—'

'Don't be silly!' said the tiger, and burst out laughing. 'He said it was the tiger who was inside the cage and the Brahmin on the street outside.'

The fox said, 'Wait a minute—the Brahmin was inside the cage and the tiger on the street outside.'

'Oh no, you fathead,' said the tiger. 'The tiger was inside and the Brahmin outside.'

'That's too much,' said the fox. 'I'm getting all mixed up. As far as I can see, the tiger

was inside the Brahmin and the cage was walking on the street—'

'I've never met a bigger fool than this,' said the tiger. 'Now listen carefully: the tiger was *inside* the cage and the Brahmin was *outside* on the street.'

The fox now scratched his head and said, 'I'm sorry, it really is too difficult for me.'

By now the tiger had quite lost his temper. He shook his fist at the fox and said, 'You've *got* to understand. Watch me now. I was *inside* the cage—like this—' The tiger stepped inside the cage as he spoke, and the moment he did so, the fox drew the belt across and locked the door. Then he turned to the Brahmin and said, 'Everything is clear to me now. And if you want to know what I want to say as a witness, it is this: never do a bad person a good turn. In this case the tiger has proved to be cleverer than you. Now hurry up if you don't want to miss that feast.'

With these words the fox went off towards the forest, and the Brahmin rushed to join in the feast.

GOOPY GYNE—A TALE OF TWO ILLUSTRATORS

[a]

[i]

[b]

[ii]

[c]

[iii]

[d]

[iv]

LEFT TO RIGHT: The story *Goopy Gyne* was serialized in six issues of *Sandesh* in 1915. It was illustrated by Upendrakishore himself [(a), (b), (c) and (d)]. Later, when the story was reprinted as *Goopy Gyne o Bagha Byne* in *Sandesh* (Puja Annual 1961), Satyajit recreated his grandfather's illustrations in his own inimitable style [(i), (ii), (iii) and (iv)].

रुपी गाहत
ॐ गंगा महंत

१

FILM TREATMENT OF *GOOPY GYNE BAGHA BYNE*

Based on Upendrakishore's story *Goopy Gyne* that was serialized in *Sandesh* from April 1915–September 1915, this film treatment by Satyajit Ray was made for the film *Goopy Gyne Bagha Byne* (1969). The previously unpublished film treatment has been transcribed from Ray's script notebook. It is to be noted that Ray has mentioned Goopy as 'Goupi' in the first draft. Later he changed it to 'Goopy.' The illustrations, taken from the script notebook, are by Satyajit Ray.

A grocery shop in a village. There is no attendant in the shop. An angry customer stands outside and shouts.

'Goupi! Kanu!'

Another customer joins him.

'What's the matter? No one in the shop?'

'So it seems . . . Kanu! Goupi!'

A man of about sixty comes into the shop, running and panting.

'I'm so sorry, sir—you must have been waiting.'

'Where have you been, Kanu—having the shop with no attendants.'

'Apologize me, sirs—I have been out looking for my worthless son.'

'Goupi? Why, what's the matter with him!'

'No mind on his job, that's the matter. He's a blot on the family's name. The only

thing he knows is music.'
'But didn't he have a hoarse voice?'
'That's the trouble, sir. He's got a voice like a frog and he thinks he's a cuckoo . . . What will it be for you, sir?'

***

A music shop in an adjacent village. A young boy of about twenty-three has just bought a second-hand tanpura, and pays thirteen rupees for it.
'It looks old,' says the old wily shopkeeper, 'but all musical instruments improve with age.'
Goupi runs his fingers on the strings.
'You're sure this will play well.'
'Second only to Narad's veena. But you have to know how to play well. It will take at least thirty-three days to tune it.'
'I am willing to give thirty-three months.'
'That's the spirit,' says the shopkeeper.
Goupi comes out of the shop with the instrument. Goupi comes marching up the village path carrying the tanpura like a hanger, and singing out *Sa-Re-Ga-Ma* with every step. Needless to say, he's a very bad singer with a very hoarse voice. Goupi is now in his own village, at a street crossing where a group of men, young and elderly, sit talking and smoking hookahs, and playing pasha below a banyan tree. Somebody calls out at the sight of Goupi.
'Hey there!'
Goupi stops.
'Who do you think you are, Bhimsen with the *gada*?'
Goupi laughs at the joke.
Another man says, 'Aren't you the son of Kanu Kyne?'
'Yes sir. My name is Gopinath. They call me Goupi.'
'But if you are such a great musician, why don't you call yourself Gyne instead of Kyne?'

Goupi likes the idea so much that his eyes shine.

'I'll certainly do that, sir. Goupi Gyne—I think it's a good name.'

Goupi is about to resume his journey, when another elderly man says, 'But why are you in a hurry to go?'

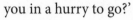

'Because otherwise my father will scold me. I'm supposed to be looking after the shop now.'

'But we are such a distinguished gathering of connoisseurs here. Won't you give us a sampling of your talent?'

They are all in a mood to pull poor Goupi's legs.

'Give us a song, give us a song.'—a chorus of request rises from the group.

'Come and sit here, we will give you an *aasan* to sit on.'

'What kind of song do you sing, Goupi? *Kheyal, Tappa, Dhrupad*!'

'I know only one song, and it is in a morning raga. But I hope to learn more.'

'Well, sing your morning song then. There's still two and a half minutes for morning to end and noon to begin.'

So Goupi settles down for a recital and sings the only song he knows—*'Look at the beauty of the world, that the sun is rising through the darkness.'* After barely half a stanza in the song, the men begin to break out in applause—

'*Shabash*! Beautiful! A golden voice! What a gift!'

The simple Goupi is deeply touched by the praise. He bows to them and takes up his tanpura, ready to resume his journey.

Then one of the men tells—'Look, I have a wonderful idea. The King is very fond of music. I thought that you sing your song to the King. I'm sure he'll reward you handsomely.'

'But how?' asks Goupi, who is excited by the idea. 'I can't just walk in at the gate and ask to sing. If you'd only tell me how I can.'

The man says, 'It's very simple. The King's bedroom is in the north-east corner of the palace. All you have to do is sit in the tomb outside the compound wall in a line with the window, and sing at the top of your voice. The King is a light sleeper and is bound to hear you. And then you'll see what happens.'

Goupi is now excited by his words. He jovially dances away, and the crowd giggle and nudge each other.

***

Goupi hums, '*Sa-ni-dha-pa-ma-ga-re-sa*!' Goupi comes hopping in and promptly puts the tanpura on the verandah of his cottage.

'*Sa-re-ga-*'

But he has to stop, because Kanu has just come in and stares down wildly at his son.

'So you've been to that music shop! And how much did you waste on that tanpura?'

'I earned this money, father, by spinning cotton and selling it in the market.'

'But why should you waste your money on a musical instrument, you who has a voice like a frog.'

'But they all said that I sing very well.'

'You stupid, you simpleton, you—'

'But,' says Goupi, 'they even suggested that I should—'

But Goupi checks himself and doesn't tell his father that he's going to sing for the Raja.

'Now go into the shop,' says Kanu. 'And if I ever find you're not there when you're supposed to be there, I'll throw that tanpura of yours into the firewood.'

Goupi goes obediently into the shop.

'A seer of mustard oil,' says a long-waiting customer.

'Yes sir,' says Goupi.

***

Dawn of the next day. Goupi is up and has just taken his tanpura. He sneaks out of the house.

***

The Raja's palace.

Goupi stands outside the compound wall looking at the palace.

'North-east . . . North-east . . .' he keeps muttering.

He now finds the North-east corner, and then sees the bedroom window. Goupi finds a place to 'sit and sing' and starts his early morning song to the accompaniment of the tanpura. The Raja's bedroom.

The Raja is inside a mosquito curtain on the Royal Bed. Goupi's hoarse voice wakes him up. Goupi sings at the top of his voice, looking at the window for signs of the King. The King now hurriedly gets out of the bed, furious. He goes to the window, looking out. There sits Goupi, singing. Goupi sees the King too, and sings even louder. The King turns away from the window and shouts for the attendant. The attendant comes hurrying in.

The King says, 'There's a human ass braying out there. I want him caught and brought to me.' We notice that the King has a voice even hoarser than Goupi.

'*Ji Huzoor*,' says the attendant and rushes out.

The Raja sits on the throne and the prisoner Goupi is brought in.

'This is the person, Your Majesty, and this is the instrument he was playing.'

'What is your name?' asks the Raja.

'Goupi Kyne—sorry, Gyne, Your Majesty.'

'Gyne? Meaning one who sings?'

'Yes, Your Majesty.'

'Hm,' says the King. 'Let me see that instrument.'

The tanpura is handed to the King, who holds it up for a moment, and then throws it high up and away. It comes down on the floor and is smashed.

Goupi's face falls. The Raja laughs out raucously.

'Set him up on a donkey and have him drummed out of the village!' he bellows.

And poor Goupi is dragged out of the hall. The drum beats, and a donkey with Goupi on its back is beaten with a stick and chased. Among the crowd of villagers who yell merrily and clap their hands, stands Kanu. There are tears in Kanu's eyes.

Goupi turns to take a last look at his father, who turns his face away to hide his tears. The donkey trots away, turns a corner and is out of sight of the villagers; who turn back—the amusement over.

Once out of sight of the villagers, Goupi dismounts and starts walking on foot. But the donkey seems to have taken a liking to him and keeps tagging along.

Goupi has great difficulty in getting rid of him. Finally, they reach a carrot field, and Goupi digs up a carrot which he holds up to the donkey, then heaves it far away in the other direction. The donkey saunters away towards the carrot and Goupi scampers off—rid of the beast at last.

***

Afternoon finds Goupi hungry and tired. He has now reached a street crossing to a village, and there's a shop in the corner which sells sweetmeats. Goupi has no money and can only stand and stare wistfully.

A fat, rich Babu arrives in the shop and buys jilebis and kachuris. They are put in sal-leaf packets and handed to the Babu. The Babu sets off homewards, Goupi looking on hungrily.

Suddenly a kite swoops down from the sky and snatches a packet from the Babu's hand with its beak and flies off.

Goupi looks up and a wad of kachuris dropping from the packet land on his upturned face. Goupi grabs hold of them before they fall on the ground, then turns to see the Babu eyeing him curiously. For a moment Goupi doesn't know what to do. Then he takes to his heels. The Babu, too fat to give chase, gives up, muttering invectives.

Making a meal of the kachuris, Goupi has the strength to continue walking.

***

Evening approaches and Goupi finds himself on the edge of a forest. Since the path leads into the forest, Goupi walks in, but doesn't have the courage to continue much further. He stops and looks around for a place to rest.

Suddenly he hears the sound of a soft, slow, regular thud—drub, drub, drub, drub . . .

Goupi looks around for the source of the sound. He walks a few steps in one direction—the sound grows softer. Then he walks in the opposite direction—the sound grows louder.

A few more steps and Goupi now knows where the sound is coming from.

A dhol is placed at the foot of a tree, and the sound coming from the regular dripping water from the leaves above. Goupi slowly comes round the trunk to find the owner of the drum, who is fast asleep in a sitting position with his back against the trunk, and the drum tied to his waist with a rope.

Goupi looks at the strange man with surprise and curiosity. Who is he? Where did he come from?

Suddenly Goupi is horror-struck to notice the head of a long snake approaching slowly towards the sleeping man. The snake reaches the right hand of the man which is placed on the ground pushed upwards. The snake slithers up on the open palm.

The man stirs a little, opens his eyes, looks down at his hand and the snake, picks up the snake, and casually flings it away. He is about to doze off again when he suddenly catches sight of Goupi. The sight of a stranger in the forest has an electrifying effect on him. He springs up to his feet, with drum stick in hand, and faces the stranger with fierce challenge in his eyes.

'Move one step forward and I'll make you forget your father's name.'

Goupi observes the man carefully, then realizes that he can't advance beyond a step or two because the weight of the drum to which he's tied himself will hold him back.

This gives Goupi courage and he takes a longish leap towards the man, shouting his father's name.

'Kanu Kyne!'

The other man rushes forward but is violently pulled up by the rope. The drum totters, but is heavy and doesn't budge. There is still a gap of six feet or so between the two. The other man, undaunted, keeps brandishing his drum stick.

'Move another step and I'll make you forget your own name.'

Goupi takes another brave leap forward, this time shouting his own name.

'Goupi Gyne!'

This time the man reacts sharply, frowning.

'Gyne? Gyne? Your name?'

'Yes.'

'What do you sing?'

'Songs.'

'Where?'

'In my village—Amloki.'

'But that's far away.'

'Yes.'

'Then why are you here?'

'I have been drummed out of the village by the King.'

'On a donkey?'

'Yes. You too?'

'Me too!'

'On a donkey?'

'On a donkey.'

The man starts laughing, and Goupi joins too. They both laugh at their own identical fates, and their laughter rings through the now dark forest, until they suddenly realize that a new voice has been added to their own. They stop laughing and immediately the

roar of a tiger is heard, which is repeated three times.

The stranger tries to be normal.

'Tiger,' he says.

'Tiger,' says Goupi.

There's a silence, then another roar.

Two more roars follow, louder and nearer now.

'There's t-tiger in my n-name too,' says the stranger.

'R-Really?' asks Goupi.

'B-Bagha B-Bagha B-Byne'.

'G-G-Good name,' says Goupi.

A tiger now appears in the forest about twenty

yards away. He stares at the sight of Goupi and Bagha.

'Wh-What can a tiger do?' says Goupi, feigning nonchalance.

'N-Nothing,' says Bagha.

The tiger keeps walking towards them.

Goupi and Bagha are now still with fright—only their teeth chattering, and the sound of the chattering is so loud that it seems to fill the forest.

Now, suddenly, the tiger seems bored and it turns and walks away, disappearing into the depths of the forest.

In enormous relief, Goupi and Bagha let out yells of delight. Bagha runs to the drum and starts drumming. Goupi begins to circle round the tree clapping hands in a wild, joyous dance, accompanying by hoarse singing to the rhythm of Bagha's drumming.

It is now wholly dark in the forest, and to the sound of drumming and singing is added the shrilling of crickets, the croaking of frogs and the occasional chorus of jackals.

In the middle of this song, suddenly Goupi and Bagha realize pairs of many lights approaching from the depths of the forest.

The lights approach and form themselves as pairs of eyes belonging to dark grotesque, two-legged forms with long, pointed ears and sharp, pointed teeth. But the teeth are formed in the broadest of grins, and somehow these demon-forms are not so terrifying.

Bagha and Goupi keep up their drumming and singing, and it appears that the demons are dancing to the rhythm of their music.

They clap their hands—some turn cartwheels, some form themselves into pairs and dance almost like Western couples; others have feathers which suggest Indian classical pattern with ornaments on their hands and limbs.

The drumming is reinforced by an unseen orchestra, and the demons join Goupi with occasional vocal reprise.

Goupi and Bagha's amazement has now given way to real excitement.

Gradually one of the demons forms a position of dominance and becomes larger and larger in size while others vanish into the background.

This demon has a sort of crown on his head and must be the King.

Finally, the frenzied dance comes to an end. The King of the Demons approaches

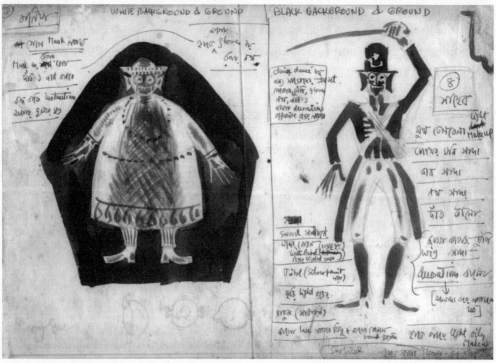

ABOVE: Draft sketches of 'Dance of the Goblins'; BELOW: Illustrations of 'Baniya' and 'Saheb' ghosts

Draft sketches from the script notebook, depicting the famous ghost dance sequence

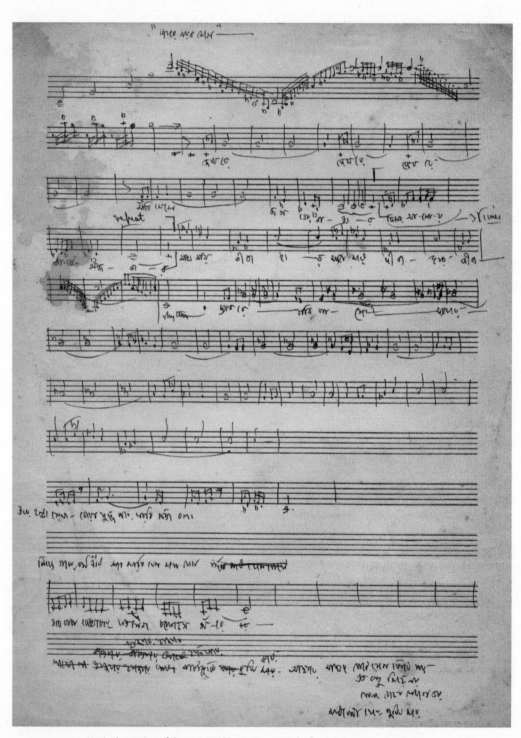

Musical notation of the song 'Dekho Re Nayan Mele' from *Goopy Gyne Bagha Byne*

Goupi and Bagha. The two boys get down on their knees.

'Did you like our music?' asks Goupi.

'Did you *really* like our music?' asks Bagha.

'Yes, but mortals won't. Not the way *you* make music.'

'No sir,' says Goupi. 'I was driven out of my village because they didn't like my singing.'

'And I was driven out of my village,' says Bagha, 'because they didn't like my drumming.'

'Well,' says the King of Demons, 'we'll see what we can do about that.'

And the King of Demons granted them four wishes.

'You will sing and play so well that as long as the music goes on, no one will be able to stir from their place. You may ask for any food you like and it will come to you. You may ask for any clothes you like and you will get them. And here's a pair of slippers for you which will take you anywhere you want to.'

Upon this, the King of Demons vanishes, leaving Goupi and Bagha in the forest. They then sense that the sky is getting lighter. Bewildered, they come out of the forest into the open. A broad river faces them. There is a glow on the eastern horizon. The first birds begin to chirp from somewhere in the forest. Goupi reacts, his eyes brightening. Then he turns to the east again. The rim of the sun begins to show. Nature had never been so beautiful to Goupi before. More birds are singing now. Goupi takes a deep breath, opens his mouth and essays the first note of song. It comes out full and clear and fills the morning air. Then Goupi sings as he had never sung before—of the beauty that is in the sky and rivers and trees and grass and flowers. Next Goupi briefly tries out the powers of his voice and sings *taan*s that range four octaves! But Bagha is now taking to try his powers too and takes up his drum and then performs some breathtaking *rela*s. Then the two of them sing a joyous song about their wonderful luck and wonderful future that lies ahead of them.

'Let us put on our slippers now and go places,' says Goupi.

'But first let us fill our hungry stomachs,' says Bagha.

So they clap their hands and wish for food—which arrives in no time on golden plates. Eating rasagolla*s* as big as cricket balls, Goupi and Bagha discuss future plans.

'Where do we go from here?' asks Bagha.

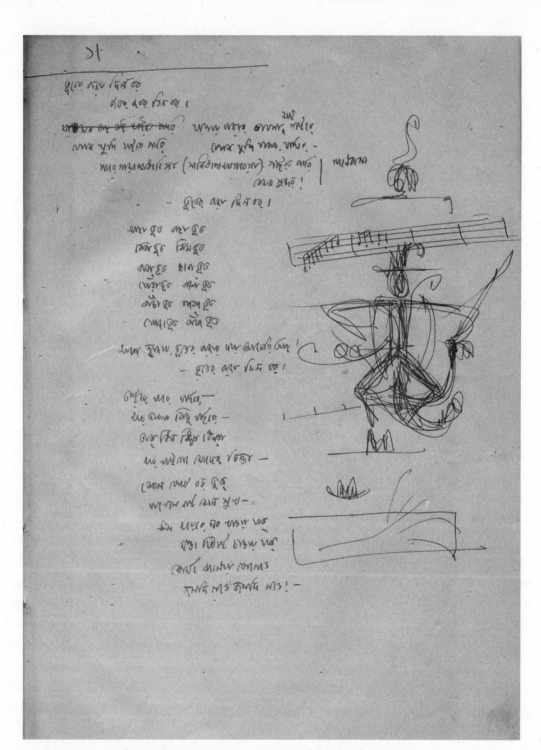

Draft lyrics of the song 'Bhooter Raja Dilo Bor' from *Goopy Gyne Bagha Byne*

Musical notation of the song 'Bhooter Raja Dilo Bor' from *Goopy Gyne Bagha Byne*

'Anywhere we like,' says Goupi.

'Yes, but where do we *like* to go?'

Goupi ponders. He is not sure himself.

'Besides,' says Bagha, 'we've got to have a place to live in. A roof over our head.'

'Yes. We can't ask for a home and get it.'

'No. And we can't live out in the open always.'

'True . . .'

'We may go to the richest kingdom in the world,' says Bagha, 'but we won't get a house there for the asking.'

'Then you think we should go back to our own villages? After all, we can sing and play now, so they won't . . .'

'Are you mad? Go back without seeing the world? And without marrying princesses?'

'What? You want to marry a princess?'

'Don't you?'

Goupi thinks.

'Why do you have to think so much?'

Goupi shakes his head.

'But a princess may not want to marry you or me.'

Bagha's face falls.

'You're right,' he says, 'I haven't thought of that.'

A noise is heard, of people walking, and horses, and a murmur of voices.

Goupi and Bagha walk in the direction of the noise and it brings them to a path along the edge of the forest. A slow procession is passing consisting of a horse-drawn carriage, in which sit a bearded old man in a turban, followed by men carrying musical instruments, and a retinue of servants.

Goupi and Bagha look on with curiosity. Then Bagha arrests a man.

'Where are you all going, sir? And who is the old man in the carriage?'

'He is the great musician Kasrat Hussain—and we are going to the State of Shundi.'

'Why?'

'The King of Shundi wants a court musician. He is very choosy. He has declared an open competition for musicians from all over the country.'

'Is the court musician given a house to live in?' asks Goupi.

'What do you mean? He gets a room in the palace itself!'

The man runs off to his place in the procession.

Goupi and Bagha exchange meaningful glances. Their eyes are glistening with hope. The procession disappears.

Bagha claps his hands.

'Off to Jhundi!' he says.

'Jhundi?' Goupi says. 'But he said Shundi.'

'Not Shundi, you fool. Jhundi.'

'All right,' says Goupi doubtfully.

'Well, let's go,' says Bagha.

'Then let's put on our slippers first.'

They put on their slippers. Then they hold each other's hands and both shout together.

'One-two-Jhundi!'

Bagha and Goupi shoot up into the air like rockets—leaving a smoke behind them. They soar through the air, with the greatest of ease and the landscape below them moves so fast that it becomes a blur in their eyes.

Whoosh!

Bagha and Goupi land in snow somewhere in the Himalayas. They shiver in the cold and keep jumping almost to keep themselves warm. Goupi is furious.

'I told you it was Shundi!'

'All right! Let's try Shundi then.'

'Shundi!' They yell again.

Zoom! They fly up. The snow below them melts in the heat of their blast.

Bulleting through the air, Bagha and Goupi now land in a picturesque country surrounded by hills and dotted with pretty houses. An old man draws water from a well. Bagha shouts to him.

'Hey, brother!'

The man turns.

'Is this the Kingdom of Shundi?'

The man nods his head but says nothing.

'Does your King want a court musician?'

The man nods again.

'Can't you open your mouth and talk?' asks Goupi with some impatience.

The man now shakes his head.

'Dumb,' says Bagha. 'Let's go and find another man.'

Bagha and Goupi walk on a little bit, and a turning brings them right in the middle of the marketplace. It is crowded with people—hundreds of them—but no one talks. The only sounds are of people's movements and the rattle of horses.

Bagha and Goupi notice that the people are using a sign language. The people stare at Goupi and Bagha because they are dressed so differently.

Bagha gets hold of another man.

'Could you direct us to the Maharaja's palace please?'

The man thinks for a moment, then asks them to follow him indicating them he is unable to give verbal directions.

Out of the bazaar they come, and then across the street up a slope. From this vantage point, the lovely turreted palace can be seen. The man points to the palace.

Goupi and Bagha thank the man. The man, too, bows with great courteousness and offers them two large apples from the basket. Goupi thanks him again and takes the apples. The man goes away. As soon as he is out of sight, Goupi and Bagha hold hands and say in a chorus:

'We want to go into the palace of the King of Shundi.'

Zoom!—And Goupi and Bagha are right inside the Durbar Hall.

The throne is yet empty but, the Hall is filled with distinguished dignitaries, and on a large carpet facing the throne sit musicians of various ages and descriptions, all obviously waiting for the King.

Goupi and Bagha put themselves suitably behind a pillar and is not immediately discovered, but they are spotted soon enough—by one of the sentries, who eyes them with a startled expression. Then he edges towards them. Goupi and Bagha stand and stare, nonplussed. Then Bagha grabs hold of Goupi's hand and they take to their heels, colliding with an upsetting sentry on the way, until they're out in the courtyard. They run off into a room in the wing of the courtyard, find an open window and jump out into the garden.

Panting, Bagha says, 'We didn't seem welcome in there!'

'How could we be, in the sort of clothes we're wearing? Did you notice what the others wore?'

'Right you are. We must get some regal uniforms. Let's wish for them.'

Goupi and Bagha wish for the costumes and almost immediately find themselves resplendently dressed.

They now walk towards the main door of the palace, and is saluted by the sentry. Goupi and Bagha march into the Durbar Hall, right into the phalanx of musicians. They take their seats and assume an air of the highest dignity.

Almost immediately a fanfare is struck up as the King arrives to assume the throne. Everybody including the musicians rises up and bows, and Goupi and Bagha have to do the same.

The King has a friendly, but tired and sad look. He stifles a yawn and declares the singing competition open by striking a gong.

Then begins a series of performances by the competing musicians—each more preposterous than the previous one. The King stops each by sounding the gong after a brief sampling. But a really tiresome and old ustad so strikes his notes that the King falls asleep and begins to snore. The ustads don't know what to do.

Goupi and Bagha exchange looks and Bagha takes his drum stick and gives a thumping rap on the drum. The bang is like a thunderclap. This wakes the King who immediately strikes the gong indicating resumption of contest.

Goupi now gets up to a drum roll by Bagha and everybody turns round to look at the pair.

The King too sits up, struck by the novelty of the drum roll. The drum roll stops and Goupi begins to sing. Everybody sits petrified while Goupi sings, and when Goupi finishes singing, it is clear that the King is pleased too. The courtiers too applaud heartily.

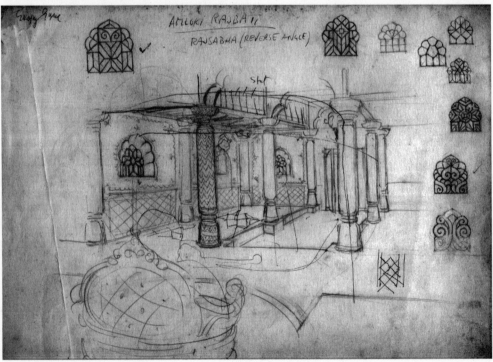

Meticulous drafts of the Durbar Hall in the kingdom of Shundi and Amloki made by Ray for the film

The King indicates end of concert by striking the gong three times. Goupi and Bagha are selected to be the court musicians.

One man among the courtiers—a very suspicious-looking man in a heavy beard coldly surveys the proceedings and quietly slips out of the Hall.

In a ballet-like sequence, Goupi and Bagha are led to their room in the palace—a luxurious affair furnished in high royal style. Servants start fanning them and massaging them and spraying them with perfume.

Goupi and Bagha help themselves to fruits from silver trays and loll on the bed.

Suddenly the King arrives, rings a bell and the servants flee.

Goupi and Bagha express their gratitude to the King, upon which the King smiles blissfully and speaks!

'I don't think I've ever heard such music in my life.'

Goupi and Bagha are astonished beyond words.

'But you can speak!' says Goupi.

'And Bengali too!' says Bagha.

'Yes, I can speak,' says the King. 'The plague didn't affect me.'

'What plague?'

'Oh—there was a plague—a strange plague which spared no one in the land. I was away on holiday with family. When I came back I found my people had lost their speech. I couldn't do anything for them, because the doctors too had lost their tongue. This made me very sad. So I also stopped speaking from that day.'

'But how is it that you speak my language?'

'Oh, I speak many languages. The King has a lot of free time, you know.'

Bagha says, 'But don't you fight battles?'

'No, I can't fight and I don't like fights, and I don't like people who like fights. So I read and learn languages, and listen to music.'

'I see.'

'So I will listen to yours from now on. You see, our musicians became dumb too!'

***

The man with the heavy, dark beard goes frantically along the corridors of a palace. This belongs to the King of Halla. He enters the room of the Prime Minister who is having his dinner.

The Minister heavily looks up from his plate saying, 'Report on your findings on Shundi.'

'Sir, they have no army, no elephants, scarcely any horses. Therefore they have no strength, so we will easily conquer them. But they have wonderful crops in their field, and fruits in their . . .'

'Yes, yes, yes, that part we know. That'll do. You may go now.'

The spy leaves, bowing and smiling ingratiatingly. The Minister finishes his meal, gets up belching and mutters, 'Must we talk to that puppet now.'

The Minister now proceeds to the King's chamber, a bunch of grapes in his hand which he eats as he walks.

The King is seated in his chamber, looking morosely out of the window. The Minister approaches him with a teasing and sinister smile and taps him on his shoulder.

The King—who bears an astonishing resemblance to the King of Shundi—wakes up from his remorse with a start and glances up at the Minister, and then longingly at the grapes which he dangles temptingly before him.

'Lovely grapes,' says the Minister.

'May I have one?' asks the King plaintively.

'Certainly.'

The Minister hands him a grape and the King puts it into his mouth.

'They make better fighters of you,' says the Minister.

'Fight?' asks the King. 'Fight what?'

'Fight a battle.'

The King's eyes open wide in fear.

'But I've never fought a battle in my life.'

'You cannot be King unless you fight battles.'

The draft illustrations of characters—the King of Shundi and the King of Halla

'But I don't want to be King. I didn't want to be King. It was you—'

'Sh-h-h,' says the Minister. 'Whatever I do, I do for your own good.'

'My own good, or your own good?'

'Shh! You mustn't talk like that. What will your subjects think if they know you are a weak King? No. We must fight this battle. We must capture the Kingdom of Shundi. It's a rich country, there are riches in its treasury. So today, in this court, you must announce that we are going to war against Shundi. Then we will send our message to the King of Shundi.'

'But our army—it is not the best army in the world.'

'It's good enough to oust Shundi. They haven't even got any army—ha ha ha!'

'But—but—how can I . . .'

'I will help you—as I've always helped you. I will put you in the right fighting mood with the help of this . . .'

And the Minister brings out of his pocket a shining amulet in a chain, and he starts swinging the amulet before the King's eyes.

The King's eyes go shiny. Then they form fierce and the King lets out a battle cry that rings through the palace . . .

The 'fierce King' of Halla enters the court grunting and stamping his feet, glancing at the sentry and at the courtiers. He is now villainy incarnate, breathing fire and venom. He ascends the throne and the court is bated with deadly silence.

'Battle!'—yells the King. 'War! Destruction!'

***

The Court of Shundi. The King is on the throne. Goupi and Bagha have just finished a song, when the messenger from the King of Halla is announced and he enters, marching up to throne.

The message is read out.

'The King of Halla hereby announces to the King of Shundi that short of surrender within three days of receipt of this message, the King of Halla will march into the Kingdom of Shundi and acquire it by force of arms.'

The King lets out a wail and strikes his forehead.

'Alas! This is the end!'

The messenger leaves. Goupi and Bagha stare at each other, perplexed by the suddenness of the event, and touched by the King's plight.

***

Later in the evening . . .

The King restlessly paces the roof of the palace wrecked by the thought of the imminent calamity.

A servant enters and announces that Goupi and Bagha would like to meet and talk with him. The King asks them to come in. Goupi and Bagha enter.

'Maharaja,' says Goupi, 'we would like to help you in your distress.'

The King laughs sadly and cynically. 'How can you help? Kill the gangsters? Halla means what he says. There's no help for it.'

'But then—if you don't want to fight—why don't you surrender?'

'That is what I think I will have to do and that is what makes me so unhappy.'

'Why?'

'Because Halla is a bad King. My people will be in great distress under him. They will not be fed and clothed and they will just wither away . . . oh, this is the end!'

Then Goupi has a sudden idea.

'Maharaja, we will go to their Kingdom and stop the war.'

The Raja laughs again.

'How can you do that?'

'We will go as spies.'

'Oh but it's a long way. It will take two days for you to reach there.'

'But,' says Bagha, 'we can fl—' and he checks himself just in time.

'At best, let us try please,' plead Goupi and Bagha.

'All right. But I'm afraid of losing my favourite musicians.'

'You won't, we assure you that.'

'Well, then you must be well stocked with provisions for the journey. My daughter will specially prepare some sweets for you.'

'Your daughter?' Goupi and Bagha both ask simultaneously. 'You have a daughter?'

'You mean you have a princess here?'

'Well, well—what's so surprising in a King having a daughter?'

'No, no—not surprising,' says Bagha.

'Not surprising,' says Goupi. 'It's only that we didn't know.'

'One daughter?' asks Bagha.

'One. And she likes your music very much.'

'Whose music?' ask Bagha and Goupi.

'Yours. Both of yours.'

'I see,' say Bagha and Goupi.

'But she's sad now, because of what is going to happen.'

Bagha and Goupi are suddenly excited.

'Nothing's going to happen. Nothing. We will prevent the war from happening.'

***

Early morning. Bagha and Goupi leave the palace to go to Halla.

As they hit the road, they turn back, and at one of the windows of the palace, they see a beautiful young girl looking at them.

Bagha and Goupi both look at her with admiration. The girl slowly withdraws from the window, and Bagha and Goupi continue on their journey.

***

Coming to a lonely spot, looking around and making sure that no one knows about them, Goupi and Bagha 'wish' to go to Halla, and behold!—they are in a strange land, with strange houses and strange towers and gateways and alleyways.

Shouts are heard and the stamping of horses.

Goupi and Bagha follow the sound until they see soldiers in action in a village square. They are rounding up people—both young and old—but all skinny and with expressions of deep resentment in their faces.

Bagha and Goupi ask a very old man why they are being rounded up and they are told that they will have to join the army to fight a war against Shundi.

Bagha and Goupi learn that nobody wants this war because they have been asked to pay new taxes for it.

'All the good things are kept in the royal family and for the family of the Prime Minister.'

Bagha and Goupi proceed further and find a row of commoners being dragged along a street with a faint rumbling noise. Again, the people who are dragging the commoners are led with wielding whips.

At another place they find a group of young and old men being dragged by ropes by another group of sentries.

Goupi and Bagha ask another old bystander and they are told that these men have refused to fight. So they are being taken to receive punishment from the King.

Bagha and Goupi fall in with the group, which is quite a large one; they are able to mingle with it without being noticed.

Soon Goupi and Bagha find themselves in the Durbar Hall where a fierce King sits on the throne meting out punishment to the offenders. The new prisoners are brought before the King and the nature of offence specified.

'These men are refusing to fight, Your Majesty.'

'Off with their heads!' shouts the King.

Goupi and Bagha exchange looks.

As the guards are about to drag the prisoners away, Bagha suddenly strikes his drum. This is a signal for Goupi to sing, who breaks into a song.

Everybody in the court, including the King, the ministers, courtiers, guards and prisoners, are stopped in mid-action.

Singing and drumming, Goupi and Bagha slowly begin to withdraw towards the entrance, until they find themselves outside, when they stop singing and 'wish' to go to the nearest field.

But among the people in the court was the spy who had heard Goupi and Bagha sing in Shundi.

He runs to the Minister and whispers into his ears about their true identity.

In the meantime, the song has broken the King's spell and he is a good and mute man again.

'Where are the men being taken?' he asks, pointing to the prisoners.

'You have just punished them, Your Majesty.'

'Why?'

'Because they won't fight the war.'

'What war? There's no war!' But by now the Minister has realized that the King's spell is broken, and he is anxious that he shouldn't be seen in the state of helplessness by his people.

He gives a hurried order to the *daroga* to capture the two musicians, who are obviously spies. Then he turns his attention to the King.

***

Goupi and Bagha are in a forest, hiding, having a good meal.

'What do you think we should do now?'

'I think we ought to do some more spying.'

'On whom!'

'I don't like that Prime Minister!'

'Neither do I.'

'But the King is a brute.'

'But did you notice how he listened to our song?'

'Yes, he had tears in his eyes.'

'Yes. So he may not be so bad after all.'

'Hmm.'

'Let's go and spy on the Prime Minister!'

'Where should we go?'

'We should go where the Prime Minister is.'

'In front of him, so he can see us?'

'No. Behind him, so he can't.'

'Let's go then.'

Goupi and Bagha clap their hands and ho—they're in the Prime Minister's room—right behind the Prime Minister, who is seated in a throne talking to a man with a pointed beard and a pointed cap and a pair of dark glasses. This is the Physician-Magician who is practically blind.

The Magician is holding up a jar in his hand containing some powder.

The Prime Minister says, 'You're sure this will give dumb men the power of speech?'

'One pinch of this in a pot of water—and that is all.'

'Good. It would be ridiculous to rule over dumb subjects. And now what about the other potion.'

'For the King?'

'Yes.'

'I have managed to make a stronger one here.'

'The only truth is that your potions have not been doing the work they're supposed to do. The King nearly weakened in court today—and you said the potion has

ABOVE: Rough sketch of the Prime Minister; BELOW: Sketch of the Prime Minister's chamber

ABOVE: Rough sketches of the Magician; BELOW: Sketch of the Magician's chamber

strength to last twelve hours.'

'But something very unusual must have happened to cause this.'

'Nothing at all. A couple of youngsters started to sing a song, and at the end of it I find the King a weak man—so I had to shut him up.'

'Song, did you say? That must have been then. It must have been a very special kind of song.'

'Well—now that you mention it, even I had a peculiar feeling when I heard that song. As if a drug has been given to me—as if I have been hypnotized.'

'That is a very bad thing, sir, you mustn't allow such singing to happen again.'

The Prime Minister suddenly remembers, 'And my God! It was sung by a couple of spies from Shundi.'

'They sound like magicians, too.'

'So they may be dangerous?'

'They may upset all my plans. I think you should arrest them immediately.'

'But how?'

'I could tell you where they are—in a moment.'

'Well—do so then!'

The Magician brings out a gadget with which he makes some odd calculations. Finally the magician announces the result of his calculations.

'They are right here, Your Highness.'

'Right here?'

'In this room. Right behind you.'

The Prime Minister whirls round, and there stand Bagha and Goupi.

The Prime Minister erupts like a volcano.

'You scoundrels!' he shouts. 'You have the nerve to come and hide in my room!'

And then he shouts for the sentry, who comes rushing in.

In the meantime, the Magician, who doesn't want to get mixed in scuffles, flees through the door.

'Arrest them!' the Prime Minister orders.

But before the sentry can take a step forward, Goupi has started a new song. Prime

Minister and the sentry stand petrified.

Singing and drumming, Bagha and Goupi leave the room—making sure of taking the jar of medicine with them. They put the jar in their bag.

Once out of the Prime Minister's room, they clap their hands and 'wish' to be in the nearest forest.

It is evening in the forest, and Goupi and Bagha have just finished a meal.

'Well, now we know who the villain is,' says Goupi.

'Yes,' says Bagha, 'but we still don't know how we will stop the war.'

'It seems like a difficult task—stopping an army from marching.'

'What do we do then?'

'Will have to think, and think quickly, because the army marches day after tomorrow.' Bagha yawns.

'But couldn't we think in the morning. I'm a little sleepy now.'

'All right, we'll think in the morning.'

'But I don't like to sleep in the forest. There are snakes and insects around!'

'Where can we sleep then? We can't go into a house.'

The two think for a while.

In the meantime, the Halla spy is scurrying the countryside for Goupi and Bagha. He looks behind bushes, up in the trunks of trees, in the ghettos in the hills.

Bagha and Goupi have fallen asleep in the forest. The spy, making his way through the forest, finds the two boys calmly asleep. The sentries arrive, and Goupi and Bagha are captured. Their struggles are of not much use, as they are cuffed immediately. In the struggle, each loses one slipper which stays behind in the forest. And so is Bagha's dhol.

Goupi and Bagha are shown into the prison and a heavy iron clanks shut behind them. Keys turn in a heavy lock and Goupi Bagha find themselves prisoners.

There is a rehearsal for battle going on in the big field in front of the Fort, and the men are being forced to march with the lashes of whips.

The King—a villain now—watches the preparation and occasionally roars with delight and the Prime Minister watches from the corner of his eyes. He is happy too — for the new medicine has worked beautifully.

***

In Shundi, the Raja paces the roof of the palace restlessly. A messenger comes and says there has been no news from Goupi and Bagha yet.

The King strikes his forehead.

The General and the Prime Minister come.

Prime Minister says, 'The only way seems is to surrender. At least we will avoid bloodshed.'

King says, 'Let us wait until tomorrow morning. I know it is practically useless but let us wait, let us wait another twenty-four hours.'

'As you wish, Your Majesty.'

***

Afternoon. In the Durbar Hall of Halla, the Raja is in a furious and villainous mood. He is brandishing his sword and taking wild swings at anybody and everybody. It is the new potion which has caused this excessive villainy, and it has made the Prime Minister greatly worried.

The potion is supposed to last till sundown, but the Sun has just gone down and the King shows no signs of weakness. He wants to march into Shundi right away.

'Tomorrow morning. Too late. Let's have the battle right now!' he yells.

***

In the Halla Prison. Goupi and Bagha sit morosely wearing a single slipper each.

'Well,' says Goupi, 'it has at least taught us not to fall asleep when we should keep awake.'

Bagha heaves a deep sigh.

'I don't think I'll ever get my drum back again.'

'And it seems we won't marry a princess after all.'

'True,' says Goupi, 'it seems a remote possibility right now. At any rate, no princess would accept a headless suitor anyway.'

Rough sketch of the Halla prison

'Headless?' asks Bagha in a tone of surprise.

'Of course,' says Goupi, 'I'm sure the King will punish us. And the only punishment he seems to know is cutting off the head.'

'It is a pity, because he really is a nice King.'

Goupi has an idea.

'Maybe we can sing a song. If the King is in a bad mood now, and if he can hear us sing, maybe he will have a change of heart, and may be he will set us free.'

'What song will you sing?'

'Well, I know a song about a sad King.'

'Go ahead and sing it. But I can't play the dhol.'

'No, you don't have to.'

So Goupi starts singing his song about the sad King, going as near as possible to the windows so that his voice can reach outside.

Goupi's magical voice does reach the Durbar Hall, where everybody is immediately spellbound. The King slumps down on the throne, and all the villainy disappears from his demeanour. As Goupi ends his song, the King is a transformed man, a good man and a peace-loving man.

The Prime Minister is now happy that he is no longer fierce, and he leads the sad King to his chamber, where he is locked up.

***

Prison. As Goupi ends his song, the Jailor brings them two pots of food, which consist of some terribly unappetizing-looking mush—and not enough of it either.

The sight of the food make Goupi and Bagha wince.

'Just as when I was feeling so hungry, they had to bring this stuff.'

Goupi turns to the Jailor and says: 'Is this the kind of food that you feed your prisoners?'

The Jailor says: 'Why prisoners? This is what everybody eats.'

'So that's why you're all so thin!' says Bagha.

The Jailor goes out of the prison cell, locking the iron gate. Then he turns to Bagha and Goupi and says, 'But you won't get thin, because you'll get only one such meal. Tomorrow morning you'll have your heads chopped off, and so you'll have nothing to eat your meals with—ha, ha!'

Goupi and Bagha survey the pots, and then look at each other. They both seem to have been struck by the same idea.

'But we don't have to have such filthy food, do we?' they whisper simultaneously.

Then they turn to the Jailor, who has kept his watchful eyes glued on them.

'Well,' says Bagha, 'we can't do anything with *him* looking on.'

'No,' says Goupi, 'we have to wait.'

'Yes, we have to be patient.'

A stamping of shoes is heard, and the Prime Minister arrives.

He stands outside the iron gate with a smile of satisfaction on his face.

'Open the door,' yells the Prime Minister.

The key turns in the lock, the gate opens and the Prime Minister enters.

'I see you haven't eaten yet,' he says, glancing at the pots.

'We're not hungry,' says Bagha.

'But you *must* eat,' says Prime Minister, his voice rasping like a razor. 'You must eat whatever you're given to eat.'

Bagha and Goupi hesitate.

The Prime Minister now bellows furiously.

'Eat, I tell you, eat it up! All of it.'

So Bagha and Goupi have to eat the terrible meal, while the Prime Minister gloats sadistically over the spectacle, himself taking a bite at a juicy grape from a bunch that he's been carrying.

The Prime Minister now leaves.

'Scoundrel,' murmurs Bagha.

'Scoundrel,' murmurs Goupi.

The Jailor again takes his position, and again turns his watchful eyes on the boys.

But now the Jailor appears sleepy, and Goupi and Bagha hold their breath.

The Jailor's head now lolls to the side, and his mouth falls open. A feeble sound of snoring can be heard.

Bagha claps his hand once, first to test the depth of the Jailor's sleep.

Then Bagha and Goupi exchange glances, 'wish' for a good, hearty meal, and it fairly fills the floor of the prison room. The plates and pots glitter, steam rises from the pulau and the aroma of the curries makes the boys nearly swoon.

Now they fall to eating with gusto, almost forgetting the existence of the Jailor.

The noise of their eating wakes the Jailor up, who looks on in wide-eyed astonishment at the fantastic meal in progress. Soon the astonishment gives way to greed, and one can almost see his mouth watering.

Bagha suddenly notices the Jailor. For a moment he is nonplussed. Then he gives a quick smile—as if nothing unusual has happened, and continues to eat. Goupi also does the same.

Next, Bagha and Goupi start discussing the food.

'Have you ever eaten such excellent rice in your life?' asks Goupi.

'Never,' says Bagha.

'And such pure ghee?'

'Never!'

'I wonder what spices they put in the korma. It tastes particularly delicious.'

'Wait till you have tasted the fish.'

By now the Jailor has lost all poise and self control. He yells—'I must have some of that food. I must!'

'Of course you will. We'll save some for you.'

'When? I can't wait any longer!'

'As soon as you let us out of here!'

The Jailor is silent for a moment.

'But what will I tell the Prime Minister?' he asks.

'Tell him that we escaped by magic!'

'Are you really magicians?'

'Of course we are. Or else how could we have all the food?'

The Jailor is now convinced—and at any rate, greedy beyond control.

He clanks open the door. Bagha and Goupi ask him to join them.

The Jailor comes and starts helping himself greedily to food.

Bagha and Goupi wash their hands, and quietly leave the prison, locking the Jailor with his meal.

Once outside the prison, they make for the forest where they lost their slippers, and the dhol.

Since they can't travel by magic, it takes them quite some time to reach the forest. Finally they find themselves in the spot, and in no time they've found their slippers as well as the dhol.

***

Early morning finds the soldiers in the battle array, ready to march into Shundi. The General marches up and down, surveying the army. The Prime Minister now appears, glances at the soldiers, and rubs his hands in satisfaction.

'This is good enough for Shundi—good enough indeed!' he says to himself.

Then to the General he says, 'The King will appear within a few minutes. In the meantime, you can give the order to advance as soon as you're ready.'

The Prime Minister goes away. The General takes his position.

***

In the King's chamber, the King is in a state of profound depression induced by the previous night's song. He is also in a belligerent and touchy mood.

The Prime Minister walks in with the magician, and the sight of them inflames the King.

'Get out of here!' he suddenly bellows, 'get out of my room!'

'But, Your Majesty, the army is about to march into Shundi!'

'Why? Why, why, why? I don't want any battle. And I don't want you two in my room. Get out!'

Then the King gives the Prime Minister instant blow on the stomach and Prime Minister topples over backwards. The Magician would run away if he could, but he is terribly hampered by his short-sightedness and begins to knock over lamps, hookahs, lecterns, etc.

***

The army is now ready to march. It is a great mess of skinny men on skinny horses—and the faces of all the sentries have a hungry look.

The General shouts—'The King has said that anybody who stays back after the order, he will have his head cut off.'

Thereupon, he raises his right hand to give the order, and at this very moment is heard Goupi's singing.

Everything, every movement, every action—has to stop now.

Goupi and Bagha come marching in, singing their song about the uselessness of war.

The end of the song has Goupi and Bagha 'wishing' a rain of sweetmeats—and they fall in hundreds from the sky. The eyes of the soldiers open wide and their mouths fall open—but they can't have it yet, because the song hasn't ended.

HALLA SOLDIERS

ABOVE AND BELOW: Detailed sketches of Halla soldiers along with Goopy and Bagha in disguise

But the moment the song ends—the soldiers make a stampede for the sweetmeats—the battle order totally forgotten. The General is completely lost in the stampede.

The great roar of the stampede reaches the King's chamber, and the Minister and the King disentangle themselves and run to the balcony.

The sight that they see astounds them.

The Minister throws up his arms in alarm and rushes out.

The King surveys the same a little longer, and the moment he realizes that there's a sort of feast going on, his eyes light up, and he too rushes out.

Goupi and Bagha run into the castle with a pot of sweets, and nearly collide with the Minister who storms out, pushing the boys aside, and makes for the scene of the stampede.

Foolishly, the Minister tries to enter into the thick of the stampede—shouting marching orders. He is nearly trampled to death.

Goupi and Bagha watch his fate with delight.

Now the Raja, running out of the castle, stops—his path guarded by Goupi and Bagha. The King and the boys stare at one another for a few moments.

Then Bagha holds up the pot of sweets to him, and the King goes for it with a plunge.

Goupi and Bagha let the King eat for a few seconds, then they slowly close in on him, and embrace him and shout 'The Durbar Hall of Shundi' and clap their hands together.

The next moment, the three are transported magically to the court of Shundi. But Halla's King is not concerned about the change of locale and keeps eating his rasagollas.

The King of Shundi nearly jumps up from his throne. Then he takes a fond look at Halla's King—who is still eating sweetmeats, and his eyes light up in recognition.

He jumps down from his throne and runs to the Halla King with open arms.

The King of Halla suddenly becomes aware of his surroundings, sees Shundi's King running up to him.

Shundi shouts: 'Udho!'

Halla shouts: 'Budho!'

Halla drops the pot of sweets and the two embrace.

Goupi and Bagha, in the background, suddenly clap their hands and disappear.

Shundi says: 'So you are the King of Halla!'

Halla says: 'So you are the King of Shundi!'

Shundi: 'I thought I had lost you forever!'

Halla: 'No, the bandits didn't kill me. They merrily put me up on a throne, and made me do the nastiest things.'

Shundi: 'You mean, you didn't want to declare war on us?'

Halla: 'Never—I hate fighting.'

Shundi: 'Wonderful!'

We find Goupi and Bagha on the edge of the hill from where they had their first glimpse of the Palace of Shundi. The hill overlooks the city.

Goupi and Bagha first light a fire with some sticks they found lying around, and put three pinches of the magic powder into it.

Then they clap their hands again, and are instantly back in the Durbar Hall.

Shundi and Halla are still talking.

Bagha walks over and taps Shundi on the shoulder. Shundi stops talking and turns to Bagha. Goupi also steps forward.

Shundi tells Halla, 'Oh! I must introduce you to these wonderful musicians—here they are.'

Bagha clears his throat and says, 'There's this little matter about the princess!'

Shundi says, 'Oh yes, of course—but the problem is—which of you is she going to marry?'

'I have a prior claim,' says Bagha.

'But you see,' says Shundi, 'I was thinking of him (pointing at Goupi) because my daughter is quite tall, and—'

Halla interrupts, 'Are you looking for a short princess?'

Bagha says, 'Do you have one?'

'Yes, indeed—I do. And she was telling me how much she liked your dhol!'

At this point, a faint noise begins to be heard. Everybody listens to it, and then walks over to the balcony to look.

The city of Shundi is enveloped in smoke, and through the smoke, the people of Shundi emerge, sneezing, shouting and jumping in joy.

Shundi turns to Halla, beaming with happiness.

'My people have got back their voices!'

Shehnai music begins to be heard over the noise of merriment, and the last image shows the wedding of Goupi and Bagha to the two pretty princesses—one short and one tall—with the two Kings in attendance and Goupi's father Kanu Kyne, and the King of Amloki.

Portrait of Sukumar drawn by Satyajit Ray.
The longhand calligraphy—'Sukumar Ray Chowdhury' by Ray has been taken from his notebook.

SATYAJIT *translates*
SUKUMAR

Studio portrait of Sukumar Ray and Suprabha Devi after their marriage

SUKUMAR

The original Bengali essay *Amar Baba* was written and read by Satyajit Ray as a radio talk broadcast by All India Radio Calcutta on 8 July 1977. It has been translated into English by Indrani Majumdar. The illustrations in the essay are by Sukumar Ray.

Soon after my birth my father fell ill. And affected by this very illness he died at the age of 36.

I was then two-and-a-half-years old. During these two and a half years when my father was ailing, whenever his condition was a little better, he was taken on a trip for a change of air. Each time, I accompanied him. It is of course questionable if memory at such a young age can be a reliable one but I do recall a few incidents of that time even though they were not very significant. Once I went to Sodhpur with my father. The house we stayed in was beside the Ganga. One day my father was sitting by the window. I sat right next to him. My father suddenly said—'There goes a steamer.' I ran out to the open compound and spotted the vessel on the Ganga. Once we visited Giridih. Whether this was before or after our visit to Sodhpur, I don't quite remember. Though my father is not part of this recollection, what I can recall vividly is the river Usri. And the presence of our senior retainer, Prayag. Prayag and I were digging into sand in search of water. At that very moment a little village girl appeared and dipped her hands into the water. I can only recall this little detail. I also remember well that both these episodes took place at dusk.

To be honest, I came to know Sukumar Ray through his writings and drawings. And also through the descriptions shared by my relatives. When I say writing I don't mean just printed words. That's only obvious. Just as I have access to his books so do many others. After all, the writer Sukumar is not just anyone's personal possession. It's been fifty years since the publication of the works, *Abol Tabol* (Rhymes without Reason) and *Ha-ja-ba-ra-la* (A Topsy-Turvy Tale). Over the past fifty years no other work has been written to match up to these two books. And the appeal of these books hasn't declined even slightly among Bengali readers. I don't know if such an observation can be made about any other books in the language.

In my opinion just within thirty pages *Ha-ja-ba-ra-la* is packed with such a stupendous amount of ideas. I doubt if in world literature any such book has been produced yet. I have the book, *Ha-ja-ba-ra-la* here right next to me and I'll flip through its pages and give you some examples right away. On the very first page we see a cat turning into a handkerchief; on the second page there's *Gechhodada* (cousin Treehopper); on the third it's *Kakkeshwar* (crow), *aar haatey roilo pencil* (carry the pencil in your hand); on the fourth—*Udo Budo* (the little old man)—*boyesh barti na komti* (is your age going upwards or downwards?); on the fifth—that strange notice put up by Kakkeshwar; on the sixth—*Hijibijbij* (Higgle-Piggle-Dee); on the seventh—*Byakaron Singh* (Grammaticus Horner, BA); on the eighth appears *Nyara* (a man with a smooth shaven head) with the line *amay gaitey bolona* (please my dear fellow, don't ask me to sing); soon after appear those strange songs—*Lal ganey neel shur* (a rose-red song with a sky-blue tune), *mishipakha shikhipakha* (the darkness looms with peacock plumes . . .), *badur boley orey o bhai shojaru* (the Bat called out to the old spark, Porcupine).

And soon after what follows is that bizarre *manhanir mokoddoma* (the wacky libel case) where one's greeted with one act of amazement after another which continues till the very end.

One major regret in my life is that I never got to see the original manuscript of *Ha-ja-ba-ra-la*. No one knows its whereabouts along with the original illustrations produced for *Abol Tabol* and *Ha-ja-ba-ra-la*.

I firmly believe that while going through manuscripts or the draft pages of a narrative one can find out many things about the writer. And in addition there are sometimes other sources like a diary, letters, etc. It's unfortunate that Sukumar Ray never kept a diary. No one in my family has ever maintained a diary. With the exception of one individual. He was my *chhoto kaka* (younger uncle)—Subimal Ray. But his diary doesn't devote any space to self-appraisal. Year after year *chhoto kaka* repeated the same format in his journal. It describes in minute details his everyday activities beginning from early morning till his bedtime at night.

Sukumar Ray maintained no diary. What he had were some notebooks, letters written to the family, two issues of a handwritten magazine, the manuscripts of a few plays, and one exercise book *(kheror khata)*. Of the oldest of these are the handwritten journals. The name of the journal was—*Sare Botrish Bhaja* (Savoury Mix). The illustrations for the jackets of these two journals were done by Sukumar Ray. At this time he was only seventeen or eighteen. This can be inferred from the mention of *Bongo-Bhongo Andolan* (Protest against Bengal Partition) in a few articles. Therefore, the years must have been 1905 or 1906.

Written by various individuals—many of whom may have then been in college. With the exception of my father, there's no way one can identify the other signatures. And each one adopted a pseudonym. The plays *Jhalapala* (Cacophony) and *Lakshmaner Shaktishel* (Lakshman and his Wonder Weapon) were written for these journals.

My father and others had formed a club. It was called the Nonsense Club.

This was organized much before the Monday Club. Amongst the various activities initiated in these journals, one was *Sare Botrish Bhaja*. Along with the other miscellaneous writings what was found were advertisements or in other words parody of advertisements. An example will make this clear. It was the advertisement of a particular medicine. The name of the medicine was clearly penned in Sukumar Ray's handwriting. The name was *Gondho Bikot Tel* (foul-smelling oil). The first few lines ran thus: So, you must have heard of this name—*Gondho Bikot Tel*. You mean you haven't? Are you deaf, sir? Needless to add the merit of the medicine, its composition, price, and distribution centres—were all mentioned in the advertisement.

One finds notes on photography and printing technology in all my father's notebooks. They include some original research notes as well. With the intention of acquiring patents a few descriptions of new discoveries also find a mention here.

The letters which are found are mostly written from England. Therefore, the year they were composed would have been 1912. My father at that time must have been twenty-four twenty-five. He'd gone to England to study Printing Technology. In all the letters written to Upendrakishore he only talks about his studies and work; from one of the letters written to his mother we gather that he can no longer survive without dried mango pulp (*amshotto*) and roasted spice/mouth freshener (*bhaja moshla*). We get to know from a letter written a few days later that these items had reached London in due course. In the missive sent to his brother, Subinoy, Sukumar requests that the journals, *Probashi*, *The Modern Review* and *Tattwokoumadi* should reach him on time; in a letter written to his younger sister, Shantilata, he mentions that within two months of settling down in London he has partially mastered the art of tying a tie—a task considered quite a challenge by him. He also reveals his eagerness to find out about the latest cricket news of Calcutta in a letter written to his uncle, Kuladaranjan. It must be mentioned here that Kuladaranjan himself was an able cricketer though we have no

knowledge whether either Upendrakishore or Sukumar played any cricket.

To me, much more than the letters, the goldmine of information comes from a kheror khata. I personally use a hardbound notebook to script all my screenplays. But this notebook of my father's can be folded and tied with a twine. Usually we refer to such writing pads as a local shopkeeper's account book. Earlier it was red in colour. Now it is a dull brown. When you open the first page you can see on the top right hand corner, engraved in English: May, 1918. Below on the right hand side of the page is written in English: Sukumar Ray. Occupying a large space in the middle, are mentioned the seven names given to this notebook: buzz notebook *(Uro Khata)*, unnecessary notebook *(Phaltu Khata)*, aimless notebook *(Emni Khata)*, account notebook *(Jabheda Khata)*, scribble notebook *(Khosra Khata)*, rubbish notebook *(Bajey Khata)*, and doodle book *(Hijibiji Khata)*. While going through these notebooks in detail one can fathom how appropriate each name was. Going through the first page, on the left hand side you can see an outline of a poem. After many layers of corrections the two lines which one can finally decipher are: *I'm i.e., Shri Gobindo / I'm no crooked fellow / I utter words with much plan / after all I don't talk blank.* There's a sketch right below this poem. An elderly turbaned and bearded fellow, wearing a short *dhoti*, a striped coat, and a shawl thrown on his shoulder. Looking daggers, this old man looks as if he is about to rebuke someone with raised arms. Opposite this page are seen the few rough lines of a song. This song is sung at many Brahmo weddings even today. And right below this is a pencil sketch of a warship in use at that time. After turning over to the next sheet you can detect the sketch of a grumpy old man with his eyes shut. Right below this is written in Bengali, a name, 'Nazimova'. Nazimova was a famous film actress of that era. The idea of associating a name like that with this sketch could come only from Sukumar. Apart from these the notebook also contains puzzles, riddles, many experimentations on the Bengali alphabet, outlines of various serious and solemn lectures, drafts of letters, poems attempted for *Sandesh*, various ideas collated for jackets of *Sandesh*; and a bunch of alliterations put together for the use of the book, *Bornomalatattwa*.

This same notebook contains an agenda of the Monday Club which must be read aloud. The agenda mentioned is: *One—the Secretary to present his annual misstatements. Two—Jibonbabu to raise a protest—Is this a report? If so, why not? Three—Sukumarbabu to move that the Secretary be dismissed. Written within brackets—a storm of protests, chorus lead by Habolbabu. And finally at the end a loud chorus—God save the Secretary.*

It's true that I never got to know my father. Yet these notebooks, papers, and letters have brought me close to him. Thanks to the presence of these items along with the books written by him which always stay near me, on no account have I felt his absence. My associations with these will never end. Hence my quest to understand him will never end either.

Note: The English translations of all the characters mentioned in *Ha-ja-ba-ra-la* and the lines of songs are taken from Sukanta Chaudhuri's translation of *Ha-ja-ba-ra-la*. The English names given to the books *Jhalapala*, *Lakshmaner Shaktishel*, *Abol Tabol* and *Ha-ja-ba-ra-la* are also his translation.

STEW MUCH!

Originally published in *Sandesh* (January 1915) as *Khichuri*. Later, it was revised when published in the book *Abol Tabol* (U. Ray & Sons, 1923). The English translation by Satyajit Ray was published in *Nonsense Rhymes* by Sukumar Ray (Writers Workshop, India, 1970). The illustrations in the poem are by Sukumar Ray.

A duck once met a porcupine; they formed a corporation
Which called itself a Porcuduck (a beastly conjugation!).
A stork to a turtle said, 'Let's put my head upon your torso;
We who are so pretty now, as Stortle would be more so!'
The lizard with the parrot's head thought: Taking to the chilli
After years of eating worms is absolutely silly.
A prancing goat—one wonders why—was driven by a need
To bequeath its upper portion to a crawling centipede.
The giraffe with grasshopper's limbs reflected: Why should I

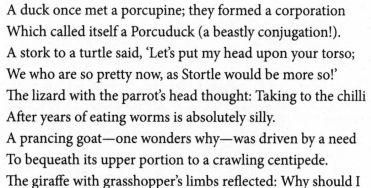

Go for walks in grassy fields, now that I can fly?
The nice contented cow will doubtless get a frightful shock
On finding that its lower limbs belong to a fighting cock.
It's obvious the Whalephant is not a happy notion:
The head goes for the jungle, while the tail turns to the ocean.
The lion's lack of horns distressed him greatly, so
He teamed up with a deer—now watch his antlers grow!

THE OLD WOODMAN

Originally published in *Sandesh* (February 1915) as *Abol Tabol*. Later, it was revised when published in the book *Abol Tabol* (U. Ray & Sons, 1923) as *Kath-Buro*. The English translation by Satyajit Ray was published in *Now*, 6 October 1967, and later compiled in *Nonsense Rhymes* by Sukumar Ray (Writers Workshop, India, 1970). The illustration in the poem is by Sukumar Ray.

The old man doesn't seem to mind
        The sun that's getting hotter,
He hums a tune and mumbles words,
He sits and licks a wooden stick
        That's just boiled in water

And, shakes his balding head;
It seems as if he's twice as wise
          As anybody dead.
'The holes you find in wood,' he says,
'Have reason to be there;
They're caused—and no one knows this yet—
          By cobwebs in the air.

But who cares for all this knowledge?'
          Screams the old man, fuming.
'A bunch of dolts—that's what they are,
          Pretending and presuming.
I've told them time and time again,
          They haven't understood,
What moonless nights are apt to do
          To holes that go with wood.'
Graphs and charts and formulae

He scribbles on the wall,
Subdividing types of wood
        And analysing all.
Tasty wood and tangy wood
        And wood that's hard to savour,
And all that lies concealed in holes
        And all the hidden flavour.
He claps the wooden sticks together
        Saying, 'These are sticks
Which hold no secrets for me now that
        I know all their tricks.
All the wooden villainy, and
        All the wooden wiles,
Wooden ills and wooden woes, and
        Beaming wooden smiles.
Some wood is wise and some is not,
        But holes are always there,
And only I can see they're caused
        By cobwebs in the air.'

THE MISSING WHISKERS

Originally published in *Sandesh* (March 1915) as *Abol Tabol*. Later, it was revised when published in the book *Abol Tabol* (U. Ray & Sons, 1923) as *Gonf Churi*. The English translation by Satyajit Ray was published in *Now*, annual issue 1965, and later compiled in *Nonsense Rhymes by Sukumar Ray* (Writers Workshop, India, 1970). The illustration in the poem is by Sukumar Ray.

They always knew the Boss Babu
To be a gentle fellow,
What happens if he in a jiffy
Turns all blue and yellow?

He was seated in his chair
Relaxed and free from care,
     Indulging in his post-meridian nap,
When, without a warning,
In the middle of his yawning,
     Something right inside him seemed to snap.

With muffled cries he rolled his eyes
     And threw his arms about.

'Alas, I'm sick. Come save me quick,'
    Was what he sputtered out.

They heard him and they all began
To cluster round the stricken man
And pondered on the safest plan
    To bring him to his senses.
'Call the police!' 'No—the Vet.'
His partner said, 'He seems upset.'
'But careful—he might bite yet,'
    Said his amanuensis.
But Boss Babu—his face all red and swollen—
Now declared, 'My moustache has been stolen.'

'Stolen whiskers?' they all cried.
'The Babu must be pacified.'

And so they held a mirror to his face.
'There, sir,' they said. 'You see
Your whiskers are where they used to be?
Who would dare to put you in disgrace?'

Babu now began to scream:
'You dunderheads, I wouldn't dream
        Of ever wearing whiskers so outrageous.
They make me look a shaggy butcher.
Know this—in the near future
        I ought to—no, I must reduce your wages.'
This he did. And then at random
He composed a memorandum,
        Herewith quoted (minus appendages):

'If you think your employees
Deserve your love—correction, please:
They don't. They're fools. No common sense.
They're full of crass incompetence.
The ones in my establishment
They show their cheek in not believing
Whiskers lend themselves to thieving.
Their moustaches, I predict,
Will soon be mercilessly picked;
And when that happens they will know
What Man is to Moustachio:
Man is slave, Moustache is master,
Losing which Man meets disaster.'

OLD TICKLER

Originally published in *Sandesh* (May 1915) as *Katukutu Buro*. Later, it was revised when published in the book *Abol Tabol* (U. Ray & Sons, 1923). The English translation by Satyajit Ray was published in *Nonsense Rhymes* by Sukumar Ray (Writers Workshop, India, 1970). The illustration in the poem is by Sukumar Ray.

Go East or West, go North or South, by land or sea or air,
But before you go, make sure old Tickler isn't there.
Tickler is a terror, and I'll tell you what he's after—
He'll have you stuffing tickle chops until you choke with laughter.
It's hard to tell just where he lives, and harder to restrict him,
He's always just around the corner looking for a victim.
His method is quite simple: he'll grab you by your sleeve
And tell you anecdotes which he insists you must believe.
He thinks they're very funny, while others find them grim,
(They have to keep on laughing, though, so as to humour him.)
One wouldn't mind the stories if they were all one had to bear,
He also uses tickle-feathers, which is most unfair,
And so he goes on cackling, 'Oh, but don't you think it's funny!—
Aunt Kitty selling pigeons' eggs and figs and cloves and honey.

The eggs are long and conical, the cloves are convoluted,
The figs have arabesques on them nicely executed.
From dawn till dusk Aunt Kitty sings a string of motley airs,
All mews and barks and brays and neighs (Aunt Kitty calls them Prayers).'
Saying so, he brings his hand behind your back to pinch you,
At which you have to laugh unless you want that he should lynch you.

UNCLE'S INVENTION

Originally published in *Sandesh* (February 1916) as *Abol Tabol*. Later, it was revised when published in the book *Abol Tabol* (U. Ray & Sons, 1923) as *Khuror Kaol*. The English translation by Satyajit Ray was published in *Now*, 6 October 1967, and later compiled in *Nonsense Rhymes* by Sukumar Ray (Writers Workshop, India, 1970). The illustration in the poem is by Sukumar Ray.

Chandidas's uncle has invented a device
Which is causing everyone to praise it to the skies.
When Uncle was a year old, or maybe even younger,
He came out with a lusty yell that sounded just like 'Goonga'.
At such an age most other tots just manage 'Glug' and 'Mum',
So 'Goonga', like a thunderbolt, struck everybody dumb.
And all who heard, said, 'Here's a boy—provided he survives—
Will one day surely bring about a change in human lives.'
It seems the day is here at last, and victory is won
With what will make a five-mile walk seem like only one.
I've seen the contrivance myself, and say with confidence
Never had invention had such great significance.
Let me tell you how it strikes the eyes of a beholder:
First of all, one notes that you must strap it to your shoulder.

An arm extends, and from its end one notes there hangs a hook
To which you bait some foodstuff which you either buy or cook.
Naturally the choice depends upon your predilections
(It's wiser to restrict yourself to hookable confections).
The sight of morsel dangling close provokes the urge to eat
Which, transcribed to motive force, soon propels the feet.
Before you know you're on the go, your mind intent on feeding,
But since the food is travelling too you never stop your speeding
The outcome, I need hardly add, will change our whole existence
Because we'll walk for nourishment, and never mind the distance.
No wonder there's a move afoot to honour Uncle soon
For bestowing on humanity an everlasting boon.

THE SONS OF RANGAROO

Originally published in *Sandesh* (May 1918) as *Hesho Na*. Later, it was revised when published in the book *Abol Tabol* (U. Ray & Sons, 1923) as *Ramgoruer Chana*. The English translation by Satyajit Ray was published in *Now*, annual issue 1965, and later compiled in *Nonsense Rhymes* by Sukumar Ray (Writers Workshop, India, 1970). The illustration in the poem is by Sukumar Ray.

To the sons of Rangaroo
      Laughter is taboo
A funny tale will make them wail:
      'We're not amused, boo-hoo!'

      They live in constant fear
      Of chuckles far and near
And start and bound at every sound
      That brings a breath of cheer.

      Their peace of mind forfeiting
      They sit and keep repeating:
'We believe in only grieving;
      Happiness is fleeting.'

They shun the summer breeze
That whispers through the trees
For fear the stir of leaf and burr
Their funny bones should tease.

They keep a wary eye
On the autumn sky
For signs of mirth above the earth
In foaming cumuli.

The darkness of the night
Brings them no respite,
As fireflies extemporize
Their dances of delight.

Those of you who're jolly
And feel to woe is folly
Must not refuse the Rangaroos
Their right to melancholy.

The Rangaroosian lair
Bereft of sun and air
Is doomed to be a monastery
Of permanent despair.

PREY FOR ME

Originally published in *Sandesh* (July 1918) as *Bhoy Kisher*. Later, it was revised when published in the book—*Abol Tabol* (U. Ray & Sons, 1923) as *Bhoy Peona*. The English translation by Satyajit Ray was published in *Prastuti Parbo*, Sukumar Ray special issue, 1982. The illustration in the poem is by Sukumar Ray.

Don't be scared, my little man—
      Think I'm going to bite you?
Silly notion! Don't you know
      I have no strength to fight you?

My heart is full of kindness
      With no anger underneath,
And all the biting that I do
      Is seldom with my teeth.

I know the horns upon my head
      Must seem a trifle shocking,
But butting pains my head, and so
      They're seldom used for knocking.

Come into my lair, little man
    And live with me a while
I'll treat you as a dear friend
    And put you up in style.

The club I'm holding in my hand—
    Now, does that cause you panic?
It's light as feather, take my word,
    It only looks titanic.

Well, well—I see you're not convinced
    By all that I have said,
It's time I grabbed you by your legs
    And knocked you on the head.

My wife and dozen kids and I
    Believe it's downright silly
To let escape a stupid man
    Who's scared willy-nilly.

THE PUNDIT'S WRATH

Originally published in *Sandesh* (June 1920) as *Ajob Saja*. Later, it was revised when published in the book *Pagla Dashu* (M.C. Sarkar & Sons, 1940). The English translation by Satyajit Ray was published in *Target* (June 1984). The illustration in the story is by Satyajit Ray for the Signet Press edition, 1946.

'Sir, Bhola is making faces at me!'

'No, sir. I was scratching my ears, which twisted my features.'

The Sanskrit pundit didn't bother to open his eyes. 'Pranks, pranks, pranks,' he drawled sleepily. 'Stand up and keep standing.'

For half a minute there was silence in the class. Then Bhola turned to Bishu and said, 'You heard him—stand up!'

'Why me?'

'It was you he asked.'

'Certainly not. Ask Ganesh. Ganesh, was it me he asked or him?'

Ganesh was not one of the bright ones. He left his desk, stole up to the teacher and called out, 'Sir!'

The pundit knitted his brows. 'What is it?'

Ganesh leaned forward earnestly. 'Who did you ask to stand up, sir?'

The pundit opened a pair of bleary eyes.

'You!' he barked out. 'Go back to your desk and keep standing.' Then he closed his eyes again.

So Ganesh kept standing.

There was another minute or so of silence. Then a loud whisper was heard. It was Bhola. 'Didn't he ask you to stand on one leg?'

'Certainly not,' snapped Ganesh. 'He only said keep standing.'

'But he raised a finger when he spoke. That surely meant he wanted you to stand on one leg.'

Ganesh couldn't deny that the pundit had raised his forefinger when shouting at him. Bishu and Bhola kept insisting. 'Come on, stand on one leg or we shall complain.' This was enough to scare Ganesh into raising a leg.

But now Bishu and Bhola broke out into a violent argument, one saying the pundit meant the right leg, while the other insisted he meant the left.

Ganesh was now in a fix. He went up to the sleeping pundit again and called out, 'Which leg did you mean, sir?'

The pundit was then in the middle of a dream and snoring. Ganesh's question shattered his siesta and sent him into a violent fit of coughing. Ganesh hadn't expected such a reaction at all, and could only mumble, 'What shall we do now?'

Bhola said, 'Run and fetch some water.'

'And pour it on the head,' added Bishu.

Ganesh ran out and came back with a carafe of water which he promptly emptied on the pundit's balding, pigtailed head. It certainly brought the fit of coughing to a quick end, but it produced a look in the pundit's eyes which made the carafe shake in Ganesh's hand.

This brought an air of solemnity into the class. Only the round-faced Shamlal appeared to be smiling because of the natural way his lips turned up at the corners. The pundit now turned his fury on him. With a roar like a hungry tiger's he said, 'Come up here, you!'

'What have I done, sir?' whimpered Shamlal. 'It was Ganesh who poured the water.'

The pundit was reasonable enough to concede that and turned to Ganesh who was still holding the carafe. Before he could be questioned Ganesh blurted out, 'It was Bhola who told me, sir.'

Bhola said, 'I only told him to bring water. Bishu suggested pouring it on your head.' Bishu retorted, 'I never said pour it on the pundit's head; I meant on Ganesh's own head.'

The pundit surveyed the class with baleful eyes for a while, and said at length, 'Very well; I'll spare you this time. But only this time.'

Everyone was relieved, but nobody could make out why the pundit went soft all of a sudden. Only the pundit knew that he was suddenly reminded of the pranks he had himself played as a schoolboy.

BABURAM THE SNAKE CHARMER

Originally published in *Sandesh* (July 1921) as *Bapre*. Later, it was revised when published in the book *Abol Tabol* (U. Ray & Sons, 1923) as *Baburam Sapure*. The English translation by Satyajit Ray was published in *Nonsense Rhymes* by Sukumar Ray (Writers Workshop, India, 1970). The illustration in the poem is by Satyajit Ray for the Signet Press edition, 1945.

Hullo there, Baburam—what have you got in there?
Snakes? Aha—and do you think there's one that you could spare?
You know, I'd love to have one, but let me tell you this—
The ones that bite aren't right for me—nor the ones that hiss.
   I'd also skip the ones that butt,
   As well as the ones that whistle,
   Or the ones that slink about
   Or show their fangs, or bristle.
As for eating habits, I think it would be nice
To go for ones that only take a meal of milk and rice.
I'm sure you know the kind of snake I want from what I've said.
Do let me have one, Baburam, so I could bash its head.

THE KING'S ILLNESS

Originally published in *Sandesh* (February 1922) as *Rajar Asukh*. The English translation by Satyajit Ray, hitherto unpublished, has been transcribed from Ray's literary notebook.

Once upon a time there was a King who had a strange illness. The doctors and hakims came in hordes and left in hordes; nobody could say what had caused the illness, and nobody could prescribe a cure for it. The King tried one medicine after another, but none worked. He put ice bags on his head, hot water bags on his stomach, but they didn't work either.

Finally the King lost his temper. He said, 'Send all the doctors away and burn all their books.'

His order was obeyed.

Everyone stayed away from the palace out of fear. But then the people began to ask themselves: Must the King die for lack of treatment?

One day a sannyasi came to the palace and said, 'I know a way to cure the king, but it's not an easy way. Do you think you will be able to follow my instructions?'

The Minister, the General, the Magistrate, the courtiers, all said, 'Why not? We'll certainly follow them even if it costs our lives.'

The sannyasi said, 'First, find a man who is without worry, who is always smiling, and who is happy at all times.'

'And then?'

'Then, if the King wears this man's clothes for a day and sleeps on his mattress for a night, he will be well again.'

Everyone said, 'But this is an excellent prescription!'

Word reached the King in no time. The king said, 'If there was such an easy cure, why was everybody going round in circles? Why didn't it strike anyone else? Go and find that happy man and bring his clothes and his mattress to me.'

People went everywhere to look for such a man, but they all came back and said, 'No sorrows, no worries, ever-smiling, ever-happy—such a man is not to be found anywhere.'

The Minister got very angry and said, 'You're all good-for-nothings. You don't even know where to look.' So he went out on his own to look for such a man.

When he came to the marketplace, he saw a large number of people gathered round an old Sethji who was doling out food and money and clothes to everybody.

The Minister thought: Why, this man looks happy enough; and he seems to have a lot of money too, so he should be free from worries. I'll go and ask for his clothes and mattress.

The Minister was about to go when he saw a beggar take alms from the Sethji without salaaming him. This so upset the Sethji that he screamed at the beggar, beat him with his shoes, took back what he had given him, and kicked him away. The minister left the marketplace in haste.

Next, he saw a man by the river who capered and sang funny songs to a crowd who roared with laughter. The antics of the man were funnier than anything the minister had ever seen, and he too was helpless with laughter. He thought: Here is a man who can laugh and make people laugh, yet none of my men came across him. 'Who is that funny man?' he asked a man standing nearby.

The man replied, 'He is Gobra the drunkard. You can see how jolly he is now, but when the sun goes down, he starts drinking and making a nuisance of himself. The people of his neighbourhood live in dread of him.'

The Minister's face fell, and he set off again looking for the happy man. He searched the whole day, but found no one. For days on end he searched, and came back home disappointed at the end of each day.

He had almost reached the end of his tether when one day he came across a crazy-looking old man sitting at the foot of a tree and laughing. The man had a shock of wild hair, a straggling beard, and a body as thin as a rake.

The Minister asked, 'What makes you laugh, old man?'

The old man said, 'But it's all so funny!—The earth spinning like a top, the grass growing in the fields, the rain falling from the sky, the birds settling on branches and then flying off again . . . I see all this happening before my eyes and it tickles me to death.'

The minister said, 'That's all very well, but you can't spend all your life sitting and laughing. I hope you do some work too.'

'Of course,' said the old man. 'I go to the river in the morning, I bathe. I watch the people coming and going and listen to them talking. Then I come and sit here in the shade of the tree. I eat when I find something to eat; when I don't, I go without food. When I feel like walking, I take a stroll; when I feel sleepy, I sleep. No worries, no problems, nothing. It's a great life.'

The minister scratched his head and said, 'But what happens when you have to go without food?'

'Nothing. I just sit quietly and watch the fun. It's more of a bother when there's something to eat. You have to use your fingers, take mouthfuls, chew the food, swallow it or wash it down with water, then wash your hands, wipe them dry—such a lot of work.'

The Minister thought: Well, I've found my man at last. He said, 'Can you lend me one of your clothes? I'll pay you whatever you ask for it.'

The old man burst into laughter. 'Clothes? My clothes? Only the other day a man gave me a wrapper, and I gave it away to a beggar. I've never cared for clothes.'

The Minister thought: What a problem! You think you've found your man, and then you find he has no clothes. He said, 'What about lending your mattress? I'll pay you anything you ask for.'

This time the old man laughed so much that he rolled on the ground. It took a long time before he could speak again. He said, 'I haven't used a bed in forty years and you ask for mattress!'

The Minister was greatly astonished, and said, 'You don't wear clothes, you never use a mattress to lie down—don't you ever fall ill?'

'Fall ill? I don't know what illness is. It's only those who are always worrying about how they are that fall ill.'

The old man leaned against the tree and started to laugh again.

The Minister went back home with his hopes dashed to the ground. The King sent for him, heard what he had to say and sent him back.

Now everyone looked at one another and shook their heads. 'There's no way to save the king,' they said.

The King, on the other hand, sat and thought: I live in right royal style, eat the best food, own the best of everything, am praised and honoured and flattered by everyone— and I had to fall ill, while the beggar who owns nothing, sits under a tree and eats what comes his way—he says he doesn't know what illness is? If he can thumb his nose at illness, why can't I?

Next morning, the king got out of bed and sent for his courtiers. 'Go and take your place in the court, you dunderheads,' he said. 'You tried and failed. Now look at me; I've cured my own illness. I'll go and sit on the throne again. If anybody dares to say a word, I'll have his head chopped off.'

THE KING OF BOMBARDIA

Originally published in *Sandesh* (November 1922) as *Keno*. It was later compiled and published in *Abol Tabol* (U. Ray & Sons, 1923) as *Bombagarer Raja*. The English translation by Satyajit Ray was published in *Now*, annual issue 1965, and later compiled in *Nonsense Rhymes* by Sukumar Ray (Writers Workshop, India, 1970). The illustrations in the poem are by Sukumar Ray.

In the land of Bombardia
The customs are peculiar:

The King, for instance, advocates
Gilded frames for chocolates,
While the Queen—who goes to bed
With pillows strapped around her head—
Insists her brothers specialize
In sticking nails in custard pies.

On moonlit nights the Bombardian—
His eyes all painted vermilion—
Keeps his silver pocket watch
Immersed in boiling butterscotch.

And if by chance he catches cold
He somersaults (if not too old).

Musicians there—a sturdy lot—
Use woollen wrappers when it's hot,
And the scholar propagates
Pasting bills on balding pates.

When the King sits on the throne
He starts hee-hawing in baritone,
And on his lap Prime Minister
Just sits and beats a canister
(The throne, you know, they decorate
With bottles of bicarbonate).

The King's old aunt (an autocrat)
Hits pumpkins with her cricket bat,
While Uncle loves to dance mazurkas
Wearing garlands strung with hookahs.

All of which, though mighty queer,
Is natural in Bombardia.

GROOMY TIDINGS

First published in the book *Abol Tabol* (U. Ray & Sons, 1923) as *Sat Patra*. The English translation by Satyajit Ray was published in *Now*, 6 October 1967, and later compiled in *Nonsense Rhymes* by Sukumar Ray (Writers Workshop, India, 1970). The illustrations in the poem are by Satyajit Ray for the Signet Press edition, 1945.

My dear sir, do let me shake your hand—
Your daughter's soon to wed, I understand.
Great news. Congrats. Now, luckily
I know this Gangaram, the groom-to-be.
Splendid chap. You've won a fair prize—
Though not so fair, ha-ha, complexion-wise!
His face reminds me of—now, let me see . . .
Ah, yes—an owl: the same rotundity.
Education, sir? Now, there's a lad
With the strength of will that's to be had.
He sat for final tests at school. No luck. He flopped.
Nineteen times he tried, and then he stopped.
Financial state, you ask? His property?
He's sunk in debts as far as I can see!

His brothers are a sorry bunch, I fear.
One's a loony, one's racketeer.

A third they put the clinkers on because
By forging money he was breaking laws.

The youngest one, I gather, plays the drum
In restaurants, and earns a paltry sum.

Gangaram himself despairs to fight his
Ailments of the spleen and hepatitis.
But mark you, sir, his noble ancestry—
Ganga branches from a princely tree.
Sham Lahiri (and it has been proved)
Is Gangaram's own cousin, thrice removed.
Looking for a future son-in-law
I daresay you could hardly ask for more.

ODOUR IN THE COURT

First published in the book *Abol Tabol* (U. Ray & Sons, 1923) as *Gondho Bichar*. The English translation by Satyajit Ray was published in *Now*, annual issue 1965, and later compiled in *Nonsense Rhymes* by Sukumar Ray (Writers Workshop, India, 1970). The illustration in the poem is by Satyajit Ray for the Signet Press edition, 1945.

The King sat down on the throne and turned to the Minister.
'What's this smell,' he asked, 'that smells so sinister?'
The Minister said, 'It's from my cloak, Your Highness—
A new perfume I've bought today. It's the finest.'
'That,' said the King, 'the Court Physician should settle.'
The Physician came and said, 'I'd prove my mettle
If a cold hadn't made my nostrils quite impassable.'
The King then turned to the ageing priest in the chasuble.
'Come here, Priest,' he said, 'and please identify
The irksome smell that the air of the court does vilify.'
The cleric said, 'I've just now taken a pinch of snuff,
Hence my nostrils aren't quite clear enough.'
The King dismissed his priest and sent for the sentinel.
The sentry marched in promptly. The King said, 'Can't you tell

What this odour is that our work does hamper?'
'Your Highness,' answered the sentry, 'the smell of camphor
In my betel still pervades my senses;
I couldn't guess what the obnoxious essence is.'
The King said, 'Off with you!' and sent for the strongman.
Bhimsing the wrestler came and proved quite the wrong man.
'Your Highness,' the wrestler said, his muscles bulging,
'I'm not in the best of health—I hate divulging.'
The King looked grim, then suddenly cried, 'By thunder,
Why not ask my distant cousin named Chunder?'
'Chunder dear,' the King implored, 'don't fail me.'
With a raucous laugh old Chunder said, 'Impale me,
Or hang me by my neck just any old season,
But forcing a man to smell, defies all reason.'
At the back of the court sat Nazir, a nonagenarian
Thinking: I'm old; I haven't much longer to carry on—
What do I care if the scent should prove to be killing?
For a sack of gold I'd smell it; I'm perfectly willing.
So Nazir hobbled to the King and said his wish.
The King said, 'Do it, Nazir. I'll give you bakshish.'
Nazir went up to the minister, and down he bent
To plant his nostrils right on the source of the scent.
Wondrous feat! The courtiers turned applauders:
'Long live Nazir—Defier of Odious Odours!'

THE DIARY OF PROF. HESHORAM HOSHIAR

Originally serialized in *Sandesh* in April and May 1923 and later compiled in the book *Pagla Dashu* (M.C. Sarkar & Sons, 1940). The English translation by Satyajit Ray was published in Sunday Review, the *Times of India*, 19 September 1982. The illustrations in the story are by Sukumar Ray.

Prof. Hoshiar has been very angry with us. We have from time to time published accounts of prehistoric animals, but never anything about the Professor's encounters with them. We admit that we have been guilty of an oversight, but the truth is, we have been wholly unaware of the Professor's exploits. However, we are very happy to publish the following extract from the Professor's diary which he has been good enough to send us. We leave it to the reader to judge the truth or otherwise of the incidents described.

JUNE 22, 1922
THE KARAKORAM TEN MILES NORTH OF THE BANDAKUSH RANGE

Our party now consists of ten people: my nephew Chandrakhai, the two shikaris, Lakkarh and Chhakkarh Singh, six porters, and myself. Our faithful dog, too, continues to keep us company.

We pitched our tents on the bank of a river, left our baggage in the care of our

All set for the shikar

porters and set out to explore, taking with us our guns, a map, and the box containing instruments and provisions.

Two hours of walking brought us to a strange place where everything around us seemed unfamiliar. The tall trees belonged to an unknown species. One had huge, crimson, wood-apple-like fruits hanging from the branches; another had white and yellow flowers, each over two feet long; yet another was covered with long, tapering vegetables whose pungent smell assailed our nostrils from fifty feet away.

We stood surveying this extraordinary scene when we suddenly heard loud, whooping noises from a nearby hilltop.

The two shikaris and I had our guns instantly on the ready, but Chandrakhai sat unconcerned and helped himself to some jam from a couple of his tins he had taken out of the box. This is one great failing of my nephew: proximity to food makes him oblivious of danger.

We stood thus for a minute or so when Lakkarh Singh spotted an animal slightly bigger than an elephant smiling down at him from its perch on the stout branch of a tree. For a moment it looked like an oversized human, then it became clear that it was neither human nor simian, but a wholly new species of fauna. It sat peeling the rind of the round, crimson fruits which it ate while grinning down at us exactly like a human being. We

A Voracitherium

managed to take quite a few photographs while the creature consumed fruit after fruit.

Chandrakhai now took up courage to advance towards the creature and offer it some more food. It happily gulped down a loaf of bread, a seer of molasses, and half a dozen boiled eggs with their shells which made loud cracking noises as he munched. It had a mind to devour the tin which contained the molasses, but after a few tentative bites it screwed up its face, broke into a whining roar and loped off into the depths of the jungle. I have decided to name the creature *Voracitherium*.

24 JULY 1922
TWENTY-ONE MILES NORTH OF BANDAKUSH

There is so much to see here, so many new species of flora and fauna, that much of our time is spent in finding and collecting them. We have managed to cull over 200 specimens of insects and butterflies and 500 varieties of fruits and flowers, besides taking numerous photographs. We are now looking for a live specimen of fauna to take back with us. Back home from our trip last time, nobody believed us when we described how we were set upon by a *Gigantodon*. A live specimen is therefore a must.

Through an oversight we had neglected to compute the height of the Bandakush peak when we climbed it. The other day both Chandrakhai and I independently worked it out with the aid of our instrument. I arrived at 16,000 ft. and Chandrakhai at 42,000 ft. Today we took fresh measurements and it came to only 2,700 ft. There is obviously something wrong with the instrument. But of one thing there is no doubt: this is a peak which has never been climbed before. Indeed, we are in a wholly unexplored territory, with no sign of human habitation anywhere. We have to make our own maps as we go along.

There was an incident this morning. Lakkarh Singh ventured to taste a new kind of fruit which grew on a tree along our route. One bite, and he was rolling on the ground

A page from Ray's literary notebook showing the drafts of *The Diary of Prof. Heshoram Hoshiar*

Extracts for the Diary of
Prof. Heshoram Hoshiar

(Prof. Hoshiar has written to us complaining that although accounts of prehistoric animals have appeared in our journal from time to time, we have never published anything about his own encounters with them animals. The truth is, we had never heard of the Professor, and as such were unaware of his encounters he mentioned. However, now that the Professor has sent us what survives of his diary, we are happy to publish some extracts from it. The reader is free to enquire whether or not of its credibility to listen upon this and what follows.)

June 26, 1922. Ten miles north of Brandakush in the Karakoram Mountains.

Party now reduced to ten members consisting of myself, my brother Chandrashekhar, two shikaris (brothers Chhotekhar & Hethkar Singh) & six coolies. My faithful dog continues to keep us company.

This morning we pitched up tents beside a stream, left the coolies to transport our luggage & set off on our exploration out to explore the region. We took with us guns, a map and a large box containing our provisions & survey instruments. Two hours of travelling brought us to a strange country. Everything about the place seemed unfamiliar. The trees were all immense & of unknown species. On bore large fruits which looked like over-blown wood-apples. A blossom tree bore

A Glumotherium

groaning. This caused Chhakkarh to break out sobbing in a fit of commiseration for his brother. This went on for ten minutes or so after which Lakkarh Singh recovered and sat up. It was then we spotted a strange animal regarding us from behind a bush with obvious and intense disapproval. It bore the look of someone for whom the world was bereft of joy, and who had no patience whatsoever with unseemly displays of grief. I instantly decided to call it *Glumotherium*. I have yet to see a creature more obviously at odds with the world. We tried to mollify it with an offer of food. The beast made a grimace, then accepted half a loaf and a couple of bananas which it consumed. But then it tried some guava jelly, and this upset it so much that it smeared jelly and butter all over itself, turned its back on us and began to butt the ground with its head.

25 AUGUST 1922
TWENTY-FIVE MILES NORTH OF BANDAKUSH

This morning we were having breakfast in the camp when we heard a funny sound coming from outside. Tip-tap . . . flop-flop . . . tip-tap . . .

We peered out and saw a strange bird hopping about in a most peculiar, zigzag fashion. It was as if the bird didn't know which way to go. If the right leg went one way, the left went the other, and if the body moved forward, the head turned towards the rear. Every dozen steps or so the legs got entangled and brought the bird down in a heap. I think its intention was to survey the camp, but as soon as it caught sight of us it got so jumpy that it promptly fell on its face. Then it scrambled to its feet, hopped a couple of yards away on one leg, twisted its neck around and stood observing us.

'Very good,' said Chandrakhai. 'This is a specimen we take back with us.'

The announcement sent a ripple of excitement over the group. I turned to Chhakkarh and said, 'Fire your gun. The noise will bring the bird down. Then four or five of us will go and grab it.'

The moment Chhakkarh fired his rifle, the bird's knees gave way and it flopped down on the ground. Then, with its eyes fixed on us, it broke into an ear-splitting crackle accompanied by a furious flapping of wings. It was enough to put us off from approaching the bird. But Lakkarh Singh, a brave fellow, ran up and gave it a hefty thwack on the chest with his umbrella.

Up on its feet at once, the bird now grabbed Lakkarh's beard with its beak and hung on to it with claws planted on the shikari's shoulders.

Seeing his brother's plight, Chhakkarh rose to the occasion. He took a mighty swipe with his gun aiming to brain the bird. Unfortunately, he missed his mark and the butt of the rifle landed on his brother's chest. This scared the bird, causing it to release its hold on Lakkarh, who forthwith launched a fierce assault on his brother, the latter resisting with equal vigour.

A Zigzagornis

For a moment it looked as if the two would fight to death, such was the fury they displayed. Aided by two porters, I was trying all the while to pull Chhakkarh away from his brother. He not only resisted, but kept raining blows at his brother's nose. Chandrakhai, a portly, well-built fellow, had wound his arms around Lakkarh's waist, which didn't prevent the latter from leaping three feet into the air and whirling his rifle over his head. It just shows that the Sikhs are a race apart.

Bent on stopping the fight, we had not realized that the bird had disappeared in the meantime. However, we managed to retrieve some feathers of what I have decided to call the *Zigzagornis*. These, along with the photographs I have taken, ought to furnish adequate proof.

1 SEPTEMBER 1922
ON THE BANKS OF THE RIVER KANKRAMOTI

Our provisions are fast running out. The stock of vegetables was exhausted some time ago. Now we have only some poultry left which provide us with our daily quota of eggs, some jam, biscuits, tinned milk and fruit, and some tinned meat and fish. Barely enough to last a fortnight. Which means we must be on our way back soon.

We were making an inventory of items left when Chhakkarh suddenly announced that his brother had gone out at dawn and hadn't come back yet. I told him not to worry. 'Where can he go?' I said. 'He's sure to be back soon.'

But two hours passed and still no sign of Lakkarh. We were discussing whether or not to go out and look for him when we suddenly saw a very large animal looming up behind a tall, bushy tree. All we saw was its head which bobbed and swayed like a drunk's. We were about to beat a hasty retreat into our tents when we heard Lakkarh call out: 'Don't run away. He's quite harmless.'

The next moment Lakkarh emerged from behind the tree. He had the huge animal in tow, having used his turban for the purpose. He said he had gone to the river to fill his pitcher and encountered the beast on his way back. Seeing him, the animal had started to roll on the ground and make whimpering noises. Lakkarh had investigated and found a thorn in the sole of the animal's foot, and blood oozing from the wound.   With great courage, Lakkarh had taken out the thorn, washed the wound and bandaged it with his handkerchief. It was when he found that the animal wouldn't be left behind but followed him limping that Lakkarh had decided to use his turban as a leash. We all said: 'Let's keep it tethered. Perhaps this is the one we can take back with us as a specimen of the *Docilosaurus*.'

This happened in the morning. In the afternoon there was another incident. A sudden, piercing screech like a chorus of kites and owls was heard from near our camp. This caused the *Docilosaurus* which lay on the grass feeding on the long leaves from the overhanging branch of a tree, to let out a jackal-like wail, tear itself free from its tether, and with a series of jerky hops disappear into the thickets beyond.

A Docilosaurus

Dazed by the suddenness of the event, we now walked gingerly across towards the source of the shrieks, and found a large beast—a cross between a fish, a snake and a crocodile—screaming away at a tiny little creature which sat right before it with its arms and legs spread out in a gesture of utter helplessness. It seemed the big animal was about to gobble up the small one—but no—all it did was to scream at it at the top of its voice.

After about ten minutes of this Lakkarh said, 'Let's put a bullet into the big one.' I shook my head. 'You might miss,' I pointed out. 'And then who knows what it might do?'

A Becharatherium and a Chillanosaurus

Our problem was solved when the beast suddenly stopped screaming and slithered off snakily towards the river. Chandrakhai said, 'Let's call that a *Chillanosaurus*,' while Lakkarh suggested *Becharatherium* for the small one.

7 SEPTEMBER 1922
ON THE BANKS OF THE RIVER KANKRAMOTI

Making our way along the river bank, we have now reached the edge of the plateau. There is no way to proceed any further. The land in front and on two sides drops sharply down 300 feet to the plains below which have the appearance of a desert with no vegetation and no sign of life.

The unnamed creature

We stood on the steps looking down when we suddenly noticed something stirring bout fifty feet below us. It was a creature the size of a smallish whale. Its head hung down like a bat's, while its tail was coiled round the stump of a tree which protruded from the cliff.

We now looked around and spotted half a dozen more such creatures. Some slept, a couple had stretched out their long necks and swung them like pendulums and one had poked its head into a crevice and appeared to be nibbling at something.

While we stood there observing the creatures, the one that we sighted first suddenly took off on its wings, swung round and came swooping down at us. We felt our limbs go numb. In our abject terror, the thought of running away didn't occur to us. In a matter of seconds the creature was right above our heads. What followed I can only dimly recall: a most unpleasant smell, a great swirl of wings, and the terrifying metallic crackle of the creature. It was a brush from its wing which finally knocked me out. The others were, if anything, in a worse state than mine. When I came to and looked around, I found all my companions bleeding from wounds. One of Chhakkarh's eyes was swollen to the point which reduced it to a mere slit. Lakkarh was groaning in pain with a twisted arm. I too felt pain in my chest and back. Only Chandrakhai seemed more intent on munching biscuits held in his right hand while with the left, which held a handkerchief, he wiped off blood from his forehead and neck.

We decided not to waste any more time, and set off on our journey back towards Bandakush.

***

This is where the extract ends. We had written to the Professor for more details. He sent along his nephew with a note saying—'this gentleman will provide you with all additional information.' Below is a verbatim account of the conversation we had with Mr Chandrakhai.

***

When can we see the specimens you brought with you?

Mr C: They're all lost.

What! Lost? All those priceless specimens lost?

Mr C: We were lucky we didn't lose our lives. You have no idea about the storms in that region. One blast sent all our stuff blowing away—our tents, our baggage, our specimens, everything. Even I was blown off the ground several times. Once I thought I was dead. The dog disappeared without a trace. You can't imagine what we went through. Maps, instruments, log books—nothing remains. You would look like porcupines with your hair standing on end if I told you how we finally got back. Struggling along without food, with nothing to guide us, it took three months to cover a distance that normally takes only a fortnight.

We take it then all the evidence has been destroyed.

Mr C: Well, I am here, my uncle is here—what more proof do you want? And here are some sketches I've brought for you. They're evidence too.

'What species of Therium are you, sir?' quipped a wag in our office.

'Bluffotherium,' said another. 'He just sits and spins yarns.'

Visibly chafing at the remark, Mr Chandrakhai scooped up a handful of cashew nuts from a plate on our desk, and strode out of the office muttering invectives.

***

পতজিৎ রায় চেধুরী

Portrait of an artist as a young man.
The longhand calligraphy—'Satyajit Ray Chowdhury'
by Ray has been taken from his notebook. This is a rare
occasion where Ray uses his ancestral title after his name.

SATYAJIT *translates*
SATYAJIT

Photograph of Satyajit Ray by Nemai Ghosh

SATYAJIT ON HIS LITERARY WORKS

Published as 'Introduction' in a compilation titled *Stories* (Secker & Warburg, 1987).

I n 1913, my grandfather Upendrakishore Ray launched a children's monthly magazine called *Sandesh*. Sandesh is the name of a popular Bengali sweetmeat; but the word also means 'information'. Upendrakishore Ray had a formidable talent as a children's writer, having already published a delightful collection of Bengali folk tales as well as children's versions of the two famous Indian epics—the Ramayana and the Mahabharata. All three were embellished with his own beautiful illustrations. The books and the magazine were published from his own press, U. Ray & Sons; my grandfather was a process engraver of the highest eminence.

Upendrakishore Ray died in 1915, six years before I was born. In the two years that he edited *Sandesh*, he filled its pages with stories, articles and illustrations. After his death, his eldest son, my father Sukumar Ray, took over. Sukumar Ray, too, had unique gifts as a children's writer and comic illustrator. Apart from school stories, plays and articles, he wrote a series of nonsense rhymes for the magazine which went on to win a permanent place in Bengali literature.

Sandesh folded four years after my father's death. Soon, U. Ray & Sons too closed down. My mother and I moved to my maternal uncle's house where I grew up, finished my education and, in 1943, joined a British advertising agency as a junior visualizer. I had no literary bent at all, and never thought that I might one day write stories. What interested me besides advertising was films, although advertising seemed more dependable as a profession. I was in advertising for twelve years before I relinquished it to brave the hazards of a career in films.

It was in 1961, after I had established myself as a filmmaker, that a poet friend of mine and I hit upon the idea of reviving *Sandesh*. The idea soon became a reality. The first issue of the revived *Sandesh* came out in the Bengali new year, in May 1961, on my fortieth birthday. As one of the two editors, I felt I had to contribute something. I produced a Bengali version of Edward Lear's *The Jumblies*. The second issue of *Sandesh* carried my first short story with my own illustration. Since then I have been writing and illustrating regularly for *Sandesh*, which celebrated its twenty-fifth anniversary this year.

Some of the stories I have written reflect my love of Verne and Wells and Conan Doyle whose works I read as a schoolboy. Professor Shonku, the scientist–inventor, may be said to be a mild-mannered version of Professor Challenger, where the love of adventure takes him to remote corners of the globe. Four of his adventures are included here. I don't think the other stories in this volume show any marked influence. Among these are straightforward tales as well as tales of the fantastic and the supernatural for which I have a special fascination.

I enjoy writing stories for its own sake and derive a pleasure from it which is quite distinct from the pleasure of the vastly more intricate business of making a film. I have written stories both during the making of a film and in the free period—usually lasting about six months—between films.

BONKUBABU'S FRIEND

The Bengali story was originally published in *Sandesh* (February 1962) as *Bonkubabur Bondhu*. The English translation by Satyajit Ray, hitherto unpublished, has been transcribed from Ray's literary notebook. The illustrations in the story, including the Bengali calligraphy in the headpiece, are by Satyajit Ray.

Nobody had ever seen Bonkubabu lose his temper. In fact, it was hard to guess how he would behave or what he would do or say if he did lose his temper.

And yet, it was not as if there were no reasons for him to be angry. For twenty-two years he had been teaching Geography and Bengali at the Kankurgachi Primary School and all these years Bonkubabu has been the victim of their jokes and pranks: drawing his caricatures on the blackboards, sticking chewing gum on his chair, setting firecrackers on him in the night of Kalipuja—had persisted all these years.

But Bonkubabu never lost his temper. At best he would clear his throat and say, 'You mustn't do that, you know.'

One reason, of course, was that if in a fit of temper he was to quit his job he would be hard put to find another job at his age. Another was that in a class full of naughty boys there were always exceptions every time. He would make friends with them, and the pleasure he got out of teaching them was enough to make his job worthwhile. In his free time, he would invite these boys over to his house. He gave them sweetmeats in a brass bowl and told them wonderful stories from all unknown and faraway places. Stories about Africa, about the discovery of the Poles, about the flesh-eating fish of Brazil, and the continent of Atlantis which had sunk in the ocean—all these Bonkubabu told in a most captivating way.

On Saturday and Sunday evenings Bonkubabu would go to zamindar Sripati Majumder's house. He has often thought that this would be the last visit. Because while he could put up with the pranks of small boys, scuffing by grownups he found hard to take. The evening sessions at Majumder's, the jokes at his expense sorely tried his patience. Hardly a couple of months ago, they were talking about ghosts. Usually Bonkubabu didn't open his mouth, but on that day he suddenly found himself saying he didn't believe in ghosts. And that did it. It was too good an opportunity for the people to pass up. So Bonkubabu had to put up with some nasty pranks on his way back home. As he was passing under a tamarind tree in Mitra's orchard, a thin lanky man all blackened with soot pounced upon him. This was doubtless a planned move of one of the elderly pranksters.

Although he was not scared, he was hurt physically. The pain in his shoulder persisted for three days. What was worse, his new shirt was not only soiled but also got badly ripped. A strange gesture indeed!

And there were other small annoyances like his shoes and umbrella hidden away, taking out the spices from his paan and putting false ones in their place, forcing a song out of him . . .

Even then he had to go to those weekend meets. Otherwise what would Mr Majumder think? Not only he was the most respected man in the village, but he was also harmful to turn and twist things his own way. On top of that, Bonkubabu's presence at his sessions was a must for him. He said you must have someone whom you could laugh at and who could be the butt of all jokes, or else what is a party? So Bonkubabu had to come.

The conversation this evening was on a celestial level; satellites were being discussed. Today just after sunset a moving light had been seen in the northern sky.

The same sort of light was also seen three months ago. Later it was learned that it was a Soviet satellite—drop-off or kick-off or some such name. It was said that the satellite was revolving around the earth at an altitude of four-hundred miles and providing scientists with a lot of new information.

Today the light was first seen by Bonkubabu. He has then pointed it out to Nidhubabu. But when Bonkubabu came to Majumder's, he found that Nidhubabu had already taken the credit himself and was bragging about it. Bonkubabu said nothing.

Nobody in the present company there knew much about satellites, but one didn't need a ticket to talk about it, nor was it considered embarrassing to do so, and everybody was adding his bit to the conversation.

Chandibabu said, 'When all is said and done, people like us merely shouldn't poke our noses into satellites. To us they are no more real than the jewel in the serpent's head. Somewhere in some corner of the heaven somebody sees a blurred light, the papers write about it, and you sit at home chewing paan and go all hysterical over it. As if you owned it; and the claps belong to you.'

Ramkanai was the youngster in the group. He said, 'It may not belong to us, but it certainly belongs to mankind. Mankind resides above all. Look at the ultimate truth.'

'Oh that's simple,' said Chandibabu, 'you don't expect a monkey to make a satellite, do you?'

Nidhubabu the pleader said, 'Very well. Leave satellites. Satellites don't have people in them. It's just a machine which goes revolving. Tops do that too. You press a switch and fans do that too. But what about rockets? That's something we can't take lightly.'

Chandibabu wrinkled his nose and said, 'Rockets? What's there to talk about rockets? It would make some sense if they made one here and shoot it up to the moon from the maidan and we went and paid for ringside seats and see it go up. To me a rocket is as real as a mare's nest.'

Bhairav Chakravarty now said, 'But suppose something from some other planet seem to come down to earth . . .'

'So what? The likes of us would never get to see it.'

'That's true.'

Everyone now turned to their tea cups, as there wasn't much left to say on the subject.

At this point Bonkubabu cleared his throat and said mildly, 'Suppose it comes here.'

Nidhubabu feigned a show of great surprise and said, 'Why, Bonku too has something to say. Dear me! What will come here, Bonku? From where?'

Bonkubabu again said softly, 'Someone or something from some other planet, perhaps.'

As with his habit, Bhairav Chakravarty gave a hefty slap on his shoulder, showed his teeth and said grinning, 'Bravo, Bonku, bravo! Men from other planets landing here? In this godforsaken place? Not London, not Moscow, not New York, not even Calcutta, land here in Kankurgachi? I must say you have high hopes.'

Bonkubabu did not say anything but it kept running in his mind—why is that is so impossible? After all, the purpose of coming from a far-away planet would be to visit earth and suppose they didn't bother where they landed? The chance of landing in Kankurgachi was just as good as landing anywhere else.

Sripatibabu hadn't opened his mouth so far. He now stirred himself; all eyes were turned on him. He put the tea cup down and spoke in a deep ringing voice of great certainty, 'Look, if anyone from any other planet chose to come down to earth, they wouldn't choose this cursed country of ours. They have better things to do than that. And they are not fools. I strongly believe they could be Europeans, and they would choose a foreign country in the West. Do you understand?'

Everybody except Bonkubabu nodded in assent.

Chandibabu poked Nidhubabu in the ribs, indicating Bonkubabu with a kidding smile and said in a mocking tone, 'I must say Bonku is right. After all, it's quite natural for them to come here if only because of Bonku. What do you say, Nidhu? Suppose they wished to take an earthly specimen back with them—what better choice than Bonku?'

Ramkanai said, 'Good enough to adorn a museum, or a zoo.'

Bonkubabu thought, you're not bad as specimens either. This Sripati, chin with camel's face; Bhairav Chakravarty with eyes like a tortoise; Nidhu with a face like a mole; Ramkanai the goat; Chandibabu the bat—and you needed men to put in a zoo . . .

Bonkubabu felt tears welling up in his eyes. He rose to go. He had looked forward to this meeting tonight, but it turned out so badly. His heart felt heavy. He couldn't stay any longer.

'You're going?' Sripati asked Bonkubabu.

'It's quite late, sir.'

'Late? But tomorrow's a holiday. Sit now, have another cup of tea.'

'No thanks, Sir. I would better go. There are some answer papers lying. Good night.'

Ramkanai said, 'Careful, Bonku. There's no moon tonight. The men of Mars are scarier than ghosts.'

***

Bonkubabu saw the light as he was halfway through Pancha Ghosh's bamboo orchard. He was not carrying a lantern himself. It was winter, so the snakes wouldn't be out. Besides, he knew the way well. It was not a path that people used much, but for him it was a short cut.

He had an odd feeling for some time. Something was not quite as it should be. But he couldn't quite pin down what made it so. Then he suddenly realized that crickets were not chirping. There was dead silence. That was what made it different. On other evenings, the deeper he moved into the orchard, the louder became the shrilling. Tonight it was just the opposite. That was what made it so eerie. Now what could be the reason? Had the crickets all gone to sleep?

He kept wondering as he walked on, and in a minute or so turned towards east, when he saw the light.

At first he thought the orchard was on fire. In an open space, where the pond was, the branches and leaves of the bamboo orchard trees were bathed in a pink glow. Down on the ground the whole area of the pond was ablaze with an intense pink light. But it was not fire, because the light didn't flicker.

Bonkubabu advanced.

He was aware of a sound on his ears, but couldn't make out what it was. It was a sort of high-pitched penetrating buzz—like ringing in the ears.

Although Bonkubabu felt a chill of fear, he walked on out of sheer curiosity.

As he crossed the large cluster of bamboo, fifteen yards or so from the pond, he saw the thing. A huge object like an overturned bowl covered the entire pond and through its translucent surface emanated a brilliant yet soothing pink light which lit up the surrounding orchard.

Even in his dreams, Bonkubabu had never seen a light like that.

He stood staring in wonder for a while, and then although at first sight the object seemed still, now there seemed to be life in it. He noticed a movement. The domed surface rose and fell as in breathing.

As Bonkubabu moved a few more steps to have a better look he suddenly felt as if a charge of electricity had passed through him. And the next moment he found himself immobilized and felt as if unseen bonds were holding him down. Drained of all energy, he could neither move forward, nor step back.

He stood for a while like this and then noticed the rise and fall of the object's surface slowly come to a stop. Along with it stopped the strange ringing sound. And then, piercing the silence of the night was heard a voice which was somewhat like human beings, although much higher in pitch. It said: 'Milipipping Khruk! Milipipping Khruk!'

Bonkubabu was shocked into speechlessness. What kind of language was this? And where was the person that spoke out?

The next shout made Bonkubabu's heart miss a beat.

'Who are you? Who are you?'

Bonkubabu gulped and shouted back, 'I am Bonkubihari Dutta sir, Bonkubihari Dutta.'

'Are you English? Are you English?'

Bonkubabu shouted again, 'No sir, Bengali Kayastha sir.'

After a few moments of silence was heard a voice that perfectly pronounced: 'Namaskar.'

Bonkubabu sighed in relief and answered back: 'Namaskar!'

And with that he could feel his unseen bonds loosening. He could run away now, but didn't, because he noticed that a section of the domed object was now opening like a door.

Through the door came out, first, a smooth round head of a creature, and then slowly emerged the rest of the body.

The thin body of the creature was covered in a shining pink covering. On its face were pairs of holes where the nose and the ears should have been, and yet another hole for the mouth. There was no trace of hair. The two yellow eyes were so bright that they looked like electric bulbs.

The creature slowly stepped forward towards Bonkubabu and stood regarding him from a distance of five feet. Inadvertently, Bonkubabu's hands came together in a gesture of Namaskar.

After looking at Bonkubabu for a minute or so, the creature spoke in his thin, fluty voice.

'You are a man?'

Bonkubabu said, 'Yes.'

'This is the Earth?'

'Yes.'

'I have guessed right—the controls are not working properly. I had a small doubt, so I questioned you first in one of the languages of Pluto. When you didn't answer, I realized I had landed on the Earth instead. What a waste of time! Having come all the way . . . The same sort of thing happened another time. I was going to Jupiter and landed up in Venus instead—heh, heh!'

Bonkubabu didn't know what to say. In any case, he was feeling very uncomfortable, because the creature had started prodding him with his thin fingers.

As he finished his examination, he said, 'I'm Ang from the planet Cranius. I belong to a much higher species than man.'

This 4-foot high creature was claiming to be of higher species than man! Bonkubabu felt like laughing.

The creature strangely though, could read Bonkubabu's thoughts and said, 'There's no point in disbelieving me. I have proof. How many languages do you know?'

Bonkubabu scratched his head and said, 'Bengali, English and eh . . . a smattering of Hindi.'

'That's two and a half.'

'Yes.'

'I know fourteen thousand. I know every language spoken in your solar system. Besides, I also know the language of planets outside your solar system. I have been to twenty-five of them myself. How old are you?'

'Fifty.'

'I am eight hundred and thirty three. Do you eat the flesh of animals?'

Only recently, on Kali Puja day, Bonkubabu had eaten meat curry. How could he say no?

Ang said, 'We don't. We gave up a few centuries ago. We used to. I might have eaten you up.'

Bonkubabu gulped.

'Ever seen this?'

Ang gave Bonkubabu something which looked like a small pebble. As soon as he took it, a tremor passed through his body, and he quickly handed that thing back.

Ang laughed, 'It was because I had this in my hand that you couldn't come near. Nobody can. There is nothing better than this to render an enemy powerless without causing him hurt.'

Bonkubabu was beginning to feel truly impressed.

Ang said, 'Are there any places or sights that you would like to see but are not able to?'

Bonkubabu thought, why, he would like to see the whole of the world, really. He taught Geography, and yet he had seen nothing besides a few towns and villages of Bengal. What has he seen even of his own province? Not the snows of Himalayas, or the ocean of Digha, or the jungles at Sunderbans; not even the Banyan tree in the Botanical Gardens at Shibpur.

He said, 'There's so much that I haven't seen. For instance, as I belong to a tropical country, I often feel a great desire to see the polar regions.'

Ang produced a swell-like tube with a lens at one end and held it before Bonkubabu's eyes. 'Take a look through it,' he said.

Bonkubabu put his eyes on the tube and felt a shiver of excitement. Was this possible? Just before his eyes was an endless stretch of ice with hillocks of snow here and

there. Up in the deep blue sky rainbow-coloured patterns kept shifting and changing in shape. Aurora Borealis. What was that? An Igloo. There—there was a group of polar bears. But what strange animal was that? Bonkubabu had a good look and recognized it, a Walrus! Not one, but two of them were locked in a fierce combat. The long, radish-like tusks of one were dug into the body of the other. Red blood dripped on the white snow.

Even in the cold December night Bonkubabu broke into a sweat.

Ang said, 'Don't you want to go to Brazil?'

Bonkubabu remembered the flesh-eating Piranha fish. Strange! How come the man was able to read his thoughts?

Bonkubabu put his eyes in the hole again.

Dense forest—the dark shadows in its depths spiked by sunlight filtering through the foliage. On one side was a gigantic tree and from its branches hung a—what was it? Good gracious! Bonkubabu could not imagine that such an enormous snake could exist.

Then suddenly he remembered about the Anaconda of Brazil. Big brother to the python. But where was the fish? Then he could see a stream. On the banks were crocodiles basking in the sun. Now one of them stirred. It was about to slip into the stream. It did so with a slithering noise—Bonkubabu could hear it. But what was that noise? The crocodile was back in the bank like a flash. But was it the same animal? Bonkubabu was horrified that the lower part of its body had almost nothing left, only bones, and the rest of its flesh was being avidly devoured by five sharp-toothed little monsters—the Piranha fish!

Bonkubabu could bear no more. His arms and legs were trembling and his head reeled.

Ang said, 'Now do you believe that we are superior?'

Bonkubabu licked his lips and said, 'Of course, certainly. No doubt about it. A hundred times superior.'

'Very well,' said Ang, 'looking at you and feeling your limbs I get the feeling that although you belong to an inferior level, you are not a bad example of human being. But the truth with you is that you are too meek, which is why you never got on in life. And to not protest against wrong and to put up with humiliation without a murmur are traits which suit no being, human or otherwise. Anyway, I am happy about the chance meeting, but I can't afford to waste time on this planet. I really must be off.'

Bonkubabu said, 'Goodbye Mr Ang. I too was very happy to—'

But before he had finished and before he knew what was happening, Ang's rocket had taken off and was out of Pancha Ghosh's bamboo orchard and had disappeared from view. Bonkubabu was now suddenly aware that the crickets had started shrilling again.

Walking homeward, Bonkubabu had a strange feeling. Even a little while ago he hadn't realized what an extraordinary event had taken place in his life. A planet tucked away in some remote corner of some solar system, nobody had ever heard of it. And from there comes this man—not man, but an Ang—and meets him and chats with him. How strange! How extraordinary! In all this earth, he was the only man this creature got to know. He—Bonkubihari Dutta, teacher of Geography and Bengali in the Kankurgachi Primary School. Today, from this moment, at least in one experience, he was, in the whole world, unique.

Bonkubabu found that he was no longer walking, but dancing.

The next day was a Sunday. The meeting in Sripatibabu's was in full swing. The news of the moving light seen in the sky the previous evening was in the papers as a very small item indeed. The news had come from only two places in Bengal, so it was just another flying saucer story.

Pancha Ghosh was among the members at today's meeting. It seemed that in the 40-bigha bamboo orchard few clusters of bamboos surrounding the pond had been scorched down in the night, and shed all their leaves. Bamboo trees do shed their dry leaves in winter, but the sudden descending was most unusual. The phenomenon was being discussed when Bhairav Chakravarty suddenly said, 'Why is Bonku so late today?'

Nobody had noticed this till now.

Nishu Moktar said, 'Bonku is unlikely to show his face just yet—after the way he was rubbed last night.'

Sripatibabu got very agitated and said, 'But that won't do. We want him here. Ramkanai, just go out and see if you can bring him along.'

Ramkanai said, 'I'll go as soon as I finish my tea,' and that very moment Bonkubabu entered the room. Entered is hardly the word for it. It was as if a tornado swept in the guise of a small man.

And then it wrecked havoc. As a prelude, Bonkubabu roared with laughter for a full minute, the likes of which no one had heard him laugh before.

Having done that, Bonkubabu cleared his throat with a loud noise and spoke.

'Friends, I am happy to announce that this is my last evening here. But before I actually part company with you, I have a few observations to make — which is why I am here. Number one—that goes for everybody—you are nothing but a bunch of windbags. People who talk of such things they know nothing about are called fools. Number two —this concerns Chandibabu—the propensity to hide shoes and umbrellas at your age is not only wrong but injustice. Please see that my umbrella and canvas shoes are sent back to my house by tomorrow. Nidhubabu, if you insist on calling me Bonkers, I shall start calling you Nitwit, and you'll have to accept that. And Sripatibabu—you are a big man, doubtless you have need for men to lick your boots. But know this, that as of today, I cease to be one of them. If you wish, I could send my pet cat Tom along; he can lick boots very well indeed. And—ah, I see Panchababu is here too. Let me inform you that one Mr Ang from the planet Cranuis came here in a rocket and landed in the pond in your bamboo orchard. I happened to get to know him. He is a delightful pers—sorry, Ang.'

With these words, and with a hefty slap on the back of Bhairav Chakravarty which sent him into a fit of coughing, Bonkubabu left the room.

At that very moment, Ramkanai dropped the full tea cup which broke into smithereens and splattering everybody's clothes with hot tea.

THE SMALL WORLD OF SADANANDA

Originally published in *Sandesh* (October 1962) as *Sadanander Khude Jagat*. The English translation by Ray was published in *Target*, annual number 1988, as *The Little World of Sadanan*da. The illustrations in the story, including the Bengali calligraphy in the headpiece, are by Satyajit Ray.

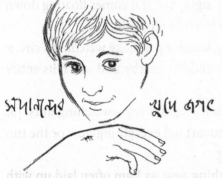

I am feeling quite cheerful today, so this is a good time to tell you everything. I know you will believe me. You are not like my people; they only laugh at me. They think I am making it up. So I have stopped talking to them.

It is midday now, so there is no one in my room. They will come in the afternoon. Now there are only two here—myself and my friend Lal Bahadur. Lal Bahadur Singh! Oh, how worried I was for his sake yesterday! I couldn't believe he would ever come back to me. He is very clever, so he was able to escape unhurt. Anyone else would have been finished by now.

How silly of me!—I have told you my friend's name, but haven't told you my own.

My name is Sadananda Chakravarty. It sounds like the name of a bearded old man, doesn't it? Actually, I am only thirteen. I can't help it if my name is old fashioned. After all, I didn't choose it; my grandma did.

If only she knew how much trouble it would cause me, she would have surely called me something else. How could she have known that people could pester me by saying, 'Why are you so glum when your name means 'ever-happy'?' Such fools! As if laughing like a jackass was the only way to show that one was happy. There are so many ways of being happy even when one doesn't smile.

For instance, suppose there's a twig sticking out of the ground and you find a grasshopper landing on its tip again and again. It would certainly make you happy to see it, but if you burst out laughing at it, people would think you were out of your mind. Like that mad uncle of mine. I never saw him, but I was told that he laughed all the time. Even when they had to put him in chains, he found it so funny that he almost split his sides laughing. The truth is, I get fun out of things which most people don't even notice. Even when I am lying in bed I notice things which make me happy. Sometimes a cotton seed will come floating in through the window. Small wispy things which the slightest breath of air sends wafting hither and thither. What a happy sight it is! If it comes floating down towards you, you blow on it and send it shooting up into the air again.

And if a crow comes and settles on the window, watching it is like watching a circus clown. I always go absolutely still when a crow comes and sits nearby, and watch its antics out of the corner of my eyes.

But if you ask me what gives me the most fun, I would say—watching ants. Of course, it is no longer just funny; it is . . . but no, I mustn't tell everything now or the fun will be spoilt. It's better that I begin at the beginning.

Once, about a year ago, I had fever. It was nothing new, as I am often laid up with fever. I catch a chill rather easily. Mother says it's because I spend so much time out of doors sitting on the grass.

As always, the first couple of days in bed was fun. A nice, chilly feeling mixed with a feeling of laziness. Added to this was the fun of not having to go to school. I lay in bed watching a squirrel climbing up the madar tree outside the window when Mother came and gave me a bitter mixture to drink. I drank it up like a good boy and then took the glass of water, drank some of it and blew the rest out of the window in a spray. I wrapped the blanket around me and was about to close my eyes for a doze when I noticed something.

A few drops of water had fallen on the window-sill, and in one of these drops a small black ant was trying desperately to save itself from drowning.

I found it so strange that I propped myself up on my elbows and leaned forward to bring my eyes-up close to the ant.

As I watched intently, it suddenly seemed as if the ant was not an ant any more but a man. In fact, it reminded me of Jhontu's brother-in-law who had slipped down the bank into a pond while fishing and, not being able to swim, wildly thrashed his arms about to keep himself afloat. In the end he was saved by Jhontu's elder brother and their servant Narahari.

As soon as I recalled the incident, I had a wish to save the ant.

Although I had fever, I jumped out of bed, ran out of the room, rushed into my father's study and tore off a piece of blotting paper from his writing pad. Then I ran back into my room, jumped on to the bed and held the blotting paper such that its edge touched the drop of water. The water was sucked up in no time.

The suddenly rescued ant seemed not to know which way to go. It rushed about this way and that for a while, and then disappeared down the drainpipe on the far side of the sill.

No more ants appeared on the sill that day.

The next day the fever went up. Around midday Mother came and said, 'Why are you staring at the window? You should try and get some sleep.'

I shut my eyes to please Mother, but as soon as she left, I opened them again and looked at the drainpipe.

In the afternoon, when the sun was behind the madar tree, I saw an ant poking its head out of the mouth of the pipe.

Suddenly it came out and started to move about briskly on the sill.

Although all black ants look alike, I somehow had the feeling that this was the same ant which had nearly drowned yesterday. I had acted as its friend, so it had come to pay me a visit.

I had made my plans beforehand. I had brought some sugar from the pantry, wrapped it up in paper and put it beside my pillow. I now opened the wrapper, took out a large grain of sugar and put it on the sill . . .

The ant seemed startled and stopped in its tracks. Then it cautiously approached the sugar and prodded it with its head from all sides. Then it suddenly made for the drainpipe and disappeared into it.

I thought, that's odd. I gave it such a nice grain of sugar and it left it behind. Why did it have to come at all if not for food?

The doctor came in a short while. He felt my pulse, looked at my tongue and placed the stethoscope on my chest and back. Then he said that I must take some more of the bitter mixture and the fever would go in a couple of days. That didn't make me happy at all. No fever meant going to school, and going to school meant not watching the drainpipe in the afternoon when the ants came out. Anyway, as soon as the doctor left, I turned towards the window and was delighted to see a whole army of black ants coming out of the drainpipe on to the sill.

The leader must be the ant I knew, and it must have informed the other ants of the grain of sugar and led them to it.

Watching for a while I was able to see for myself how clever the ants were. All the ants now banded together to push the grain towards the drainpipe. I can't describe how funny it was, I imagined that if they had been coolies pushing a heavy weight, they'd have shouted, 'All together, heave ho! A little further, heave ho! That's the spirit, heave ho!'

After my fever was gone, school was a bore for a few days. My thoughts would go back again and again to the window-sill. There must be ants coming there every afternoon. I would leave a few grains of sugar on the sill every morning before going to school, and when I returned in the afternoon I would find them gone.

In the class I used to sit at a desk towards the middle of the room. Beside me sat Sital. One day I was a little late and found Phani sitting in my place. So I had no choice but to sit at the back of the class, in front of the wall. In the last period before recess, we read history. In his thin, piping voice Haradhanbabu the history teacher was describing how brave Hannibal was. Hannibal had led an army from Carthage and had crossed the Alps to invade Italy.

As I listened, I suddenly had the feeling that Hannibal's army was in the classroom and was on the march very close to me.

I looked around and my eyes travelled to the wall behind me. Down the wall ran a long line of ants—hundreds of small black ants, exactly like a mighty army on the way to battle.

I looked down and found a crack in the wall near the floor through which the ants were going out.

As soon as the bell rang for the recess, I ran out to the back of our classroom and spotted the crack. The ants were coming out of it and making their way through the grass towards a guava tree.

I followed the ants and found, at the foot of the guava tree, something which can only be described as a castle.

It was a mound of earth with a tiny opening at the base through which the ants entered.

I had a great urge to look inside that castle.

I had my pencil in my pocket, and with its tip I began to dig carefully into the mound. At first, I found nothing inside, but on digging a little further, I had the surprise of my life. I found there were countless small chambers inside the mound, and a maze of passages leading from one chamber to another. How very strange! How could the ants build such a castle with their tiny arms and legs? How could they be so clever? Did they have schools where they were taught? Did they also learn from books, draw pictures, build things? Did that mean they were no different from human beings except in looks? How was it that they could build their own house while tigers, elephants, bears and horses couldn't? Even Bhulo, my pet dog, couldn't.

Of course, birds build nests. But how many birds can live in a single nest? Can the birds build a castle where thousands of them can live?

Because I had spoilt a part of the mound, there was a great flurry amongst the ants. I felt sorry for them. I thought, now that I have done them harm, I must make up by doing them a good turn, or they will look upon me as their enemy, which I am not. I was truly their friend.

So the next day I took half of a sweetmeat which Mother gave me to eat, wrapped

it up in a sal leaf and carried it in my pocket to school. Just before the bell rang for the classes to begin, I put the sweetmeat by the anthill. The ants would have to travel to find food; today they'd find it right at their doorstep. Surely this was doing them a good turn.

In a few weeks the summer holidays began and my friendship with ants began to grow. I would tell the elders about my observations of how ants behaved, but they paid no attention to me. What really put my back up was that they laughed at me. So I decided not to tell anybody anything. Whatever I did, I would do on my own and keep what I learned to myself.

One day, in the afternoon, I sat by the compound wall of Pintu's house watching a hill made by red ants. People will say that you can't sit near red ants for long because they bite. I had been bitten by red ants myself, but of late I had noticed that they didn't bite me anymore. So I was watching them without fear when I suddenly saw Chhiku striding up.

I haven't mentioned Chhiku yet. His real name is Srikumar. He is in the same class as me, but he must be older than me because there's a thin line of moustache above his lips. Chhiku is a bully, so nobody likes him. I usually don't meddle with him because he is stronger than me. Chhiku saw me and called out, 'You there, you silly ass, what are you doing squatting there on the ground?' I didn't pay any attention to him. He came up towards me. I kept my eyes on the ants.

Chhiku drew up and said, 'Well, what are you up to? I don't like the look of it.'

I made no attempt to hide what I was doing and told him the truth. Chhiku made a face, and said, 'What do you mean—watching ants? What is there to watch? And aren't there ants in your own house that you have to come all the way here?'

I felt very angry. What was it to him what I did? Why did he have to poke his nose into other people's affairs?

I said, 'I'm watching them because I like doing so. You know nothing about ants. Why don't you mind your own business? Why come and bother me?'

Chhiku hissed like an angry cat and said, 'So you like watching ants, eh? Well—there! There!' Before I could do or say anything, Chhiku had levelled the anthill with three vicious jabs of his heel, thereby squashing at least five-hundred ants.

Chhiku gave a hollow laugh and was about to walk away when something suddenly happened to me. I jumped up on Chhiku's back, grabbed hold of his hair, and knocked his head four or five times against Pintu's compound wall. Then I let go of him. Chhiku burst into tears and went off.

When I got back home, I learnt that Chhiku had already been there to complain against me.

But I was surprised when at first Mother neither scolded nor beat me. Perhaps she hadn't believed Chhiku, because I had never hit anyone before. Besides, Mother knew that I was scared of Chhiku. But when Mother asked what had happened, I couldn't lie to her.

Mother was very surprised. 'You mean you really bashed his head against the wall?'

I said, 'Yes, I did. And why only Chhiku? I would do the same to anyone who trampled on anthills.' This made Mother so angry that she slapped me.

It was a Saturday. Father came back from the office early. When he heard from Mother what had happened, he locked me up in my room. Although my cheeks smarted from the slaps, I wasn't really sorry for myself. I was very sorry for the ants. Once in Sahibgunge where cousin Parimal lives, there was a collision between two trains which killed three-hundred people. Today it took Chhiku only a few seconds to kill so many ants!

It seemed so wrong, so very, very wrong.

As I lay in bed thinking of all that had happened, I suddenly felt a little chilly and had to draw the blanket over myself.

And then I went off to sleep. I was awakened by a strange noise. A thin, high-pitched sound, very beautiful, going up and down in a regular beat, like a song.

My ears pricked up and I looked around but couldn't make out where the sound came from. Probably someone far away was singing. But I had never heard such singing before.

Look who's here! Coming out of the drainpipe while I was listening to the strange sound.

This time I clearly recognized it—the ant I had saved from drowning. It was facing me and salaaming me by raising its two front legs and touching its head with them. What shall I call this black creature? Kali, Krishna? I must think about it. After all, one can't have a friend without a name. I put my hand on the window-sill, palm upwards. The ant brought his legs down from his head and crawled slowly towards my hand. Then it climbed up my little finger and started scurrying over the crisscross lines on my palm.

Just then I started as I heard a sound from the door, and the ant clambered down and disappeared into the drainpipe.

Now Mother came into the room and gave me a glass of milk. Then she felt my forehead and said I had fever again.

Next morning the doctor came. Mother said, 'He has been restless the whole night, and kept saying 'Kali' again and again.' Mother probably thought I was praying to the Goddess Kali, because I hadn't told her about my new friend.

The doctor had put the stethoscope on my back when I heard the song again. It was louder than yesterday and the tune was different. It seemed to come from the window, but since the doctor had asked me to keep still, I couldn't turn my head to see.

The doctors finished his examination, and I cast a quick glance towards the window. Hello there! It was a large black ant this time, and this one too was salaaming me. Are all ants my friends then? And was it this ant which was singing? But Mother said nothing about a song. Did it mean that she couldn't hear it?

I turned towards Mother to ask her, and found her staring at the ant with fear in her eyes. The next moment she picked up my arithmetic notebook from the table, leaned over me and with one slap of the book squashed the ant. The same moment the singing stopped.

'The whole house is crawling with ants!' said Mother. 'Just think what would happen if one crawled inside your ear.'

The doctor left after giving me an injection. I looked at the dead ant. He was killed while singing a beautiful song. Just like my great-uncle Indranath. He too used to sing classical songs, which I didn't understand very well. One day he was playing the tanpura and singing when he suddenly died. When he was taken to the crematorium in a procession, a group of kirtan singers went along singing songs. I watched it and still remember it, although I was then very small.

And then a strange thing happened. I fell asleep after the injection and dreamed that, like the funeral of great-uncle Indranath, a dozen or so ants were bearing the dead ant on their shoulders while a line of ants followed singing a chorus.

I woke up in the afternoon when Mother put her cool hand on my forehead.

I glanced at the window and found that the dead ant was no longer there.

This time the fever kept on for several days. No wonder, because everyone in the house had started killing ants. How can the fever go if you have to listen to the screaming of ants all day long?

And there was another problem. While the ants were being killed in the pantry, hordes of ants turned up on my window-sill and wept. I could see that they wanted me to do something for them—either stop the killing or punish those who were doing the misdeed. But since I was laid up with fever, I could do nothing about it. Even if I were well, how could a small boy like me stop the elders from what they were doing?

But one day, I was forced to do something about it. I don't exactly remember what day it was, but I do remember that I had woken up at the crack of dawn and right; away heard Mother announcing that an ant had got into Phatik's ear and bitten him.

I was tickled by the news but just then I heard the slapping of brooms on the floor and knew that they were killing ants.

Then a very strange thing happened. I heard thin voices shouting, 'Help us! Help us, please!' I looked at the window and found that a large group of ants had gathered on the sill and were running around wildly.

Hearing them cry out I could no longer keep calm. I forgot about my fever, jumped out of bed and ran out of the room. At first I didn't know what to do. Then I took up a clay pot which was lying on the floor and smashed it. Then I started to smash all the things I could find which would, break. It was a clever ruse because it certainly stopped the killing of ants. But it made my parents, my aunt, my cousin Sabi all come out of their rooms, grab hold of me, put me back on my bed and lock the door of my room.

I had a good laugh, though, and the ants on my window kept saying, 'Thank you! Thank you!' and went back into the drainpipe again.

Soon after this, I had to leave home. The doctor examined me one day and said I should be sent to hospital for treatment.

Now I am in a hospital room. I've been here these last four days. The first day I felt very sad because the room was so clean that I knew there couldn't be any ants in it. Being a new room, there were no cracks or holes in the walls. There wasn't even a cupboard for ants to hide under or behind it. But there was a mango tree just outside the window, and one of its branches was within reach.

I thought if there was a place to find ants it would be on that branch.

But the first day I couldn't get near the window. How could I, since I was never alone? Either the nurse, or the doctor, or someone from my house was always in the room. The second day too was just as bad. I was so upset that I threw a medicine bottle on the floor and broke it. It made the doctor quite angry. He was not a nice doctor, this new one. I could tell that from his bristling moustache and from the thick glasses he wore.

On the third day, something happened. There was only a nurse in my room then, and she was reading a book. I was in bed wondering what to do. I heard a thud and saw that the book had slipped from the nurse's hand and fallen on the floor. The nurse had dozed off. I got down from the bed and tiptoed to the window. Leaning out of the window and stretching my body as far as it would go, I grabbed hold of the mango branch and began to pull it towards me.

This made a noise which woke up the nurse, and then the fireworks started.

The nurse gave a scream, came rushing towards me and, wrapping her arms around me, dragged me to the bed and dumped me on it. Others too came into the room just then, so I could do nothing more.

The doctor promptly gave me an injection.

I could make out from what they were saying that they thought I had meant to throw myself out of the window. Silly people! If I had thrown myself from such a height, all my bones would have been crushed and I would have died.

After the doctor left, I felt sleepy. I thought of the window by my bed at home and felt very sorry. Who knew when I would be back home again?

I had nearly fallen asleep when I heard a thin voice saying, 'Sepoys at your service, sir—sepoys at your service!'

I opened my eyes and saw two large red ants standing with their chests out by the medicine bottle on the bedside table.

They must have climbed on to my hand from the mango branch without my knowing it.

I said, 'Sepoys?'

The answer came, 'Yes, sir—at your service.'

'What are your names?' I asked them.

One said, 'Lal Bahadur Singh.' And the other said, 'Lal Chand Pandey.'

I was very pleased. But I warned them to go into hiding when people came into the room, or they might be killed. Lal Chand and Lal Bahadur salaamed and said, 'Very well, sir.' Then the two of them sang a lovely duet which lulled me to sleep.

I must tell you right away what happened yesterday, because it's nearly five and the doctor will be here soon. In the afternoon I was watching Lal Chand and Lal Bahadur wrestling on the table while I lay in bed. I was supposed to be asleep, but the pills and the injection hadn't worked. Or, to be quite truthful, I wilfully kept myself awake. If I slept in the afternoon, when would I play with my new friends?

The two ants fought gamely and it was hard to say who would win when suddenly there was a sound of heavy footsteps. The doctor was coming!

I made a sign and Lal Bahadur promptly disappeared below the table. But Lal Chand had been thrown on his back and was thrashing his legs about, so he couldn't run away. And that was what caused the nasty incident.

The doctor came, saw the ant, and saying some rude words in English, swept it off the table with his hand.

I could tell from Lal Chand's scream that he was badly hurt, but what could I do? By that time the doctor had grabbed my wrist to feel my pulse. I tried to get up, but the nurse held me down.

After the examination, the doctor as usual made a glum face and scratched the edge of his moustache. He was about to turn towards the door when he suddenly screwed up his face, gave a leap and yelled 'Ouch!'

Then all hell broke loose. The stethoscope flew out of his hand, his spectacles jumped off his nose and crashed on to the floor. One of the buttons of his jacket came off as he struggled to take it off, his tie wound tighter around his neck and made him gasp and sputter before at last he managed to pull it free, the hole in his vest showed as he

yanked off his shirt, jumping around and yelling all the time. I was speechless.

The nurse said, 'What is the matter, sir?'

The doctor continued to jump about and yelled, 'Ant! Red ant! It crawled up my arm—ouch!'

Well, well, well! I knew this would happen, and it serves you right! Lal Bahadur had taken revenge on his friend's behalf.

If they saw me now they would know how deliriously happy Sadananda could be.

PATOLBABU, FILM STAR

Originally published in *Sandesh* (August 1963) as *Patolbabu Film Star*. It was translated by the author himself to be part of the compilation titled *Stories* (Secker & Warburg, 1987). The illustrations in the story, including the Bengali calligraphy in the headpiece, are by Satyajit Ray.

Patolbabu had just hung his shopping bag on his shoulder when Nishikantobabu called from outside the main door. 'Patol, are you in?' 'Oh, yes,' said Patolbabu. 'Just a minute.'

Nishikanto Ghosh lived three houses away from Patolbabu in Nepal Bhattacharji Lane. He was a genial person.

Patolbabu came out with the bag. 'What brings you here so early in the morning?'

'Listen, what time will you be back?'

'In an hour or so. Why?'

'I hope you'll stay in after that—today being Tagore's birthday. I met my youngest brother-in-law in Netaji Pharmacy yesterday. He is in the film business, in the production department. He said he was looking for an actor for a scene in a film they're now shooting. The way he described the character—fiftyish, short, bald-headed—it reminded me of you. So I gave him your address and asked him to get in touch with you directly. I hope you won't turn him away. They'll pay you, of course.'

Patolbabu hadn't expected such news at the start of the day. That an offer to act in a film could come to a fifty-two-year-old nonentity like him was beyond his wildest dreams.

'Well, yes or no?' asked Nishikantobabu. 'I believe you did some acting on the stage at one time?'

'That's true,' said Patolbabu. 'I really don't see why I should say no. But let's talk to your brother-in-law first and find out some details. What's his name?'

'Naresh. Naresh Dutt. He's about thirty. A strapping young fellow. He said he would be here around ten-thirty.'

Buying provisions in the market, Patolbabu mixed up his wife's orders and bought red chillies instead of onion seeds. And he quite forgot about the aubergines. This was not surprising. At one time Patolbabu had a real passion for the stage; in fact, it verged on obsession. In Jatras, in amateur theatricals, in plays put up by the club in his neighbourhood, Patolbabu was always in demand. His name had appeared in handbills on countless occasions. Once it appeared in bold type near the top: 'Sitalakanto Ray (Patolbabu) in the role of Parasar'. Indeed, there was a time when people bought tickets especially to see him.

That was when he used to live in Kanchrapara. He had a job in the railway factory there. In 1934, he was offered higher pay in a clerical post with Hudson and Kimberley, in Calcutta, and was also lucky to find a flat in Nepal Bhattacharji Lane. He gave up his factory job and came to Calcutta with his wife. It was quite smooth sailing for some years, and Patolbabu was in his boss's good books. In 1943, when he was just toying with the idea of starting a club in his neighbourhood, sudden retrenchment in his office due to the war cost him his nine-year-old job. Ever since then Patolbabu had struggled to make a living. At first he opened a variety store which he had to wind up after five years. Then he had a job in a Bengali firm which he gave up in disgust when his boss began to treat him in too high-handed a fashion. Then, for ten long years, starting as an insurance salesman, Patolbabu tried every means of earning a livelihood without ever succeeding in improving his lot. Of late he has been paying regular visits to a small establishment dealing in scrap iron where a cousin of his has promised him a job.

And acting? That has become a thing of the remote past; something which he recalls at times with a sigh. Having a good memory, Patolbabu still remembers lines from some of his better parts. 'Listen, O listen to the thunderous twang of the mighty bow Gandiva engaged in gory conflict, and to the angry roar of the mountainous club whizzing through the air in the hands of the great Brikodara!' It sent a shiver down his spine just to think of such lines.

Naresh Dutt turned up at half past twelve. Patolbabu had given up hope and was about to go for his bath when there was a knock on the front door.

'Come in, come in, sir!' Patolbabu almost dragged the young man in and pushed the broken-armed chair towards him. 'Do sit down.'

'No, thanks. I—er—I expect Nishikantobabu told you about me?'

'Oh yes. I must say I was quite taken aback. After so many years . . .'

'I hope you have no objection?'

'You think I'll be all right for the part?' Patolbabu asked with great diffidence.

Naresh Dutt cast an appraising look at Patolbabu and gave a nod. 'Oh yes,' he said. 'There is no doubt about that. By the way, the shooting takes place tomorrow morning.'

'Tomorrow? Sunday?'

'Yes, and not in the studio. I'll tell you where you have to go. You know Faraday House near the crossing of Bentinck Street and Mission Row? It's a seven-storey office building. The shooting takes place outside the office in front of the entrance. We'll expect you there at eight-thirty sharp. You'll be through by midday.'

Naresh Dutt prepared to leave. 'But you haven't told me about the part,' said Patol babu anxiously.

'Oh yes, sorry. The part is that of a—a pedestrian. An absent-minded, short-tempered pedestrian. By the way, do you have a jacket which buttons up to the neck?'

'I think I do. You mean the old-fashioned kind?'

'Yes. That's what you'll wear. What colour is it?'

'Sort of nut-brown. But woollen.'

'That's okay. The story is supposed to take place in winter, so that would be just right. Tomorrow at 8.30 a.m. sharp. Faraday House.'

Patolbabu suddenly thought of a crucial question.

'I hope the part calls for some dialogue?'

'Certainly. It's a speaking part. You have acted before, haven't you?'

'Well, as a matter of fact, yes . . .'

'Fine. I wouldn't have come to you for just a walk-on part. For that we pick people from the street. Of course, there's dialogue and you'll be given your lines as soon as you show up tomorrow.'

After Naresh Dutt left, Patolbabu broke the news to his wife.

'As far as I can see, the part isn't a big one. I'll be paid, of course, but that's not the main thing. The thing is—remember how I started on the stage? Remember my first part? I played a dead soldier! All I had to do was lie still on the stage with my arms and legs spread. And remember how I rose from that position? Remember Mr Watts shaking me by the hand? And the silver medal which the chairman of our municipality gave me? Remember? This is only the first step on the ladder, my dear better-half! Yes—the first step that would—God willing—mark the rise to fame and fortune of your beloved husband!'

'Counting your chickens again before they're hatched, are you? No wonder you could never make a go of it.'

'But it's the real thing this time! Go and make me a cup of tea, will you? And remind me to take some ginger juice tonight. It's very good for the throat.'

The clock in the Metropolitan building showed seven minutes past eight when Patolbabu reached Esplanade. It took him another ten minutes to walk to Faraday House.

There was a big crowd outside the building. Three or four cars stood on the road. There was also a bus which carried equipment on its roof. On the edge of the pavement there was an instrument on three legs around which there was a group of busy people. Near the entrance stood—also on three legs—a pole which had a long arm extending from its top at the end of which was suspended what looked like a small oblong beehive. Surrounding these instruments was a crowd of people among which Patolbabu noticed some non-Bengalis. What they were supposed to do he couldn't tell.

But where was Naresh Dutt? He was the only one who knew him.

With a slight tremor in his heart, Patolbabu advanced towards the entrance. It was the middle of summer, and the warm jacket buttoned up to his neck felt heavy. Patolbabu could feel beads of perspiration forming around the high collar.

'This way, Atulbabu!'

Atulbabu? Patolbabu spotted Naresh Dutt standing at the entrance and gesturing towards him. He had got his name wrong. No wonder, since they had only had a brief meeting. Patolbabu walked up, put his palms together in a namaskar and said, 'I suppose you haven't yet noted down my name. Sitalakanto Ray—although people know me better by my nickname Patol. I used it on the stage too.'

'Good, good. I must say you're quite punctual.'

Patolbabu rose to his full height.

'I was with Hudson and Kimberley for nine years and wasn't late for a single day.'

'Is that so? Well, I suggest you go and wait in the shade there. We have a few things to attend to before we get going.'

'Naresh!'

Somebody standing by the three-legged instrument called out.

'Sir?'

'Is he one of our men?'

'Yes, sir. He is—er—in that shot where they bump into each other.'

'Okay. Now, clear the entrance, will you? We're about to start.'

Patolbabu withdrew and stood in the shade of a paan shop.

He had never watched a film shoot before. How hard these people worked! A youngster of twenty or so was carrying that three-legged instrument on his shoulder. Must weigh at least sixty pounds.

But what about his dialogue? There wasn't much time left, and he still didn't know what he was supposed to do or say.

Patolbabu suddenly felt a little nervous. Should he ask somebody? There was Naresh Dutt there; should he go and remind him? It didn't matter if the part was small, but, if he had to make the most of it, he had to learn his lines beforehand. How small he would feel if he muffed in the presence of so many people! The last time he acted on stage was twenty years ago.

Patolbabu was about to step forward when he was pulled up short by a voice shouting 'Silence!'

This was followed by Naresh Dutt loudly announcing with hands cupped over his mouth: 'We're about to start shooting. Everybody please stop talking. Don't move from your positions and don't crowd around the camera, please!'

Once again the voice was heard shouting 'Silence! Taking!' Now Patolbabu could see the owner of the voice. He was a stout man of medium height, and he stood by the camera. Around his neck hung something which looked like a small telescope. Was he the director? How strange!—he hadn't even bothered to find out the name of the director!

Now a series of shouts followed in quick succession—'Start sound!' 'Running!' 'Camera!' 'Rolling!' 'Action!'

Patolbabu noticed that as soon as the word 'Action' was said, a car came up from the crossing and pulled up in front of the office entrance. Then a young man in a grey suit and pink make-up shot out of the back of the car, took a few hurried steps towards the entrance and stopped abruptly. The next moment Patolbabu heard the shout 'Cut!' and immediately the hubbub from the crowd resumed.

A man standing next to Patolbabu now turned to him. 'I hope you recognized the young fellow?' he asked.

'Why, no,' said Patolbabu.

'Chanchal Kumar,' said the man. 'He's coming up fast. Playing the lead in four films at the moment.'

Patolbabu saw very few films, but he seemed to have heard the name Chanchal Kumar. It was probably the same boy Kotibabu was praising the other day. Nice make-up the fellow had on. If he had been wearing a Bengali dhoti and panjabi instead of a suit, and given a peacock to ride on, he would make a perfect God Kartik. Monotosh of Kanchrapara—who was better known by his nickname Chinu—had the same kind of looks. He was very good at playing female parts, recalled Patolbabu.

Patolbabu now turned to his neighbour and asked in a whisper, 'Who is the director?'

The man raised his eyebrows and said, 'Why, don't you know? He's Baren Mullick. He's had three smash hits in a row.'

Well, at least he had gathered some useful information. It wouldn't have done for him to say he didn't know if his wife had asked in whose film he had acted and with which actor.

Naresh Dutt now came up to him with tea in a small clay cup. 'Here you are, sir — the hot tea will help your throat. Your turn will come shortly.'

Patolbabu now had to come out with it. 'If you let me have my lines now . . .

'Your lines? Come with me.'

Naresh Dutt went towards the three-legged instrument with Patolbabu at his heels. 'I say, Sosanko.'

A young fellow in a short-sleeved shirt turned towards Naresh Dutt. 'This gentleman wants his lines. Why don't you write them down on a piece of paper and give it to him? He's the one who—'

'I know, I know.'

Sosanko now turned to Patolbabu.

'Come along, Grandpa. I say, Jyoti, can I borrow your pen for a sec? Grandpa wants his lines written down.'

The youngster Jyoti produced a red dot pen from his pocket and gave it to Sosanko. Sosanko tore off a page from the notebook he was carrying, scribbled something on it and handed it to Patolbabu.

Patolbabu glanced at the paper and found that a single word had been scrawled on it—'Oh!'

Patolbabu felt a sudden throbbing in his head. He wished he could take off his jacket. The heat was unbearable.

Sosanko said, 'What's the matter, Grandpa? You don't seem too pleased.'

Were these people pulling his leg? Was the whole thing a gigantic hoax? A meek, harmless man like him, and they had to drag him into the middle of the city to make a laughing stock of him. How could anyone be so cruel?

Patolbabu said in a hardly audible voice, 'I find it rather strange.'

'Why, Grandpa?'

'Just "Oh"? Is that all I have to say?'

Sosanko's eyebrows shot up.

'What are you saying, Grandpa? You think that's nothing? Why, this is a regular speaking part! A speaking part in a Baren Mullick film—do you realize what that means? Why, you're the luckiest of actors. Do you know that till now more than a hundred persons have appeared in this film who have had nothing to say? They just walked past the camera. Some didn't even walk; they just stood in one spot. There were others whose faces didn't register at all. Even today—look at all those people standing by the lamp post; they all appear in today's scene but have nothing to say. Even our hero Chanchal Kumar has no lines to speak today. You are the only one who has—see?'

Now the young man called Jyoti came up, put his hand on Patolbabu's shoulder and said, 'Listen, Grandpa. I'll tell you what you have to do. Chanchal Kumar is a rising young executive. He is informed that an embezzlement has taken place in his office, and he comes to find out what has happened. He gets out of his car and charges across the pavement towards the entrance. Just then he collides with an absent-minded pedestrian. That's you. You're hurt in the head and say 'Oh!', but Chanchal Kumar pays no attention to you and goes into the office. The fact that he ignores you reflects his extreme preoccupation—see? Just think how crucial the shot is.'

'I hope everything is clear now,' said Sosanko. 'Now, if you just move over to where you were standing . . . the fewer people crowd around here, the better. There's one more shot left before your turn comes.'

Patolbabu went slowly back to the paan shop. Standing in the shade, he glanced down at the paper in his hand, cast a quick look around to see if anyone was watching, crumpled the paper into a ball and threw it into the roadside drain.

Oh . . .

A sigh came out of the depths of his heart.

Just one word—no, not even a word; a sound—'Oh!'

The heat was stifling. The jacket seemed to weigh a ton. Patolbabu couldn't keep standing in one spot anymore; his legs felt heavy.

He moved up to the office beyond the paan shop and sat down on the steps. It was nearly half past nine. On Sunday mornings, songs in praise of the Goddess Kali were sung in Karalibabu's house. Patolbabu went there every week and enjoyed it. What if he were to go there now? What harm would there be? Why waste a Sunday morning in the company of these useless people, and be made to look foolish on top of that? 'Silence!'

Stuff and nonsense! To hell with your 'silence'! They had to put up this pompous show for something so trivial! Things were much better on the stage. The stage . . . the stage . . .

A faint memory was stirred up in Patolbabu's mind. Some priceless words of advice given in a deep, mellow voice: 'Remember one thing, Patol; however small a part you're offered, never consider it beneath your dignity to accept it. As an artist your aim should be to make the most of your opportunity, and squeeze the last drop of meaning out of your lines. A play involves the work of many and it is the combined effort of many that makes a success of the play.'

It was Mr Pakrashi who gave the advice. Gogon Pakrashi, Patolbabu's mentor. A wonderful actor, without a trace of vanity in him; a saintly person, and an actor in a million.

There was something else which Mr Pakrashi used to say. 'Each word spoken in a play is like a fruit in a tree. Not everyone in the audience has access to it. But you, the actor, must know how to pluck it, get at its essence, and serve it up to the audience for their edification.'

The memory of his guru made Patolbabu bow his head in obeisance.

Was it really true that there was nothing in the part he had been given today? He had only one word to say—'Oh!', but was that word so devoid of meaning as to be dismissed summarily?

Oh, oh, oh, oh, oh—Patolbabu began giving the exclamation a different inflection each time he uttered it. After doing it for a number of times he made an astonishing discovery. The same exclamation, when spoken in different ways, carried different shades of meaning. A man when hurt said 'Oh' in quite a different way. Despair brought forth one kind of 'Oh', while sorrow provoked yet another kind. In fact, there were so many kinds of Oh's—the short Oh, the long-drawn Oh, Oh shouted and Oh whispered, the high-pitched Oh and the low-pitched Oh, and the Oh starting low and ending high, and the Oh starting high and ending low . . . Strange! Patolbabu suddenly felt that he could write a whole thesis on that one monosyllabic exclamation. Why had he felt so disheartened when this single word contained a gold-mine of meaning? The true actor could make a mark with this one single syllable.

'Silence!'

The director had raised his voice again. Patolbabu could see the young Jyoti clearing the crowd. There was something he had to ask him. He went quickly over to him.

'How long will it be before my turn comes, brother?'

'Why are you so impatient, Grandpa? You have to learn to be patient in this line of business. It'll be another half an hour before you're called.'

'That's all right. I'll certainly wait. I'll be in that side street across the road.'

'Okay—so long as you don't sneak off.'

'Start sound!'

Patolbabu crossed the road on tiptoe and went into the quiet little side street. It was good that he had a little time on his hands. While these people didn't seem to believe in rehearsals, he himself would rehearse his own bit. There was no one about. These were office buildings, so very few people lived here. Those who did—such as shopkeepers—had all gone to watch the shooting.

Patolbabu cleared his throat and started enunciating the syllable in various ways. Along with that he worked out how he would react physically when the collision took place—how his features would be twisted in pain, how he would fling out his arms, how his body would crouch to express pain and surprise—all these he performed in various ways in front of a large glass window.

Patolbabu was called in exactly half an hour. Now he had completely got over his apathy. All he felt now was a keen anticipation and suppressed excitement. It was the feeling he used to feel twenty years ago just before he stepped on to the stage.

The director Baren Mullick called Patolbabu to him. 'I hope you know what you're supposed to do?' he asked.

'Yes, sir.'

'Very good. I'll first say "Start sound". The recordists will reply by saying "Running". That's the signal for the camera to start. Then I will say "Action". That will be your cue to start walking from that pillar, and for the hero to come out of the car and make a dash for the office. You work out your steps so that the collision takes place at this spot, here. The hero ignores you and strides into the office, while you register pain by saying 'Oh!', stop for a couple of seconds, then resume walking—okay?'

Patolbabu suggested a rehearsal, but Baren Mullick shook his head impatiently. 'There's a large patch of cloud approaching the sun,' he said. 'This scene must be shot in sunlight.'

'One question please.'

'Yes?'

An idea had occurred to Patolbabu while rehearsing; he now came out with it.

'Er—I was thinking—if I had a newspaper open in my hand, and if the collision took place while I had my eyes on the paper, then perhaps—'

Baren Mullick cut him short by addressing a bystander who was carrying a Bengali newspaper. 'D'you mind handing your paper to this gentleman, just for this one shot? Thanks . . . Now you take your position beside the pillar. Chanchal, are you ready?'

Baren Mullick raised his hand, then brought it down again, saying, 'Just a minute. Keshto, I think if we gave the pedestrian a moustache, it would be more interesting.'

'What kind, sir? Walrus, Ronald Colman or Butterfly? I have them all ready.'

'Butterfly, butterfly—and make it snappy!' The elderly make-up man went up to Patolbabu, took out a small grey moustache from a box, and stuck it on with spirit-gum below Patolbabu's nose.

Patolbabu said, 'I hope it won't come off at the time of the collision?'

The make-up man smiled. 'Collision?' he said. 'Even if you were to wrestle with Dara Singh, the moustache would stay in place.'

Patolbabu had a quick glance in a mirror which the man was holding. True enough, the moustache suited him very well. Patolbabu inwardly commended the director's perspicacity. 'Silence! Silence!'

The business with the moustache had provoked a wave of comments from the spectators which Baren Mullick's shout now silenced.

Patolbabu noticed that most of the bystanders' eyes were turned towards him. 'Start sound!'

Patolbabu cleared his throat. One, two, three, four, five—five steps would take him to the spot where the collision was to take place. And Chanchal Kumar would have to walk four steps. So if both were to start together, Patolbabu would have to walk a little faster than the hero, or else—

'Running!'

Patolbabu held the newspaper open in his hand. What he had to do when saying 'Oh!' was mix sixty parts of irritation with forty parts of surprise.

'Action!'

Clop, clop, clop, clop, clop—Wham!

Patolbabu saw stars before his eyes. The hero's head had banged against his forehead, and an excruciating pain had robbed him of his senses for a few seconds.

But the next moment, by a supreme effort of will, Patolbabu pulled himself together, and mixing fifty parts of anguish with twenty-five of surprise and twenty-five of irritation, cried 'Oh!' and, after a brief pause, resumed his walk.

'Cut!'

'Was that all right?' asked Patolbabu anxiously, stepping towards Baren Mullick.

'Jolly good! Why, you're quite an actor! Sosanko, just take a look at the sky through the dark glass, will you.'

Jyoti now came up to Patolbabu and said, 'I hope Grandpa wasn't hurt too badly?'

'My God!' said Chanchal Kumar, massaging his head, 'you timed it so well that I nearly passed out!'

Naresh Dutt elbowed his way through the crowd, came up to Patolbabu and said, 'Please go back where you were standing. I'll come to you in a short while and do the necessary.'

Patolbabu took his place once again by the paan shop. The cloud had just covered the sun and brought down the temperature. Nevertheless, Patolbabu took off his woollen jacket, and then heaved a sigh of relief. A feeling of total satisfaction swept over him.

He had done his job really well. All these years of struggle hadn't blunted his sensibility. Gogon Pakrashi would have been pleased with his performance. But all the labour and imagination he had put into this one shot—were these people able to appreciate that? He doubted it. They just got hold of some people, got them to go through certain motions, paid them for their labours and forgot all about it. Paid them, yes, but how much? Ten, fifteen, twenty rupees? It is true that he needed money very badly, but what was twenty rupees when measured against the intense satisfaction of a small job done with perfection and dedication?

Ten minutes or so later Naresh Dutt went looking for Patolbabu near the paan shop and found that he was not there. That's odd—the man hadn't been paid yet. What a strange fellow!

'The sun has come out,' Baren Mullick was heard shouting. 'Silence! Silence!—Naresh, hurry up and get these people out of the way!'

BIPIN CHOUDHURY'S LAPSE OF MEMORY

Originally published in *Sandesh* (Puja Annual 1963) as *Bipin Choudhurir Smritibhram. The English translation by Ray was published in *Target* (July 1984). The illustrations in the story, including the Bengali calligraphy in the headpiece, are by Satyajit Ray.

বিপিন চৌধুরীর স্মৃতিভ্রম

Every Monday, on his way back from work, Bipin Choudhury would drop in at Kalicharan's in New Market to buy books. Crime stories, ghost stories and thrillers. He had to buy at least five at a time to last him through the week. He lived alone, was not a good mixer, had few friends, and didn't like spending time in idle chat. Those who called in the evening got through their business quickly and left. Those who didn't show signs of leaving would be told around eight o'clock by Bipinbabu that he was under doctor's orders to have dinner at 8.30 p.m. After dinner he would rest for half an hour and then turn in for the night with a book. This was a routine which had persisted unbroken for years.

Today, at Kalicharan's, Bipinbabu had the feeling that someone was observing him from close quarters. He turned round and found himself looking at a round-faced, meek-looking man who now broke into a smile.

'I don't suppose you recognize me.'

Bipinbabu felt ill at ease. It didn't seem that he had ever encountered this man before. The face seemed quite unfamiliar.

'But you're a busy man. You must meet all kinds of people all the time.'

'Have we met before?' asked Bipinbabu.

The man looked greatly surprised. 'We met every day for a whole week. I arranged for a car to take you to the Hundru falls. In 1958. In Ranchi. My name is Parimal Ghosh.'

'Ranchi?'

Now Bipinbabu realized that it was not he but this man who was making a mistake. Bipinbabu had never been to Ranchi. He had been at the point of going several times, but had never made it. He smiled and said, 'Do you know who I am?'

The man raised his eyebrows, bit his tongue and said, 'Do I know you? Who doesn't know Bipin Chowdhury?'

Bipinbabu now turned towards the bookshelves and said, 'Still you're making a mistake. One often does. I've never been to Ranchi.'

The man now laughed aloud.

'What are you saying, Mr Chowdhury? You had a fall in Hundru and cut your right knee. I brought you iodine. I had fixed up a car for you to go to Netarhat the next day, but you couldn't because of the pain in the knee. Can't you recall anything? Someone else you know was also in Ranchi at that time. Mr Dinesh Mukerjee. You stayed in a bungalow. You said you didn't like hotel food and would prefer to have your meals cooked by a bawarchi. Mr Mukerjee stayed with his sister. You had a big argument about the moon landing, remember? I'll tell you more: you always carried a bag with your books in it on your sightseeing trips. Am I right or not?'

Bipinbabu spoke quietly, his eyes still on the books.

'Which month in fifty-eight are you talking about?'

The man said, 'Just before the Pujas. October.'

'No, sir,' said Bipinbabu. 'I spent Puja in fifty-eight with a friend in Kanpur. You're making a mistake. Good day.'

But the man didn't go, nor did he stop talking.

'Very strange. One evening I had tea with you on the verandah of your bungalow. You spoke about your family. You said you had no children, and that you had lost your wife ten years ago. Your only brother had died insane, which is why you didn't want to visit the mental hospital in Ranchi . . .'

When Bipinbabu had paid for the books and was leaving the shop, the man was still looking at him in utter disbelief.

Bipinbabu's car was safely parked in Bertram Street by the Lighthouse cinema. He told the driver as he got into the car, 'Just drive by the Ganga, will you, Sitaram.' Driving up the Strand Road, Bipinbabu regretted having paid so much attention to the intruder. He had never been to Ranchi—no question about it. It was inconceivable that he should forget such an incident which took place only six or seven years ago. He had an excellent memory. Unless—Bipinbabu's head reeled.

Unless he was losing his mind.

But how could that be? He was working daily in his office. It was a big firm, and he had a responsible job. He wasn't aware of anything ever going seriously wrong. Only today he had spoken for half an hour at an important meeting. And yet . . .

And yet that man knew a great deal about him. How? He even seemed to know some intimate details. The bag of books, wife's death, brother's insanity . . . The only mistake was about his having gone to Ranchi. Not a mistake; a deliberate lie. In 1958, during the pujas, he was in Kanpur at his friend Haridas Bagchi's place. All Bipinbabu had to do was write to—no, there was no way of writing to Haridas. Bipinbabu suddenly remembered that Haridas had not left his address.

But where was the need for proof? If it so happened that the police were trying to pin a crime on him which had taken place in Ranchi in 1958, he might have needed to prove he hadn't been there. He himself was fully aware that he hadn't been to Ranchi—and that was that.

The river breeze was bracing, and yet a slight discomfort lingered in Bipinbabu's mind.

Around Hastings, Bipinbabu had the sudden notion of rolling up his trousers and taking a look at his right knee.

There was the mark of an old inch-long cut. It was impossible to tell when the injury had occurred. Had he never had a fall as a boy and cut his knee? He tried to recall such an incident, but couldn't.

Then Bipinbabu suddenly thought of Dinesh Mukerjee. That man had said that Dinesh was in Ranchi at the same time. The best thing surely would be to ask him. He lived quite near—in Beninandan Street. What about going right now? But then, if he had really never been to Ranchi, what would Dinesh think if Bipinbabu asked for a confirmation? He would probably conclude Bipinbabu was going nuts. No—it would be ridiculous to ask him. And he knew how ruthless Dinesh's sarcasm could be.

Sipping a cold drink in his air-conditioned living room, Bipinbabu felt at ease again. Such a nuisance the man was! He probably had nothing else to do, so he went about getting into other people's hair.

After dinner, snuggling into bed with one of the new thrillers, Bipinbabu forgot all about the man in New Market.

Next day, in the office, Bipinbabu noticed that with every passing hour, the previous day's encounter was occupying more and more of his mind. That look of round-eyed surprise on that round face, the disbelieving snigger . . . If the man knew so much about the details of Bipinbabu's life, how could he be so wrong about the Ranchi trip?

Just before lunch—at five minutes to one—Bipinbabu couldn't check himself any more. He opened the phone book. He had to ring up Dinesh Mukerjee. It was better to settle the question over the phone; at least the embarrassment on his face wouldn't show.

Two-three-five-six-one-six.

Bipinbabu dialled the number.

'Hello.'

'Is that Dinesh? This is Bipin here.'

'Well, well—what's the news?'

'I just wanted to find out if you recalled an incident which took place in fifty-eight.'

'Fifty-eight? What incident?'

'Were you in Calcutta right through that year? That's the first thing I've got to know.'

'Wait just a minute . . . fifty-eight . . . just let me check in my diary.'

For a minute there was silence. Bipinbabu could feel that his heartbeat had gone

up. He was sweating a little.

'Hello.'

'Yes.'

'I've got it. I had been out twice.'

'Where?'

'Once in February—nearby—to Krishnanagar to a nephew's wedding. And then . . . but you'd know about this one. The trip to Ranchi. You were there too. That's all. But what's all this sleuthing about?'

'No, I just wanted to—anyway, thanks.'

Bipinbabu slammed the receiver down and gripped his head with his hands. He felt his head swimming. A chill seemed to spread over his body. There were sandwiches in his tiffin box, but he didn't feel like eating them. He had lost his appetite. Completely.

After lunchtime, Bipinbabu realized that he couldn't possibly carry on sitting at his desk and working. This was the first time something like this had happened in his twenty-five years with the firm. He had a reputation for being a tireless, conscientious worker. The men who worked under him all held him in awe. In the worst moments of crisis even when faced with the most acute problems, Bipinbabu had always kept his cool and weathered the storm. But today his head was in a whirl.

Back home at two-thirty, Bipinbabu shut himself up in his bedroom, lay down in bed and tried to gather his wits together. He knew that it was possible to lose one's memory through an injury to the head, but he didn't know of a single instance of someone remembering everything except one particular incident—and a fairly recent and significant one at that. He had always wanted to go to Ranchi; to have gone there, done things, and not to remember was something utterly impossible.

At seven, Bipinbabu's servant came and announced that Seth Girdhariprasad had come. A rich businessman—and a VIP—this Girdhariprasad. And he had come by appointment. But Bipinbabu was feeling so low that he had to tell his servant that it was not possible for him to leave his bed. To hell with VIPs.

At seven-thirty, the servant came again. Bipinbabu had just dozed off and was in the middle of an unpleasant dream when the servant's knock woke him up. Who was it this time? 'Chunibabu, sir. Says it's very urgent.'

Bipinbabu knew what the urgency was. Chunilal was a childhood friend of his. He had fallen on bad times recently, and had been pestering Bipinbabu for a job. Bipinbabu had kept fobbing him off, but Chuni kept coming back. What a persistent bore!

Bipinbabu sent word that not only was it not possible for him to see Chuni now, but not in several weeks as well.

But as soon as the servant stepped out of the room, it struck Bipinbabu that Chuni might remember something about the fifty-eight trip. There was no harm in asking him.

He sped downstairs. Chuni had got up to leave. Seeing Bipinbabu, he turned round with a flicker of hope in his eyes. Bipinbabu didn't beat about the bush.

'Listen, Chuni—I want to ask you something. You have a good memory, and you've been seeing me off and on for a long time. Just throw your mind back and tell me—did I go to Ranchi in fifty-eight?'

Chuni said, 'Fifty-eight? It must have been fifty-eight. Or was it fifty-nine?'

'You're sure that I did go to Ranchi?'

Chuni's look of amazement was not unmixed with worry.

'D'you mean you have doubts about having gone at all?'

'Did I go? Do you remember clearly?'

Chuni was standing up; he now sat down on the sofa, fixed Bipinbabu with a long, hard stare and said, 'Bipin, have you taken to drugs or something? As far as I know, you had a clean record where such things were concerned. I know that old friendships don't mean much to you, but at least you had a good memory. You can't really mean that you've forgotten about the Ranchi trip?'

Bipinbabu had to turn away from Chuni's incredulous stare. 'D'you remember what my last job was?' asked Chunilal.

'Of course. You worked in a travel agency.'

'You remember that and you don't remember that it was I who fixed up your booking for Ranchi? I went to the station to see you off; one of the fans in your compartment was not working—I got an electrician to fix it. Have you forgotten everything? Whatever is the matter with you? You don't look too well, you know.'

Bipinbabu sighed and shook his head.

'I've been working too hard,' he said at last. 'That must be the reason. Must see about consulting a specialist.'

Doubtless it was Bipinbabu's condition which made Chunilal leave without mentioning anything about a job.

Paresh Chanda was a young physician with a pair of bright eyes and a sharp nose. He became thoughtful when he heard about Bipinbabu's symptoms. 'Look, Dr Chanda,' said Bipinbabu desperately, 'you must cure me of this horrible illness. I can't tell you how it's affecting my work. There are so many kinds of drugs these days; isn't there something specific for such a complaint? I can have it sent from abroad if it's not to be had here. But I must be rid of these symptoms.'

Dr Chanda shook his head.

'You know what, Mr Chowdhury,' he said, 'I've never had to deal with a case such as yours. Frankly, this is quite outside my field of experience. But I have one suggestion. I don't know if it'll work, but it's worth a try. It can do no harm.'

Bipinbabu leaned forward anxiously.

'As far as I can make out,' said Dr Chanda, 'and I think you're of the same opinion—you have been to Ranchi, but due to some unknown reason, the entire episode has slipped out of your mind. What I suggest is that you go to Ranchi once again. The sight of the place may remind you of your trip. This is not impossible. More than that I cannot do at the moment. I'm prescribing a nerve tonic and a tranquilizer. Sleep is essential, or the symptoms will get more pronounced.'

It may have been the sleeping pill, and the advice which the doctor gave, which made Bipinbabu feel somewhat better the next morning.

After breakfast, he rang up his office, gave some instructions, and then procured a first-class train ticket to Ranchi for the same evening.

Getting off the train at Ranchi next morning, he realized at once that he had never been there before.

He came out of the station, hired a taxi and drove around the town for a while. It was clear that the streets, the buildings, the hotels, the bazaars, the Morabadi Hill

were all unfamiliar—with none of these had he the slightest
acquaintance. Would a trip to the Hundru Falls help? He didn't
believe so, but, at the same time, he didn't wish to leave
with the feeling that he hadn't tried hard enough. So he
arranged for a car and left for Hundru in the afternoon.

At five o'clock the same afternoon in Hundru,
two Gujarati gentlemen from a group of picnickers
discovered Bipinbabu lying unconscious beside a
boulder. When the ministrations of the two gentlemen
brought him around, the first thing Bipinbabu
said was, 'I'm finished. There's no hope left.'

Next morning, Bipinbabu was back
in Calcutta. He realized that there was truly no
hope for him. Soon he would   lose
everything: his will to work, his
confidence, his ability, his balance of
mind. Was he going to end up in the
asylum at Ranchi . . .? Bipinbabu couldn't
think anymore.

Back home, he rang up Dr Chanda and asked him to come over. Then, after a shower, he got into bed with an ice bag clamped to his head. Just then the servant brought him a letter which someone had left in the letter box. A greenish envelope with his name in red ink on it. Above the name it said 'Urgent and Confidential'. In spite of his condition, Bipinbabu had a feeling that he ought to go through the letter. He tore open the envelope and took out the letter. This is what he read—

Dear Bipin,

I had no idea that affluence would bring about the kind of change in you that it has done. Was it so difficult for you to help out an old friend down on his luck? I have no money, so my resources are limited. What I have is imagination, a part of which is used in retribution of your unfeeling behaviour. The man in New Market is a neighbour and acquaintance of mine and a capable actor who played the part I wrote for him. Dinesh Mukerjee has never been particularly well-disposed towards you: so he was quite willing to help. As for the mark on your knee, you will surely recall that you tripped on a rope in Chandpal Ghat back in 1939.

Well, you'll be all right again now. A novel I've written is being considered by a publisher. If he likes it enough, it'll see me through the next few months.

Yours,

Chunilal

When Dr Chanda came, Bipinbabu said, 'I'm fine. It all came back as soon as I got off the train at Ranchi.'

'A unique case,' said Dr Chanda. 'I shall certainly write about it in a medical journal.'

'The reason why I sent for you,' said Bipinbabu, 'is that I have a pain in the hip from a fall I had in Ranchi. If you could prescribe a painkiller . . .'

The first page of the draft script that Ray prepared for *Professor Shonku and Khoka*

PROFESSOR SHONKU AND KHOKA— DRAFT SCRIPT

Originally published in *Sandesh* (July 1967) as *Professor Shonku o Khoka*. The hitherto unpublished script was developed from that story to be telecast for the TV series *Satyajit Ray Presents*. However, it was not filmed. The illustrations in the story, including the Bengali calligraphy in the headpiece, are by Satyajit Ray.

PART 1

[Prof. Shonku's laboratory. Morning]

Prof. Shonku is in his laboratory working with test tubes, flasks, retorts, while a Bunsen burner burns. Shonku is mixing liquids, which produces strong reaction, resulting in smoke and vapour. Shonku's servant Prahlad comes into the laboratory.

Prahlad: Sir, two gentlemen have come to see you.

Shonku: Who are they?

Prahlad: One of them says he knows you. He is a doctor. Doctor Bose. They say they only want five minutes of your time.

Shonku: Have you told them I'm working?

Prahlad: Yes, but they say it's very urgent. They are in the sitting room.

[Shonku's sitting room]

The two men rise as Shonku enters. One is tall, wears glasses and is in a white suit, while the other is meek-looking and small and is dressed in dhoti and panjabi (kurta). *Shonku greets the tall man.*

    Shonku: Hello, Dr Bose, what brings you here?

    Bose: Let me apologize for coming without an appointment.

    Shonku: That's all right.

    Bose: This is Mr Mitter, who lives in Bhowanipore.

    Shonku: Namaskar.

Mitter folds his hands in a namaste with great diffidence.

    Bose: You see, it's Mr Mitter's son. He is eight years old—a rather delicate boy, who has suddenly undergone a strange transformation.

    Shonku: Transformation?

    Bose: Well, that's the only way I can put it. He slipped and fell in the courtyard of his house and hurt his head. There's a lump there, but no other injury. Ever since then he has been talking strangely.

    Shonku: What do you mean—talking strangely?

    Mitter: Well, half the time we don't know what he's talking about. He is not in pain, he has no fever. Dr Bose has examined him twice. In all other respects he is quite normal except in that what he says.

    Shonku: Can you give an example?

    Bose: The moment I entered the room, he said Sagittarius. It so happens that I am a Sagittarian. Then when I began to examine him, he said pulse rate 82, temperature 97.6. Indeed his pulse rate was 82 and temperature 97.6, and as far as I could see there was nothing wrong with him.

    Mitter: And he said something about a crow that sat on the window.

    Bose: Yes, he said *Corvus splendens*.

    Shonku: But that is the Latin name for the crow!

    Bose: Yes.

    Shonku: And you say that boy is eight years old?

    Mitter: Eight years or so. He was eight last June.

Shonku: Well, I am very keen to see this boy. I have never heard anything like this before.

Bose: I have brought my car. We can go right away.

Shonku: Very well.

∗∗∗

[Mitter's house. Bedroom]

The boy, Ajay, is lying in bed. A pale boy, with large eyes and fair skin. 'Delicate' describes him perfectly. His mother approaches his bed and pulls her sari over her head. Dr. Bose introduces Shonku. Shonku has his eyes fixed on the boy. The boy is also looking at Shonku.

Shonku: Where was he hurt in the head?

Boy: Os temporale.

Shonku raises his eyebrows.

Shonku: Why, he even knows the name of the bone!

Bose: And nobody told him.

Shonku bends down for the boy to look at him more carefully.

Boy: Six and seven point four.

Bose and Shonku are left puzzled for a moment. Then Shonku realizes.

Shonku: He is talking about my spectacles. They are the powers of my lenses.

Bose: How extraordinary!

Shonku turns to the parents.

Shonku: I hope he hasn't lost his appetite.

Mitter: No, he sleeps all right. The only thing he has stopped is talking to us. He says things of which we don't know the meaning.

Shonku turns to the boy.

Shonku: Will you come and stay with me for a few days? Do you know who I am?

Boy: Trilokeshwar Shonku. A scientist and inventor.

Shonku: Then you know me already. We shall be good friends.

Shonku turns to the parents.

Shonku: Do you mind if I take him with me to my house for a few days? His 'case' is certainly worth studying.

Mitter: Do what you like, sir, but return him to me as he was before. I don't like the way he has changed. He is not my son anymore and we can't lose our son. He was just a simple boy, like any other boy. This boy is a stranger to me. It is as if we have lost him.

Shonku: Let me see what I can do. But you must be patient. A very radical change has come over him, and to return him to normal may take a little time. I shall of course see that a neurosurgeon examines him. I know a very good one.

***

[Shonku's house. Bedroom]

The boy is in bed, Shonku is seated in a chair beside him.

Shonku: Are you missing your parents?

Boy: No.

Shonku: You like to be here?

Boy: Yes, it is all right.

Shonku: I'm going to ask you a few questions—will you answer them?

Boy: Yes.

Shonku: What are the planets of the solar system?

Boy: Mercury, Venus, Earth, Mars, Jupiter, Saturn, Uranus, Neptune, Pluto.

Shonku: Do you know what is the nearest star?

Boy: Alpha centauri.

Shonku: Do you know what is the earliest ancestor of man called?

Boy: Australopithecus afarensis.

Shonku: Do you know Einstein's formula of relativity?

Boy: $E = mc^2$

Shonku: Very good. As I said before, a doctor will come to examine you today.

Boy: Neurosurgeon.

Shonku: Yes, a neurosurgeon.

Boy: There is no need of a doctor. I know what has happened to me.

Shonku: What is it?

Boy: It has no name yet.

Shonku: Is there a cure for it?

Boy: I don't know yet.

Shonku: The doctor might know.

Boy: No, he won't. No one knows but I may know in a day or two. My knowledge is increasing.

Shonku: I see.

The phone rings. Shonku takes the call.

Shonku: Shonku speaking.

Man: Good morning. I am the local correspondent of the *Calcutta Morning Gazette.*

Shonku: Yes?

Man: I believe an eight-year-old boy has come and is staying with you, and that he has unusual powers of intellect.

Shonku: Look, I can't comment anything on the subject.

Man: But we already know about it, sir, and it's going to be out in the papers tomorrow.

Shonku: But that would be wrong.

Man: I'm sorry Prof. Shonku, we have no choice in the matter. I only wanted a little more information from you.

Shonku: Sorry, I cannot give you any more information at all.

Man: Very well. Goodbye.

PART 2

[Shonku's bedroom]

Newspaper Headline: 'An Extraordinary Child Prodigy'. There is also a picture of the boy which they obviously got from his parents. Shonku throws aside the paper and rushes to the telephone. He rings up the police headquarters.

Shonku: Hello, I want to speak to Inspector Shome—yes . . . Hello—Inspector

Shome, this is Trilokeshwar Shonku. I suppose you have read in the papers about the boy who is staying in my house.

Shome: Yes sir.

Shonku: Well, I fear that there will be a stampede in my house to catch a glimpse of him. I would request you to arrange for a police force outside my house. Nobody is to be allowed in.

Shome: Very well, Prof. Shonku.

Shonku: Thank you very much. I hope you realize that this is urgent.

[Shonku's sitting room]

Shonku has finished reading the paper, folds it up, puts it aside and drinks coffee. There is a knock on the door. Shonku reacts, and is tensed. He opens the door after a second knock. It is an old neighbour of his—Abinashbabu.

Shonku: Come in, Abinashbabu. I thought you were a journalist.

Abinash: But what is all this in the paper?

Shonku: It is true, and that is why I was so panicky.

Abinash: And where is this boy?

Shonku: His name is Ajay.

Abinash: At least let me see him. You can't hide him from an old friend like me.

Shonku calls out.

Shonku: Ajay!

The boy enters the room solemnly. Shonku introduces him to the visitor and neighbour.

Shonku: This is an old friend and neighbour of mine, Abinash Majumder.

Abinash: What is your name?

The boy keeps looking at Abinashbabu, saying nothing. Abinashbabu repeats his question.

Abinash: What is your name?

Ajay: Ectomorphic cerebretonic.

Abinash: My goodness! What kind of a name is that?

Shonku smiles.

Shonku: That's not his name. He is only describing the type of person you are. It's a

Admiral: But what is all this in the boxes?

Shotover: It is true, & that is why I am to disaster.

Admiral: But what is this boy?

Shotover: He was in my library, ...

The boy enters the room solemnly. Shotover introduces him to the visitor.

Shotover: This is the old ... of mine, Admiral ...

Admiral: What is your name?

Boy: Entomoscopic Cockburnstown

Admiral: My soul! What kind of a name is that?

Shotover writes.

Shotover: That's not his name. He is only describing the ... from physiology. ... known there. His name is ...

Admiral: Don't tell me you have taken to teaching ...

Boy: He has taught me nothing.

Shotover: That is true, I have taught him nothing.

... a ladder — Shotover opens it. It is ...

Shotover: ... everything is very fine.

Shotover: Thank you very much

Shotover: The sea never has spread very wide, & I fear the worst ...

A page from the draft script

A page from the draft script

technical term from physiology. His name is Ajay Kumar Mitra.

Abinash: Don't tell me you have taken to teaching jawbreaking scientific names to kids.

Ajay: He has taught me nothing.

Shonku: That is true. I have taught him nothing.

Just then a police jeep draws up outside the house. There is a knock at the door—Shonku opens it. It is Inspector Shome.

Shome: I just came to assure you that everything is being done.

Shonku: Thank you very much.

Shome: The news has spread very wide and I fear the worst.

Shonku: That is what I thought, so I decided to call you first thing in the morning.

Shome: Well, I will take my leave. I don't think you'll have to worry about anything.

Shome goes out.

Abinash: It looks like trouble. Well, I had better get going too. Good day, Professor.

Shonku: Good day.

Abinash takes his leave too. Shonku turns to Ajay.

Shonku: How do you feel today?

Ajay: All right.

Shonku: Is there anything special you would like to do? We can go for a drive in my car, you know.

Ajay: I don't want to go out.

Shonku: Then what do you want to do?

Ajay: I want to see your laboratory.

Shonku: My laboratory?

Ajay: Yes.

Shonku: But there are dangerous things in it. It is not a safe place for a small boy, you know.

Ajay: It is quite safe. I know what I want. I want you to take me there. Please take me.

Shonku: All right, if you insist.

Shonku takes the boy out of the room.

[The laboratory]

Shonku opens the lock with a key, and enters with the boy in tow. The boy goes towards the table—various kinds of apparatus fill the room. He also murmurs at the same time and passing his hand over the various instruments.

Ajay: Micropipe . . . Test tube . . . Flasks . . . Retorts . . . Bunsen burner . . .

The boy now looks up at the shelf where a range of bottles stand.

Ajay: Sulphuric acid . . . Nitric acid . . . Prussic acid . . . Salicylic acid . . .

The boy approaches the shelf for a closer look and is about to take down the bottle of sulphuric acid when Shonku stops him.

Shonku: Don't do that! Don't touch that bottle, Ajay! That is a very poisonous acid. If a drop falls on your skin, it will be burnt. Do you know that?

Ajay: Yes, I do.

Shonku: Well, I think you have seen enough, you'd better come up and rest. You have walked about quite a bit.

They come out of the laboratory. Shonku locks the door with the key.

***

[Upstairs. Bedroom]

Shonku and Ajay come in. Shonku puts the key in a drawer—Ajay notices it. Ajay gets into bed. Shonku turns to Ajay.

Shonku: You still don't miss your parents?

Ajay: No.

Shonku eyes the boy for a few seconds.

Shonku: But your mother must be missing you.

Ajay: I can't do anything about that.

***

[Mitter's House]

A man knocks at the door. This is an impresario, Mr Bhowmick. Mitter opens the door.

Bhowmick: Mr Mitter?

Mitter: Yes—

Bhowmick: May I talk to you for a few minutes?

Mitter: Certainly—come in.

The two sit in the small sitting room.

Bhowmick: I have been reading about your son in the papers.

Mitter: I see.

Bhowmick: My name is Bhowmick and I am an impresario. I work as the manager of people who give performances on the stage.

Mitter: I see.

Bhowmick: Is your son here?

Mitter: No—he is staying with the scientist Prof. Shonku. Why do you ask?

Bhowmick: You see, I feel your son would be a sensation on the stage. He could give answers to questions—the most difficult questions—an eight-year-old boy with the wisdom and knowledge of an eighty year old. Can you imagine how people would go crazy? And he would be a source of extra income to you. I know you are a clerk in the post office. Don't you want to add to your income? He will have the box office of the biggest film star.

Mrs Mitter has been listening from behind the curtain.

Mrs Mitter: But this won't bring back our *khoka* to us. He will remain as he is now—a stranger. What will we do with money when we have lost our boy?

Bhowmick: But with money you can afford the treatment. Then maybe you will get back the son you have lost. But in the meantime let us make the best of the opportunity. He is unique Mrs Mitter, don't let this chance go. He will be famous and you will be rich. How much does your husband earn as a post office clerk? He will earn a hundred times more!

Mitter: But he is not with us, you know. He is with Prof. Shonku.

Bhowmick: I'll talk to the Professor. The main thing is to talk to the boy. If he agrees, the Professor will say nothing.

***

[Outside Shonku's room]

About a hundred people have gathered asking to see the boy. The police is keeping them at bay, but they are having a tough time of it.

   Police: Get back, get back—you can't go in.

   Man 1: We want to catch a glimpse of him.

   Man 2: Yes, just a glimpse.

Inside the house, Shonku is pacing the floor of the sitting room. There is a knock on the door. Shonku opens it. There is a police officer.

   Officer: They just want to take a look at him, and then they said they will go. If you could just bring him to the door.

Ajay is seated in a sofa in a corner of the room.

   Shonku: All right, but I hope they keep their word. Come Ajay, we'll stand at the door—the two of us.

Ajay and Shonku open the door and stand facing the crowd. There is a big applause from the crowd.

   Officer: Well, that's enough—now get going—get going, *(to Shonku)* you two go back inside.

Shonku and Ajay get back in and shut the door again.

✱✱✱

[Shonku's house. Sitting room]

Mr Mitter and Mr Bhowmick have come to see Prof. Shonku.

   Prof. Shonku: Well, what I can say is that if the boy agrees to it then you can go ahead. But too much strain may be bad for him.

   Bhowmick: He will be the last item in the magic show. He will be on stage no more than fifteen or twenty minutes.

Shonku calls the boy. Ajay comes and stands before Mitter and Bhowmick, says nothing.

   Mitter: How are you?

   Ajay: All right.

   Mitter: This is Mr Bhowmick. He wants you to perform on the public stage and answer questions from the audience.

Ajay stares at Bhowmick.

Ajay: Everyday?

Bhowmick: For a fortnight only!

Ajay: How many questions?

Bhowmick: As many as you can answer in fifteen or twenty minutes.

Ajay: And after that?

Bhowmick: After that we would bring you back here. All right?

Ajay: All right.

Bhowmick: You see, you are a famous boy now, and everybody wants to see you.

PART 3

[Stage]

The magician is dressed as usual in a turban and sherwani. He picks little pieces of paper from a container. Ajay is seated in a chair at one side with an expressionless face.

Magician: I have a bunch of questions here from the members of the audience. I shall read them out one by one to our Wonder Boy. Let us see if he knows the answers. The first question—what is the name of the court musician of Akbar?

Ajay: Tansen.

The audience claps. Shonku is seen seated amongst the audience.

Magician: Second question—what is the name of the second highest mountain in the world?

Ajay: Mount Godwin Austin.

Magician: That is correct.

Applause. Magician takes another paper.

Magician: Who wrote *Mrichhakatikam*?

Ajay: Susruta.

Magician: Correct.

Applause. Magician picks up another paper.

Magician: Who discovered the malarial vector?

Ajay: Dr Ronald Ross.

Applause.

***

[Another Day]

Ajay is wearing a different shirt now. Magician is as usual picking up papers from a bag.

    Magician: What is the value of pi?

    Ajay: About 3.14159

    Magician: Correct.

Applause.

    Magician: What was the longest of the prehistoric animals?

    Ajay: Brontosaurus.

    Magician: Correct!

Applause.

    Magician: Which was the oldest civilization in Ancient India?

    Ajay: Mohenjo Daro.

Applause.

***

[Another day]

    Magician: Which year was the first battle of Panipat fought?

    Ajay: Fifteen twenty-six.

Applause.

    Magician: Who painted the Sistine Chapel?

    Ajay: Michelangelo.

Applause.

    Magician: What is the commonest element in nature?

Ajay does not answer.

    Magician: Ajay—what is the commonest element in nature?

Ajay still keeps quiet.

Magician: Ajay—the audience is waiting.

Shonku reacts, he is tense and restless.

Magician: Ajay—the audience is waiting.

Ajay: I don't want to answer.

Magician: Please Ajay, you've done so well so far.

Ajay: I—don't—want—to—answer.

There is consternation amongst the audience. Shonku keeps looking.

Magician: I'm afraid Ajay is not feeling well tonight. So we'll have to stop here.

The curtain drops.

***

[Shonku's bedroom]

Ajay is lying in bed. Shonku paces the room. Shonku stops and turns to Ajay.

Shonku: Were you not feeling well?

Ajay does not answer. Shonku repeats the question.

Ajay: I was all right.

Shonku: Then why did you not answer?

Ajay: I'm not a clown in a circus.

Shonku: I see. So that is why you stopped.

Ajay: Yes.

Shonku: Well, I think you did the right thing.

Ajay says nothing. Shonku keeps looking at Ajay.

Shonku: Do you wish to go back home now—to your parents?

Ajay: No.

Shonku: You prefer to stay with me?

Ajay: Yes. And I don't want to answer any more questions.

Shonku: You don't have to. I'm not going to ask you anything.

Ajay: Good.

Prahlad comes.

Prahlad: Sir, there is a gentleman to see you.

Shonku: What is his name?

Prahlad: He says Banerjee, Jagadish Banerjee. He wants to see you for a few minutes.

Shonku: Tell him I'm coming.

Prahlad goes away. Shonku turns to Ajay.

Shonku: You rest in here while I'll see what this gentleman wants.

[Sitting room]

Shonku comes in. A middle aged man in dhoti and panjabi gets up and folds his hands in a namaskar.

Banerjee: I'm very sorry to disturb you, but I couldn't help coming to you.

Shonku: What can I do for you?

Banerjee: You see, my son, my only son, who is seventeen, has been severely ill for over a month. The doctors have tried but have failed.

Banerjee stops.

Shonku: But I'm not a doctor.

Banerjee: I know, and it's not you I have come to see.

Shonku: Then?

Banerjee: It is the boy who is staying with you. I have been watching his performance. This is not possible unless the boy is possessed of a great spiritual power.

Shonku: It is still not clear what you want.

Banerjee: I want you to bring that boy to my house so he can see my son. I'm sure a word from him will help him. Please Mr Shonku, do not let me down.

Shonku: I think you are suffering from a delusion. That boy knows no magical cure, nor is he practising witchcraft. Please excuse me. Goodbye.

Shonku gets up. The man takes his leave. Shonku goes back into the bedroom. He is still irritated about the visitor.

Shonku: Silly fool!

Now Ajay talks.

Ajay: Carcinosis.

Shonku: What?

Ajay: Carcinosis. That young man will not live.

***

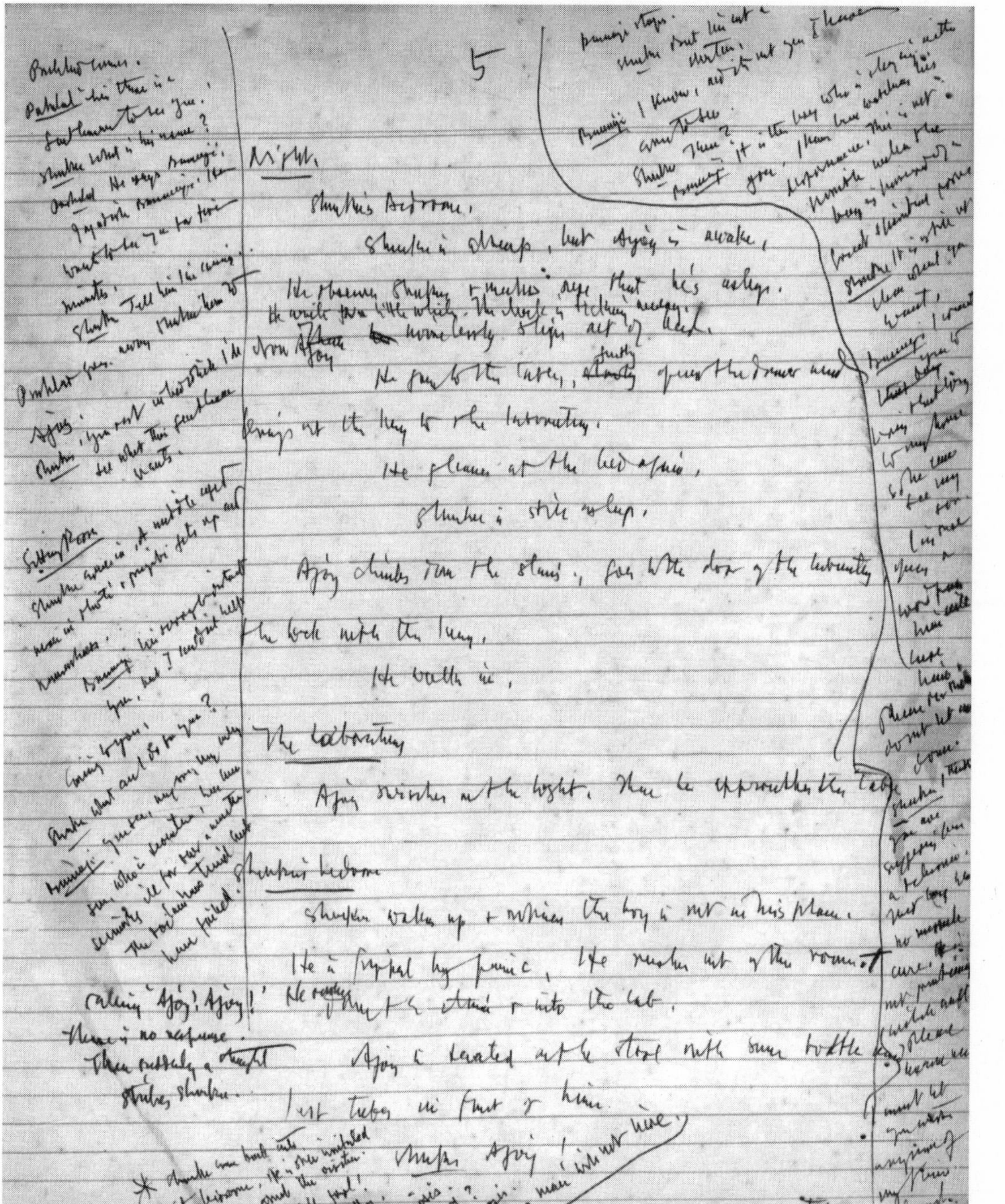

<u>Night</u>

Shankar's Bedroom.

Shankar is asleep, but Ajoy is awake.

He observes Shankar + makes sure that he's asleep. He waits for a little while. The house is perfectly silent. He rises at last.

He goes to the table, slowly opens the drawer and brings out the key to the laboratory.

He glances at the bed again.

Shankar is still asleep.

Ajoy climbs down the stairs, goes to the door of the laboratory. He locks with the key.

He walks in.

<u>The laboratory</u>

Ajoy switches on the light. Then he approaches the table.

<u>Shankar's bedroom</u>

Shankar wakes up and notices the boy is not in his place.

He is gripped by panic. He rushes out of the room, calling "Ajoy! Ajoy!" He reaches the stairs + into the lab.

There is no response. Then suddenly a thought strikes Shankar.

Ajoy is seated at the stool with some bottles + test tubes in front of him.

Shankar: Ajoy! ... Ajoy! ...

[marginal and surrounding notes largely illegible]

A page from the draft script

[Night. Shonku's bedroom]

Shonku is asleep, but Ajay is awake. He observes Shonku and makes sure that he's asleep. He waits for a little while. The clock is ticking away. Now Ajay noiselessly slips out of bed. He goes to the table, quietly opens the drawer and brings out the key to the laboratory. He glances at the bed again. Shonku is still asleep. Ajay climbs down the stairs; goes to the door of the laboratory, opens the lock with the key. He walks in.

[The laboratory]

Ajay switches on the light. Then he approaches the table.

[Shonku's bedroom]

Shonku wakes up and notices the boy is not in his place. He is gripped by panic. He rushes out of the room calling 'Ajay! Ajay!' There is no response. Then suddenly a thought strikes Shonku. He rushes down the stairs and goes towards the laboratory. Ajay is seated on the stool with some bottle and test tubes in front of him.

[The laboratory]

Shonku: Ajay!

Ajay swirls around. He picks up a bottle of sulphuric acid and raises his hand.

Ajay: Don't come near me or I'll throw this at you.

Shonku: But—but—you'll kill yourself, I told you.

Ajay: I know, and I know exactly what to do. If you come a step near me I'll throw this acid at you. You just stand and watch.

Shonku stands helplessly.

Shonku: Ajay—I beg of you—don't do that.

Ajay picks up the Annihilin. He mixes three acids in a test tube—a hissing smoke issues from the liquid. Then Ajay takes the test tube and drinks the mixture. Then his hand lolls on the table. Shonku rushes to Ajay.

Shonku: Ajay! Ajay! My God!

But Ajay is not dead. He slowly opens his eyes.

Shonku: Ajay—are you all right? Are you all right?

Ajay: Where is my mother? I want to go to my mother.

Freeze on Ajay.

NIGHT OF THE INDIGO

Originally published in *Sandesh* (Puja Annual 1968) as *Neel Atanko*. It was translated by the author himself to be part of the compilation titled *Stories* (Secker & Warburg, 1987). The illustrations in the story, including the Bengali calligraphy in the headpiece, are by Satyajit Ray.

My name is Aniruddha Bose. I am twenty-nine and a bachelor. For the last eight years I've been working in an advertising agency in Calcutta. With the salary I get I live in reasonable comfort in a flat in Sardar Shankar Road. It consists of two rooms on the first floor facing south. Two years ago, I bought an Ambassador car which I drive myself. I do a bit of writing in my spare time. Three of my stories have been published in magazines and have earned the praise of my acquaintances, but I know I cannot make a living by writing alone. The last few months I haven't written at all, but have read a lot about indigo plantations in Bengal and Bihar in the nineteenth century. I am something of an authority on the subject now: how the English started the cultivation of indigo here; how they exploited the poor peasants; how the peasants rose in revolt, and how, finally, with the invention of synthetic indigo in Germany, the cultivation of indigo was wiped out from our country—all this I know by heart. It is to describe the terrible experience which instilled in me this interest in indigo that I have taken up my pen today.

At this point I must tell you something about my past.

My father was a well-known physician in Monghyr, a town in Bihar. That is where I was born and that is where I went to a missionary school. I have a brother five years older than me. He studied medicine in England and is now attached to a hospital in a suburb of London called Golders Green. He has no plans to return to India.

My father died when I was sixteen. Soon after his death, my mother and I left Monghyr and came to Calcutta where we stayed with my maternal uncle. I went to St Xavier's College and took my bachelor's degree. Soon after that I got my job with the advertising agency. The backing of my uncle helped, but I wasn't lacking in qualities as a candidate myself. I had been a good student, I spoke English fluently, and I had the ability to carry myself well in an interview.

The fact that I had spent my early years in Monghyr will help to explain one of my traits. From time to time I long to get away from the hectic life of Calcutta. I have done so several times ever since I bought my car. On weekends I have made trips to Diamond Harbour, to Port Canning, to Hassanabad along the Dum Dum Road. Each time I have gone alone because, to be quite honest, I don't really have a close friend in Calcutta. That is why Promode's letter made me so happy. Promode had been my classmate in Monghyr. After I came away to Calcutta, we continued to keep in touch for three or four years. Then, perhaps it was I who stopped writing. Suddenly the other day when I came back from work, I found a letter from Promode waiting for me on my desk. He had written from Dumka—'I have a job in the Forest Department here. I have my own quarters. Why don't you take a week's leave and come over . . .?'

Some leave was due to me, so I spoke to my boss, and on the twenty-seventh of April—I shall remember the date as long as I live—I packed my bags and set off for Dumka.

Promode hadn't suggested that I go by car; it was my idea. Dumka was two hundred miles away, so it would take about five or six hours at the most. I decided to have an early lunch, set off by ten and reach there before dusk.

At least that was the plan, but there was a snag right at the start. I had my meal and was about to toss a paan into my mouth when my father's old friend Uncle Mohit suddenly turned up—a man of grave deportment whom I was meeting again after ten years. So there was no question of giving him short shrift. I had to offer him tea and listen to him chat for over an hour.

I saw Uncle Mohit off and shoved my suitcase and my bedding into the back seat of my car. Just then I saw my ground floor neighbour Bholababu walking up with his four-year-old son Pintu in tow.

'Where are you off to all by yourself?' Bholababu asked. When I told him, he said with some concern, 'But that's a long way. Shouldn't you have arranged for a driver?'

I said I was a very cautious driver myself, and that I had taken such care of my car that it was still as good as new—'So there's nothing to worry about.'

Bholababu wished me luck and went into the house. I glanced at my wrist watch before turning the ignition key. It was ten minutes past eleven.

Although I avoided Howrah and took the Bally Bridge road, it took me an hour and a half to reach Chandannagore. Driving through dingy towns, these first thirty miles were so dreary that the fun of a car journey was never in evidence. But from here on, as the car emerged into open country, the effect was magical. When did one see such clear blue sky free from chimney smoke, and breathe air so pure and so redolent of the smell of earth? At about half past twelve, when I was nearing Burdwan, I began to feel the consequence of having an early lunch. I felt hungry. I pulled up by the station which fell on the way, went into a restaurant and had a light meal consisting of toast, omelette and coffee. Then I resumed my journey. I still had a hundred and thirty-five miles to go.

Twenty miles from Burdwan was the small town of Panagarh. There I will have to leave the Grand Trunk Road and take the road to Illambazar. From Ilambazar the road went via Suri and Massanjore to Dumka.

The military camp at Panagarh had just come into view when there was a bang from the rear of my car. I had a flat tyre.

I got down from the car. I had a spare tyre and could easily fit it. The thought that other cars would go whizzing by and that their occupants would laugh at my predicament was not a pleasant one. Nevertheless I brought out the jack from the boot and set to work.

By the time I finished putting the new tyre on, I was dripping with sweat. My watch showed half past two. It had turned muggy in the meantime. The cool breeze which was blowing even an hour ago, and which made the bamboo trees sway, had stopped. Now everything was still. As I got back into the car I noticed a blue-black patch in the west above the tree tops. Cloud. Did it portend a storm? A nor'wester? It was useless to speculate. I must drive faster. I helped myself to some hot tea from the flask and resumed my journey.

Before I had crossed Ilambazar, I was caught in the storm. I had enjoyed such nor'westers in the past, sitting in my room, and had even recited Tagore poems to chime with the mood. I had no idea that, driving through open country, such a nor'wester could strike terror into the heart. Thunderclaps always make me uncomfortable. They seem to show a nasty side of nature; a vicious assault on helpless humanity. It seemed as if the shafts of lightning were all aimed at my poor Ambassador, and one of them was sure to find its mark sooner or later.

In this precarious state I passed Suri and was well on my way to Massanjore when there was yet another bang which no one could mistake for a thunderclap, I realized that one more of my tyres had decided to call it a day.

I gave up hope. It was now pouring with rain. My watch said half past five. For the last twenty miles I had had to keep the speedometer down to fifteen, or I would have been well past Massanjore by now. Where was I? Up ahead nothing was visible through the rainswept windscreen. The wiper was on but its efforts were more frolicsome than effective. Being April, the sun should still be up, but it seemed more like late evening.

I opened the door on my right slightly and looked out. What I saw didn't suggest the presence of a town, but I could make out a couple of buildings through the trees. There was no question of getting out of the car and exploring, but one thing was clear enough: there were no shops along the road as far as the eye could see.

And I had no more spare tyres.

After waiting in the car for a quarter of an hour, it struck me that no other vehicles had passed in all this time. Was I on the right road? There had been no mistake up to Suri, but suppose I had taken a wrong turning after that? It was not impossible in the blinding rain.

But even if I had made a mistake, it was not as if I had strayed into the jungles of Africa or South America. Wherever I was, there was no doubt that I was still in the district of Birbhum, within fifty miles of Shantiniketan, and as soon as the rain stopped my troubles would be over—I might even find a repair shop within a mile or so.

I brought out my packet of Wills from my pocket and lit a cigarette. I recalled Bholababu's warning. He must have been through the same trying experience, or how could he have given me such sound advice? In future—

'Honk! Honk! Honk!'

I turned round and saw a truck standing behind. But why was it blowing its horn? Was I standing right in the middle of the road?

The rain had let up a little. I opened the door, got out and found that it was no fault of the truck's. When my tyre burst the car had swerved at an angle and was now blocking most of the road. There was no room for the truck to pass.

'Take the car to one side, sir.'

The Sikh driver had by now come out of the truck.

'What's the matter?' he asked. 'A puncture?'

I shrugged to convey my state of helplessness. 'If you could lend a hand,' I said, 'we could move the car to one side and let you pass.'

The Sikh driver's helper too came out. The three of us pushed the car to one side of the road. Then I found out by asking that this was not the road to Dumka at all. I had indeed taken a wrong turning. I will have to drive back three miles to get back on the right track. I also learnt that there were no repair shops nearby.

The truck went on its way. As its noise faded away, the truth struck me like a hammer blow.

I had reached an impasse.

There was no way I could reach Dumka tonight, and there was no knowing how and where I would spend the night.

The roadside puddles were alive with the chorus of frogs. The rain had now been reduced to a light drizzle.

I got back into the car. I was about to light a second cigarette when I spotted a light through the window on my side. I opened the door again. Through the branches of a tree I saw a rectangle of orange light. A window. Just as smoke meant the presence of fire, a kerosene lamp meant the presence of a human being. There was a house nearby and there were occupants in it.

I got out of the car with my torch. The window wasn't too far away. I had to go and investigate. There was a narrow footpath branching off from the main road which seemed to go in the direction of the house with the window.

I locked the door of the car and set off.

I made my way avoiding puddles as far as possible. As I passed a tamarind tree, the house came into view. Well, hardly a house. It was a small cottage with a corrugated tin roof. Through an open door I could see a hurricane lantern and the leg of a bed.

'Is anybody there?' I called out.

A stocky, middle-aged man with a thick moustache came out of the room and squinted at my torch. I turned the spot away from his face.

'Where are you from, sir?' the man asked.

In a few words I described my predicament. 'Is there a place here where I can spend the night?' I asked, 'I shall pay for it, of course.'

'In the dak bungalow, you mean?'

Dak bungalow? I didn't see any dak bungalow.

But immediately I realized my mistake. Because of the presence of the lantern, I had failed to look around. Now I turned the torch to my left and immediately a large, one-storey bungalow came into view. 'You mean that one?' I asked.

'Yes sir, but there is no bedding. And you can't have meals here.'

'I'm carrying my own bedding,' I said, 'I hope there's a bed there?'

'Yes sir. A charpoy.'

'And I see there's an oven lighted in your room. You must be cooking your own meal?'

The man broke into a smile and asked if I would care for coarse chapati prepared by him and urut-ka-dal cooked by his wife. I said they would do very nicely. I liked all kinds of chapatis, and urut was my favourite dal.

I don't know what it was like in its heyday, but now it was hardly what one understood by a dak bungalow. But belonging to the time of the Raj, the bedroom was large and the ceiling was high. The furniture consisted of a charpoy, a table set against the wall on one side, and a chair with a broken arm.

The chowkidar, or the caretaker, had in the meantime lighted a lantern for me. He brought it and put it on the table. 'What is your name?' I asked.

'Sukhanram, sir.'

'Has anybody ever lived in this bungalow or am I the first one?'

'Oh, no sir, others have come too. There was a gentleman who stayed here two nights last winter.'

'I hope there are no ghosts here,' I said in a jocular tone.

'God forbid!' he said, 'No one has ever complained of ghosts.'

I must say I found his words reassuring. If a place is spooky, and old dak bungalows have a reputation for being so, it will be so at all times. 'When was this bungalow built?' I asked.

Sukhanram began to unroll my bedding and said, 'This used to be a sahib's bungalow, sir.'

'A sahib?'

'Yes, sir. An indigo planter. There used to be an indigo factory close by. Now only the chimney is standing.'

I knew indigo was cultivated in these parts at one time. I had seen ruins of indigo factories in Monghyr too in my childhood.

It was ten-thirty when I went to bed after dining on Sukhan's coarse chapatis and urut-ka-dal. I had sent a telegram to Promode from Calcutta saying that I would arrive this afternoon. He would naturally wonder what had happened. But it was useless to think of that now. That I had found a shelter, and that too without much trouble, was something I could congratulate myself on. In future I would do as Bholababu had advised. I had learnt a lesson, and a lesson learnt the hard way goes deeper.

I put the lantern in the adjoining bathroom. The little light that seeped through the door which I kept slightly ajar was enough. I can't sleep if there's a light on in my room, and yet what I most badly needed now was sleep. I was worried about my car which I had left standing on the road, but it was certainly safer to do so in a village than in the city.

The sound of drizzle had stopped. The air was now filled with the croaking of frogs and the shrill chirping of crickets. Lying in this ancient bungalow in this remote village, the city seemed to belong to another planet. Indigo . . . I thought of the play by Dinabandhu Mitra—*The Mirror of Indigo*. As a college student I had watched a performance of it in a theatre in Cornwallis Street.

I didn't know how long I had slept, but I was suddenly awakened by a sound. It was a sound of scratching which came from the door. The door was bolted. Must be a dog or a jackal. In a minute or so the sound stopped.

I shut my eyes in an effort to sleep, but only for a short while. The barking of a dog put an end to my efforts. This was not the bark of a stray village dog, but the unmistakable bay of a hound. I was familiar with it. Two houses away from us in Monghyr lived Mr Martin. He had a hound which bayed just like this. Who on earth kept a pet hound here? I thought of opening the door to find out because the sound came from quite near. But then I thought; why bother? It was better to get some more sleep. What time was it now?

A faint moonlight came in through the window. I raised my left hand to glance at the wrist watch, and gave a start. There was no wrist watch.

And yet, because it was an automatic watch, I always wore it to bed. Where did it disappear? And how? Are there thieves around? What will happen to my car then?

I felt beside my pillow for my torch and found that was gone too.

I jumped out of bed, knelt on the floor and looked underneath it. My suitcase too had disappeared.

My head started spinning. Something had to be done about it. I called out: 'Chowkidar!' There was no answer.

I went to the door and found it was still bolted. The window had bars. So how did the thief enter?

As I was about to unfasten the bolt, I glanced at my hand and experienced an odd feeling.

Had whitewash from the wall got on to my hand? Or was it white powder? Why did it look so pale?

I had gone to bed wearing a vest; why then was I wearing a long-sleeved silk shirt?

I felt a throbbing in my head. I opened the door and went out on the verandah. 'Chowkidar!'

The word that came out was spoken with the unmistakable accent of an Englishman. And where was the chowkidar, and where was his little cottage? There was now a wide open field in front of the bungalow. In the distance was a building with a high chimney. The surroundings were unusually quiet.

And they had changed.

And so had I.

I came back into the bedroom in a sweat. My eyes had got used to the darkness. I could now clearly make out the details. The bed was there, but it was covered with a mosquito net. I hadn't been using one. The pillow too was unlike mine. This one had a border with frills; mine didn't. The table and the chair stood where they did, but they had lost their aged look.

The varnished wood shone even in the soft light. On the table stood not a lantern but a kerosene lamp with an ornate shade.

There were other objects in the room which gradually came into view: a pair of steel trunks in a corner, a folding bracket on the wall from which hung a coat, an unfamiliar type of headgear and a hunting crop. Below the bracket, standing against the wall was a pair of galoshes.

I turned away from the objects and took another look at myself. Till now I had only noticed the silk shirt; now I saw the narrow trousers and the socks. I didn't have shoes on, but saw a pair of black boots on the floor by the bed.

Now I passed my right hand over my face and realized that not only my complexion but my features too had changed. I didn't possess such a sharp nose, nor such thin lips or narrow chin. I felt the hair on my head and found that it was wavy and that there were sideburns which reached below my ears.

Along with surprise and terror, I felt a great urge to find out what I looked like. But where to find a mirror?

I strode towards the bathroom, opened the door with a sharp push and went in.

I had earlier noticed that there was nothing there but a bucket. Now I saw a metal bath tub, and a mug kept on a stool beside it. The thing I was looking for was right in front of me: an oval mirror fixed to a dressing table. Although I stood facing the mirror, the person reflected in it was not me. By some devilish trick I had turned into a nineteenth-century Englishman, with a sallow complexion, blond hair and light eyes which showed a strange mixture of hardness and suffering. How old would the Englishman be? Not more than thirty, but it looked as if either illness or hard work or both had aged him prematurely.

I went closer and had a good look at 'my' face. As I looked, a deep sigh rose from the depths of my heart.

The voice was not mine. The sigh, too, expressed not my feelings but those of the Englishman.

What followed made it clear that all my limbs were acting of their own volition. And yet it was surprising that I—Aniruddha Bose—was perfectly aware of the change in identity. But I didn't know if the change was temporary or permanent or if there was any way to regain my lost self.

I came back to the bedroom.

Now I glanced at the table. Below the lamp was a notebook bound in leather. It was open at a blank page. Beside it was an inkwell with a quill pen dipped in it.

I walked over to the table. Some unseen force made me sit in the chair and pick up the pen with my right hand. The hand with the pen now moved towards the left-hand page of the notebook. Now the silent room was filled with the scratching noise of a quill pen writing on the blank page. This is what I wrote:

April 27, 1868

Those fiendish mosquitoes are singing in my ears again. So that's how the son of a mighty Empire had to meet his end — at the hands of a tiny insect. What strange will of God is this? Eric has made his escape. Percy and Tony too left earlier. Perhaps I was

greedier than them. So in spite of repeated attacks of malaria I couldn't resist the lure of indigo. No, not only that. One mustn't lie in one's diary. My countrymen know me only too well. I didn't lead a blameless life at home either; and that they surely have not forgotten. So I do not dare go back home. I know I will have to stay here and lay down my life on this alien soil. My place will be beside the graves of my wife Mary and my dear little son Toby. I have treated the natives here so badly that there is no one to shed a tear at my passing away. Perhaps Mirjan would miss me—my faithful trusted bearer Mirjan. And Rex? My real worry is about Rex. Alas, faithful Rex! When I die, these people will not spare you. They will either stone you or club you to death. If only I could do something about you!'

I could write no more. The hands were shaking. Not mine, but the diarist's.

I put down the pen.

Now my right hand came down from the table, moved to the right and made for the handle of the drawer.

The drawer opened.

Inside there was a pin cushion, a brass paperweight, a pipe and some papers.

Now the drawer opened a little more. A metal object glinted in the half light.

It was a pistol, its butt inlaid with ivory.

The hand brought out the pistol. The shaking stopped.

A group of jackals cried out. It was as if in answer to the jackal's cry that the hound bayed again.

I left the chair and advanced towards the door. Then through the door out on to the verandah.

The field in front was bathed in moonlight.

About ten yards from the verandah stood a large greyhound. He wagged his tail as he saw me.

'Rex!'

It was the same deep English voice. The echo of the call came floating back from the faraway factory and bamboo grove—Rex! Rex!

Rex came up towards the verandah.

As he stepped from the grass on to the cement, my right hand rose to my waist, the pistol pointing towards the hound. Rex stopped in his tracks, his eye on the pistol. He gave a low growl.

My right forefinger pressed the trigger.

As the gun throbbed with a blinding flash, smoke and the smell of gunpowder filled the air.

Rex's lifeless, blood-spattered body lay partly on the verandah and partly on the grass.

The sound of the pistol had wakened the crows in the nearby trees. A hubbub now rose from the direction of the factory.

I came back into the bedroom, bolted the door and sat on the bed. The shouting drew near.

I placed the still hot muzzle of the pistol to my right ear. That is all I remember.

I woke up at the sound of knocking.

'I've brought your tea, sir.'

Daylight flooded in through the window. Out of sheer habit my eyes strayed to my left wrist.

Thirteen minutes past six. I brought the watch closer to my eyes to read the date, April the twenty-eighth.

I now opened the door and let Sukhanram in.

'There's a car repair shop half an hour down the road, sir,' he said, 'it'll open at seven.'

'Very good,' I said, and proceeded to drink my tea.

Will anyone believe me when they hear of my experience on the one hundredth anniversary of the death of an English indigo planter in Birbhum?

THE LIFE AND DEATH OF ARYASEKHAR

Originally published in *Amrita* (Puja Annual 1968) as *Aryashekharer Janmo O Mrityu*.
The English translation by Ray has not been published earlier and is transcribed from Ray's
literary notebook. The illustration in the story is by Satyajit Ray.

Aryashekhar was what one would call a 'child prodigy' in English. He was ten years old when his eyes caught a sentence near the bottom of a page in *The Statesman*—'Sun rises today at 6.13 a.m.' Aryashekhar presented himself to his father, Soumyashekhar, along with the newspaper.

— Father

— Yes?

— There's something in the newspaper.

— What?

— It says the sun rose at thirteen minutes past six.

— Yes, of course. It did rise on time.

— You checked the clock?

— No need for that.

— Why?

— It would, everybody knows.

— How?

— That has to do with science. With astronomy.

— What if it didn't?

— The clock must have been wrong.

— What if it wasn't?

— Then? It'd mean the end of the world.

The day marked the beginning of Aryashekhar's passion for science. Two years later, Aryashekhar found himself going to his father again, with another question.

— Father

— Hmm.

— Are the Sun and the moon the same size?

— Don't be silly.

— Then?

— The Sun's far bigger.

— How much bigger?

— Millions of times.

— But they do look the same size?

— Because the sun is further away.

— Exactly so far away that it looks just the same as the moon?

— Hmm.

— How did that happen?

— I have no idea, son. I'm not exactly the Creator, you know.

We must remind ourselves at this point that Soumyashekhar was not a scientist. His profession was Law.

The talk with his father had made it eminently clear to Aryashekhar that the sun and the moon's apparent similarity in size was a chance occurrence. This chance occurrence instilled in him a great sense of wonder. He forgot all about his schoolbooks, unlocked his father's bookshelves, and began reading up the stars and planets from the ten volumes which comprised *Harmsworth's Popular Science*. It goes without saying that he had to take frequent recourse to the dictionary in his endeavour. But he did not lose heart, since his character was a rare blend of the imaginative and the single-minded.

On his fourteenth birthday, Aryashekhar opened a drawer in his father's table and took out three unused diaries, and wrote on the first page of the largest—*Though there might be living creatures on the other planets of our solar system, in my opinion, they can never be the same as humans, because no other planet has a Sun and a Moon like we do. Had there been, there could have been human beings. I believe it is the Sun and the Moon which make humans human.*

A year later, he began solving difficult mathematical problems offhand, for fun. Additions, subtractions, multiplications and divisions were there of course, but there were some problems which definitely fell under advanced mathematics. For example, he would look at a kite circling in the sky and calculate its speed, its height from the earth's surface, even the circumference of its flight path. Manilal Majumder, his private tutor, felt embarrassed by his student's sudden proficiency and resigned from his post. Soumyashekhar, too, was simultaneously astonished by and elated at his son's achievements. His own, and a few of his clients', effort succeeded in directing the gaze of the city's renowned mathematicians towards Aryashekhar's genius. Jibanananda Dhar, Professor of Mathematics at the Presidency College, arrived at their residence and tested Aryashekhar over a period of three and a half hours, and left behind a lengthy certificate of merit. It read something like this, 'I will not be surprised if Aryashekhar surpasses Somesh Basu in near future, in solving mathematical problems viva voce. I wish this divinely gifted boy a long life.'

Most people, even the rich, find it difficult to ignore an extra source of income if it presents itself. Soumyashekhar was only reasonably well-off and so it should not come as a surprise that he tried to enhance his income, if only slightly, by exhibiting his son's extraordinary talent. But he had no intention of doing anything without asking for his son's consent, and so he sent for Aryashekhar.

— Err, I've something on my mind.

— What?

— The way things are with me—I mean, the times are such—it's not really, err, in proportion to the—just about breaking even, I mean. But you seem to have this, err, and everybody is full of praise, it's a kind of magic really! What if we could share it with the people around us—I mean, we could look up a nice place, and arrange things . . .

But his son's startled and offended expression made him recoil. He stayed silent for a few seconds and then took up a different tune.

— Of course there's no question if you have any reservations.

— Shows aren't meant for a genius, father.

His father's actions sparked off a new set of questions. How was it possible that a prodigious boy like him had such a mean-minded father? Was this dichotomy an everyday fact or was it an exception?

And if it was an exception indeed, what would be the scientific reason behind it? Aryashekhar had no dearth of free time, because his father had taken him away from school soon after his genius had manifested itself. Aryashekhar immersed himself in the study of heredity and genetics at his leisure. Soon he became familiar with the glory of genes. The secrets of a person's physical form and nature were hidden inside certain atoms of the human body. Amazing!

Aryashekhar presented himself to his father once again.

— Father, don't we have a family tree?

— Family tree? Why?

— Do we have one?

— Would have been eaten by termites already, if we do. But why, do you feel you've suddenly developed the symptoms of somebody who can remember past lives?

— No, I was wondering whether any of my forefathers had shown signs of genius. Of course I know about you and grandfather. But what about those who came before you?

— Certainly not in the past seven generations. I can guarantee that. But I can't vouch for the rest.

Aryashekhar came back to his room and sat immersed in thought. Nobody on his father's side, not for the past five generations. On his mother's side, no better—in fact the chances were even less on his mother's side. Neeharika Devi was extremely unextraordinary as far as talent went. Aryashekhar avoided her at all times for she

UPENDRAKISHORE RAY CHOWDHURY (1863–1915)

ABOVE FROM LEFT: Content pages of *Mukul,* 1896 and 1898 respectively; cover of *Sandesh* (1913) edited and illustrated by Upendrakishore Ray Chowdhury.

ABOVE: The masthead of *Sakha.*

RIGHT: The introductory pages of the children's magazines *Sakha* (1884) and *Sathi* (1894). The magazines later merged to form *Sakha o Sathi.* Upendrakishore's early writings were published in these magazines—*Mukul, Sakha, Sathi* and *Sakha o Sathi.*

ABOVE FROM LEFT: The introductory pages of *Sakha o Sathi,* fourteenth volume, first and second issue (1897).

ABOVE: First cover of *Tuntunir Boi* by
Upendrakishore Ray Chowdhury
(U. Ray & Sons, 1910).

RIGHT: The book cover of *Tuntunir Boi*
by Satyajit Ray (Signet Press, 1954).

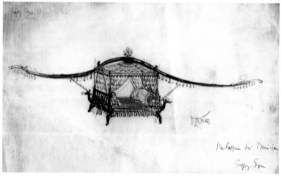

ABOVE: Colour illustration of the palanquin used in the film *Goopy
Gyne Bagha Byne*, taken from Ray's notebook.

LEFT: The book cover of *Goopy Gyne o Bagha Byne* by Satyajit Ray
(Indian Associated Publishing Company, 1963).

Decorative headpiece illustration by Upendrakishore Ray Chowdhury for *Sandesh* (First volume, first issue, 1913).

Illustration by Upendrakishore Ray Chowdhury for *Goopy Gyne Bagha Byne* (*Sandesh*, 1915).

Satyajit Ray

3 Lake Temple Road, Calcutta 29   Phone 46-1817

Upendrakishore Ray

U. Ray was born in 1862 and died in 1915.

He was writer, painter, musician and scientist — and made outstanding contributions in each capacity.

He was a pioneer of children's literature in Bengal. The children's magazine SANDESH which he founded in 1913 set an incredibly high standard in form and content. He wrote illustrated versions of Ramayana & Mahabharata for children which Tagore thought unsurpassed. He also wrote tender versions of Bengali folk tales, & a fascinating series of accounts of prehistoric animal life.

As a musician, he composed many wonderful children's songs and Brahmo Samaj hymns which are still regularly sung. He also wrote text books on the playing of various musical instruments which were models of their kind.

As a scientist, his main contributions — new by Western reckoning — were in the field of printing and block-making. In fact, he was the first to introduce half tone blocks into India, and in time, incorporated improvements in its methods which were adopted in Western countries. This is particularly astonishing in view of the fact that he never had a chance to go abroad, and was completely self-taught.

ABOVE: An unpublished draft of the bio-sketch 'Upendrakishore Ray' by Satyajit Ray (c. 1963).

ABOVE FROM TOP: Cover of Leela Majumder's book, *Upendrakishore*, designed by Satyajt Ray (New Script, 1963). This book contains Ray's wonderful illustrations of bygone 'Calcutta' as well as vignettes from Upendrakishore's life. (See pages 7–12)

SUKUMAR RAY (1887–1923)

Various covers of *Sandesh* (1915–23) edited and illustrated by Sukumar Ray.

Various covers and inserts of *Sandesh* (1915–23) edited and illustrated by Sukumar Ray.

The original cover of *Abol Tabol* (U. Ray & Sons, 1923), illustrated and designed by Sukumar Ray, is a landmark in Indian publishing as it used an innovative horizontal book format.

Frontispiece illustration by Sukumar Ray as printed in the original *Abol Tabol* (U. Ray & Sons, 1923).

Cover of *Abol Tabol,* later published by Signet Press (1945), used a more regular format.

Book cover of *Pagla Dashu* (M.C. Sarkar & Sons, 1940); this is also the first book cover by Satyajit Ray.

Book cover of *Pagla Dashu* designed by Annada Munshi and illustrated by Satyajit Ray (Signet Press, 1946).

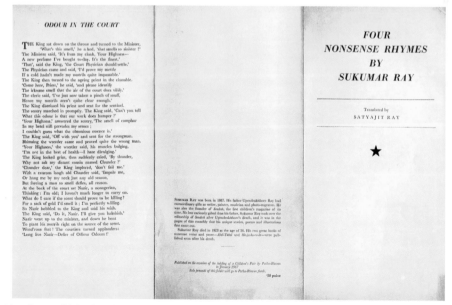

A brochure published on the occasion of a children's fair by Patha Bhavan School, Kolkata (January 1967).

THE SONS OF RANGAROO

TO the sons of Rangaroo
Laughter is taboo
A funny tale will make them wail :
'We're not amused, boo hoo!'

They live in constant fear
Of chuckles far and near
And start and bound at every sound
That brings a breath of cheer.

Their peace of mind forfeiting
They sit and keep repeating :
'We believe in only grieving ;
Happiness is fleeting.'

They shun the summer breeze
That whispers through the trees
For fear the stir of leaf and bur
Their funnybones should tease.

They keep a wary eye
On the autumn sky-
For signs of mirth above the earth
In foaming cumuli.

The darkness of the night
Brings them no respite
As fireflies extemporise
Their dances of delight.

Those of you who're jolly
And feel to woe is folly
Must not refuse the Rangaroos
Their right to melancholy.

The Rangaroosian lair
Bereft of sun and air
Is doomed to be a monastery
Of permanent despair.

THE MISSING WHISKERS

THEY always knew the Boss Babu
To be a gentle fellow,
What happens if he in a jiffy
Turns all blue and yellow ?

He was seated in his chair
Relaxed and free from care,
Indulging in his post-meridian nap,
When, without a warning,
In the middle of his yawning,
Something right inside him seemed
to snap.

With muffled cries he rolled his eyes
And threw his arms about,
'Alas, I'm sick. Come save me quick',
Was what he sputtered out.

They heard him and they all began
To cluster round the stricken man
And pondered on the safest plan
To bring him to his senses.
'Call the police !' 'No—the Vet.'
His partner said, 'He seems upset.'
But careful—he might bite yet,'
Said his amanuensis.

But Boss Babu—his face all red and
swollen—
Now declared, 'My moustache has
been stolen.'

'Stolen whiskers ?' they all cried,
'The Babu must be pacified.'
And so they held a mirror to his face
'There, sir,' they said, 'You see
Your whiskers where they used to be ?
Who would dare to put you in
disgrace ?'

Babu now began to scream :
'You dunderheads, I wouldn't dream
Of ever wearing whiskers so out-
rageous.
They make me look a shaggy butcher
Know this—in the near future
I ought to—no, I must reduce your
wages.'
This he did. And then at random
He composed a memorandum,
Herewith quoted (minus appen-
dages) :

'If you think your employees
Deserve your love—correction, please!
They don't. They're fools. No com-
nonsense.

They're full of crass incompetence.
The ones in my establishment
Deserve the highest punishment.
They show their cheek in not be-
lieving
Whiskers lend themselves to thieving.
Their moustaches, I predict,
Will soon be mercilessly picked;
And when that happens they will
know
What Man is to Moustachio :
Man is slave, Moustache is master,
Losing which Man meets disaster.'

THE KING OF BOMBARDIA

In the land of Bombardia
The customs are peculiar:

The King, for instance, advocates
Gilded frames for chocolates,
While the Queen—who goes to bed
With pillows strapped around her
head—
Insists her brothers specialise
In sticking nails in custard pies,

On moonlit nights the Bombardian—
His eyes all painted vermilion—
Keeps his silver pocket watch
Immersed in boiling butter scotch.
And if by chance he catches cold
He somersaults (if not too old).

Musicians there—a sturdy lot—
Use woollen wrappers when it's hot,
And the scholar propagates
Pasting bills on balding pates.

When the King sits on the throne
He starts hee-hawing in baritone,
And on his lap P. Minister
Just sits and beats a cannister.
(The throne, you know, they decorate
With bottles of bicarbonate).

The King's old aunt (an autocrat)
Hits pumpkins with her cricket bat,
While uncle loves to dance mazurkas
Wearing garlands strung with hookahs.

All of which, though mighty queer,
Is natural in Bombardia.

Inside pages of the brochure (January 1967).

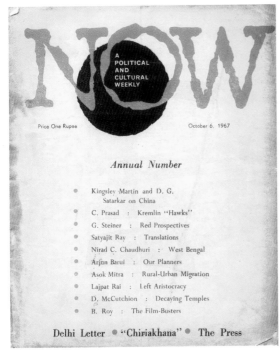

NOW

A POLITICAL AND CULTURAL WEEKLY

Price One Rupee   October 6. 1967

Annual Number

- Kingsley Martin and D. G. Satarkar on China
- C. Prasad : Kremlin "Hawks"
- G. Steiner : Red Prospectives
- Satyajit Ray : Translations
- Nirad C. Chaudhuri : West Bengal
- Arjun Barui : Our Planners
- Asok Mitra : Rural-Urban Migration
- Lajpat Rai : Left Aristocracy
- D. McCutchion : Decaying Temples
- B. Roy : The Film-Busters

Delhi Letter ● "Chiriakhana" ● The Press

Nonsense Rhymes

BY SUKUMAR RAY

Translated by

SATYAJIT RAY

Groomy Tidings

MY dear sir, do let me shake your hand—
Your daughter's soon to wed, I understand.
Great news. Congrats. Now, luckily
I know this Gangaram, the groom-to-be.
Splendid chap. You've won a fair prize-
Though not so fair, ha ha, complexion-wise !
His face reminds me of—now, let me see . . .
Ah, yes—an owl : the same roundity.
Education, sir ? Now, there's a lad
With all the strength of will that's to be had.
He sat for final tests at school. No luck. He flopped.
Nineteen times he tried, and then he stopped.
Financial state, you ask ? His property ?
He's sunk in debts as far as I can see !
His brothers are a sorry bunch, I fear.
One's a loony, one's a racketeer.
A third they put the clinkers on became
By forging money he was breaking laws.
The youngest one. I gather, plays the drum
In restaurants, and earns a paltry sum.
Gangaram himself despairs to fight his
Ailments of the spleen and hepatitis.
But mark you, sir, his noble ancestry—
Ganga branches from a princely tree.
Sham Lahiri (and it has been proved)
Is Gangaram's own cousin, thrice removed.
Looking for a future son-in-law
I daresay you could scarcely ask for more.

The Old Woodman

THE old man doesn't seem to mind
The sun that's getting hotter
He hums a tune and mumbles words
He sits and licks a wooden stick
That's just been boiled in water.
And shakes his balding head ;
It seems as if he's twice as wise
As anybody dead.
'The holes you find in wood', he says,
'Have reason to be there :
They're caused—and no one knows this yet—
By cobwebs in the air.
'But who cares for all this knowledge ?'
Screams the old man, fuming.
'A bunch of dolts—that's what they are,
Pretending and presuming.
I've told them time and time again.
They haven't understood,
What moonless nights are apt to do
To holes that go with wood.'
Graphs and charts and formulas
He scribbles on the wall.
Subdividing types of wood
And analysing all.
Tasty wood and tangy wood
And wood that's hard to savour
And all that lies concealed in holes
And all the hidden flavour
He claps the wooden sticks together
Saying, 'These are sticks
Which hold no secrets for me now that
I know all their tricks,
'All the wooden villainy, and
All the wooden wiles.
Wooden ills and wooden woes, and
Beaming wooden smiles.
'Some wood is wise and some is not,
But holes are always there,
And only I can see they're caused
By cobwebs in the air.'

Pages from the English periodical *Now* (6 October 1967).

A page from the manuscript of *Chalachitto-Chanchari*—a drama written by Sukumar Ray, published in *Bichitra*, 1927.

In the land of Bombardia
The customs are peculiar.
The King, for instance, advocates
Picture frames for chocolats.

who seldom

The Courtiers, both young and old,
Turn somersaults when they have a cold.

On moonlit nights the Bombardian,

And when the King sits upon the throne

A page from Satyajit Ray's literary notebook with a draft translation of Sukumar Ray's *The King of Bombardia*.

SATYAJIT RAY (1921–22)

ABOVE: Satyajit Ray with poet Subhas Mukhopadhyay. They decided to revive *Sandesh* in 1961.
Photograph by Amanul Huq

ABOVE: Cover of *Sandesh* (1964) by Satyajit Ray.

LEFT: The cover of the first edition of the revived *Sandesh* (1961) edited by Satyajit Ray and Subhas Mukhopadhyay.

Various covers of *Sandesh* (1961–92) edited and illustrated by Satyajit Ray.

Original artwork of *Sandesh* cover (1990) by Satyajit Ray.

Various logos and letterings of *Sandesh* (1961–92) designed by Satyajit Ray.

Original artwork of *Ratanbabu and that Man* by Satyajit Ray, published in *Sandesh* (1970).

Original artwork of *Khagam* by Satyajit Ray, published in *Sandesh* (1973).

Original artworks of *The Unicorn Expedition* by Satyajit Ray, published in *Sandesh* (1973–74).

Illustration of *Bonkubabu's Friend* by Satyajit Ray, published in *Sandesh* (1962).

Illustration of *Professor Shonku and Khoka* by Satyajit Ray, published in *Sandesh* (1967).

Colour illustration of *Corvus* by Satyajit Ray, published in *Anandamela* (1972).

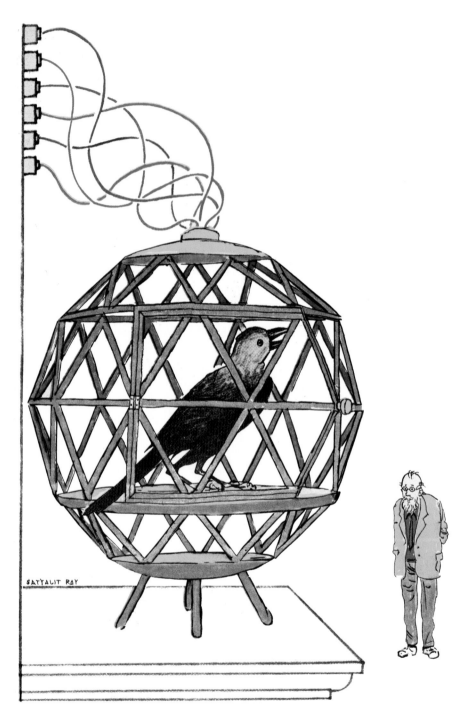

Colour illustration of *Corvus* by Satyajit Ray, published in *Anandamela* (1972).

Colour illustration of *Corvus* by Satyajit Ray,
published in *Anandamela* (1972).

Colour illustration of *The Duel* by Satyajit Ray, published in *Sandesh* (1984).

ABOVE: Headpiece of *The Duel* by Satyajit Ray, published in *Sandesh* (1984); BELOW: Colour illustration of *The Duel*.

insisted on calling him 'baby' even now.

It would be difficult to put it down to heredity. To his surroundings? To environment? Could one recommend thirty-three Patuatolla Lane for environment? Not really? Then?

But were calculations a sure proof? One could go with a family tree thing as back as the beginning of time, from father to father. Weren't genes coming down as far back as that? Who knew who or what Aryashekhar's forefathers were twenty thousand years ago! One of them might well have painted the bison in that cave in Altamira. Shouldn't these cave-painters be recognized for their genius? Or those who had planned the cities of Harappa and Mohenjo Daro? And the ones who had written the Vedas and the Upanishads? Things would of course fall in place if one of them was a distant relation of Aryashekhar. But something kept pricking his peace of mind. He could not justify, by any amount of science, that an unimaginative, materialist and coarse creature like Soumyashekhar was his father.

And then, suddenly, a possibility came and hit him on the face like a bludgeon.

What if he was an illegitimate son? What if he had not been begotten by Soumyashekhar?

Aryashekhar immediately realized that his father alone was capable of answering this query and he found it impossible to rest until he had seen the bottom of things. He had complete faith in the natural right of a son to ask any question to his father on his quest for truth.

Soumyashekhar, immersed in a massive, nine-hundred-and-twenty-six-page law digest, had difficulty understanding the question.

— Twins? Who are you referring to?

— Not twins. I meant misbegotten. I want to know whether I'm misbegotten.

Soumyashekhar's lips parted at these words. A faint tremor shook his hands. The tremor soon spread itself to other parts of his body. Then his tremulous right hand fixed itself upon the object nearest at hand, a heavy glass paperweight, and hurled it at Aryashekhar. Aryashekhar screamed and fell to the floor, blood dripping from his head.

Once he had recovered, it was discovered that his miraculous gift with numbers had been irreparably damaged. But his scientific rigour persisted.

Aryashekhar was nineteen years old when, one evening, he sat under a siris tree on the bank of the Ganga, and a piece of excrement emanated from a tree-borne bird and came to rest upon his left shoulder, instantly reminding him of the infallibility of gravitation. As expected, he embarked upon a thorough study of the subject. He had always believed that the story of Newton and his apple was no more than a myth. But a reference to the incident in *Principia*, by Newton himself, changed his views. Starting from Tycho Brahe and Galileo, through Copernicus, Kepler and Leibniz, he soon reached Einstein. His knowledge was inadequate for a proper assimilation of Einstein, but he had an incredible capacity for reading everything from beginning to end, be it readable or not. In this case, however, there was an added interest; he wanted to see whether the last word on gravitation had already been pronounced. From what he could make of Einstein, he saw that the 'what' of gravitation had been explained, but its 'why' still eluded mankind. Aryashekhar decided that this 'why' was going to be his life's goal.

He decided that from now on he would keep a sharp lookout for insignificant events that occurred in his vicinity. He remembered that many scientific discoveries had been sparked off by insignificant incidents, like that of Newton's apple.

Unfortunately, even after watching over more than a thousand insignificant occurrences, he could not identify a single one which had not been already explained by science. Aryashekhar decided upon following a different course. Meditation was at the root of all realization—inspired by this, he decided to go up to the attic and immerse himself in meditation, with dedication.

On the very first day—it was a Sunday—just as he was going to close his eyes as he sat on a cot in the attic, an insignificant incident on the terrace next door fell in his line of vision. Dolly, the daughter of neighbour Fanindranath Basak, was elevating her arms to the wash line to hang out the washing. The sight immediately sparked off a new dawn, a new strain of scientific thought in his mind.

He scripted his realization in an essay which took up one hundred and thirty pages of foolscap paper. This concise report is too short for a detailed description, but its main subject was the following: *Life was created in opposition to gravitation, because all life force is aimed upward, but gravitation manifests itself by pulling things down. But how was it possible that Life was created at all, in spite of the presence of such potent anti-life forces, like that of gravitation? Because of the Sun. But the Sun does not have a permanent effect and the material manifestation of ever-present gravitation defeats it slowly. Old age creeps in, followed by death, destroying the life force. Insensate matter, alone, is not the sole site of such conflict; the dichotomy is present everywhere—in all of mankind's actions, thoughts, passions and interrelationships. Each and every meanness attributed to mankind, every one of its evils, wrongs, miseries, poverty, the war-and-bloodshed which human society is witness to, is a progeny of gravity. And all that is beautiful and fresh, improving and good, is so because of the Sun. The Earth will never be rid of her blemishes as long as gravity holds sway. She would have been destroyed long ago, had it not been for the Sun. The processes of creation have been going on hand in hand with those of destruction, from the beginning of time.*

Once the essay was finished, Aryashekhar came out of his room and offered a silent prayer of thanks to the Sun, and then to Dolly. At that moment, Bharadwaj the servant appeared, and informed him that his old man was expecting him below.

Soumyashekhar had been worrying over his son these past few days. Wife Neeharika had passed away last year. She had lamented, in her deathbed, the fact that she was leaving without seeing her son settled in some way.

Aryashekhar rolled up the sheets and came and stood in front of his old man, clutching the roll.

— Can you explain what's become of you? Are you a snake, a toad or a pain in the neck?

— That will be difficult to explain until I study the true nature of my existence.

— True nature of what?

— Genes.

— I don't understand half the things you say.

— Not everybody understands everything. I don't understand much about legal practices, do I?

— I hope you understand that you are eating off it? It's time you remember that it's no honour at your age to idle away your father's money. Don't come to me with your genes and the rest. Remember no matter what you do in that attic of yours, you are no better than any of those jobless pests with their wild ways. I'll let you have another year. Find a job, any job. I don't expect much of you since you could not even get a degree. But you must learn to stand on your own feet. You may do as you wish once you've learnt to do that.

— Then do what?

— It's time you thought about procreation. Or have you already decided against marriage?

— Yes I have.

— You won't marry?

— No.

— May I know why?

— Primarily because I doubt my procreating abilities.

Soumyashekhar was afflicted by a sudden fit of hiccups. Aryashekhar allowed him time to recover his poise.

— Secondly, I am at the high noon of my life, when the Sun is its most active, and I have no intention of letting anything distract me from my work, and thoughts, at this point of time.

— Have you been initiated into some religion, or something of that kind?

— You could say that.

— Which religion?

— My personal religion. I haven't been able to name it yet.

For a second Soumyashekhar had hoped that he had deciphered the enigma called his son. But he soon realized that he was far off the mark. He stared at his son for some time. Especially at his eyes. Were those eyes giving away any sign of madness? Soumyashekhar's great grandfather had once appeared at the village *chandimandap* on the great eighth day of Durga Puja, completely naked, and in full view of the entire local population. He had not shared this bit of information with Aryashekhar. A tender pity welled in his mind. After all, despite his thousand faults, Aryashekhar was his one and only son, the apple of his eye. Let him do whatever he wants—as long as he keeps alive and breathing. And as long as he doesn't lose his mind.

— Alright. You may go now.

Aryashekhar had written the essay in English—for he did not believe that such a work would find sympathy with Bengali readers. Now he set to typing four copies of the essay, painstakingly and with inexperienced hands, on Soumyashekhar's derelict Remington. It was finally finished but he could feel that his hands, legs, back and waist were aching from the strain. Moreover, his prolonged incarceration had induced a feeling of suffocation.

Aryashekhar came down from the terrace. He had just stepped out of his home with a mind to take a quick stroll around Goldighi, when he noticed a white-skinned young man in a saffron kurta and pyjama, with a beard and whiskers and long hair, standing right in front of his house and glancing around.

The young man saw Aryashekhar and immediately asked whether he knew the whereabouts of the Mahabodhi Society. 'Come, I'll show you the way.' Aryashekhar offered, 'I'm headed that way.'

Aryashekhar introduced himself to the young man on his way to his destination. His name was Bob Goodman. He was a resident of Toledo, Ohio. He had renounced university education and come to India in search of love and enlightenment.

Aryashekhar liked the boy. He gave him a copy of his essay that very night. And said, 'You'll be the first to read my work. I'd like to know if you have any comments.'

Goodman appeared the next morning, chewing on peanuts, the sheaf of foolscap nestled in his satchel—'It's great, great. Yeah—you got something there—yeah.'

Aryashekhar thanked him under his breath but Goodman added, 'Why have you put such a lot of pessimism in your work? You have the means of defeating gravitation in your own country. Don't you know about levitation? Haven't you heard of the yogis?'

Goodman now took out a crumpled ball of paper and handed it to Aryashekhar. The package was opened and a cube of white sugar was found inside. At least it looked like sugar! It was a sugar cube, Goodman explained, 'But with an atom of acid added to it. There was nothing like it to suppress gravitation. Taste it. The reactions will be manifold— don't panic. I have a feeling that you'll be rid of your pessimism once you've had this.'

Aryashekhar returned home with the package given him by Goodman and went straight up to the second floor terrace. He sat cross-legged on a red mat in the soft sun of the Ashwin afternoon and inserted the sugar cube into his mouth, then began chewing on it.

Nothing happened the first few hours. Then came a time when Aryashekhar could feel himself being elevated towards the Sun. An indescribable euphoria pervaded his sense. He looked down and the dust-and-smoke-smeared city of Calcutta unrolled itself like a brilliant and fascinating carpet from Tehran. The sky above his head was teeming with numerous blocks of colour, hurtling along serpentine courses. Aryashekhar knew that those were kites, but not like any he had seen before. A mass of colour flew towards him. Aryashekhar felt an intense pang of kinship and stretched his arms out, before launching himself at it. He had no recollection of what happened afterwards.

Before starting off for Mihijam, with the express purpose of reviving his health, under Dr Bagchi's orders, Aryashekhar had his essay typed out by a professional typist and mailed fifty copies of it to select scientists and intellectuals of most countries of the world. A reply from one of those lucky few reached Aryashekhar's hand the day before he was to leave for Mihijam. English physicist and Nobel laureate, Prof. Carmichael, had thanked him for his essay, and written—*I found it most intriguing*. The Mihijam episode was short, and so its description must necessarily be so:

19th October, the day after Aryashekhar had reached Mihijam, he wrote in his diary—'Bird bird bird bird. Bird *is* bird. *Most intriguing*; which creature goes nearest the Sun? Bird. *O Bird, how your flight flouts gravity!*'

2nd November, Bharadwaj, the servant, notices that Aryashekhar has brought back a weaverbird's nest from somewhere and is looking at it intently, deciphering its weaving techniques.

The next morning, Aryashekhar himself brought over some sticks and twigs and began fashioning a weaverbird nest with his own hands. That night he wrote in his diary—'Man's highest achievement would be to rise to the level of birds.'

13th November, Bharadwaj wonders why *babu* is being so late and so goes out in search of him. After a half hour's search, he finds Aryashekhar lying unconscious under a babla tree, at the edge of a paddy field.

The local doctor diagnosed sunstroke. Soumyashekhar arrived from Calcutta. There were three days of severe delirium and then Aryashekhar passed away, in the presence of his father and servant.

He uttered one single word before breathing his last—'Maa!'

MAGIC BOX OF BAGHDAD

Originally published in *Sandesh* (March–April 1970) as *Professor Shonku o Baghdader Baksa*. The English translation by Ray has not been published earlier and is transcribed from Ray's literary notebook. The illustrations in the story, including the Bengali calligraphy in the headpiece, are by Satyajit Ray.

15 NOVEMBER

Goldstein has just gone to the post office to mail a letter, which gives me the opportunity to bring my diary up to date. Goldstein is such a windbag that it is impossible to do anything but listen to him while he is around. Prof. Petrucci is also with us, sitting across the table from me, but ever since he lost his hearing aid in the hotel yesterday, he has stopped talking to people. He knows Arabic well, which explains the local newspaper open in his hand.

We are sitting in a café in Baghdad, very Persian, with tables and chairs under an awning on the pavement. Coffee has been ordered and should arrive soon.

The reason for our coming to Baghdad is an international conference of inventors. There are scientific conferences of all kinds taking place around the world all the time; but this is the first inventors' conference ever. It goes without saying that amongst those who have been invited, I hold a position of prominence. Those who have come have all brought their latest inventions with them, and one of the aims of the conference is to give these inventions world-wide publicity. I have brought my omniscope with us. This has created quite a stir among the delegates. This is a viewer which is worn like spectacles, and which can be used with adjustments as a microscope, a telescope or an X-ray scope

The conference ended yesterday. Many of the delegates left for home this morning. The three of us will stay for a few more days. I had decided from the beginning to extend my stay for at least a week; that I found two others to keep me company was pure luck. Last night there was a dinner given by the university. On the way back to the hotel Goldstein asked, 'Are you going back tomorrow?' I replied, 'To come to Haroun-al-Rashid's country and go back after three days is absurd. I have a mind to stay a few more days and look around a bit. I want to see some of the relics of the ancient civilization of Iraq.'

Goldstein was delighted. 'That's great!' he said. 'I've found a companion. But why do talk only of Haroun-al-Rashid? Haroun reigned only a thousand years ago. Think of the times before that.'

I said, 'That's very true. We Indians pride ourselves in our ancient civilization, but what has been known about Sumerian civilization goes back seven thousand years. Even Egypt didn't have a civilization that far back in time.'

Goldstein said, 'I suppose you realize that there's a special significance in holding the inventors' conference here. It was here that writing evolved for the first time five thousand years ago, and true civilization begins with the invention of writing.'

Iraq is part of what was once known as Mesopotamia. It is situated by the twin rivers Tigris and Euphrates. The first civilized human beings appeared close to where Baghdad is now. This was the Sumerian civilization. Many stone slabs with inscriptions on them have been dug up by archaeologists around Baghdad. It has been possible through the untiring efforts of specialists to decipher these inscriptions.

The Sumerian civilization is marked by many ups and downs. Four thousand years ago the Sumerians were invaded by Semites. The war ended in the defeat of the Sumerians. The next stage was marked by the rise of Babylon and Assyria. We read of famous kings—Nebuchadnezzar, Belshazzar, Sennacherib, Assurbanipal. Some of them were noble and benevolent, while others were tyrants.

Even in such ancient times, the largest palace in Babylon was a thousand feet high. The city had so many palaces that from a distance it looked like the Kingdom of Gods. Even at night the beauty of the city was undiminished because as early as four thousand years ago Babylonians had learnt to extract petroleum from the soil and use it to illuminate their city.

Two thousand five hundred years ago the Persians invaded Babylon and ousted the Semites. We hear of great monarchs among the Persians—Darius, Cyrus, Xerxes— some high-minded, some incredibly cruel. It was about this time that a nomadic tribe from Persia came to India through Baluchistan. They were the Aryans. Actually, there is no difference between Aryans and Iranians.

Thus, how can we deny that there was a close affinity between India and the country where we are at the present? Which educated Indian has not been fascinated by the stories of the Arabian Nights? The Baghdad that we find described in the time of Haroun appears to have been a thriving place. The Baghdad of today may not resemble that very much, but those possessing imagination are bound to feel that aura of romance that the memories of these stories evoke.

I can see Goldstein returning. There is an elderly man with him I haven't seen before. Appears to be a local man from the red fez he is wearing. Who can this stranger be?

19 NOVEMBER, 11 P.M.

In my travels I have met some very interesting people in various parts of the world. Although in many cases I haven't had the opportunity to renew their acquaintance, they have nevertheless carved a permanent niche in my mind through their uniqueness.

I met one such unique person today: the gentleman who came with Goldstein. His name is Al Habbal and he is, as I suspected, an Iraqi. He turned out to be considerably older than me, but his movements were remarkably agile, and there was a youthful glint in his eyes.

As Goldstein introduced him, the gentleman bowed Moslem-fashion, took a seat beside me and said, 'You're the first Indian I have met. I consider myself very fortunate, because I never forget the bond that exists between the two nations.'

I gave a suitably polite reply and was wondering why Goldstein had brought him when the gentleman himself provided the answer. He said: 'I was delighted that scientists from all over the world had come to our city. I saw your picture in the papers and was very keen to meet you; but I didn't know how to go about it. I ran into this gentleman in the post office quite accidentally and promptly introduced myself.'

It didn't seem from the newcomer's behaviour that he was in a hurry to leave, so we ordered another cup of coffee. From the rings he wore in both hands he appeared to be a man of means. Even his dress proclaimed that.

He opened a gold cigarette case and, after offering us, helped himself to a black Sobranie. 'What I wished to ask you,' he said after lighting the cigarette, 'is this: You are all world-famous inventors; but do you know of the extraordinary inventions that took place in our country thousands of years ago?'

I replied: 'Well, thanks to the archaeologists, we do know about some of them. For instance, the Sumerian invention of writing, the early advances you made in Astrology, the four thousand year old petroleum lamps . . .'

Al Habbal suddenly broke out in a high-pitched ripple of laughter. 'Yes yes yes,' he said, 'the sahibs all write about these things in their books. I have read them. But that is nothing!'

'Nothing?' Both Goldstein and I cried out simultaneously. Petrucci had put down his newspaper and was now staring hard at Al Habbal, probably trying to lip-read him.

Al Habbal cast a look around him and said, 'Restaurants are too crowded, and the streets are so noisy that it is difficult to make oneself heard without shouting. If you finished your coffee, why can't we go to a quiet place and talk?'

Goldstein paid the bill and the four of us left the café.

Walking in the shade of the palm trees lining the promenade by the Tigris, Al Habbal resumed the conversation.

'I hope you are familiar with the Arabian Nights?'

'Who isn't?' I replied. 'Such a wealth of stories exists only in your country outside India. Nearly everybody in India knows at least some of the stories.'

'How do the stories strike you?'

'They certainly prove what enchanting stories the human imagination is capable of concocting.'

Once again that high-pitched ripple of laughter greeted my remark. 'Imagination?' chuckled Al Habbal. 'That's what it is, eh? Everybody believes so. What can it be but imagination? How can such things happen in real life? And yet you had this conference here and each of you brought something you had invented, some of them extraordinary, even mind-boggling. But you wouldn't call them products of the imagination, would you? Since you see them with your own eyes, you take them to be real. Isn't that so?'

Goldstein and I exchanged glances. A boat with a striped sail passed close to the bank, bringing back memories of our own rivers. Al Habbal said, 'Let us go and sit on that bench.'

I glanced at my watch. It was half past eleven. Perhaps the man was dotty? The feeling had been growing in my mind ever since I heard his strange high-pitched laughter.

Al Habbal lighted another Sobranie as we sat on the bench and said, 'If you promise not to tell anyone about it, nor make any attempts to possess it, I will show you something—'

I interrupted Al Habbal. 'What a strange notion! Why should anyone want to possess something that belongs to you?'

Al Habbal gave a cynical smile and said, 'I was not thinking of you, but—' 'he cast a sidelong glance at Goldstein—'some of the best examples of our civilization are in the museums of the West. In fact, the best part of our treasure is gone. So, even if you do not want to possess it yourself, you may set the dogs of the museum on me.'

Goldstein managed with effort to keep his cool and said with force: 'Why should we do that? I give you my word. We shan't breathe a word to anyone. But what kind of object are you talking about?'

I knew that even if Goldstein didn't talk to the museums, if the object was exciting enough, he himself might covet it. He was considerably wealthy. Science was a hobby with him; his real interest was collecting antique. In the few days that we have been here, Goldstein has bought in my presence at least a thousand dollars worth of sundry art objects.

Al Habbal now said in a measured voice, 'I am talking of a scientific invention dating back to the pre-Christian times. We will have to go to a hundred and ten kilometres from here to see it. I shall take you in my own car.'

More than this Al Habbal wouldn't say.

He will come with his car at nine tomorrow morning. I had a talk with my two companions after Al Habbal left. Both of them feel that Al Habbal is a crackpot. Not yet ripe for the asylum, perhaps, but the day was not far when he would be.

I said, 'If we can make a trip to the countryside at someone else's expense, why should we mind?'

I had a little rest in bed in the afternoon. The climate here is delightful. I already feel full of vim and vigour.

20 NOVEMBER

That we should have an interesting experience in an interesting city like Baghdad was to be expected; but what actually happened went far beyond our expectation. Fairy tales belong in the world of imagination. The pleasure that one gets from reading them is of a special kind. But if one suddenly finds elements from the fairy tales existing in the real world, then one's notions get badly mixed up.

Let me now describe today's events.

True to his word, Hassan Al Habbal arrived at the hotel in his green Citroen at nine in the morning. Not only was he providing transport, he was also carrying a wicker basket which contained our lunch. 'You are my guests for the whole day,' he said.

By nine-fifteen we were out on the road. Petrucci had looked desperately in every shop and had at last managed to procure a hearing aid. As a result his whole personality has changed. Occupying the front seat, Goldstein turned to me and said with a wink, 'It feels like we're going out on a picnic as we used to when we were kids.' It was clear that he hadn't believed a word of what Al Habbal had said. He has come just because he had nothing better to do, and expects nothing more than an enjoyable outing.'

We crossed the bridge over Tigris and drove on westwards. There wasn't much vegetation around, which gave the place a desert-like appearance. But being November, it was cool. 'We're going to a spot,' said Al Habbal, sitting at the wheel, 'where the distance between Tigris and Euphrates is only forty kilometres. One reason for Babylon's glory was the proximity of the two rivers.'

I now asked him something I had been curious to find out since yesterday.

'Are you a scientist?' I asked. 'An archaeologist, perhaps?'

'If you men are scientists with a degree,' said Al Habbal, 'then I'm not one. But if by archaeologist you mean someone who assesses the value of ancient treasures, then I am certainly one.'

Our car was now leaving the flat country and climbing up. A range of hills could be made out in the distance. Al Habbal said, 'Those hills mark the boundary of Iraq. Beyond them lies Iran.'

The landscape was changing. Within a few minutes we found ourselves in a pass. Steep boulders rose on both sides. I had read up a little on Iraq before coming to Baghdad. I asked, 'Are we in Abu Guyaib?' Al Habbal nodded. 'You're right. Another ten miles and we will have reached our destination.'

The sunlight didn't penetrate into the mountain pass, so I was feeling a little chilly. I wrapped the muffler around my neck. Petrucci hadn't spoken a word yet. It was hard to make him out. Goldstein appeared to be dozing off.

We crossed the mountain pass and found that the landscape had changed again. There was vegetation ahead dotted with huge chunks of grey boulders.

The car now turned left from the main road. Al Habbal was humming an Iraqi tune which sounded very much like our Indian music. How old would he be? It was hard to guess. There were numerous crow's feet at the corners of his eyes which suggested a fairly advanced age. But what energy he had! He had already driven over a hundred kilometres but showed no signs of tiredness. Within ten minutes the car had got off the road onto yellowed grass and had pulled up by a fir tree. 'The rest of the way we walk,' announced

Al Habbal. 'Not far—only half a kilometre.'

The surroundings were unusually quiet. Trees abounded—willow, oak, fir, date palm and so on—in fact, a forest of sorts. An occasional boulder reared its head from out of the vegetation. Bird calls could be heard, of which the bulbul reminded me of home. The grass underfoot was dappled with sunlight penetrating through the foliage.

Now we noticed a boulder looming up ahead. It occupied a large area and reached the height of an average four-storeyed building.

As we reached the boulder, Al Habbal announced, 'Here we are.'

Where were we? I could see some pine trees on the left and the steep wall of the boulder on the right. What was there to see here?

Turning to Al Habbal I found that his whole countenance had changed. His eyes were shining and his body was tense. Suddenly he broke into his now familiar rippling laughter, glanced at the three of us and said in a suppressed voice, 'So you are all inventors? Great scientists of the twentieth century, eh? Very well, now see what our scientists at the dawn of history were capable of—*Open Sesame!*'

Al Habbal had of course used the Arabic word 'Sim-sim' for Sesame, but the effect of these two words were magical. A huge, loose chunk of rock resting on the boulder began to move aside with a deep rumbling and revealed an entrance into what turned out to be a cave. The three of us watched dumbfounded.

Al Habbal relished our amazement for a little while, then bowed, stretched out his left hand towards the entrance and said, 'Be pleased to enter the cave of Ali Baba!'

We followed Al Habbal into the cave. Now he called out again in Arabic: 'Close Sesame!'

Immediately the loose rock rumbled back into place and we were plunged in the deepest darkness. What was the old man up to? There was a strong whiff of black art in the whole thing which didn't please me at all.

Now we heard the sound of a match being struck, and the next moment a pale yellow glow lit up the interior of the cave. Al Habbal had lighted a lamp. A look around the cave now told me that a scene imagined in my childhood had suddenly appeared before me as reality. The only description that fitted the place was Ali Baba's cave, straight out of the pages of Arabian Nights. Around us were shelves carved out of the rocks. Boxes, caskets, pots, pitchers, vases were stacked on them. All were made of metal; some even seemed to be of gold, and each was set with precious stones which reflected the light from the lamp and created a many-hued radiance which permeated the cave.

We were watching the scene spellbound when Goldstein suddenly cried out: 'You think we're all fools, eh? Trying to pull a fast one on us, are you?'

I was surprised to see that the harsh words didn't ruffle Al Habbal at all. In the tremulous light of the lamp I saw that he was smiling at Goldstein and gently shaking his head. 'Can any of you read a five-thousand-year-old Sumerian inscription?' he asked at length.

Petrucci said, 'I can. I used to be an archaeologist. Twelve years ago I was digging in the desert in Iran when I nearly died of sunstroke. I have given up digging since then. But why do you ask?'

Al Habbal carried the lamp towards a corner of the cave. I saw a grey slab of stone nearly as high as me and about two feet wide resting against the wall of the cave. There were inscriptions on it. Al Habbal said, 'See if you can read what it says here.'

Petrucci took the lamp in his own hand and got down on his knees. At first he just mumbled to himself. Then, after nearly ten minutes, he got up and said, 'Where did you get this stone? It doesn't belong here.'

Al Habbal said, 'First tell us what is inscribed there.'

'It describes this cave,' said Petrucci, 'indicates its location, and tells how its door can be opened. It also says that the cave contains the grave of the great magician Gemal Nishahir, as well as a magic box of his making.'

'Is that all?'

I noticed that a suppressed excitement had crept into Al Habbal's usually calm voice.

'No, there is more.'

'What?'

'It says the box will work as living history, and those who disbelieve the history, or do harm to the box, will suffer the wrath of the god of ziggurat.'

Al Habbal gravely nodded.

Now Goldstein bellowed again.

'Open this gate, I say! I can't stay in this cave any longer. There's poison in the air here.'

I felt Goldstein was overreacting. Al Habbal paid no attention to his ravings. Petrucci said, 'It appears that this stone slab has been brought here from Kish. I'm curious to know how it fell into your hands.'

Al Habbal's reply astonished me. He spoke without a trace of excitement in his voice. 'You must be aware that Sir John Hollingsworth had come to Kish several years ago for archaeological excavations. I was with the team as official interpreter. This slab was among the things dug up at that time. I read the inscription before Sir John had the time to do so, and I lost no time in removing it. I saw nothing wrong in doing so, and I don't do so even now. After all, the thing belongs to our country, to our culture. If it had fallen into the hands of foreigners, it wouldn't have remained in Baghdad; it would have ended up in some museum in the West. I have kept it here, where no harm can ever come to it.'

Goldstein had been sitting on a rock. He now seemed to lose all patience and jumped up screaming: 'Blackguard! Swindler! I don't know about that chunk of stone and the knick-knacks on those shelves out there, but do you claim that the door opens and shuts by means of some device which is five thousand years old? You mean there's no modern gadgetry involved here? That there are no cables running through those cracks?'

Al Habbal raised his right hand to calm Goldstein and said, 'The way you are screaming, I am afraid you might upset the skeleton which has been resting in this cave for fifty centuries. Please, Mr Goldstein, restrain yourself.'

'Skeleton?'

Goldstein seemed a little taken aback.

Al Habbal picked up the lamp and stepped towards the right. We followed him and found that the cave here had turned into a sort of chamber. In the middle of the floor was a rectangular pit about four feet deep. Al Habbal put the lamp down into the pit. The light revealed a skeleton lying on its back with some copper objects strewn about it.

Al Habbal now pointed towards the skeleton and said in a tone of great reverence: 'The king of magicians—Gemal Nishahir al Hararit!'

Beads of perspiration had appeared on Goldstein's forehead. He made a wry face and said, 'I don't see why we have to put up with all this mumbo-jumbo. Will you open the door or not?'

Al Habbal calmly transferred his gaze from the skeleton to Goldstein.

Goldstein didn't wait for Al Habbal. He cried out, 'Open Sesame!'

For a few seconds we all stood facing the door. Nothing happened. Now Goldstein lunged towards Al Habbal and took him by the scruff of his neck.

'Open the door at once, I tell you!'

Petrucci and I managed to get Goldstein's hands off the Iraqi. Al Habbal straightened his tie and said in a measured tone: 'Prof. Goldstein, you will gain nothing by losing your temper. The door won't open unless the command is given in a particular tone of voice. Only I know that tone, that pitch. It took me three weeks after finding the cave to master the right pitch. Therefore—'

'All right,' said Goldstein impatiently, 'you say it. I can't stay cooped up here anymore.'

Al Habbal said, 'But how can I open the door without telling you why I brought you here? Suppose you don't keep your word?'

'What word?'

Al Habbal now moved over towards the centre of the cave. The lamplight showed a stone pedestal standing on the ground. On moving closer we saw that on the pedestal was placed a strange-looking object. It appeared to be a box made of copper with gold and silver decorations on it studded with precious stones which sparkled in the lamplight. Although I call it a box, it didn't seem as if it could be opened, because there didn't appear to be a lid.

'What's that?' asked Goldstein.

'Is this the box mentioned in the inscription?' asked Petrucci.

Al Habbal nodded.

'When I first discovered the cave, there was nothing but this box and skeleton in it.'

I said, 'But what about the living history preserved in it?'

Al Habbal's eyes twinkled mischievously in the lamplight.

'I can only say that the claim is just one,' he said. 'But it is fitting that, being scientists, you should discover for yourself why I say so. The box doesn't yield its secret easily, but I am sure that if you gentlemen tried, you would succeed in fathoming that secret.'

'Leave me out of it,' said Goldstein. 'I don't believe there is anything in that box.'

Goldstein picked up the box and observed it frowning. Al Habbal didn't protest, but said with quiet emphasis, 'If you defile that, you will be incurring the displeasure of the god of ziggurat.'

Goldstein put down the box with an air of disdain. Now I took it up and turned it around in my hand. Petrucci stood by my side.

Al Habbal moved closer with the lamp.

The box was quite heavy. I shook it gently and heard something rattle inside; obviously a loose element.

At last I said, 'I don't think the mystery can be solved in the cave. Do you mind if we take it to the hotel with us? I promise I shan't defile it in any way.'

Al Habbal fixed me with a long stare. Then he asked, 'Do you believe in the supernatural power of the god of ziggurat?'

I said, 'I have great respect for ancient artefacts, especially when they are as beautiful as this one.'

Al Habbal smiled.

'That is enough for me.'

He now turned round to face the door and in his strange musical voice commanded: 'Open Sesame!'

Once again there was that rumbling sound, and the door opened ponderously to let the daylight in. We came out and breathed deeply.

Lunching on delicious fruits, sweets, bread and cheese, we started on our journey back just before sunset, and came back to the hotel with the box around seven in the evening. Goldstein was still grumbling. He resented the fact that I had listened to Al Habbal, behaved decently with him, and undertaken to solve the mystery of the box. As soon as we got out of the car, he turned to Al Habbal and said, 'If it turns out that you've been pulling our leg, then I will go to the police. You have yourself admitted that you are a thief; so it shouldn't be difficult for us to have you convicted. Remember that.'

Al Habbal smiled.

'What punishment can you give a man of eighty-two, Mr Goldstein? I have only one wish left: to display to you the wonders of that box. If you fail to fathom its secret, I shall come to your aid. After that it doesn't matter whether I am punished or not, whether I live or die.'

Then he turned to me and said, 'You will find it difficult to get in touch with me, because I am not on the phone. I will come myself tomorrow and see you.'

With these words, Al Habbal salaamed, stepped out of the hotel onto the street, and got lost in the darkness.

It is half past ten now. In the last two hours, working with the box, Petrucci and I have discovered only one thing. Of the jewels set on the surface of the box, one, a large carnelian, has been screwed on. In other words, it can be taken off by unscrewing. We have done that and found a small container behind it, black in colour. We have also found that it smells of paraffin. This paraffin had obviously been lighted, accounting for the blackness of the container. We tried to obtain some paraffin, but it wasn't possible at such a late hour. We will have to postpone our investigation until tomorrow morning.

Goldstein hasn't shown his face at all. I phoned him. He said he had a headache. If the god of ziggurat has any power, perhaps he has already started working his curse on Goldstein.

Who knows!

21 NOVEMBER, 6.30 A.M.

A remarkable incident happened half an hour ago.

I am an early riser by habit, going for daily walks by the river Usri at five in the morning when at home. Today I got up even earlier, perhaps because of a feeling of unease in my mind. I took a shower, had a cup of coffee, and stood at the window. It was already light. The sky was filled with choppy white clouds. The play of colours on them reminded me of Ali Baba's cave and the magic words 'Open Sesame'. Through a purely involuntary action, I uttered the two words softly in Arabic several times. Suddenly, a clicking sound behind me made me swivel round.

The box was kept on the bedside table. Now there seemed to be something sticking out of its side. I hurried to it and found that a lapis lazuli, about an inch in diameter and provided with a metal rim and a hinge, had swung open, revealing a circular aperture on the side of the box. How strange!—the same command opened both the cave and the box, only the latter called for a different pitch. I had struck the right pitch quite inadvertently.

I looked through the aperture. The inside of the box was filled with intricate machinery. It included metal elements as well as what looked like glass beads. It was impossible to guess what function they performed, because I had never seen anything like it before. I used my omniscope as a microscope, but it didn't help.

I now picked up the box, took it near the window and, for the first time, had a good look at it in the daylight. I noticed that opposite to the side where the carnelian was, there was a small hole, and the opening of the hole was covered by a tiny jewel. Was it a diamond? It looked like that, but its function escaped me.

Petrucci called an hour later and learned of the discoveries I had made. He has promised to get some paraffin as soon as the shops open. I hope that will shed some light, not only literally but also figuratively. I have encountered many strange pieces of machinery, but never one as curious as this.

22 NOVEMBER, 8 P.M.

Glory to Haroun's Baghdad! Glory to the Sumerian civilization! Glory to the wizard Gemal Nishahir al Hararit!

My jubilation is entirely due to the fact that I have discovered a scientific genius whose brilliance puts into shade all our achievements. I am almost ready to toss my omniscope into the waters of the Tigris before I leave here. The state of my mind is a strange mixture of thrill, wonder, despair and awe—something I have never felt before.

Yesterday morning, soon after Petrucci left, Al Habbal rang up. 'Well?' he asked. 'Have you been able to make out anything?'

When I described what had happened, he said, 'I'll come right away and bring paraffin. Ask Petrucci not to bother.' The three of us delegates had breakfast together. Goldstein had only a cup of coffee. He wasn't looking well at all. 'I didn't sleep well last night,' he said, 'and the little sleep that I did have was full of horrible dreams.'

Petrucci light-heartedly brought up the subject of the curse which only added fuel to the fire. 'You're so superstitious,' he snapped, 'that you don't deserve to be called scientists. I'm feeling low only because I was shut up in that goddam cave yesterday. There's no other reason.'

Perhaps because he had nothing else to do that he came into my room and sat down on the sofa. Within a minute Al Habbal came with the paraffin. 'I should like to congratulate you, sir!' he said, addressing me. 'It took me more than a week of trial and error before I reached the stage that you have reached in less than twenty-four hours.'

We locked the door to keep out intruders and set to work.

First I unscrewed the carnelian, took out the blackened container and filled it with paraffin. Then I tore off a portion of my handkerchief, rolled it into a wick and dipped it in the paraffin oil. I set fire to the wick and put the container back in place. We were now surprised to see Goldstein, who sat facing the box, now bathed in a large area of light.

How was this possible?

I now suddenly remembered the small diamond-like jewel in front of the box. There was now no doubt that the jewel served as a lens.

I glanced at Al Habbal. His eyes were like points of fire. Goldstein too seemed bewildered. He got up and moved away from the area of light. Al Habbal now ran up and pushed the sofa aside so that the light now fell directly on the wall. Now we could see that the light was in the shape of a disc.

Petrucci suddenly exclaimed in his mother tongue: 'La Lanterna Magica!'

Yes, a magic lantern. But where was the picture?

I now gave my attention to the door which had swung open in the morning. It was still open. Carefully, I inserted my right forefinger through the hole, twiddled it for a while until I came into contact with what felt like the point of a pencil. A little pressure on the point, and something happened which makes my hair stand on just to think of it.

The pressure set things in motion in the box. I looked at the wall and saw a vibration had been set up in the disc of light. Then patterns appeared in the disc.

Petrucci rushed to the window and shut it. The room was completely dark now but for the light which came out of the box.

And on the wall. We were speechless to see that moving pictures had appeared in the circle of light. They were not very clear, but there was no difficulty in making out what they showed. There was actually no difference between this and the cinema of our time except that the image here was circular.

But what were we seeing now? What city was this? Who were those people? Why were there so many of them, and what was the great occasion?

Petrucci cried out, 'It's a funeral. Somebody famous must have died! There, that's the coffin!'

Quite so. And behind the coffin followed an immense crowd of people. How many? At least ten thousand. And strangely were they dressed and strange was their hairstyle. I noticed that many of them carried fans which they all waved together. One could also see four-wheeled conveyances mingled with the crowd. They were being drawn by animals which looked like bullocks.

It was Petrucci again who exclaimed, 'I know! That must be Ur. Some king of Ur must have died. When a king died there, fifty other persons had to kill themselves by taking poison. And everybody had to be buried at the same time.'

I could barely keep my eyes on the images. My head was swimming. I moved away from the table and sat down on the bed. The seven-thousand-year-old motion picture has been a mind-blowing experience.

I don't know how long the thing ran. I suddenly saw Al Habbal blowing out the paraffin lamp. 'Gentlemen!' he said triumphantly, 'I hope you will all admit the truth of my claim.' The three of us were still too overwhelmed by the experience to speak. Al Habbal continued, 'My last wish has been fulfilled. I feel honoured that I have been able to show you what our ancient civilization was capable of. But I have one request. You must not tell anyone about this box. Even if you do, nobody is likely to believe you. Mr Goldstein called me a swindler; you will be called crazy. And you won't be able to prove anything, because the box goes back where it has been these last four thousand years . . .

Well, gentlemen, I will take your leave then. Salaam Aleikum!'

Al Habbal had brought his wicker basket with him. He now put the box in it and left.

For a while the three of us sat open-mouthed, not saying a word. Then Petrucci turned to Goldstein. 'Well, do you think the man is a fraud?' he asked.

Goldstein appeared to have come out of his stupor. His eyes had a glint in them. He got up from his chair, paced about restlessly for a while and suddenly turned to me.

'A thing like that cannot be allowed to stay in that cave!' was his comment.

I didn't like what he said at all. I said, 'There are lots of wonderful things from earlier civilizations still lying buried in the ground. Just forget that anything special happened today.'

'Impossible!' cried Goldstein. 'There's no doubt that the man is a thief. He has no right to decide what happens to the box. I want it. I'll get it no matter how much it costs.'

Before we could do anything, Goldstein had stormed out of the room.

Petrucci shook his head and said, 'Goldstein is making a mistake. I don't like it at all.'

After a few more minutes of pacing about, Petrucci went back to his room. I sat on the bed for some more time. I could still see in my mind's eye the funeral of the dead king of Ur. I was never more acutely aware of the extraordinary advances in science made by past civilizations.

In the afternoon, Petrucci called to say that Goldstein hadn't returned yet. I had also rung up Goldstein's room half an hour ago and got no reply. There was nothing more we could do now. We would have to wait till the next morning. I was thinking of Ishtar, the god of ziggurat, and feeling more and more worried about Goldstein.

23 NOVEMBER

I never imagined that our adventure in Baghdad would end like this. This was a demonstration of where excessive greed can lead one. The only consolation is that my presence helped to avert an even greater disaster.

An early morning call told me that Goldstein hadn't returned last night. I immediately got in touch with Petrucci. Both of us realized that we should have to return to the cave.

Al Habbal had gone there, and Goldstein must have followed him.

The manager of the hotel Mr Farouqi arranged for a car as soon as we told him that we wanted to go sightseeing. By half past six we were out.

It took an hour and a half to do the one hundred and twenty kilometres. We stopped where Al Habbal had stopped, asked the driver to wait and set off on foot.

We found the door of the cave closed. I had expected this, but Petrucci seemed disappointed. He said, 'We've come for nothing. I see no way of opening the door without blasting it with dynamite.'

I said, 'Before that I should like to test my memory.'

Petrucci was highly sceptical. 'You don't mean to say you can exactly reproduce Al Habbal's tone?'

In answer, I cupped my hands over my mouth, raised my voice several pitches and let go in Arabic.

'Open Sesame!'

For a few seconds nothing happened. Then the rumbling started. A lizard close by raised its tail and scampered off. We saw the door opening slowly to reveal the darkness beyond.

After the door had fully opened, the two of us entered the cave with our hearts in our throats.

We both had electric torches with us. When we switched them on, at first we could see nothing but the glitter of the varied coloured gems. Then we aimed our torches at the pedestal in the middle of the hall. The box was not on it.

Meanwhile, Petrucci had advanced towards the corner. A sudden gasp from him made me rush towards him.

Petrucci's torch was pointed towards the pit on the ground. In it lay Goldstein with staring eyes. Now I lit my torch too, and the whole corner of the cave was lit up. The sight that met my eyes froze my blood.

About a yard away from Goldstein lay Al Habbal, grasping to his chest the four-thousand-year-old movie projector, while beside him lay the skeleton of Gemal Nishahir, just as we had found it.

I heaved a sigh of relief when I felt Goldstein's pulse. He was not dead, but in pretty bad shape. He must be taken out of the cave and back to Baghdad at once.

And Al Habbal? Well, his life was over. He had been dead for quite a while, because we tried to dislodge the box from his grasp but couldn't. His lifeless hands would hang on to the box for all time to come.

***

We brought Goldstein back to the hotel an hour ago. He had regained consciousness. The doctor who examined him said there was nothing wrong with him physically, but we know that a special kind of change has come over him, because when we asked him what happened yesterday, he gave a broad smile and said, '*Open Sesame!*'

Ever since then, to every question he has been asked, Goldstein has given the same smile and the same answer—*Open Sesame*!

RATANBABU AND THAT MAN

Originally published in *Sandesh* (November–December 1970) as *Ratanbabu r Sei Lokta*.
It was translated by the author himself to be part of the compilation titled *Stories* (Secker & Warburg, 1987). The illustrations in the story, including the Bengali calligraphy in the headpiece, are by Satyajit Ray.

Stepping out of the train on the platform, Ratanbabu heaved a sigh of relief. The place seemed quite inviting. A shirish tree reared its head from behind the station house, and there was a spot of red in its green leaves where a kite was caught in a branch. The few people around seemed relaxed and there was a pleasant earthy smell in the air. All in all, he found the surroundings most agreeable.

As he had only a small holdall and a leather suitcase, he didn't need a coolie. He lifted his luggage with both hands and made for the exit.

He had no trouble finding a cycle rickshaw outside.

'Where to, sir?' asked the young driver in striped shorts.

'You know the New Mahamaya hotel?' asked Ratanbabu.

The driver nodded. 'Hop in, sir.'

Travelling was almost an obsession with Ratanbabu. He would go out of Calcutta whenever the opportunity came, not that it came so often. Ratanbabu had a regular job. For twenty-four years, he had been a clerk in the Calcutta Office of the Geological Survey. He could really get away only once a year, when he would latch his yearly leave on to the

Puja holidays and set off all by himself. He never took anyone with him, nor would it have occurred to him to do so. There was a time when he had felt the need of companionship; in fact, he had once talked about it to Keshabbabu who occupied the adjacent desk in his office. It was a few days before the holidays; in the planning stage. 'You're pretty much on your own, like me,' he had said. 'Why don't we go off together somewhere this time?'

Keshabbabu had stuck his pen in his ear, put his palms together and said with a wry smile, 'I don't think you and I have the same tastes, you know. You go to places no one has heard of, places where there's nothing much to see, nor any decent places to stay or eat at. No sir, I'd sooner go to Harinabhi and visit my brother-in-law.'

In time, Ratanbabu had come to realize that there was virtually no one who saw eye to eye with him. His likes and dislikes were quite different from the average person's, so it was best to give up hopes of finding a suitable companion.

There was no doubt that Ratanbabu possessed traits which were quite unusual. Consider these trips of his. Keshabbabu had been quite right: Ratanbabu was never attracted to places where people normally went for vacations. 'All right', he would say, 'so there is the sea in Puri and there is the temple of Jagannath; and you can see the Kanchanjungha from Darjeeling, and there are hills and forests in Hazaribagh and the Hundru falls in Ranchi. So what? You've heard them described so many times that you almost feel you've seen them yourself.'

What Ratanbabu looked for was a little town somewhere with a railway station not too far away. Every year before the holidays he would open the timetable, pick such a town and sally forth. No one bothered to ask where he was going and he never told anyone. In fact, there had been occasions when he had gone to places he had never even heard of, and whenever he had gone he had discovered things to delight him. To others, such things might appear trivial, like the old fig tree in Rajabhatkhaoa which coiled itself around a kul and a coconut tree; or the ruins of the indigo factory in Maheshgunj; or the delicious dal barfi sold in a sweet shop in Moina . . .

This time Ratanbabu has come to a town called Shini, fifteen miles from Tatanagar. Shini was not picked from the timetable; it was his colleague Anukul Mitra who had mentioned it. The New Mahamaya hotel, too, was recommended by him.

To Ratanbabu, the hotel seemed quite adequate. His room wasn't large, but that didn't matter. There were windows to the east and the south with pleasant views of the countryside. The servant Pancha seemed an amiable sort. Ratanbabu was in the habit of bathing twice a day in tepid water throughout the year, and Pancha had assured him that there would be no trouble about that. The cooking was passable, and this was all right too, because Ratanbabu was not fussy about food. There was only one thing he insisted on: he needed to have rice with the fish curry and chapati with dal and vegetables. He had informed Pancha about this as soon as he had arrived, and Pancha had passed on the information to the manager.

Another habit of Ratanbabu's when he arrived in a new place was to go for a walk in the afternoon. The first day at Shini was no exception. He finished the cup of tea brought by Pancha and was out by four.

After a few minutes' walk he found himself in open country. The terrain was uneven and criss-crossed with paths. Ratanbabu chose one at random and after half an hour's walk, discovered a charming spot. It was a pond with water lilies growing in it and a large variety of birds in and around it. Of these there were some—cranes, snipes, kingfishers, magpies—which Ratanbabu recognized, the others were unfamiliar.

Ratanbabu could cheerfully have spent all his afternoons sitting beside this pond, but on the second day he took a different path in the hope of discovering something new. Having walked a mile or so, he had to stop for a herd of goats to cross his path. As the road cleared, he went on for another five minutes until a wooden bridge came into view. Going a little further, he realized it had railway lines passing below it. He went and stood on the bridge. To the east could be seen the railway station; to the west the parallel lines stretched as far as the eye could see. What if a train were suddenly to appear and go thundering underneath? The very thought thrilled Ratanbabu.

Perhaps because he had his eyes on the tracks, he failed to notice another man who came and stood beside him. Ratanbabu looked around and gave a start.

The stranger was clad in a dhoti and shirt, carried a snuff-coloured wrapper on his shoulder, wore bifocals and brown canvas shoes. Ratanbabu had an odd feeling. Where had he seen this person before? Wasn't there something familiar about him? Medium height, medium complexion, a pensive look in his eyes . . . How old could he be? Surely not over fifty.

The stranger smiled and folded his hands in greeting. Ratanbabu was about to return the greeting when he realized in a flash why he had that odd feeling. No wonder the stranger's face seemed familiar. He had seen that face many, many times—in his own mirror. The resemblance was uncanny. The squarish jaw with the cleft chin, the way the hair was parted, the carefully trimmed moustache, the shape of the earlobes—they were all strikingly like his own. Only the stranger seemed a shade fairer, his eyebrows a little bushier and the hair at the back a trifle longer.

Now the stranger spoke, and Ratanbabu had another shock. Sushanto, a boy from his neighbourhood, had once recorded his voice in a tape recorder and played it back to him. There was no difference between that voice and the one that spoke now.

'My name is Manilal Majumdar. I believe you're staying at the New Mahamaya?'

Ratanlal—Manilal . . . the names were similar too. Ratanbabu managed to shake off his bewilderment and introduced himself.

The stranger said, 'I don't suppose you'd know, but I have seen you once before.'
'Where?'
'Weren't you in Dhulian last year?'
Ratanbabu's eyebrows shot up. 'Don't tell me you were there too!'
'Yes, sir. I go off on trips every Puja. I'm on my own. No friends to speak of. It's fun to be in a new place all by yourself. A colleague of mine recommended Shini to me. Nice place, isn't it?'

Ratanbabu swallowed, and then nodded assent. He felt a strange mixture of disbelief and uneasiness in his mind.

'Have you seen the pond on the other side where a lot of birds gather in the evening?' asked Manilalbabu.

Ratanbabu said yes, he had.

'Some of the birds I could recognize,' said Manilalbabu, 'others I have never seen before in Bengal. What d'you think?'

Ratanbabu had recovered somewhat in the meantime. He said, 'I had the same feeling; some birds I didn't recognize either.'

Just then a booming sound was heard. It was a train. Ratanbabu saw a point of light growing bigger as it approached from the east. Both Ratanbabu and Manilalbabu moved up close to the railing of the bridge. The train hurtled up and passed below them, causing the bridge to shake. Both men now crossed to the other side and kept looking until the train disappeared from view. Ratanbabu felt the same thrill as he did as a small boy. 'How strange!' said Manilalbabu, 'Even at this age watching trains never fails to excite me.'

On the way back Ratanbabu learnt that Manilalbabu had arrived in Shini three days ago. He was staying at the Kalika Hotel. His home was in Calcutta where he had a job in a trading company. One doesn't ask another person about his salary, but an indomitable urge made Ratanbabu throw discretion to the wind and put the question. The answer made him gasp in astonishment. How was such a thing possible? Both Ratanbabu and Manilalbabu drew exactly the same salary—four hundred and thirty-seven rupees a month—and both had received exactly the same Puja bonus.

Ratanbabu found it difficult to believe that the other man had somehow found out all about him beforehand and was playing some deep game. No one had ever bothered about him before; he had kept very much to himself. Outside his office he spoke only to his servant and never made called on anyone. It was just possible for an outsider to find out about his salary, but such details as when he went to bed, his tastes in food, what newspapers he read, what plays and films he had seen lately—these were known only to himself. And yet everything tallied exactly with what this man was saying.

He couldn't tell this to Manilalbabu. All he did was listen to what the man had to say and marvel at the extraordinary similarity. He revealed nothing about his own habits.

They came to Ratanbabu's hotel first, and stopped in front of it. 'What's the food here like?' asked Manilalbabu.

'They make a good fish curry,' replied Ratanbabu, 'the rest is just adequate.'

'I'm afraid the cooking in my hotel is rather indifferent,' said Manilalbabu, 'I've heard they make very good luchis and chholar dal at the Jagannath Restaurant. What about having a meal there tonight?'

'I don't mind,' said Ratanbabu, 'shall we meet around eight then?'

'Right. I'll wait for you, then we'll walk down together.'

After Manilalbabu left, Ratanbabu roamed about in the street for a while. Darkness had fallen. It was a clear night, indeed, so clear that the Milky Way could be seen stretching from one end of the star-filled sky to the other. What a strange thing to happen! All these years Ratanbabu had regretted that he couldn't find anyone to share his tastes and become friends with him. Now at last in Shini he has run into someone who might be said to be an exact replica of himself. There was a slight difference in looks, perhaps, but in every other respect such identity was rare even amongst twins.

Did it mean that he had found a friend at last?

Ratanbabu couldn't find a ready answer to the question. Perhaps he would find it when he got to know the man a little better. One thing was clear—he no longer had the feeling of being isolated from his fellow men. All along there had been another person exactly like him, and he had quite by chance come to know him.

In the Jagannath Restaurant, sitting face to face across the table, Ratanbabu observed that, like him, Manilalbabu ate with a fastidious relish; like him, didn't drink any water during the meal; and like him, he squeezed lemon into the dal. Ratanbabu always had sweet curd to round off his meals, and so did Manilalbabu.

While eating, Ratanbabu had the uncomfortable feeling that diners at other tables were watching them. Did they observe how alike they were? Was the identity so obvious to onlookers? After dinner, Ratanbabu and Manilalbabu walked for a while in the moonlight. There was something which Ratanbabu wanted to ask, and he did so now. 'Have you turned fifty yet?'

Manilalbabu smiled. 'I'll soon be doing so,' he said, 'I'll be fifty on the twenty-ninth of December.'

Ratanbabu's head swam. They were both born on the same day: the twenty-ninth of December, 1916.

Half an hour later, as they were taking leave, Manilalbabu said, 'It has been a great pleasure knowing you. I don't seem to get on very well with people, but you're an exception. I can now look forward to an enjoyable vacation.'

Usually, Ratanbabu was in bed by ten. He would glance through a magazine, and gradually feel drowsiness stealing over him. He would put down the magazine, turn off the bed lamp and within a few minutes would start snoring softly. Tonight he found that sleep wouldn't come. Nor did he feel like reading. He picked up the magazine and put it down again. Manilal Majumdar . . .

Ratanbabu had read somewhere that of the billions of people who inhabited the earth, no two looked exactly alike. And yet everyone had the same number of features—eyes, ears, nose, lips and so on. But even if no two persons looked alike, was it possible for them to have the same tastes, feelings, attitudes—as in the present case? Age, profession, voice, gait, even the power of their glasses—were identical. One would think such a thing impossible, and yet here was proof that it was not, as Ratanbabu had learnt again and again in the last four hours.

At about midnight, Ratanbabu got out of bed, poured some water from the carafe and splashed it on his head. Sleep was impossible in his feverish state. He passed a towel lightly over his head and went back to bed. At least the wet pillow would keep his head cool for a while.

Silence had descended over the neighbourhood. An owl went screeching overhead. Moonlight streamed in through the window and on to the bed. Presently, Ratanbabu's mind regained its calm and his eyes closed of their own accord.

As sleep had come late, it was almost eight when Ratanbabu woke up next morning. Manilalbabu was supposed to come at nine. Today was Tuesday—the day when the weekly market or haat was held at a spot a mile or so away. The night before the two had almost simultaneously expressed a wish to visit the haat, more to look around than to buy anything.

It was almost nine when Ratanbabu finished breakfast. He helped himself to a pinch of mouri from the saucer on the table, came out of the hotel and saw Manilalbabu approaching.

'I couldn't sleep for a long-time last night,' were Manilalbabu's first words. 'I lay thinking how alike you and I were. It was five to eight when I woke this morning. I am usually up by six.'

Ratanbabu refrained from commenting. The two set off towards the haat. They had to pass some youngsters standing in a cluster by the roadside. 'Hey, look at Tweedledum and Tweedledee!' one of them cried out. Ratanbabu tried his best to ignore the remark and went on ahead. It took them about twenty minutes to reach the haat.

The haat was a bustling affair. There were shops for fruits and vegetables, for utensils, clothes and even livestock. The two men wove their way through the milling crowd casting glances at the goods on display.

Who was that there? Wasn't it Pancha? For some reason, Ratanbabu couldn't bring himself to face the hotel servant.

That remark about Tweedledum and Tweedledee had made him realize it would be prudent not to be seen alongside Manilalbabu.

As they jostled through the crowd, a thought suddenly occurred to Ratanbabu. He realized he was better off as he was—alone, without a friend. He didn't need a friend. Or, at any rate, not someone like Manilalbabu. Whenever he had spoken to Manilalbabu, it had seemed as if he was carrying on a conversation with himself. It was as if he knew all the answers before he asked the questions. There was no room for argument, no

possibility of misunderstanding. Were these signs of friendship? Two of his colleagues, Kartik Ray and Mukunda Chakraborty, were bosom friends. Did that mean they had no arguments? Of course, they did. But they were still friends—close friends.

It struck him again and again that it would have been better if Manilalbabu hadn't come into his life. Even if there existed two identical men, it was wrong that they should meet. The very thought that they might continue to meet even after returning to Calcutta made Ratanbabu shudder.

One of the shops was selling cane walking sticks. Ratanbabu had always wanted to possess one, but seeing Manilalbabu haggling with the shopkeeper, he checked himself. Manilalbabu bought two sticks and gave one to Ratanbabu saying, 'I hope you won't mind accepting this as a token of our friendship.'

On the way back to the hotel, Manilalbabu spoke a lot about himself—his childhood, his parents, his school and college days. Ratanbabu felt that his own life story was being recounted.

The plan came to Ratanbabu in the afternoon as the two were on their way to the railway bridge. He didn't have to talk much, so he could think. He had been thinking since midday of getting rid of this man, but he couldn't decide on a method. Ratanbabu had just turned his eye to the clouds gathering in the west when the method suddenly appeared to him with a blazing clarity. The vision he saw was of the two of them standing by the railing of the bridge. In the distance the mail train was approaching. When the engine approached to within twenty yards, Ratanbabu gathered his strength and gave a hefty push—

Ratanbabu inadvertently closed his eyes. Then he opened them again and shot a glance at his companion. Manilalbabu seemed quite unconcerned. But if the two had so much in common, perhaps he too was thinking of a way to do him in?

But his looks didn't betray any such thoughts, as a matter of fact, he was humming a Hindi film tune which Ratanbabu himself was in the habit of humming from time to time.

The dark clouds had just covered the sun which would in any case set in a few minutes. Ratanbabu looked about and saw they were quite alone. Thank God for that. Had there been anyone else, his plan wouldn't have worked.

It was strange that even though his mind was bent on murder, Ratanbabu couldn't think of himself as a culprit. Had Manilalbabu possessed any traits which endowed him with a personality different from his own, Ratanbabu could never have thought of killing him. He believed that there was no sense in both of them being alive at the same time. It was enough that he alone should continue to exist.

The two arrived at the bridge.

'Bit stuffy today,' commented Manilalbabu. 'It may rain tonight, and that could be the start of a cold spell.'

Ratanbabu stole a glance at his wrist-watch. Twelve minutes to six. The train was supposed to be very punctual. There wasn't much time left. Ratanbabu contrived a yawn to ease his tension. 'Even if it does rain,' he said, 'it is not likely to happen for another four or five hours.'

'Care for a betel nut?'

Manilalbabu had produced a small round tin box from his pocket. Ratanbabu too was carrying a metal box with betel nuts in it, but didn't mention the fact to Manilalbabu. He helped himself to a nut and tossed it into his mouth. Just then was heard the sound of the train.

Manilalbabu advanced towards the railing, glanced at his watch and said, 'Seven minutes before time.'

Because of the thick cloud in the sky, it had grown a little darker than usual. This made the headlight seem brighter in contrast. The train was still far away but the light was growing brighter every second.

'Krrrring . . . Krrring . . .

A cyclist was approaching from the road towards the bridge. Good god! Was he going to stop?

No. Ratanbabu's apprehension proved baseless. The cyclist rode swiftly past them and disappeared into the gathering darkness down the other side of the road.

The train was hurtling up at a great speed. It was impossible to gauge the distance owing to the blinding glare of the headlight. In a few seconds the bridge would start shaking. Now the sound of the train was deafening. Manilalbabu was looking down with his hands on the railings. A flash of lightning in the sky—and Ratanbabu gathered all his strength, flattened his palms against the back of Manilalbabu, and heaved. Manilalbabu's body vaulted over the four-foot-high railing and plummeted down towards the on-rushing engine. That very moment the bridge began to shake.

Ratanbabu didn't wait to see the train vanishing into the horizon. Like the bridge, he too felt a tremor within himself. The cloud had spread from the west and there were occasional flashes of lightning.

Ratanbabu wound his wrapper tighter and started on his way back.

Towards the end of his journey he had to break into a run in a vain effort to avoid being pelted by the first big drops of rain. Panting with the effort, he rushed into the hotel.

As soon as he entered he felt there was something wrong.

Where had he come? The lobby of the New Mahamaya was not like this at all—the tables, the chairs, the pictures on the wall . . .

Looking around, his eye was suddenly caught by a signboard on the wall. What a stupid mistake! He had come into the Kalika Hotel instead. Isn't this where Manilalbabu was staying?

'So you couldn't avoid getting wet?'

Somebody had put the question to him. Ratanbabu turned round and saw a man with curly hair and a green shawl—probably a resident of the hotel looking at him with a cup of tea in his hand. 'Sorry,' said the man, seeing Ratanbabu's face, 'for a moment I thought you were Manilalbabu.'

It was this mistake which raised the first doubts in Ratanbabu's mind. Had he been careful enough about the crime he had committed? Many must have seen the two of them going out together, but had they really noticed? Would they remember what they had seen? And if they did, would the suspicion then fall on him? That no one had seen them after they had reached the outskirts of the town he was sure of. And after reaching the bridge—oh, yes, the cyclist. He must have seen them both. But by that time it had turned quite dark. The cyclist passed by at a high speed. Was it likely that he would remember their faces? Certainly not.

The more Ratanbabu pondered, the more reassured he felt. There was no doubt that Manilalbabu's dead body would be discovered. But that it would lead to him being suspected of the crime, that he would be tried, found guilty, and brought to the gallows—all this he just could not believe.

Since it was still raining, Ratanbabu stayed for a cup of tea. Around seven-thirty the rain stopped and Ratanbabu went directly to the New Mahamaya. He found it almost funny the way he had blundered into the wrong hotel.

At dinner, he ate well and with relish; then he slipped into bed with a magazine, read an article on the aborigines of Australia, turned off the bed lamp and closed his eyes with not a worry in his mind. Once again, he was on his own; and unique. He didn't have a friend, and didn't need one. He would spend the rest of his days in exactly the same way he had done so far. What could be better?

It had started to rain again. There were flashes of lightning and peals of thunder. But none of it mattered. Ratanbabu had already started to snore.

'Did you buy that stick from the haat, sir?' asked Pancha when he brought Ratanbabu his morning tea. 'Yes,' said Ratanbabu.

'How much did you pay for it?'

Ratanbabu mentioned the price. Then he asked casually, 'Were you at the haat too?'

Pancha broke into a broad smile. 'Yes, sir,' he said, 'and I saw you. Didn't you see me?'

'Why, no.'

That ended the Pancha episode.

Finishing tea, Ratanbabu made his way to the Kalika Hotel. The curly-haired man was talking to a group of people outside the hotel. Ratanbabu heard Manilalbabu's name and the word 'suicide' mentioned several times. He edged closer to hear better. Not only that, he was bold enough to put a question.

'Who has committed suicide?'

The curly-haired man said, 'It was the same man I had mistaken you for yesterday.'

'Suicide, was it?'

'It looks like that. The dead body was found by the railway tracks below the bridge. Looks as if he threw himself from it. An odd character, he was. Hardly spoke to anyone. We used to talk about him.'

'I suppose the dead body . . .?'

'In police custody. Came here for a change of air from Calcutta. Didn't know anyone here. Nothing more has been found out.'

Ratanbabu shook his head, made a few clucking noises and went off.

Suicide! So nobody had thought of murder at all. Luck was on his side. How simple it was, this business of murder! He wondered what made people quail at the thought.

Ratanbabu felt quite light-hearted. After two whole days he would now be able to walk alone again. The very thought filled him with pleasure.

It was probably while he pushed Manilalbabu yesterday that a button from his shirt had come off. He found a tailor's shop and had the button replaced. Then he went into a store and bought a tube of Neem toothpaste.

Walking a few steps from the store he heard the sound of kirtan coming from a house. He stood for a while listening to the song, then made for the open terrain outside the town. He walked a mile or so along a new path, came back to the hotel about eleven, had his bath and lunch, and took his afternoon nap.

As usual he woke up around three, and realized almost immediately that he had to pay another visit to the bridge that evening. For obvious reasons he had not been able to enjoy the sight of the train yesterday. The sky was still cloudy but it didn't seem that it would rain. Today he would be able to watch the train from the moment it appeared till it vanished into the horizon.

He had his afternoon tea at five and went down into the lobby. The manager Shambhubabu sat at his desk by the front door. He saw Ratanbabu and said, 'Did you know the man who was killed yesterday?'

Ratanbabu looked at Shambhubabu, feigning surprise. Then he said, 'Why do you ask?'

'Well, it's only that Pancha mentioned he had seen you two together in the haat.'

Ratanbabu smiled. 'I haven't really got to know anyone here,' he said calmly. 'I did speak to a few people in the haat, but the fact is, I don't even know which person was killed.'

'I see,' said Shambhubabu, laughing. He was prone to laughter, being jovial by nature. 'He too had come for a change,' he added. 'He put up at the Kalika.'

'I see.'

Ratanbabu went out. It was a two-mile walk to the bridge. If he didn't hurry he might miss the train.

In the street nobody cast suspicious glances at him. Yesterday's youngsters were not in their usual place. That remark about Tweedledum and Tweedledee had nettled him. He wondered where the boys were. The sound of drums could be heard from somewhere close by. There was a puja on in the neighbourhood. That's where the boys must have gone. Good.

Today he was all by himself on the path in the open field. He was a contented person even before he had met Manilalbabu; but today he felt more relaxed than ever before.

There it was—the babla tree. A few minutes' walk from the tree was the bridge.

The sky was still overcast, but not with thick black clouds like yesterday. These were grey clouds, and there being no breeze, the whole sky stood ashen and still.

Ratanbabu's heart leaped with joy at the sight of the bridge. He quickened his pace. Who knows, the train might turn up even earlier than yesterday. A flock of cranes passed overhead. Migratory cranes? He couldn't tell.

As he stood on the bridge, Ratanbabu became aware of the stillness of the evening. Straining his ears, he could hear faint drumbeats from the direction of the town. Otherwise all was quiet.

Ratanbabu moved over to the railing. He could see the signal, and beyond that, the station. What was that now? Lower down the railing, in a crack in the wood was lodged a shiny object. Ratanbabu bent down and prised it out. A small round tin box with betel nuts in it. Ratanbabu smiled and tossed it over the railing. A metallic clink was heard as it hit the ground. Who knows how long it would lie there?

What was that light?

Ah, the train. No sound yet, just an advancing point of light. Ratanbabu stood and stared fascinated at the headlight. A sudden gust of wind whipped the wrapper off his shoulder. Ratanbabu wrapped it properly around him once more.

Now he could hear the sound. It was like the low rumble of an approaching storm.

Ratanbabu suddenly had the feeling that somebody had come and stood behind him. It was difficult to take his eyes away from the train, but even so he cast a quick glance around. Not a soul anywhere. Being not so dark as yesterday, the visibility was much better. No, except for himself and that approaching train, there was no one for miles around.

The train had now approached within a hundred yards. Ratanbabu edged further towards the railing. Had the train been an old-fashioned one with a steam engine, he couldn't have gone so close to the edge as the smoke would have got into his eyes. This was a smokeless diesel engine. There was only a deep, earth-shaking rumble and the blinding glare of the headlight.

Now the train was about to go under the bridge.

Ratanbabu placed his elbows on the railing and leaned forward to watch.

At that very moment a pair of hands came up from behind and gave him a savage push. Ratanbabu went clean over the four-foot high railing.

As usual, the train made the bridge shudder as it passed under it and sped towards the west where the sky had just begun to turn purple.

Ratanbabu is no longer on the bridge, but as a token of his presence a small shining object is stuck in a crack in the wooden railing.

It is an aluminium box with betel nuts in it.

FRITZ

Originally published in *Sandesh* (January-February 1971). The English translation by Ray was published in *Science Today*, December 1986. The illustration in the story, including the Bengali calligraphy, is by Satyajit Ray.

I had been observing Jayanta for some time, and at last said, 'You seem to be a bit mopish today. What's the matter? I hope you're not unwell?'

Jayanta pulled himself together and said, smiling, 'Oh, no. On the contrary, I already feel refreshed. I love this place.'

'But you've been here before; didn't you know it was a nice place?'

'I'd almost forgotten.' Jayanta took a deep breath. 'It's all coming back slowly. The Circuit House seems exactly as it was then, even the rooms look more or less the same. Some of the old furniture is still around, such as these cane chairs.'

The bearer brought tea and biscuits. It wasn't 4 p.m. yet, but the sun was already down. I began pouring the tea. 'When were you here last?' I asked.

'Thirty-one years ago,' replied Jayanta. 'I was only six then.'

We were sitting on the lawn of the Circuit House at Bundi in Rajasthan. We had arrived yesterday. Jayanta is a very old friend of mine. We were at school and college together. He is the assistant editor of a newspaper, while I teach in a school. Although we

belong to different professions, it hasn't affected our friendship. We have been planning this trip to Rajasthan for a long time, but it was proving rather difficult for both of us to get leave at the same time. However, Jayanta finally managed to wangle a week's leave during my autumn vacation. Usually visitors to Rajasthan start off with cities like Jaipur, Udaipur, and Chittor, but Jayanta had insisted on Bundi from the very beginning. I didn't object, because the prospect of seeing with our own eyes the fortress which Tagore's poem had familiarized us with from our schooldays was a pleasant one. There was more colourful history bound up with Jaipur, Udaipur and Chittor, but if one looked for beauty, then Bundi had much to offer.

At first it had struck me as a bit odd that Jayanta should insist on Bundi; it was on our way in the train that I found our the reason: Jayanta had wanted to compare his boyhood memories with his impressions of today. Jayanta's father Animesh Dasgupta had been in the Archaeological Survey. His job often took him to places of historical interest. Jayanta had accompanied him on one of his trips to Bundi.

The Circuit House was splendid. It dated back to the days of the Raj, and was almost a hundred years old. It was a one-storeyed building with sloping tiled roofs. The ceiling was high, and there were skylights which one could open or shut by means of ropes. On the eastern side was a wide verandah which faced a large compound with a rose garden in it. Towards the back of the compound were large trees which in the daytime were alive with the cry of birds; parakeets being the most plentiful. One could also hear the wail of peacocks, but it came from outside the compound.

In the morning we had a drive around the town. The famous fortress is set like a jewel on the slope of a hill. We had a distant view today; tomorrow we plan to go inside. But for the electric poles, the town gives the impression of being unchanged over the centuries. With its cobbled alleys, its ornate balconies jutting out of stone facades, its carved wooden doors, it is hard to imagine we are living in the twentieth century.

I have been noticing that Jayanta is less communicative here than he usually is. Perhaps he is wrapped up in his memories; it is not unusual for someone returning to a place he knew as a child to feel wistful. As it is Jayanta is a bit more of an introvert than the average person.

Jayanta put down the tea cup and said, 'You know, Shankar, it is very strange; when I came here the first time, I remember I used to sit cross-legged in these chairs. It felt like sitting on a throne. Now they seem quite ordinary—both in size and in looks. The drawing room looked twice as large as it does now. If I hadn't come back the childhood impressions would have remained.'

I said, 'That's only natural. When we ourselves are small, the objects around us seem large. We grow in size, but the objects don't.'

We were taking a stroll in the garden after tea when Jayanta suddenly stopped on his tracks and said, 'Deodar'.

I turned to him in surprise. 'A deodar tree,' he repeated. 'Should be somewhere down there.'

Jayanta suddenly started walking towards a corner of the compound. What was so special about a deodar tree that he should remember it?

Within a few seconds I heard his shout.

'It's here! Just where I thought it would be.'

I caught up with him and said, 'A tree is apt to stick in one place, you know.'

Jayanta shook his head impatiently.

'It's not that I thought that the tree would change its place in thirty-one years, I'm only pleased to find it where I expected to find it.'

'But why did you suddenly think of this tree?'

Jayanta slowly shook his head and said, 'I can't remember why. I had come to this tree for some reason . . . and done something . . . a foreigner . . .'

'Foreigner?'

'Sorry, I can't remember anything else. Memory is an odd thing . . .'

While we were having dinner at the oval dining table, Jayanta said, 'The cook during our first trip was called Dilwar. He had a scar down his left cheek—a cut from a dagger—and his eyes were always bloodshot. But he cooked wonderful meals.'

Sitting in the drawing room after dinner, more memories began to come back to Jayanta. Where his father would sit and smoke cheroot, where his mother sat and knitted, what magazines lay strewn on the table and so on.

And then in the end he remembered Fritz.

An uncle of his had brought back from Switzerland a footlong puppet, an old man in native Swiss costume. It looked exactly like a miniature man, and it had movable limbs. There was a smile on the puppet's face, and on its head was a Swiss mountaineer's hat with a yellow feather stuck in it. Even the clothes of the puppet, down to the buckles on the shoes, were most life-like.

Jayanta was given the puppet a few months before his first visit to Bundi. His uncle had bought it from an old man in a Swiss village. 'His name is Fritz,' the old man said laughing. 'He won't answer to any other name.' Jayanta said, 'I had lots of toys as a child. It was probably because I was an only child that my parents never stinted on toys. But when my uncle gave me Fritz, I quite forgot my other toys. I used to play with Fritz all day. In fact, there came a time when I would keep talking to him for hours on end. The conversation was one-sided, of course, but the smile on Fritz's face and the look in his eyes were such that it seemed he could perfectly follow what I said. Sometimes I felt that if I spoke in German and not in Bengali, he would have answered me. It sounds like childish prank now, but at that time the thing was very real to me. My parents would try to stop me but I wouldn't listen. I had not joined school yet, so I had plenty of time for Fritz.'

Jayanta paused. I glanced at my watch. It was half past nine. Bundi was now quiet. We were still sitting in the drawing room.

I said, 'What happened to the puppet?'

Jayanta was still lost in thought. His answer came so late that I had begun to think he hadn't heard the question. 'I had brought the puppet to Bundi. It was spoilt here.' 'Spoilt? How?'

Jayanta sighed. 'We were having tea in the garden one afternoon. I had put the puppet down on the grass by my chair. Some street dogs had come into the compound and were romping about nearby. I was not supposed to have tea at that age, but I had urged my parents to give me some. The upshot was that I spilled some on my trousers and had to run to my room to change. When I came back I found Fritz no longer there. I looked about frantically and found two of the street dogs playing tug-of-war with it. The thing was so strongly built that it didn't come apart, but it was horribly disfigured, and its clothes were in tatters. In other words, Fritz didn't exist for me anymore. He was dead.'

'And then?' I was fascinated by the story of Jayanta's puppet.

'What more? I gave him a decent burial.'

'What d'you mean?'

'I buried him below that deodar tree. I wanted a coffin for him; after all he was a Christian. Even a plain cardboard box would have done. But I couldn't find one. I just buried him as he was.'

At last the mystery of the deodar tree was cleared up.

It was about ten when we turned in. We slept in two separate beds in a large bedroom. The long walks through the town had made me quite tired, and sleep came quickly.

I don't know what time it was, but I was awakened in the middle of the night by a sound. I turned to Jayanta and found him sitting bolt upright on his bed, with the table lamp on by his side. In the light I could see the look of anxiety in his eyes. I said, 'What's the matter?'

Instead of answering, Jayanta put a question to me. 'Are there cats or mice in the

Circuit House?'

'I shouldn't be surprised if there were,' I answered. 'Why do you ask?'

'Something walked across my chest. That is what woke me up.'

I said, 'Mice usually come in through the drain pipes. But I've never heard of mice climbing on to beds.'

Jayanta said, 'I woke up once before, and heard a scratching sound coming from the window.'

'Then it is more likely to have been a cat.'

'But then . . .'

Jayanta still seemed puzzled. I said, 'Couldn't you see anything after you put on the light?'

'No. But then, I didn't put it on as soon as I woke up. I was quite upset, you see. To be honest, I was a bit scared. But I saw nothing after I put on the light.'

'Then whatever came in must still be in the room.'

'That's possible, since both the doors are locked.'

I got out of bed and made a quick search under the beds and furniture and behind the suitcases. I found nothing. The bathroom door was shut; still I went in to have a look when I heard Jayanta calling out in a stifled voice.

'Shankar!'

I came back. Jayanta was staring down at the yellow blanket. I walked over to him. He held a portion of the blanket under the lamp and said, 'Look.'

There were some roundish, brown marks on the blanket. 'Those could be from a cat's paws,' I said.

Jayanta kept staring at the marks. My watch said 2.30 a.m. I needed to sleep well to get over the day's fatigue, and there was more outing tomorrow. So I assured him that there was nothing to fear with me in the room, and those marks must have been there already. Then I put out the light and went back to bed. I had little doubt that what Jayanta described was part of a dream. This was only a result of Bundi stirring up old memories.

If anything more happened during the night, I was not aware of it. But looking at Jayanta in the morning, I could see that he hadn't slept well. It turned out that Jayanta wasn't carrying any sleeping pills, so I decided to give him one of mine.

As we had planned, we went to see the Bundi Fort after breakfast.

Even here, a flood of childhood memories came back to Jayanta. Fortunately, none of it was connected with the puppet. In fact, his excitement on seeing the fort almost made it seem that he had forgotten about the puppet. So many memories were being roused that he would cry out again and again—'There's that elephant over the gate.' 'There's the silver bed!' 'There's the throne!' . . .

However, in a few hours his enthusiasm waned. I was so absorbed myself that I wasn't aware of it at first. I was walking down a big hall and observing the chandeliers in the ceiling when I suddenly noticed that Jayanta was not by my side. Where had he disappeared?

There was a guide with us who said that Jayanta had gone out on to the terrace.

I came out of the hall and found Jayanta on the far side of the terrace, standing quietly by the parapet. He was so distrait that he didn't even react when I went and stood by his side. At last I had to call him by his name. He gave a start and turned to me. I said, 'You must tell me what is the matter with you. I can't bear the sight of you so glum-faced in such glorious surroundings.'

'If you have finished looking, can we go now?'

Had I been on my own, I'd probably have stayed a little longer, but for the sake of my friend I decided to return to the Circuit House.

The metalled road back into town ran by the hillside. The two of us sat quietly in the back of the car. I offered Jayanta a cigarette, but he refused. The way he cracked his fingers and bit his nails clearly showed that he was overwrought. I must say it made me most uncomfortable because as a rule Jayanta was unflappable.

I bore it for ten minutes or so, and then said, 'You know, Jayanta, you might feel better if you told me what was eating you.'

Jayanta shook his head. 'There's no point in telling you, because you won't believe me.'

'I could at least discuss it with you.'

Jayanta turned to face me.

'Fritz was in my room last night,' he said. 'Those marks on the blanket were his footprints.'

This was a bit much. I felt like shaking him by the shoulders to bring him back to his senses. How could you argue with a man who had such notions? I said, 'You actually didn't see him, did you?'

'No, but I did feel that the thing that was walking over me had two legs, not four.'

By the time we reached the Circuit House, I had already decided that Jayanta needed a dose of nerve tonic. It was ridiculous that a childhood memory should so upset a man of thirty-seven.

While taking a shower, I hit upon a plan. If the puppet had been buried thirty-one years ago, and if the place of burial was known, digging there might reveal some remnants of it. If Jayanta could be shown that was all that was left of his puppet, it might help to drive away the absurd notion that was plaguing him now. Otherwise, if the notion persisted that his puppet was paying him nightly visits, it would end up driving him out of his mind.

When I described my plan to Jayanta, he seemed to react favourably. He pondered for a few seconds and said, 'But who will dig! Where will you get a spade?'

I laughed.

'When they have a garden, they obviously have a gardener too. And the gardener must have a spade or a shovel. If we pay him, it is hard to believe that he would refuse to do a little digging for us.'

Jayanta didn't give his assent immediately, and I too didn't insist on it. Normally he had a good appetite, but today he took only a couple of chapattis and a little curry. After lunch we went out on the verandah and sat down in the cane chairs. We were the only occupants in the Circuit House now. A stillness hung in the air. On our right, beyond the gravelled road, was a flame-of-the-forest tree with langurs capering on its branches. They made whooping noises from time to time.

About 3 p.m., an old man with white hair and moustache came to the garden with a watering can.

'Who will tell him—you or I?'

I raised a reassuring hand at Jayanta, left my chair and made for the gardener. When I asked him if he would do a little digging for us, the gardener looked at me suspiciously. I could see that no one had ever asked him to do a thing like that. To his question: 'But why, sir?' I put my hand on his shoulder and said, 'Never mind that. We will give you five rupees for it. Just do as we tell you.'

Needless to say, the man not only agreed but showed his teeth in a broad smile.

I signalled Jayanta to join me. He left his chair and walked over. As he came close, I noticed that he was looking very pale indeed. I fervently hoped that the digging would reveal some remnants of the puppet.

The gardener had meanwhile procured a shovel. The three of us walked towards the deodar tree.

Jayanta pointed to a spot about a yard from the base of the tree and said, 'Here.'

'I hope your memory can be trusted?' I asked.

Jayanta gave a brief nod.

'How far below the ground did you bury it?'

'About a foot.'

The gardener got busy with his shovel. The man had a sense of humour. Between digs he asked us if we were hoping to find buried treasure, and in case we did, if we would let him have a share. I smiled, but Jayanta stayed grim. It was cool in Bundi in October, but Jayanta was wet around the collar. His eyes were fixed on the ground. The gardener went on digging. Why was there no sign of the puppet yet?

I had turned my head at a call from a peacock, when a strangled cry from Jayanta made me turn sharply towards him.

With his eyes bulging out of their sockets, he extended an arm and pointed with his fingers towards the ground.

Then came the question in a hoarse voice.

'What on earth is that?'

The shovel dropped from the gardener's hand.

I looked down at the pit, and my jaw dropped in horror mingled with utter disbelief.

In the pit, half embedded in the earth lay with its arms and legs spread, a footlong, white, human skeleton.

THE SAHARA MYSTERY

Originally published in *Sandesh* (May-June 1972) as *Maru Rahasya*. Translated by the author himself to be part of the compilation titled *Stories* (Secker & Warburg, 1987). The illustrations in the story, including the Bengali calligraphy in the headpiece, are by Satyajit Ray.

3 JANUARY

Distressing news in the New Year: Demetrius is missing. Professor Hektor Demetrius, the famous Greek biologist. Demetrius lived in Iraklion, the largest city in the island of Crete. I had never met him, but had written to him when I came to know that he was doing research on ancient medicine. When I sent

him some information on our own Ayurvedic medicine, he replied at once, thanking me profusely, with elegant handwriting and considerable command of English. I later learned from my friend John Summerville that Demetrius had studied in Cambridge. It was Summerville's letter which informed me yesterday of Demetrius's disappearance and this is what the letter revealed.

On the thirty-first of December, at nine in the morning, Demetrius had left his home with a suitcase in his hand. His servant had seen him go out, but didn't know where he was going. When his master hadn't returned by evening, he had informed the police. Investigations had revealed that Demetrius had taken a taxi to the airport and caught a plane at ten-thirty in the morning. The plane was bound for Cairo. In Cairo, Demetrius had checked into the Alhambra hotel and stayed there one night. After that the police had drawn a blank. Summerville, who had written from Iraklion, was a friend of Demetrius. He had gone to Athens to give a lecture, and had decided to go back by way of Crete. He heard of Demetrius's disappearance while still in Athens, had dropped everything and gone straight to Iraklion. Now he has decided to carry on his own investigation and wants me to help him. I have been to Greece twice before but not to Crete. The urge to go is strong.

8 JANUARY

I arrived in Iraklion this morning. The town is situated on the northern coast of the island. Demetrius's home is in the outskirts of the town at the foot of a hill, surrounded on three sides by an olive orchard. At the back of the house, beyond the orchard, is a forest of cypress and fir. On the whole a picturesque setting.

Summerville is worried, and there is plenty of cause for that. Firstly, there has been no further news from Cairo. Secondly, no reason has been found for Demetrius's sudden disappearance. Examination of the papers in his laboratory has given no indication of what he had been working on. A notebook has been found which, it appears, he had been using of late. It is filled with writing, but the strange script has baffled us completely. Some of the letters look English, but the whole thing makes no sense at all. I asked Summerville if there was any possibility of it being a code. Summerville replied, 'I shouldn't be surprised. He had a special interest in languages. Are you familiar with Linear A?'

I knew that Cretan stone inscriptions dating back to 2000 BC have been christened Linear A by archaeologists; Summerville said Demetrius had been studying this script for a long time. Perhaps the notebook contains important conclusions drawn from that study. Demetrius's servant Mikhaili says his master had been making frequent trips to ancient Cretan cities. He would stay a week or so in each place and come back with stone slabs bearing inscriptions. We have, of course, seen quite a few of these slabs strewn about the house.

Something else which Mikhaili said caused Summerville much concern. The day before Demetrius left, Mikhaili had heard a gunshot in the evening. It came from the direction of the forest behind the house. Demetrius was not at home then, but had returned a little later. Demetrius himself possessed a gun which hadn't been used for a long time. That gun was missing.

Mikhaili has a son about ten years old. I don't know if one can trust his words, but he says that a little before the gunshot, he had heard the roar of a tiger from the forest. Since the presence of tigers was impossible in Crete, I asked the boy how he could recognize the roar. He said he had once heard a tiger roaring in a circus which had come to Iraklion. There was no reason to doubt the truth of this.

We have decided to make a trip to the forest after lunch; it is important to find out what happened there.

9 JANUARY

I am writing this in the lounge of the Iraklion airport. They have announced that the Cairo flight will be delayed by two hours, so I am taking this opportunity to record yesterday's event.

Yesterday after lunch Summerville and I went out to explore the forest.

Although walking through the forest for twenty minutes revealed nothing suspicious, I detected a smell that raised my hopes. Summerville had a cold which had blocked his nostrils, but I could clearly make out the presence of a dead animal in the vicinity. I proceeded in the direction of the smell with Summerville following on my heels. Soon enough Summerville too became aware of the smell.

He asked in a whisper, 'Are you carrying a weapon?' I produced my Stun Gun from my pocket and showed it to him. It was obvious that Summerville was apprehensive of the presence of live animals as well as the dead one.

We advanced cautiously. It was Summerville who spotted the vultures first. In a clearing amidst the cypresses, a dozen or so of these ungainly birds were making a meal of a dead animal. We were still about thirty yards away, so we couldn't make out what the animal was except that it was black in colour. A few paces later, my eyes fell on a tuft of jet black fur lying on the grass beside a cluster of white wild flowers.

'Bear?' I asked tentatively.

'Most unlikely,' said Summerville. I too was aware that the presence of a bear in this region was an impossibility.

Meanwhile Summerville had picked up some of the fur.

As we advanced another ten yards or so, the head of the animal came into view. Although part of the head had been devoured by the vultures, it was clear that the animal belonged to the tiger species.

One of the vultures hopped aside with a flapping of wings at our approach, revealing the white of the exposed bones and the black of the pelt sticking to the angry red of the raw flesh. The vultures were having a great time. Have they ever tasted the flesh of a black panther in Crete? Although I am using the term panther, I know that no panther ever possessed such long and thick fur.

Summerville finally said, 'I suppose we'll have to call it a brand new species of tiger.'

'But was this the one killed with the gun?'

'So it would seem. But the question is whether it was Demetrius who used the gun.'

When we later described the beast to Mikhaili, he was quite surprised. 'A black beast looking like a tiger? The only black beasts I have seen around here are a cat and a dog.'

In the evening we found something very valuable in a drawer of Demetrius's desk: a brand new diary bound in leather containing two entries in Greek on December the twenty-seventh and the twenty-eighth, and in Demetrius's own hand. Between the two of us we soon translated it. Although brief, the comments were as mysterious as they were intriguing. The entry for December the twenty-seventh runs:

'I have always noticed that in my life happiness and sorrow go hand in hand. Which is why even success brings me no peace. I must never again undertake any experiment without first considering its possible consequences.'

The entry for December twenty-eight says:

'In a fair at Knossos ten years ago, a gypsy woman told me my fortune. She said that some danger might befall me on my sixty-fifth birthday, and that it might prove fatal. There are only sixteen days to my sixty-fifth birthday on the thirteenth of January. When the gypsy's other prophecies have come true, I can assume that this one too will. Perhaps the experiment I am about to undertake will be the cause of my death. If I achieve success before I die, I will have no regrets. But this small, crowded island is most unsuitable for what I am about to do. I need the vast open spaces. I need the—Sahara!'

There is a double underline below the word Sahara. This makes the reason for the trip to Cairo clear; but the nature of the experiment, and why a desert should be needed for it, are not clear. Perhaps our trip to Cairo will shed some light.

9 JANUARY, 5 P.M.

Cairo. We are staying in the same hotel as Demetrius—the Alhambra. I noticed Demetrius's name when I was writing my own in the register. Summerville did something very sleuth-like: he asked for us the same room—No. 313—in which Demetrius had stayed. Luckily the room was free. The possibility of the existence of any clues is remote, because in the last eleven days many guests have occupied the room, and it has been cleaned many times. But in the end it has turned out to be a very lucky decision. The room-boy who came and made our beds a little while ago provided us with some useful information. It was Summerville who questioned him.

'How long have you been working in this hotel?'

'Four years, sir.'

'Do you remember the guests who come here for short stays?'

'I certainly remember the ones who tip me well.'

I could see the boy had a sense of humour. Summerville said, 'A Greek gentleman came and stayed here for a night ten days ago. He was a man of about sixty-five, bald-headed, with thick black eyebrows and a high pointed nose. Can you recall him?'

Although I had never met Demetrius, a photo on the mantelpiece in his study had familiarized me with his features.

The boy grinned broadly. 'He tipped me seventy-five piastres; how can I forget him?'

Seventy-five piastres is almost fifteen rupees. No wonder the boy was happy.

'The gentleman was here for just one night, wasn't he?' asked Summerville.

'Yes, sir, and he had the *Do Not Disturb* sign hanging on his doorknob most of the time.'

'Did he say where he was going from here?'

'He asked me about camels. He said he wanted to go to the desert and asked me where he could hire camels. I said there was a caravan track from El Giza which runs a thousand miles into the desert. I said he could hire a camel in El Giza.'

That's all the information we could elicit from the room-boy. The news about Giza was most important. Cairo was on the eastern bank of the Nile, while at Giza, on the west, were the famous pyramids and the Sphinx.

We shall make a few more enquiries in Cairo, then proceed to Giza tomorrow morning.

10 JANUARY, 12.30 PM

We are with a caravan of about five hundred camels on our way to the Baharia oasis. The caravan consists almost entirely of traders. They are taking wool and other products from the city into the villages in the deep interior of the desert. They will exchange their wares mainly for dates. This has been going on for centuries.

We halted by an oasis about ten minutes ago, and will continue after a brief rest. This is a valley. An occasional limestone hill rears its head from an endless stretch of sand. There is a pool nearby surrounded by date palms and tents set up by the Bedouins.

Strewn about are ruined fragments of ancient Egyptian architecture. I am leaning against a headless pillar as I write.

We left the hotel at seven-thirty this morning after an early breakfast. It took us half an hour to reach Giza. We hired our camels in a marketplace, where we also got news of Demetrius from an old fruit seller. I know Arabic, which is why I was able to describe Demetrius to a shopkeeper and ask him if he had seen him. He pointed to the old fruit seller. 'Ask Mehmood, he might know.' As soon as we questioned the old man, he burst into an angry tirade against Demetrius. Apparently, Demetrius had bought dates from him and paid him in coins which contained two Greek leptas. Later he had looked for Demetrius and found that he was gone. Summerville was obliged to make good his loss by paying him in local currency. Well, it is clear that we have done the right thing by coming to Giza. Demetrius had obviously set off from here on a camel towards the desert. The question is whether he has gone all the way with the caravan or had veered off on his own.

I have taken with me enough of my nutriment pills to last us a fortnight. I hope our mission will be over by then, and that we will find Demetrius alive. The gypsy woman's prophecy keeps rankling in my mind. I have found such prophecies coming true at times, although I have never found a rational explanation for it. January the thirteenth is Demetrius's birthday; today is the tenth.

11 JANUARY, 6.30 P.M.

I don't know how far we have travelled in thirty-six hours. My guess is about a hundred miles. We have now halted for the day, and will resume our journey tomorrow morning. The travellers have pitched their tents and lit fires. The camels are all seated around making occasional gurgling noises. The cry of jackals can be heard; once I heard what sounded like a hyena's laughter. On the way we have seen wild hare and field rats darting out of the bushes. The only birds we have seen so far are hawks and kites.

We are now seated in our tent, lit by my Luminimax lamp; the fuel is a naphthalene-like ball which when set alight gives off the same amount of light as a two-hundred-watt bulb. One ball lasts the whole night.

Let me now describe what happened this afternoon.

It had been a bit stuffy during the day, although not too warm. Clouds had gathered in the west, and I thought it would rain. The two or three days' rain that takes place in this region every year usually does so in winter. But it didn't rain. Instead, a wind rose from the direction of the clouds. We were thankful for it, as it can be very hot in the desert in the daytime. But the wind brought with it a sound which greatly perplexed us. It went 'dub—thump . . . dub—thump . . . dub—thump . . .' as if a gigantic drum was being beaten, although to produce a sound so deep and low, the drum would have to be the size of a pyramid.

In a little while it was clear that the sound had produced a commotion among both men and beasts comprising the caravan. A dozen or so of the camels flopped down on the ground with the riders on their backs. As long as the wind held up the eerie sound continued 'dub—thump . . . dub—thump . . . dub—thump . . .' I worked out that there was a gap of two seconds between the 'dub' and the 'thump', and three seconds between the 'thump' and the next 'dub'. The rhythm and timing were maintained right through.

Both of us dismounted.

'What do you make of it?' I asked Summerville.

Summerville listened intently for a while. 'It seems to have a subterranean quality,' he said.

I too had the same feeling. The sound had strength and body, but lacked clarity. But there was no way of finding out the distance of the source.

Meanwhile, great agitation seemed to have spread among the Bedouins. An old wool merchant with a coppery skin and a heavily wrinkled face came up to me and started talking about demons and ogres. Not only that, he started a whispering campaign against us, accusing us of having brought them bad luck. If all the five hundred traders suddenly took it into their heads that we were responsible for those infernal drumbeats, there would be real trouble.

I could feel the wind dropping and the beats becoming fainter. I decided to cash in on it. I turned towards the wind, stretched my arms forward, and with various appropriate gestures started intoning Sanskrit verses. Around the middle of the fifth verse the wind stopped, and along with it the drumbeats too. We had no more trouble from our fellow travellers after this.

But there is no denying that the drumming has caused both of us great bewilderment. Not that this is likely to have any connection with Demetrius. Summerville thinks it could be large tribal tom-toms distorted and magnified by the vagaries of the desert atmosphere. Perhaps he is right. Whatever it was, I don't think we have to worry about it any more.

12 JANUARY, 10.30 A.M.

We were forced to break away from the caravan which proceeded south-west to Baharia while we went west. Let me explain.

This morning, after travelling from 6 a.m. for four and a half hours, we suddenly noticed, some two hundred yards to our right, a group of vultures gathered over a sand dune. I caught my breath. I didn't like the sight. I looked behind and found Summerville too surveying the same scene. Our caravan was by-passing it, but I felt a burning desire to find out what the birds were up to. I turned to our camel drivers and said, 'We should like to go and take a look at those vultures. We'll rejoin the caravan afterwards.'

The men readily agreed, doubtless because they too were impressed with my performance yesterday and had taken me for a prophet.

We left the caravan and headed towards the vultures. It took five minutes for our curiosity to be satisfied. The vultures were making a meal of a dead camel.

No, not just a camel. There was another carcass lying alongside, and this was human. Like the two men with us, this too was a camel driver. Man and beast had strayed from a caravan and met their end. But was it a natural death, or was somebody else responsible for it?

What was that lying on the sand a couple of yards away? I dismounted and walked over to investigate. What was shining in the midday sun was the barrel of a rifle, the rest of it being buried in the sand.

I picked up the weapon. It was a Mauser. There was no doubt that bullets from it had killed these two creatures, and there was every reason to believe that the man who had done the killing was none other than Professor Hektor Demetrius. I was also sure that the same gun had been used by the same man to kill the unnamed black beast in the forest in Iraklion.

So this was the camel that Demetrius hired. At this point, he had no more use for his mount; so he had killed it as well as its owner. Wherever Demetrius had gone from here, he must have gone on foot.

We now looked at the two Arabs. Their faces had turned white. This was not only because of the scene of carnage, but because gusts of wind had started blowing from the west again, bringing with them the eerie sound—'dub—thump . . . dub—thump . . . dub—thump . . .'

We realized we should have to mount our camels again and follow the sound to its source. Both of us now believed that it must have some connection with Demetrius.

The camel men agreed after some persuasion backed by baksheesh.

For three hours we travelled while the sound grew louder and louder, until a strange sight obliged us to stop and dismount.

In the middle of the desert stood a huge sand-covered mound shaped somewhat like a pyramid. If it was a relic of ancient Egypt, neither of us had ever seen it mentioned in any book.

We have pitched our tent at a considerable distance from the mound. We shall get a proper idea of its dimensions when we go closer to it. We have asked the camel drivers about it, but they seem to have been struck dumb; perhaps the insistent drumming has made them speechless. From here the deep pounding can be heard all the time, even when there is no wind blowing. It is as if the sound was part of the ambience of the place. We have been here an hour; not once has the pounding stopped or its rhythm changed.

Summerville's guess is that the mound is an ancient monument. We have decided to take a little rest and then go up to it to take a close look. Summerville seems just as puzzled as I am about the pounding, but he was right about one thing: the source of the sound is subterranean. It was proved when we placed our ears on the sand. This incessant pounding may disturb our concentration. We can only wait and see what happens.

Clouds have gathered in the west again, and a wind is raising the sand.

12 JANUARY, 4 P.M.

A terrible sandstorm nearly blew away our tents. On top of that there was an earthquake.

I noticed something strange about the tremor: it was not sideways like an ordinary earthquake. At the first impact, it felt as if the ground had suddenly subsided. It was like pulling a chair from under someone. I know that some earthquakes are accompanied by a rumbling sound; I myself heard it in the Bihar earthquake of 1934. But I doubt if anything like the sound which accompanied the earthquake today had ever been heard before. It was as if the whole earth was groaning in unbearable agony. Even I found myself breaking out in a cold sweat. Murad and Suleiman, our two camel men, both fainted from sheer fright. They were revived with medication, but I doubt if they'll ever be able to speak again. The two camels seem petrified with their looks fixed towards the mysterious edifice. I feel quite confused. The only constant thing in all this is the great, pounding drumbeats.

We shall wait for some time. If no other calamity takes place we shall go out. We must get close to the mound to investigate.

5.15 P.M.

I am writing this sitting by the sand hill, which now seems twice as high as it did from the camp. Its highest point is certainly higher than the highest pyramid at Giza. The drumbeat here is deafening. We have to use a sign language to communicate with each other. But the strange thing is that one begins to get used to a sound of even such deafening intensity. It doesn't bother me anymore nor does it interfere with my thoughts.

First let me try to explain what the hill looks like. Here is a diagram of it—

ABC, the northern face, is vertical, and roughly the shape of an equilateral triangle. ABD and ACD are respectively the eastern and western faces, while BCD is the base—in the shape of an isosceles triangle—on which the structure stands. We both believe that removing the sand would reveal a solid structure, probably of sandstone, representing an ancient Egyptian monument as yet unknown to the civilized world.

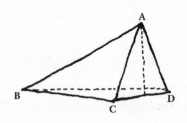

On the way to the mound we discovered two highly interesting and mysterious objects. Summerville is now busy with one of them. What we first came across looked like a length of very stout brown cable sticking out of the sand. We had never seen anything like it before, and it was impossible to guess what it was made of. Both of us pulled hard at it, but it stuck, fast. In the end Summerville sliced off a portion of the cable with his knife with a view to testing it.

What baffled us even more was something which looked like the segment of a disc-like object, pink in colour, and with furrows on its curved surface. This too proved impossible to dislodge. My guess is that, had the whole surface been revealed, it would have proved large enough to hold a tennis court.

Both the objects were so out of place in the desert and so unlikely in their connection with ancient Egypt, that it has set a new problem for us.

I wonder if the two objects, the colossal mound, and the pounding drumbeats, have an extra-terrestrial origin! They all seem to be on a superhuman scale. Perhaps the pounding emanates from an underground factory or laboratory where Demetrius is

working under the guidance of an alien intelligence!

Summerville is making for the vertical northern face of the mound. I must go with him. If something should happen to one of us, the other would feel very helpless indeed.

11.20 P.M.

A great many strange happenings in the last five hours.

First of all, let me say that by digging with our hands we have been able to locate a tunnel on the vertical northern face of the mound. The inside of it is pitch dark. We flashed a powerful torch into it and looked through binoculars. There was nothing to see. Great gusts of wind blew out of the tunnel every so often and it made our work very difficult, but we persisted. We gave up only after it became too dark to work, and came back to our tent. Tomorrow, if we find that the layer of sand has thinned down a bit, we shall make an attempt to enter the tunnel. I strongly believe that the answer to the mystery lies in the depths of that darkness.

Back at camp, we made ourselves some coffee. My pills take care of both our thirst and hunger, but don't provide the satisfaction of a cup of hot coffee at the end of a day's work. Summerville has brought some excellent Brazilian coffee, which is what we drank. But let me now describe what happened after coffee.

Summerville was sitting with Demetrius's notebook open before him. Half an hour's effort to decipher the script had failed. I too sat beside him recalling the strange events of the past few days, when my eyes fell on the notebook. Summerville's spectacles were resting on it on their rims. I noticed that Demetrius's writing was reflected in the glasses as in a mirror. The very next moment, I saw that I could read the writing and that it was a language we both knew. It was not Greek, but the all-too-familiar English! Demetrius had guarded himself against others having access to his notes by using mirror writing. I recalled that Da Vinci also wrote his notes in this fashion. In the last couple of hours, we have been able to read most of Demetrius's notes with the help of Summerville's shaving mirror. Here is what the notes have revealed—

In Knossos, in the ruins of a 5,000-year-old temple, Demetrius had found a stone inscription. On deciphering it, he had found that it was the formula for a miraculous drug which was supposed to induce a god's power into a human being. Demetrius had proceeded to prepare the drug, and the note suggests that he had succeeded in doing so. Not only that; on the twenty-sixth of December he had tried out the drug on someone called Felix. Demetrius does not say who this Felix was, but both Summerville and I know that although some people are called Felix, it can also be the name for a cat, *felis* being the Latin term for the genus cat. Does that name—no, it is not possible to continue writing. A storm seems to be building up.

16 JANUARY

It is about two hours since we arrived in Cairo. My hands are not steady, yet I must write down the terrible events of the last two days. We have lost a whole day waiting for a caravan. Our own camels, along with their owners, are missing, probably dead. We had to trek three and a half hours across the desert in our pitiful state to reach the caravan track. My Miracurol has worked wonders to the extent of mending Summerville's broken elbow. But the state of our minds is far from normal. By great good fortune, my two phials of medicine, my diary, fountain pen, wallet, duplicate spectacles and my pistol were all in the pockets of my jacket. Everything else, including Demetrius's notebook, has been blown away without a trace.

I have already recorded how on January the twelfth a storm interrupted my writing. As a matter of fact, it was a combination of rain and storm, the like of which I have never experienced in all my life. The first thing to go was the Luminimax lamp. The camels had started to scream at the top of their voices, and I peeped out of the tent and saw in three successive flashes of lightning, Murad and Suleiman lying prostrate on the sand desperately invoking the name of Allah.

About a quarter to midnight—the radium dial on my watch could at least tell me the time—the storm seemed to subside a little. Our tents had, of course, collapsed long ago, and were now wrapped around us. We clung on to them in the hope that we would be able to set them up again when the weather cleared.

Precisely at midnight, after an ear-splitting thunderclap, the convulsions of a terrible earthquake started. With the very first shock, I found that I was no longer on the ground but had been hoisted skyward like a cricket ball from a mighty drive. I sailed for a full five seconds through the air before landing on wet sand as cold as a slab of ice. I had nothing over my head now, nor was Summerville by my side. Where Summerville was, whether he was still alive, where the camels and the camelmen were, whether they were alive—there was no way of knowing.

And now there was a sudden jolt, and the earth was still.

The rain too had stopped, and there was silence.

No sound at all! Not even the drumbeats!

No, not even those. Incredibly enough, the pounding had stopped.

Instead of that there was an almost palpable silence.

I raised my head and looked around. It wasn't dark any more. How could there be so much light? How was it that I could see everything clearly?

Now I realized that the sky was clear but for a wisp of cloud which was slowly revealing the moon—the full moon.

And now the moon was out. Never had I seen such resplendent moonlight.

Who was that to my left—about a couple of yards away? Wasn't it Summerville?

Yes, Summerville. He was standing. I shouted, 'John! John!'

No answer. Had he turned deaf? Or mad? What was he staring at so intently?

I too turned my eyes in the same direction, towards the mound.

The mound was clear of sand now. But what was it that was revealed in its nakedness?

I staggered towards Summerville. I could not take my eyes off the mound. The incredibility of it all took my breath away. I could see that the enormous thing that raised itself towards the sky was something well known to me. And the two enormous cavities on the vertical northern face, those which we thought were tunnels into a subterranean factory, they were known to me too. The cavities were nostrils, and the mound was the nose of a man lying on the ground, and the two dense semi-circles of dark foliage were the two eyebrows on the two sides of the nose bridge, and the huge convexities below them were the two closed eyelids.

'Demetrius!'

Summerville's whispered utterance seemed to echo in the stillness of the vast moonlit expanse of the Sahara.

'Demetrius! Demetrius!'

Yes, Demetrius. I know that now from his photo. Those eyes I have seen open; now they were closed in death. Now I know that the brown cable was a hair of his body, and the pink segment of a disc was one of his fingernails.

'Do you realize the reason for the earthquake?' asked Summerville.

I said, 'Yes. They were caused by Demetrius in the throes of death.'

'And the pounding drumbeats?'

'Demetrius's heartbeat, of course . . . He had first tried out his drug on his black cat Felix. The cat grew to an enormous size, forcing Demetrius to use the gun.'

'But he didn't wish to stop his own growth. Like a true scientist, he wanted to find out the limit of the drug's power.'

'Yes. He believed he would grow into a Colossus. So he wanted the limitless expanse of the Sahara for his experiment.'

'Have you tried to work out how big he had grown?'

I said, 'If the vertical wall with the nostrils is a hundred feet high, then the whole body should be at least sixty times more.'

'That is more than a mile.'

Summerville sighed.

'So the old gypsy woman wasn't wrong,' he said.

'In fact, she was dead right. Today is the thirteenth. The pounding stopped exactly at midnight.'

We had to wait for the day.

As soon as it turned light, I saw a horrible sight. The sky was filled with hundreds of vultures circling slowly down. It was as if all the vultures in the world had joined forces to devour the six-thousand-foot-long carcass.

I took out my pulverising pistol from my pocket, aimed it at the swarm and pressed the trigger.

In a few seconds the swarm disappeared and the spotless, rain-washed blue sky of the Sahara smiled down at us.

Originally published in *Anandamela* (Puja Annual 1972). Translated by the author himself to be part of the compilation titled *Stories* (Secker & Warburg, 1987). The illustrations in the story, including the Bengali calligraphy in the headpiece, are by Satyajit Ray.

15 AUGUST

Birds have fascinated me for a long time. When I was a boy, we had a pet mynah which we taught to pronounce clearly more than a hundred Bengali words. I knew, of course, that although some birds could talk, they didn't understand the meaning of what they said. But one day our mynah did something so extraordinary that I was forced to revise my opinion. I had just got back from school, Mother had brought me a plate of halwa, when the mynah suddenly screeched, 'Earthquake! Earthquake!' We had felt nothing but next day the papers reported that a slight tremor had indeed been recorded by the seismograph.

Ever since then I have felt a curiosity about the intelligence of birds, although in my preoccupation with various scientific projects, I have not been able to pursue it in any way. My cat, Newton, contributed to this neglect. Newton doesn't like birds, and I don't wish to do anything that would displease him. Lately, however—perhaps because of age—Newton has grown increasingly indifferent to birds. Which is probably why my laboratory is being regularly visited by crows, sparrows and *shaliks*. I feed them in the morning, and in anticipation of this they begin to clamour outside my window from well before sunrise.

Every creature is born with skills peculiar to its species. I believe such skills are more pronounced and more startling in birds than in other creatures. Examine a weaver bird's nest, and it will make you gasp with astonishment. Given the ingredients to construct such a nest, a man would either throw up his hands in despair or take months of ceaseless effort to do so.

There is a species of birds in Australia called the malleefowl which builds its nest on the ground. Sand, earth and vegetable matter go into the making of this hollow mound which is provided with a hole for entry. The bird lays its eggs inside the mound but doesn't sit on them to hatch. Yet without heat the eggs won't hatch, so what is the answer? Simply this: by some amazing and as yet unknown process, the malleefowl maintains a constant temperature of 78° Fahrenheit inside the mound regardless of whether it is hot or cold outside.

Nobody knows why a bird called the Grebe should pluck out its feathers to eat them and feed their young with them. The same Grebe while floating in water can, by some unknown means, reduce its own specific gravity at the sight of a predator so that it floats with only its head above the water.

We all know of the amazing sense of direction of the migratory birds, the hunting prowess of eagles and falcons, the vultures' keen sense of smell, and the enchanting gift of singing possessed by numerous birds. It is for this reason that I have been wanting for some time to devote a little more time to the study of birds. How much can a bird be taught beyond its innate skills? Is it possible to instil human knowledge and intelligence in one? Can a machine be constructed to do this?

20 SEPTEMBER

I believe in the simple method, so my machine will be a simple one. It will consist of two sections: one will be a cage to house the bird; the other will transmit intelligence to the bird's brain by means of electrodes.

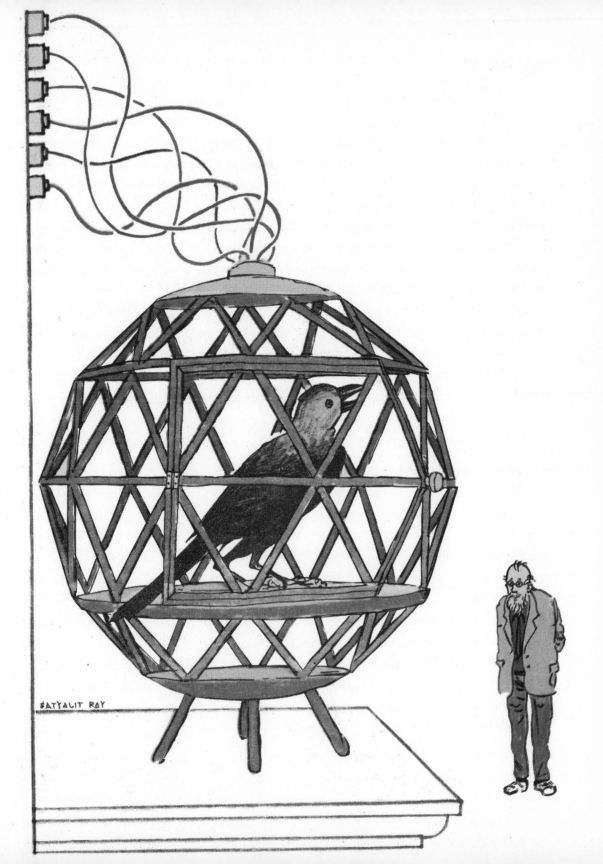

For the past month I have been carefully studying the birds which come into my laboratory for food. Apart from the ubiquitous crows and sparrows and shaliks, birds such as pigeons, doves, parakeets, and bulbuls also come. Amongst all these, one particular bird has caught my attention, a crow. Not the jet black raven, but the ordinary crow. I can easily make him out from the other crows. Apart from the tiny white spot below the right eye which makes him easily recognizable, his behaviour, too, marks him out from other crows. For instance, I have never seen a crow hold a pencil in its beak and make marks on the table with it. Yesterday he did something which really shook me. I was working on my machine when I heard a soft rasping noise. I turned round and saw that the crow had taken a matchstick from a half-open matchbox and, holding it in his beak, was scraping it against the side of the box. When I shooed him away, he flew across, sat on the window and proceeded to utter some staccato sounds which bore no resemblance to the normal cawing of a crow. In fact, for a minute I thought the crow was laughing!

27 SEPTEMBER

I finished assembling my Ornithon machine today. The crow has been in the lab since morning, eating breadcrumbs and hopping from window to window. As soon as I placed the cage on the table and opened the door, the crow flew over and hopped inside, a sure sign that he is extremely eager to learn. Since a familiarity with language is essential for the bird to follow my instructions, I have started with simple Bengali lessons. All the lessons being pre-recorded, all I have to do is press buttons. Different lessons are in different channels, and each channel bears a different number. I have noticed a strange thing; as soon as I press a button the crow's eyes close and his movements cease. For a bird as restless as a crow this is unusual indeed.

A conference of ornithologists is being held in November in Santiago, the capital of Chile. I have written to my ornithologist friend Rufus Grenfell in Minnesota. If my feathered friend is able to acquire some human intelligence, I should like to take him to the conference for a lecture-demonstration.

4 OCTOBER

Corvus is the Latin name for the genus crow. I have started calling my pupil by that name. In the beginning he used to answer my call by a turn of the head in my direction. Now he responds vocally. For the first time I heard a crow saying 'ki' (what?) instead of 'caw'. But I don't expect speech will ever be his forte. Corvus will never turn into a talking crow. Whatever intelligence he acquires will show in his actions.

Corvus is learning English now; if I do go abroad for a demonstration, English would help. Lessons last an hour between eight and nine in the morning. The rest of the day he hangs around the lab. In the evening he still prefers to go back to the mango tree in the north-east corner of my garden.

Newton seems to have accepted Corvus. After what happened today, I shouldn't be surprised if they end up friends. It happened in the afternoon. Corvus for once was away somewhere. I sat in the armchair scribbling in my notebook, and Newton was curled up on the floor alongside when a flapping sound made me turn towards the window. It was Corvus. He had just come in with a freshly cut piece of fish in his beak. He dropped it in front of Newton, went back to the window, and sat surveying the scene with little twists of his neck.

Grenfell has replied to my letter. He says he is arranging to have me invited to the ornithologists' conference.

20 OCTOBER

Unexpected progress in the last two weeks. With a pencil held in his beak, Corvus is now writing English words and numerals. The paper is placed on the table, and Corvus writes standing on it. He wrote his own name in capital letters: C-O-R-V-U-S. He can do simple addition and subtraction, write down the capital of England when asked to, and can even write my name. Three days ago I taught him the months, days, and dates; when asked what day of the week it was today, he wrote in clear letters: F-R-I-D-A-Y.

That Corvus is clever in his eating habits too was proved today. I had kept some pieces of toast on one plate and some guava jelly on another in front of him; each time he put a piece in his mouth, he smeared some jelly on it first with his beak.

22 OCTOBER

I had clear proof today that Corvus now wants to stay away from other crows. There was a heavy shower and after an ear-splitting thunderclap I looked out of the window and saw the simul tree outside my garden smouldering. In the afternoon, after the rain stopped, there was a tremendous hue and cry set up by the neighbourhood crows who had all gathered around the simul tree. I sent my servant Prahlad to investigate. He came back and said, 'Sir, there's a dead crow lying at the foot of the tree; that's why there is such excitement.' I realized the crow had been struck by lightning. But strangely enough, Corvus didn't leave my room at all. He held a pencil in his beak and was absorbed in writing the prime numbers: 1 2 3 5 7 11 13 . . .

7 NOVEMBER

Corvus can now be proudly displayed in scientific circles. Birds can be taught to do small things, but a bird as intelligent and educated as Corvus is unique in history. The Ornithon has done its job well. Questions which can be answered in a few words, or with the help of numbers, on subjects as diverse as mathematics, history, geography and the natural sciences, Corvus is now able to answer. Along with that Corvus has spontaneously acquired what can only be termed human intelligence, something which has never been associated with birds. I shall give an example. I was packing my suitcase this morning in preparation for my trip to Santiago. As I finished and closed the lid, I found Corvus standing by with the key in his beak.

Another letter from Grenfell yesterday. He is already in Santiago. The organizers of the conference are looking forward to my visit. Till now these conferences have only dealt with birds in the abstract; never has a live bird been used as an illustration. The paper I have written is based on the priceless knowledge I have gathered in the last two months about bird behaviour. Corvus will be there in person to silence my critics.

10 NOVEMBER

I'm writing this on the plane to South America. I have only one incident to relate. As we were about to leave the house, I found Corvus greatly agitated and obviously anxious to get out of the cage. I couldn't make out the reason for this; nevertheless, I opened the cage door. Corvus hopped out, flew over to my desk and started pecking furiously at the drawer. I opened it and found my passport still lying in it.

I have had a new kind of cage built for Corvus. It maintains the temperature that best suits the bird. For his food, I have prepared tiny globules which are both tasty and nutritious. Corvus has aroused everyone's curiosity on the plane as they have probably never seen a pet crow before. I haven't told anyone about the uniqueness of my pet—I prefer to keep it secret. Corvus too, probably sensing this, is behaving like any ordinary crow.

14 NOVEMBER

Hotel Excelsior, Santiago, 11 p.m. I have been too busy these last couple of days to write. Let me first describe what happened at the lecture, then I shall come to the disconcerting events of a little while ago. To cut a long story short, my lecture has been another feather in my cap. My paper took half an hour to read; then followed an hour's demonstration with the crow. I had released Corvus from the cage and put him down on the table as soon as I ascended the podium. It was a long mahogany table behind which sat the organizers of the conference, while I stood to one side speaking into the microphone. As long as I spoke, Corvus listened with the utmost attention, with occasional nods to suggest that he was getting the drift of my talk. To the applause that followed my speech, Corvus made his own contribution by beating a tattoo with his beak on the surface of the table.

The demonstration that followed gave Corvus no respite. All that he had learnt in the past two months he now demonstrated to the utter amazement of the delegates who all agreed that they had never imagined a bird could be capable of such intelligent behaviour. The evening edition of the local newspaper Correro de Santiago splashed the news on the front page with a picture of Corvus holding a pencil in his beak.

After the meeting, Grenfell and I went on a sightseeing tour of Santiago with the chairman Signor Covarrubias. It is a bustling, elegant metropolis to the east of which the Andes range stands like a wall between Chile and Argentina. After an hour's drive Covarrubias turned to me and said, 'You must have noticed in our programme that we have made various arrangements for the entertainment of our delegates. I should particularly like to recommend the show this evening by the Chilean magician Argus. His speciality is that he uses a lot of trained birds in his repertory.'

I was intrigued, so Grenfell and I have been to the Plaza theatre to watch Senor Argus. It is true that he uses a lot of birds. Ducks, parrots, pigeons, hens, a four-foot-high crane, a flock of humming birds—all these Argus deploys with much evidence of careful training. But none of these birds comes anywhere near Corvus. Frankly, I found the magician himself far more interesting than his birds. Over six feet tall, he has a parrot-like nose, and his hair, parted in the middle, is slick and shiny as a new gramophone record. He wears spectacles so high-powered that they turn his pupils into a pair of tiny black dots, and out of the sleeves of his jet-black coat emerges a pair of hands whose pale, tapering fingers cast a spell on the audience with their sinuous movements. Not that the conjuring was of a high order, but the conjuror's presence and personality were well worth the price of admission. As I came out of the theatre, I remarked to Grenfell that it wouldn't be a bad idea to show Senor Argus some of Corvus's tricks now that he had shown us his.

Dinner was followed by excellent Chilean coffee and a stroll in the hotel garden with Grenfell. It was past ten when I returned to my room. I changed into my nightclothes, put out the lamp and was about to turn in when the phone rang.

'Senor Shonku?'

'Yes—'

'I'm calling from the reception. Sorry to trouble you at this hour, sir, but there's a gentleman here who is most anxious to see you.'

I said I was too tired to see anybody, and that it would be better if the gentleman could make an appointment over the phone next morning. I was sure it was a reporter. I had already been interviewed by four of them. Some of the questions they asked tried the patience of even a placid person like me. For instance, one of them asked if crows too, like cows, were held sacred in India!

The receptionist spoke to the caller and came back to me.

'Senor Shonku, the gentleman says he wants only five minutes of your time. He has another engagement tomorrow morning.'

'This person—is he a reporter?' I asked.

'No, sir. He is the famous Chilean magician Argus.'

When I heard the name, I was left with no choice but to ask him to come up. I turned on the bedside lamp. Three minutes later the buzzer sounded.

The man who confronted me when I opened the door had seemed like a six-footer on stage, now he looked a good six inches taller. In fact, I had never seen anyone so tall before. Even when he bowed he remained a foot taller than me.

I asked him in. He had discarded his stage costume and was now dressed in an ordinary suit, but this one too was black. When he entered, I saw the evening edition of the Correro sticking out of his pocket. We took our seats after I had congratulated him on his performance. 'As far as I can recall,' I said, 'there was a gifted person in Greek mythology who had eyes all over his body and who was called Argus. An apt name for a magician, I think.'

Argus smiled, 'Then I'm sure you also remember that this person had some connection with birds.'

I nodded, 'The Greek goddess Hera had plucked out Argus's eyes and planted them on the peacock's tail—which is supposed to account for the circular markings on the tail. But what I'm curious about are your eyes. What is the power of your glasses?'

'Minus twenty,' he replied. 'But that doesn't bother me. None of my birds are short-sighted.'

Argus laughed loudly at his own joke, then suddenly froze open-mouthed. His eyes had strayed to the plastic cage kept on a shelf in a corner of the room. Corvus was asleep when I came in, but was now wide awake and staring fixedly at the magician.

Argus, his mouth still open, let his chair and tiptoed towards the cage. He stared at the crow for a full minute. Then he said, 'Ever since I read about him in the evening papers, I've been anxious to meet you. I haven't had the privilege of hearing you speak.

I'm not an ornithologist, you know, but I too train birds.'

The magician looked worried as he returned to his seat. 'I can well appreciate how tired you must be,' he said, 'but if you could just let your bird out of the cage . . . just one sample of his intelligence . . .'

I said, 'It's not just I who is tired; Corvus is too. I shall open the cage door for you, but the rest is up to the bird. I can't force him to do anything against his wish.'

'All right, fair enough.'

I opened the cage door. Corvus came out, flapped up to the bedside table, and with an unerring peck of his beak, switched off the lamp.

The room was plunged into darkness. Intermittent flashes of pale green light from the neon sign of the Hotel Metropole across the street glared through the open window. I sat silent. Corvus flew back to his cage and pulled the door shut with his beak.

The green light played rhythmically across Argus's face making his snake-like eyes look even more reptilian through the thick lenses of his gold-rimmed spectacles. I could see that he was struck dumb with amazement, and that he could read the meaning behind Corvus's action. Corvus wanted to rest. He didn't want light in the room. He wanted darkness; he wanted to sleep.

From under his thin moustache a soft whisper escaped his lips—'Magnifico!' He had brought his hands below his chin with his palms pressed together in a gesture of frozen applause.

Now I noticed his nails. They were unusually long and shiny. He had used nail polish—silver nail polish—the kind that would under glaring stage lights heighten the play of his fingers. The green light was now reflected again and again on those silver nails.

'I want that crow!'

Argus spoke in English in a hoarse whisper. All this time he had been speaking in Spanish. Although, as I write this down, I realize that it probably sounds like unashamed greed, but in fact Argus was pleading with me.

'I want that crow!' Argus repeated.

I regarded him in silence. There was no need to say anything just now. I waited instead to hear what else he had to say.

Argus had been looking out of the window. Now he turned to me. I was fascinated by the alternation of darkness and light on his face. Now he was there, now he wasn't. Like magic again.

Argus moved his fingers and pointed them at himself.

'Look at me, Professor. I am Argus. I am the world's greatest magician. In every city of North and South America, anyone who knows about magic knows me. Men, women and children—they all know me. Next month I go on a world tour. Rome, Madrid, Paris, London, Athens, Stockholm, Tokyo . . . Every city will acclaim my genius. But do you know what can make my wonderful magic a thousand times more wonderful? It is that crow—that Indian crow. I want that bird, Professor, I want that bird! I do . . .'

As Argus spoke, he waved his hands before my eyes like snakes swaying to a charmer's flute, his silver nails catching the green light from the neon flashing on and off. I couldn't help being amused. If it had been anyone else in my place, Argus would have accomplished his object and got his hands on the bird. I now had to tell Argus that his plan wouldn't work with me.

I said, 'Mr Argus, you're wasting your time. It is useless to try to hypnotize me. I cannot accede to your request. Corvus is not only my pupil, he is like a son to me, and a friend—a product of my tireless effort and experiment.'

'Professor!'—Argus's voice was much sharper now, but he softened it the very next moment and said, 'Professor, do you realize that I am a millionaire? Do you know that I own a fifty-room mansion in the eastern end of this city? That I have twenty-six servants and four Cadillacs? Nothing is too expensive for me, Professor. For that bird I am willing to pay you ten thousand escudos right now.'

Ten thousand escudos meant about fifteen thousand rupees. Argus did not know that just as expenses meant nothing to him, money itself meant nothing to me. I told him so. Argus made one last attempt.

'You're an Indian. Don't you believe in mystic connections? Argus—Corvus . . . how well the two names go together! Don't you realize that the crow was fated to belong to me?'

I couldn't bear with him anymore. I stood up and said, 'Mr Argus, you can keep your cars, houses, wealth and fame to yourself. Corvus is staying with me. His training is not over yet, I still have work left to do. I am extremely tired today. You had asked for five minutes of my time, and I have given you twenty. I can't give you any more. I want to sleep now and so does my bird. Therefore, good night.'

I must say I felt faint stirrings of pity at the abject look on his face; but I didn't let them surface. Argus bowed once again in continental style and, muttering good-night in Spanish, left the room.

I closed the door and went to the cage to find Corvus still awake. Looking at me, he uttered the single syllable 'kay' (who?) in a tone which clearly suggested a question.

'A mad magician,' I told him, 'with more money than is good for him. He wanted to buy you off, but I turned him down. So you may sleep in peace.'

16 NOVEMBER

I wanted to record the events of yesterday last night, but it took me the better part of the night to get over the shock.

The way in which the day began held no hint of impending danger. In the morning there was a session of the conference in which the only notable event was the stupendously boring extempore speech by the Japanese ornithologist Morimoto. After speaking for an hour or so, Morimoto suddenly lost the thread of his argument and started groping for words. It was at this point that Corvus, whom I had taken with me, decided to start an applause by rapping with his beak on the arm of my chair. This caused the entire audience to burst out laughing, thus putting me in an acutely embarrassing position.

In the afternoon there was lunch in the hotel with some delegates. Before going there, I went to my room, number seventy-one, put Corvus into the cage, gave him some food and said, 'You stay here. I'm going down to eat.'

The obedient Corvus didn't demur.

By the time I finished lunch and came up, it was two-thirty. As I inserted the key into the lock, a cold fear gripped me. The door was already open. I burst into the room and found my worst fears confirmed: Corvus and his cage were gone.

I was back in the corridor in a flash. Two suites down was the room-boys' enclosure. I rushed in there and found the two of them standing mutely with glazed looks in their eyes. It was clear that they had both been hypnotized.

I now ran to one-hundred-and-seven—Grenfell's room. I told him everything and we went down to the reception together. 'No one had asked us for your room keys, sir,' said the clerk. 'The room-boys have the duplicate keys. They might have given them to someone.'

The room-boys didn't have to give the keys to anyone. Argus had cast his spell over them and helped himself to the keys.

In the end we got the real story from the concierge. He said Argus had arrived half an hour earlier in a silver Cadillac and gone into the hotel. Ten minutes later he had come out carrying a cellophane bag, got into his car and driven off.

A silver Cadillac. But where had Argus gone from here? Home? Or somewhere else?

We were now obliged to turn to Covarrubias for help. He said, 'I can find out for you in a minute where Argus lives; but how will that help? He is hardly likely to have gone home. He must have gone into hiding somewhere with your crow. But if he wants to leave the city, there's only one road leading out. I can fix up a good car and driver and police personnel to go with you. But time is short. You must be out in half an hour and take the highway. If you're lucky, you may still find him.'

We were off by 3.15 p.m. Before leaving I made a phone call from the hotel and found out that Argus had not returned home. We went in a police car with two armed policemen. One of them, a young fellow named Carreras, turned out to be quite well-informed about Argus. He said Argus had several hideouts in and around Santiago; that he had at one time hobnobbed with gypsies; and that he had been giving magic shows from the age of nineteen. About four years ago he had decided to include birds in his repertory, and this had given his popularity a great boost.

I asked Carreras if Argus was really a millionaire.

'So it would seem,' Carreras replied. 'But the man's a tightwad, and trusts nobody. That's why he has few friends left.'

As we left the city and hit the highway we ran into a small problem. The highway branched into two — one led north to Los Andes, and the other west to the port of Valparaiso. There was a petrol station near the mouth of the fork. We asked one of the attendants there and he said, 'A silver Cadillac? Senor Argus's Cadillac? Sure, I saw it take the road to Valparaiso a little while ago.'

We shot off in pursuit. I knew Corvus would not come to any harm, as Argus needed him badly. But Corvus's behaviour last night had clearly indicated that he hadn't liked the magician at all. So it pained me to think how unhappy he must be in the clutches of his captor.

We came across two more petrol stations on the way, and both confirmed that they had seen Argus's Cadillac pass that way earlier.

I am an optimist. I have emerged unscathed from many a tight corner in the past. To this day none of my ventures has ever been a failure. But Grenfell, sitting by my side, kept shaking his head and saying, 'Don't forget, Shonku, that you're up against a fiendishly clever man. Now that he's got his hands on Corvus, it's not going to be easy for you to get your bird back.'

'And Senor Argus may be armed,' added Carreras. 'I've known him use real revolvers in his acts.'

The highway sloped downwards. From Santiago's elevation of sixteen hundred feet we were now down to a thousand. Behind us the mountain range was becoming progressively hazier. We had already done forty miles; another forty and we would be in Valparaiso. Grenfell's glum countenance was already beginning to make a dent in my armour of optimism. If we did not find Argus on the highway, we would have to look for him in the city, and it would then be a hundred times more difficult to track him down.

The road now rose sharply. Nothing could be seen beyond the hump. We sped along, topped the rise, and saw the road ahead dipped gently down as far as the eye could see. A few trees dotted its sides; a village could be made out in the distance; buffaloes grazed in a field. Not a human being in sight anywhere. But what was that up ahead? It was still quite far away, whatever it was. At least a quarter of a mile.

Not more than four hundred yards away now. A car, gleaming in the sunlight, parked at an angle by the roadside. We drew nearer. A Cadillac! A silver Cadillac!

Our Mercedes drew up alongside. Now we could see what had happened: the car had swerved and dashed against a tree. Its front was all smashed up.

'It is Senor Argus's car,' said Carreras. 'There is only one other silver Cadillac in Santiago. It belongs to the banker, Senor Galdames. I can recognize this one by its number.' The car was there; but where was Argus? What was that next to the driver's seat? I poked my head through the window. It was Corvus's cage. Its key was in my pocket. I hadn't locked it that afternoon—merely, put the door to. Corvus had obviously come out of the cage by himself. But after that?

Suddenly we heard someone scream in the distance. Carreras and the other policeman raised their weapons, but our driver turned out to be a milksop. He dropped on his knees and started to pray. Grenfell's face had fallen too. 'Magicians as a tribe make me most uncomfortable,' he groaned. I said, 'I think you'd better stay in the car.'

The screams came closer. They seemed to be coming from behind some bushes a little way ahead to the left of the road. It took me some time to recognize the voice, because last night it had been dropped to a hoarse whisper. It was the voice of Argus. He was pouring out a string of abuse in Spanish. I clearly heard 'devil' in Spanish a couple of times along with the name of my bird.

'Where is that devil of a bird? Corvus! Corvus! Damn that bird to hell! Damn him!'

Suddenly Argus stopped, for he had seen us. We could see him too. He stood with a revolver in each hand near some bushes some thirty yards away.

Carreras shouted, 'Lower your weapons, Senor Argus, or—' With an ear-splitting sound a bullet came crashing into the door of our Mercedes. This was followed by three more shots, the bullets whizzing over our heads. Carreras now raised his voice threateningly. 'Senor Argus, we are fully armed. We are the police. If you don't drop your guns, we'll be forced to hurt you.'

'Hurt me?' moaned Argus in a hoarse voice. 'You are the police? I can't see anything!'

Argus was now within ten yards of us. Now I realized his plight. He had lost his spectacles, and that is why he was shooting at random.

Argus now threw down his weapons and came stumbling forward. The policemen advanced towards him. I knew that none of Argus's tricks would work in this crisis. He was in a pitiful state. Carreras retrieved the revolvers from the ground, while Argus kept groaning, 'That bird is gone—that Indian crow! That devil of a bird! But how damnably clever!'

Grenfell had been trying to say something for some time. Now at last I could make out what he was saying. 'Shonku, that bird is here.'

What did he mean? I couldn't see Corvus anywhere. Grenfell pointed to the top of a bare acacia tree across the road.

I looked up—and sure enough—there he was: my friend, my pupil, my dear old Corvus, perched on the topmost branch of the tree and looking down at us calmly.

I beckoned, and he swooped gracefully down like a free-floating kite and alighted on the roof of the Mercedes. Then, carefully, as if he was fully aware of its worth, he placed before us the object he had been carrying in his beak: Argus's high-powered, gold-rimmed spectacles.

KHAGAM

Originally published in *Sandesh* (March-April 1973). It was translated by the author himself to be part of the compilation titled *Stories* (Secker & Warburg, 1987). The illustrations in the story, including the Bengali calligraphy in the headpiece, are by Satyajit Ray.

We were having dinner by the light of the petromax lamp. I had just helped myself to some curried egg when Lachhman, the cook and caretaker of the rest house, said, 'Aren't you going to pay a visit to Imli Baba?

I had to tell him that since we were not familiar with the name of Imli Baba, the question of paying him a visit hadn't arisen. Lachhman said the driver of the Forest Department jeep which had been engaged for our sightseeing would take us to the Baba if we told him. Baba's hut was in a forest and the surroundings were picturesque. As a holy man he was apparently held in very high regard; important people from all over

India came to him to pay their respects and seek his blessings. What really aroused my curiosity was the information that the Baba kept a king cobra as a pet which lived in a hole near his hut and came to him every evening to drink goat's milk.

Dhurjatibabu's comment on this was that the country was being overrun by fake holy men. The more scientific knowledge was spreading in the west, he said, the more our people were heading towards superstition. 'It's a hopeless situation, sir. It puts my back up just to think of it.'

As he finished talking, he picked up the fly swatter and brought it down with unerring aim on a mosquito which had settled on the dining table. Dhurjatibabu was a short, pale-looking man in his late forties, with sharp features and grey eyes. We had met in the rest house in Bharatpur; I came here by way of Agra before going to my elder brother in Jaipur to spend a fortnight's holiday with him. Both the Tourist Bungalow and the Circuit House being full, I had to fall back on the Forest Rest House. Not that I regretted it; living in the heart of the forest offers a special kind of thrill along with quiet comfort.

Dhurjatibabu had preceded me by a day. We had shared the Forest Department jeep for our sightseeing. Yesterday we had been to Deeg, twenty-two miles to the east from here, to see the fortress and the palace. The fortress in Bharatpur we saw this morning, and in the afternoon we saw the bird sanctuary at Keoladeo. This was something very special: a seven-mile stretch of marshland dotted with tiny islands where strange birds from far corners of the globe come and make their homes. I was absorbed in watching the birds, while Dhurjatibabu grumbled and made vain efforts to wave away the tiny insects buzzing around our heads. These *unki*s have a tendency to settle on your face, but they are so small that most people can ignore them. Not Dhurjatibabu.

Finishing dinner at half past eight, we sat on cane chairs on the terrace admiring the beauty of the forest in moonlight. 'That holy man the servant mentioned,' I remarked, 'what about going and taking a look at him?'

Flicking his cigarette towards a eucalyptus tree, Dhurjatibabu said, 'King cobras can never be tamed. I know a lot about snakes. I spent my boyhood in Jalpaiguri, and killed many snakes with my own hand. The king cobra is the deadliest, most vicious snake there is. So the story of the holy man feeding it goat's milk must be taken with a pinch of salt.'

I said, 'We see the fortress at Bayan tomorrow morning. In the afternoon we have nothing to do.'

'I take it you have a lot of faith in holy men?'

I could see the question was a barbed one. However, I answered in a straightforward way.

'The question of faith doesn't arise because I've never had anything to do with holy men. But I can't deny that I am a bit curious about this one.'

'I too was curious at one time, but after an experience I had with one . . .'

It turned out that Dhurjatibabu suffered from high blood pressure. An uncle of his had persuaded him to try a medicine prescribed by a holy man. Dhurjatibabu had done so, and as a result had suffered intense stomach pain. This had caused his blood pressure to shoot up even more. Ever since then he had looked upon ninety per cent of India's holy men as fakes.

I found this allergy quite amusing, and just to provoke him I said, 'You said it wasn't possible to tame king cobras; I'm sure ordinary people like us couldn't do it, but I've heard of sadhus up in the Himalayas living in caves with tigers.'

'You may have heard about it, but have you seen it with your own eyes?'

I had to admit that I hadn't.

'You never will,' said Dhurjatibabu. 'This is the land of tall stories. You'll hear of strange happenings all the time, but never see one yourself. Look at our Ramayana and Mahabharata. It is said they're history, but actually they're no more than a bundle of nonsense. The ten-headed Ravan, the Monkey-God Hanuman with a flame at the end of his tail setting fire to a whole city, Bhim's appetite, Ghatotkach, Hidimba, the flying chariot Pushpak, Kumbhakarna—can you imagine anything more absurd than these? And the epics are full of fake holy men. That's where it all started. Yet everyone—even the educated—swallows them whole.'

We lunched in the rest house after visiting the fortress at Bayan and, after a couple of hours' rest, reached the holy man's hermitage a little after four. Dhurjatibabu didn't object to the trip. Perhaps he too was a little curious about the Baba. The hermitage was in a clearing in the forest below a huge tamarind tree, which is why he was called Imli Baba by the local people, Imli being the Hindi word for tamarind. His real name was not known.

In a hut made of date palm leaves, the Baba sat on a bearskin with a lone disciple by his side. The latter was a young fellow, but it was impossible to guess the Baba's age. There was still an hour or so until sunset, but the dense covering of foliage made the place quite dark. A fire burnt before the Baba, who had a ganja pipe in his hand. We could see by the light of the fire a clothesline stretched across the wall of the hut from which hung a towel, a loin cloth, and about a dozen sloughed-off snake skins.

Dhurjatibabu whispered in my ear: 'Let's not beat about the bush; ask him about the snake's feeding time.'

'So you want to see Balkishen?' asked the Baba, reading our minds and smiling from behind his pipe. The driver of the jeep, Din Dayal, had told us a little while ago that the snake was called Balkishen. We told Baba that we had heard of his pet snake and we were most anxious to see it drink milk. Was there any likelihood of our wish being fulfilled?

Imli Baba shook his head sadly. He said, as a rule Balkishen came every day in the evening in answer to Baba's call, and had even come two days ago. But since the day before he had not been feeling well. 'Today is the day of the full moon,' said the Baba, 'so he will not come. But he will surely come again tomorrow evening.'

That snakes too could feel indisposed was news to me. And yet, why not? After all, it was a tame snake. Weren't there hospitals for dogs, horses and cows?

The Baba's disciple gave us another piece of news: red ants had got into the snake's hole while it lay ill, and had been pestering it. Baba had exterminated them all with a curse. Dhurjatibabu gave a sidelong glance at me at this point. I turned my eyes towards Baba. With his saffron robe, his long, matted hair, his iron earrings, *rudraksh* necklaces and copper amulets, there was nothing to distinguish him from a host of other holy men. And yet in the dim light of dusk, I couldn't take my eyes away from the man on the bearskin.

Seeing us standing, the disciple produced a pair of reed mats and spread them on the floor in front of the Baba. But what was the point of sitting down when there was no hope of seeing the pet snake? Delay would mean driving through the forest in the dark, and we knew there were wild animals about; we had seen herds of deer while coming. So we decided to leave. We bowed in namaskar to the Baba who responded by nodding without taking the pipe away from his mouth. We set off for the jeep parked about two hundred yards away on the road. Only a little while ago, the place had been alive with the call of birds coming home to roost. Now all was quiet.

We had gone a few steps when Dhurjatibabu suddenly said, 'We could at least have asked to see the hole where the snake lives.'

I said, 'For that we don't have to ask the Baba; our driver Din Dayal said he had seen the hole.'

'That's right.'

We fetched Din Dayal from the car and he showed us the way. Instead of going towards the hut, we took a narrow path by an almond tree and arrived at a bush. The stone rubble which surrounded the bush suggested that there had been some sort of an edifice here in the past. Din Dayal said the hole was right behind the bush. It was barely visible in the failing light. Dhurjatibabu produced from his pocket a small electric torch, and as the light from it hit the bush, we saw the hole. But what about the snake? Was it likely to crawl out just to show its face to a couple of curious visitors? To be quite honest, while I was ready to watch it being fed by the Baba, I had no wish to see it come out of the hole now. But my companion seemed devoured by curiosity. When the beam from the torch had no effect, he started to pelt the bush with clods of dirt.

I felt this was taking things too far, and said, 'What's the matter? You seem determined to drag the snake out, and you didn't even believe in its existence at first.'

Dhurjatibabu now picked up a large clod and said, 'I still don't. If this one doesn't drag him out, I'll know that a cock-and-bull story about the Baba has been spread. The more such false notions are destroyed, the better.'

The clod landed with a thud on the bush and destroyed a part of the thorny cluster. Dhurjatibabu had his torch trained on the hole. For a few seconds there was silence but for a lone cricket which had just started to chirp. Now there was another sound added to it: a dry, soft whistle of indeterminate pitch. Then there was a rustle of leaves and the light of the torch revealed something black and shiny slowly slipping out of the hole.

Now the leaves of the bush stirred, and the next moment, through a parting in them emerged the head of a snake. The light showed its glinting eyes and its forked tongue flickering out of its mouth again and again. Din Dayal had been pleading with us to go back to the jeep for some time; he now said, 'Let it be, sir. You have seen it: now let us go back.'

It was perhaps because of the light shining on it that the snake had its eyes turned towards us and was flicking its tongue from time to time. I have seen many snakes, but never a king cobra at such close quarters. And I have never heard of a king cobra making no attempt to attack intruders.

Suddenly the light of the torch trembled and was whisked away from the snake. What happened next was something I was not prepared for at all. Dhurjatibabu swiftly picked up a stone and hurled it with all his force at the snake. Then he followed it in quick succession with two more such missiles. I was suddenly gripped by a horrible premonition and cried out, 'Why on earth did you have to do that, Dhurjatibabu?'

The man shouted in triumph, panting, 'That's the end of at least one vicious reptile!'

Din Dayal was staring open-mouthed at the bush. I took the torch from Dhurjatibabu's hand and flashed it on the hole. I could see a part of the lifeless form of the snake. The leaves around were spattered with blood.

I had no idea that Imli Baba and his disciple had arrived to take their place right behind us. Dhurjatibabu was the first to turn round, and then I too turned and saw the Baba standing with a staff in his hand a dozen feet behind us. He had his eyes fixed on Dhurjatibabu. It is beyond me to describe the look in them. I can only say that I have never seen such a mixture of surprise, anger and hatred in anyone's eyes.

Now Baba lifted his right arm towards Dhurjatibabu. The index finger now shot out to pinpoint the aim. I now noticed for the first time that Baba's fingernails were over an inch long. Who did he remind me of? Yes, of a figure in a painting by Ravi Varma which I had seen as a child in a framed reproduction in my uncle's house. It was the sage Durbasha cursing the hapless Shakuntala. He too had his arm raised like that, and the same look in his eyes.

But Imli Baba said nothing about a curse. All he said in Hindi in his deep voice was: 'One Balkishen is gone; another will come to take his place. Balkishen is deathless . . .'

Dhurjatibabu wiped his hands with his handkerchief, turned to me and said, 'Let's go.' Baba's disciple lifted the lifeless snake from the ground and went off, probably to arrange for its cremation. The length of the snake made me gasp; I had no idea king cobras could be that long. Imli Baba slowly made his way towards the hut. The three of us went back to the jeep.

On the way back, Dhurjatibabu was gloomy and silent. I asked him why he had to kill the snake when it was doing him no harm. I thought he would burst out once more and fulminate against snakes and Babas. Instead he put a question which seemed to have no bearing on the incident.

'Do you know who Khagam was?'

Khagam? The name seemed to ring a bell, but I couldn't think where I had heard it. Dhurjatibabu muttered the name two or three times, then lapsed into silence.

It was half past six when we reached the rest house. My mind went back again and again to Imli Baba glowering at Dhurjatibabu with his finger pointing at him. I don't know why my companion behaved in such a fashion. However, I felt that we had seen the end of the incident, so there was no point in worrying about it. Baba himself had said Balkishen was deathless. There must be other king cobras in the jungles of Bharatpur. I was sure another one would be caught soon by the disciples of the Baba.

Lachhman had prepared curried chicken, lentil and chapatis for dinner. One feels hungry after a whole day's sightseeing. I find I eat twice as much here as I eat at home. Dhurjatibabu, although a small man, is a hearty eater; but today he seemed to have no appetite. I asked him if he felt unwell. He made no reply. I now said, 'Do you feel remorse for having killed the snake?'

Dhurjatibabu was staring at the petromax. What he said was not an answer to my question. 'The snake was whistling,' he said in a soft, thin voice. 'The snake was whistling . . .' I said, smiling, 'Whistling, or hissing?'

Dhurjatibabu didn't turn away from the light. 'Yes, hissing,' he said. 'Snakes speak when snakes hiss . . .

Yes, Snakes speak when snakes hiss . . .
I know this. I know this . . .'

Dhurjatibabu stopped and made some hissing noises himself. Then he broke into rhyme again, his head swaying in rhythm.

'Snakes speak when snakes hiss
I know this. I know this,
Snakes kill when snakes kiss
I know this. I know this . . .
What is this? Goat's milk?'

The question was directed at the pudding in the plate before him.

Lachhman missed the 'goat' bit and answered, 'Yes, sir—there is milk and there is egg.'

Dhurjatibabu is by nature whimsical, but his behaviour today seemed excessive. Perhaps he himself realized it, because he seemed to make an effort to control himself. 'Been out in the sun too long these last few days,' he said. 'Must go easy from tomorrow.'

It was noticeably chillier tonight than usual; so instead of sitting out on the terrace, I went into the bedroom and started to pack my suitcase. I was going to catch the train next evening. I would have to change in the middle of the night at Sawai Madhopur and arrive in Jaipur at five in the morning.

At least that was my plan, but it came to nothing. I had to send a wire to my elder brother saying that I would be arriving a day later. Why this was necessary will be clear from what I'm about to say now. I shall try to describe everything as clearly and accurately as possible. I don't expect everyone will believe me, but the proof is still lying on the ground fifty yards away from the Baba's hut. I feel a cold shiver just to think of it, so it is not surprising that I couldn't pick it up and bring it as proof of my story. Let me now set down what happened.

I had just finished packing my suitcase, turned down the wick of my lantern and got into my pyjamas when there was a knock on the door on the east side of the room. Dhurjatibabu's room was behind that door.

As soon as I opened the door the man said in a hoarse whisper: 'Do you have some Flit, or something to keep off mosquitoes?'

I asked: 'Where did you find mosquitoes? Aren't your windows covered with netting?'

'Yes, they are.'

'Well, then?'

'Even then something is biting me.'

'How do you know that?'

'There are marks on my skin.'

It was dark at the mouth of the door, so I couldn't see his face clearly. I said, 'Come into my room. Let me see what kind of marks they are.'

Dhurjatibabu stepped into my room. I raised the lantern and could see the marks immediately. They were greyish, diamond-shaped blotches. I had never seen anything like them before, and I didn't like what I saw. 'You seem to have caught some strange disease,' I said. 'It may be an allergy, of course. We must get hold of a doctor first thing tomorrow morning. Try and go to sleep and don't worry about the marks. And I don't think they're caused by insects. Are they painful?'

'No.'

'Then don't worry. Go back to bed.'

He went off. I shut the door, climbed into bed and slipped under the blanket. I'm used to reading in bed before going to sleep, but this was not possible by lantern light. Not that I needed to read. I knew the day's exertions would put me to sleep within ten minutes of putting my head on the pillow.

But that was not to be tonight. I was about to drop off when there was the sound of a car arriving, followed soon by English voices and the bark of a dog. Foreign tourists obviously. The dog stopped barking at a sharp rebuke. Soon there was quiet again except for the crickets. No, not just the crickets; my neighbour was still awake and walking about. And yet through the crack under the door I had seen the lantern either being put out, or removed to the bathroom. Why was the man pacing about in the dark?

For the first time I had a suspicion that he was more than just whimsical. I had known him for just two days. I knew nothing beyond what he had himself told me. And yet, to be quite honest, I had not seen any signs of what could be called madness in him until only a few hours ago. The comments that he had made while touring the forts at Bayan and Deeg suggested that he was quite well up on history. Not only that, he also knew quite a bit about art, and spoke knowledgeably about the work of Hindu and Moslem architects in the palaces of Rajasthan. No—the man was obviously ill. We must look for a doctor tomorrow.

The radium dial on my watch said a quarter to eleven. There was another rap on the east side door. This time I shouted from the bed.

'What is it, Dhurjatibabu?'

'S-s-s-s-'

'What?'

'S-s-s-s-'

I could see that he was having difficulty with his speech. A fine mess I had got myself into. I shouted again: 'Tell me clearly what the matter is.'

'S-s-s-sorry to bother you, but—'

I had to leave the bed. When I opened the door, the man came out with such an absurd question that it really annoyed me.

'Is s-s-s-snake spelt with one "s"?'

I made no effort to hide my annoyance.

'You knocked on the door at this time of the night just to ask me that?'

'Only one "s"?' he repeated.

'Yes, sir. No English word begins with two s's.'

'I s-s-see. And curs-s-s-e?'

'That's one "s" too.'

'Thank you. S-s-s-sleep well.'

I felt pity for the poor man. I said, 'Let me give you a sleeping pill. Would you like one?'

'Oh no. I s-s-s-sleep s-s-s-soundly enough. But when the s-s-sun was s-s-s-setting this evening—'

I interrupted him. 'Are you having trouble with your tongue? Why are you stammering? Give me your torch for a minute.'

I followed Dhurjatibabu into his room. The torch was on the dressing table. I flashed it on his face and he put out his tongue.

There was no doubt that something was wrong with it. A thin red line had appeared down the middle.

'Don't you feel any pain?'

'No. No pain.'

I was at a loss to know what the matter was with him.

Now my eye fell on the man's bed. Its clean appearance made it clear that he hadn't got into bed at all. I was quite stern about it. I said, 'I want to see you turn in before I go back. And I urge you please not to knock on my door again. I know I won't have any sleep in the train tomorrow, so I want to have a good night's rest now.'

But the man showed no signs of going to bed. The lantern being kept in the bathroom, the bedroom was in semi-darkness. Outside there was a full moon. Moonlight flooded in through the north window and fell on the floor. I could see Dhurjatibabu in the soft reflected glow from it. He was standing in his nightclothes, making occasional efforts to whistle through parted lips. I had wrapped the blanket around me when I left my bed, but Dhurjatibabu had nothing warm on him. If he caught a chill then it would be difficult for me to leave him alone and go away. After all, we were both away from home; if one was in trouble, it wouldn't do for the other to leave him in the lurch and push off.

I told him again to go to bed. When I found he wouldn't, I realized I should have to use main force. If he insisted on behaving like a child, I had no choice but to act the stern elder.

But the moment I touched his hand I sprang back as if from an electric shock.

Dhurjatibabu's body was as cold as ice. I couldn't imagine that a living person's body could be so cold.

It was perhaps my reaction which brought a smile to his lips. He now regarded me with his grey eyes wrinkled in amusement. I asked him in a hoarse voice: 'What is the matter with you?'

Dhurjatibabu kept looking at me for a whole minute. I noticed that he didn't blink once during the whole time. I also noticed that he kept sticking out his tongue again and again. Then he dropped his voice to a whisper and said, 'Baba is calling me—"Balkishen! . . . Balkishen! . . ." I can hear him call.' His knees now buckled and he went down on the

floor. Flattening himself on his chest, he started dragging himself back on his elbows until he disappeared into the darkness under the bed.

I was drenched in a cold sweat and shivering in every limb. It was difficult for me to keep standing. I was no longer worried about the man, all I felt was a mixture of horror and disbelief. I came back to my room, shut the door and bolted it. Then I got back into bed and covered myself from head to toe with the blanket. In a while the shivering stopped and I could think a little more clearly. I tried to realize where the matter stood, and the implication of what I had seen with my own eyes. Dhurjatibabu had killed Imli Baba's pet cobra by pelting it with stones. Immediately after that Imli Baba had pointed to Dhurjatibabu with his finger and said: 'One Balkishen is gone. Another will come to take his place.' The question is: was the second Balkishen a snake or a man? Or a man turned into a snake?

What were those diamond-shaped blotches on Dhurjatibabu's skin?

What was the red mark on his tongue?

Did it show that his tongue was about to be forked?

Why was he so cold to the touch?

Why did he crawl under the bed?

I suddenly recalled something in a flash. Dhurjatibabu had asked about Khagam. The name had sounded familiar, but I couldn't quite place it. Now I remembered. A story I had read in the Mahabharata when I was a boy. Khagam was the name of a sage. His curse had turned his friend into a snake. Khagam—snake—curse—it all fitted. But the friend had turned into a harmless non-poisonous snake, while this man . . .

Somebody was knocking on the door again. At the foot of the door this time. Once, twice, thrice . . . I didn't stir out of the bed. I was not going to open the door. Not again.

The knocking stopped. I held my breath and waited.

A hissing sound now, moving away from the door.

Now there was silence, except for my pounding heartbeat.

What was that sound now? A squeak. No, something between a squeak and a screech. I knew there were rats in the bungalow. I saw one in my bedroom the very first night. I had told Lachhman, and he had brought a rat-trap from the pantry to show me a rat in it. 'Not only rats, sir, there are moles too.'

The screeching had stopped. There was silence again. Minutes passed. I glanced at my watch. A quarter to one. Sleep had vanished. I could see the trees in the moonlight through my window. The moon was overhead now.

The sound of a door opening. It was the door of Dhurjatibabu's room which led to the verandah. The door was on the same side as my window. The line of trees was six or seven yards away from the edge of the verandah.

Dhurjatibabu was out on the verandah now. Where was he going? What was he up to? I stared fixedly at my window.

The hissing was growing louder. Now it was right outside my window. Thank God the window was covered with netting!

Something was climbing up the wall towards the window. A head appeared behind the netting. In the dim light of the lantern shone a pair of beady eyes staring fixedly at me.

They stayed staring for a minute; then there was the bark of a dog. The head turned towards the bark, and then dropped out of sight.

The dog was barking at the top of its voice. Now I heard its owner shouting at it. The barking turned into a moan, and then stopped. Once again there was silence. I kept my senses alert for another ten minutes or so. The lines of a verse I had heard earlier that night kept coming back to me—

> *Snakes speak when snakes hiss*
> *I know this. I know this,*
> *Snakes kill when snakes kiss*
> *I know this. I know this . . .*

And then the rhyme grew dim in my mind and I felt a drowsiness stealing over me.

I woke up to the sound of agitated English voices. My watch showed ten minutes to six. Something was happening. I got up quickly, dressed and came out on the verandah. A pet dog belonging to two English tourists had died during the night. The dog had slept in the bedroom with its owners who hadn't bothered to lock the door. It was surmised that a snake or something equally venomous had got into the room and bitten it.

Instead of wasting my time on the dog, I went to the door of Dhurjatibabu's room at the other end of the verandah. The door was ajar and the room empty. Lachhman gets up every morning at five to light the oven and put the tea-kettle on the boil. I asked him. He said he hadn't seen Dhurjatibabu.

All sorts of anxious thoughts ran in my head. I had to find Dhurjatibabu. He couldn't have gone far on foot. But a thorough search of the woods around proved abortive.

The jeep arrived at half past ten. I couldn't leave Bharatpur without finding out what had happened to my companion. So I sent a cable to my brother from the post office, got my train ticket postponed for a day and came back to the rest house to learn that there was still no sign of Dhurjatibabu. The two Englishmen had in the meantime buried their dog and left.

I spent the whole afternoon exploring around the rest house. Following my instruction, the jeep arrived again in the afternoon. I was now working on a hunch and had a faint hope of success. I told the driver to drive straight to Imli Baba's hermitage.

I reached it about the same time as we did yesterday. Baba was seated with the pipe in hand and the fire burning in front of him. There were two more disciples with him today.

Baba nodded briefly in answer to my greeting. The look in his eyes today held no hint of the blazing intensity that had appeared in them yesterday. I went straight to the point: Did the Baba have any information on the gentleman who came with me yesterday? A gentle smile spread over Baba's face.

He said, 'Indeed I have! Your friend has fulfilled my hope. He has brought back my Balkishen to me.'

I noticed for the first time the stone pot on Baba's right hand side. The white liquid it contained was obviously milk. But I hadn't come all this way to see a snake and a bowl of milk. I had come in quest of Dhurjatibabu. He couldn't simply have vanished into thin air. If I could only see some sign of his existence!

I had noticed earlier that Imli Baba could read one's mind. He took a long pull at the pipe of ganja, passed it on to one of his disciples and said, 'I'm afraid you won't find your friend in the state you knew him, but he has left a memento behind. You will find that fifty steps to the south of Balkishen's home. Go carefully; there are thorny bushes around.'

I went to the hole where the king cobra lived. I was not the least concerned with whether another snake had taken the place of the first one. I took fifty steps south through grass, thorny shrubs and rubble, and reached a bel tree at the foot of which lay something the likes of which I had seen hanging from a line in Baba's hut a few minutes ago.

It was a freshly sloughed-off skin marked all over with a pattern of diamonds.

But was it really snake skin? A snake was never that broad, and a snake didn't have arms and legs sticking out of its body.

It was actually the sloughed-off skin of a man. A man who had ceased to be a man. He was now lying coiled inside that hole. He is a king cobra with poison fangs.

There, I can hear him hissing. The sun has just gone down. I can hear the Baba calling—'Balkishen—Balkishen—Balkishen.'

THE UNICORN EXPEDITION

Originally written in Bengali as *Ekshringa Abhijan* and published in *Sandesh* (December 1973–April 1974). It was translated by the author himself to be part of the compilation titled *Stories* (Secker & Warburg, 1987). The illustrations in the story, including the Bengali calligraphy in the headpiece, are by Satyajit Ray.

1 JULY

E xciting news. A diary belonging to Charles Willard has been found. Only a year ago, while on his way back from Tibet, this English explorer was waylaid by a gang of Khampa robbers who made off with most of his belongings.

B y a supreme effort, Willard was able to reach the town of Almora in India in a state of near collapse. He died there soon after. All this I had read in the papers. Today I had a letter from London from my geologist friend Jeremy Saunders. He says that among the few personal effects that Willard left behind was a diary which is now in Saunders' possession. The diary mentions a most unusual event. Knowing of my great interest in Tibet and the Tibetan language, Saunders has passed the information on to me. Here is an extract from his letter:

'You know that Willard had been an old friend of mine. I called on his widow Edwina a couple of days back. She mentioned that among Willard's possessions sent her from Almora was a diary. I borrowed the diary from her. Unfortunately, much of the writing has been washed away, but the very last entry is quite legible. It records an incident which took place on March the nineteenth. Only two lines describe it: "I saw a herd of unicorns today. I write this in full possession of my senses." Seeing a storm coming up, Willard had stopped writing at this point. I am most curious to know what you feel about the extraordinary statement.'

Willard had to assert that he was in his right senses; like the dragon of the east and the west, the unicorn has been known as a product of human imagination. But I have some hesitation in using the word imagination. I have a book open before me on my desk which is about the ancient civilization of Mohenjo Daro. Apart from pottery, toys, figurines and ornaments, diggings at Mohenjo Daro have revealed a large number of rectangular clay and ivory seals bearing carvings of, amongst other things, animals such as elephants, tigers, bulls and rhinoceroses. In addition to these familiar animals, there are representations of a beast unknown to us. It is shown as a bull-like creature with a single curved horn growing out of its forehead. Archaeologists have taken it to be a creature of fantasy, although I see no point in depicting an imaginary creature when all the others shown are real.

There is another reason for thinking that the unicorn may not, after all, be a fantastic animal. Two thousand years ago, the Roman scholar Pliny clearly stated in his famous treatise on animals that in India there exist cows and donkeys with a single horn. Aristotle, too, maintained that there were unicorns in India. Would it be wrong to conclude from this that in India there did exist, in ancient times, a species of unicorn which became extinct here, but which still survives in some parts of Tibet? What if Willard had accidentally stumbled upon a herd of them? It is true that in the last two hundred years many foreign explorers have visited Tibet none of whom mention the unicorn. But what does that prove? There are still many unexplored regions in Tibet. Who knows what species of animal may exist there?

I must pass my thoughts on to Saunders.

15 JULY

Here is Saunders' reply to my letter:

> *Dear Shonku,*
> *Thanks for your letter. I have managed to decipher some of Willard's entries towards the end of his diary, and am even more astonished. On March the sixteenth he writes:*

'Today I flew with the two-hundred-year-old lama.' What on earth does he mean? Flying in an aeroplane? That sounds most unlikely when Tibet lacks even railways. Does he mean flying without the aid of an aircraft? Like a bird? But is such a thing possible? Such a statement raises doubts about Willard's sanity. And yet the doctor— Major Horton—who examined Willard in Almora categorically stated that Willard's brain had not been affected. The entry of March the thirteenth mentions a monastery called Thokchum Gompa. According to Willard: 'A wonderful monastery. No European has ever been here before.' Have you heard of this monastery? Anyway, the upshot is that Willard's diary has fired me with a great impulse to visit Tibet. My German friend Wilhelm Kroll is also enthusiastic. He has been particularly intrigued by the mention of the flying lama. I suppose you know that Kroll has done important research on magic and witchcraft. He is also an excellent mountaineer. It goes without saying that it would be wonderful if you too could come with us. Let me know what you decide.
With best wishes,
Yours,
Jeremy Saunders

A flying lama! I have read the autobiography of the Tibetan saint Milarepa. He was able to perform supernatural feats by tantra and yogic meditation. One of the feats he became adept at was flying. Did Willard fly with the help of such a yogi?

I haven't been to Tibet; but I have read about it and learned the Tibetan language. Willard's diary has raised my curiosity to a high pitch. That is why I'm thinking of joining Saunders' party. It would actually help them if I did, because I have inventions of mine which would considerably reduce the strain of such a journey.

27 JULY

My friend and neighbour Mr Abinash Majumder threw up his hands when I told him I was going to Tibet. Having accompanied me twice on my trips abroad, his wanderlust had been aroused. I had to tell him about the hazards of such a journey. He replied, 'So what? What more could a devout Hindu like me want than to have a glimpse of Lord

Shiva's own mountain Kailash?' Although Mr Majumder knew about Kailash, he didn't know about the holy lake at its foot. 'What!' he exclaimed, 'Lake Mansarovar in Tibet? I always thought it was in Kashmir.'

I didn't mention the unicorn and the flying lama to Mr Majumder because I do have doubts about them, but when I mentioned the Khampa bandits, Mr Majumder calmly said, 'Don't worry, Lord Shiva will protect you from harm.'

We have decided to start our journey from Kathgodam. I have sent a wire to Saunders saying that I shall arrive in Kathgodam on the first of August. We will, of course, have to travel light. When I told this to Mr Majumder, he said, 'What about my pillows? I can't sleep without them.' I have promised to make him a couple of inflatable ones. For high altitude wear I'm taking vests made of Shanklin fabric. In case anyone has breathing trouble, we are taking small portable oxygen cylinders. In all, the luggage shouldn't weigh more than ten kilograms. Suitable footwear we could buy on the way in Almora.

It has been quite stuffy here these last few days. Possibly a portent of heavy rains. Once we cross over into Tibet, we shall be out of reach of the monsoon.

10 AUGUST
GARBAYANG

I haven't had any time for my diary these last few days. We left Kathgodam on the third by taxi for Almora. Thereafter we have travelled a hundred and fifty miles on horseback to reach Garbayang yesterday evening.

Garbayang is a Bhutia village at an altitude of ten thousand feet. We are still in India. To our east runs the river Kali. Across the river one can see the dense pine forests of Nepal. Twenty miles to the north one has to negotiate a pass in order to reach Lipudhura. Beyond Lipudhura is Tibet.

Mount Kailash and the Lake Mansarovar are about forty miles from the Tibetan border. Not a great distance, but the terrain is difficult and the cold bitter. Besides, there are other unforeseen hazards which have discouraged ninety-nine per cent of Indians from venturing into this region. And yet the landscape we have passed through even at

Jeremy Saunders

Wilhelm Kroll

Ivan Markovitch

this early stage gives a foretaste of the grandeur that lies ahead.

Let me describe our party now. Besides Saunders and Kroll, a third European has joined us. His name is Ivan Markovitch; he is a Russian by birth but lives in Poland. He speaks English quite well but with an accent. He is the youngest in our group, and the tallest. He has blue eyes, a headful of unruly brown hair, thick eyebrows and a drooping moustache. We met him in Almora. He was also bound for Tibet, the reason being sheer wanderlust. He joined our party as soon as he learnt that we were also headed the same way. He seems a reasonably decent individual, although I have noticed that he seldom smiles, and even when he does, his lips curl up but his eyes remain unsmiling: a sure sign of a closed mind, which is probably why Kroll has taken a dislike to him.

Wilhelm Kroll is a round, ruddy individual no taller than five foot six inches, and with no hair on his head except for a few golden tufts about the ears. It is impossible to guess by looking at him that he has climbed the Matterhorn four times. A highly qualified anthropologist, Kroll makes no secret of his deep interest in the occult. He fully believes that the unicorn and flying lamas may well exist in Tibet. I have noticed that Kroll has a habit of lapsing into absent-mindedness, so that you have to call him thrice before he answers.

Saunders is five years younger than me. He is a well-built handsome man with intelligent blue eyes and a broad forehead. He has read about a dozen books on Tibet in the last couple of weeks to prepare himself for the journey. He doesn't believe in magic or yogic powers; even reading about Tibet hasn't converted him. There is nothing he relishes more than a lively argument with Kroll and he indulges in it at every opportunity.

My neighbour Mr Majumder has come for the sole purpose of pilgrimage. He is now seated a few yards away from us sipping Tibetan tea from a copper bowl, with his eyes on a yak tethered to a nearby pole. Only this morning he remarked, 'All our lives we have seen the yak's tail at the end of a silver handle being waved at religious ceremonies. Now, for the first time, I see where it really belongs.' Actually, it is the tail of the white yak which is used in rituals. The yaks here are mostly black. They are invaluable as carriers of luggage. We are taking with us four yaks, six ponies and eight porters.

Mr Majumder has warned me that I shouldn't expect him to hobnob with my foreign friends. 'You may know sixty-four languages; I know only one. I can say 'good morning' and 'good evening' all right; and if one of them should slip and fall into an abyss I could even say 'goodbye'. But that is all. You can tell them I am one of those Indian sadhus who observe a vow of silence, and my only purpose in coming is pilgrimage.' The three Europeans and myself are now seated in front of a Bhutiya shop, having our breakfast of tea and tsampa. Tsampa is a ball of ground wheat which you soak in tea or water and eat. The tea is not like our Indian tea at all. It comes from China and is known as brick tea. Instead of milk and sugar, this tea is taken with butter and salt. It is poured into a cylindrical bamboo cup and stirred with a bamboo stump till the three ingredients are thoroughly mixed. Tibetans drink it at least thirty times a day. They also eat the meat of goat and yak. We are carrying with us a large stock of rice, lentils, vegetables, coffee and tinned food. If and when we run out of stock, we shall have to fall back on my nutriment pills.

Having now read Willard's diary myself, my curiosity has increased a hundredfold. A group of Tibetan wool merchants has arrived here. I asked one of them about unicorns. He only grinned at me as if I was a child asking a stupid question. When asked about flying lamas, he said all lamas could fly. I don't think anything will come out of talking to these people. We doubt if we will have Willard's luck, but we're all hoping that we will. In his entry for March the eleventh, Willard talks about a place whose name he doesn't mention, but whose geographical position he gives as Lat. 33°3' N and Long. 84° E. The map shows it to be roughly one hundred miles north-east of Mount Kailash in a region called Chang Thang. This is supposed to be a particularly hostile terrain, quite bereft of vegetation. Some nomadic tribes pass through it once in a while, but no one lives here. The place is also known for blizzards which bore through seven layers of woollens to freeze one's bones.

We are prepared to put up with everything provided we achieve our goal. Mr Majumder says, 'You mustn't worry. My faith in the Lord of Mount Kailash will guarantee the success of your mission.'

14 AUGUST
PURANG VALLEY

We have set up camp beside a torrential river at an altitude of about twelve-thousand feet. It is afternoon now, and the sun is about to go down behind the high, snow-clad mountains which surround us, making the atmosphere chillier by the minute. Surprisingly enough, although the nights here can be extremely cold, in the daytime the temperature often rises to 90° Fahrenheit.

Since I knew we would be climbing high, I reminded everyone that we were carrying oxygen. Saunders and Mr Majumder needed it. Kroll didn't since he was from the mountain resort of Meiningen, and therefore used to heights. Markovitch too said he was used to heights. He was to realize later that he had done something very foolish. We were proceeding quite peacefully with five of us up front on our ponies, followed by our porters and the yaks loaded with our baggage. As we crossed the Gurup La pass at sixteen-thousand feet we heard a strange noise above the clatter of hooves and the whistling of the wind. Someone amongst us had broken out in a wild laughter.

I looked about and realized that the laughter emanated from the man at the head of the group, Mr Ivan Markovitch. We all stopped.

Markovitch had pulled up too. He now dismounted, still laughing, and stood swaying perilously close to the edge of the road which dropped two thousand feet into a gorge. If he went over, Mr Majumder would surely have an opportunity to say 'goodbye'.

Saunders, Kroll and I dismounted and hurried towards Markovitch. The man's eyes looked glazed and, like his laughter, suggested a mind bereft of sense. It was clear what had happened. Above twelve-thousand feet, the oxygen content in the atmosphere begins to thin. This causes some people to feel no more than a slight discomfort in breathing, others faint, or show symptoms of insanity by weeping or laughing hysterically. Markovitch belonged to the last category. Our porters had probably never encountered such an exhibition before, for they too had started to laugh. The mountains around now echoed with the laughter of nine men.

Kroll suddenly came up to me and said, 'What about giving him a sock on the jaw?'

I was bewildered. 'Why sock him?' I asked. 'It is lack of oxygen which is making him laugh like that.'

'Precisely,' said Kroll. 'You can't make him take any oxygen in this state. If I knock him out, you can force it down his nose.' Before I could answer him, Kroll had turned round and delivered a mighty blow on the man's jaw. I got busy with the medication, and in ten minutes Markovitch had regained consciousness. He looked about with a puzzled expression, rubbed his jaw, and got back on to his pony without any more fuss. We resumed our journey.

Sitting around the fire, we fell to talking about fantastic creatures. What strange beings the human imagination had concocted in the past ages! Of course, some scholars say that they are not wholly imaginary. Remnants of the memory of creatures seen in prehistoric times are said to persist for ages in the collective human consciousness. By adding his imagination to such shreds of memory, man creates new species. Perhaps the pterodactyl and the aepyornis are really the progenitors of our mythical Garuda and Jatayu, and the Roc in the tale of Sinbad, a giant bird whose young fed on elephants. In the folk tales of Egypt one reads of the bird Ti-Bennu which became the Phoenix of later European myths. Then there is the dragon which occurs both in the myths of the east and the west. The difference is that the dragon of western mythology is a malignant demon, while that of the far east is a benevolent god.

It was I who finally changed the subject and raised the question of Markovitch, who was away resting in his tent. We hadn't yet told him the real reason for our expedition; it was my feeling that we should tell him now. We should also make clear to him the terrible hazards of the Chang Thang region. If after knowing of the risks involved he still wants to come with us, then let him do so. If not, he should either branch off on his own or get back to India.

'You're right,' said Kroll. 'Why should we burden ourselves with someone who can't even mix properly? Let's have it out with him right now.'

The three of us went into Markovitch's tent. He sat crouching on the far side dimly visible in the half light. Without beating about the bush, Saunders told him about Willard's diary and our search for the unicorn. Even before he had finished, Markovitch blurted out, 'Unicorns? Why, I have seen dozens of unicorns. Even today I saw one. Didn't you see it?'

We exchanged glances. It didn't seem as if Markovitch was being facetious. Kroll left the tent humming a German tune. He had obviously given up Markovitch as a bad case. Now the two of us came out too. Kroll lit his pipe and said in a mocking tone, 'You don't think it's lack of oxygen that makes him talk like that, do you?' Saunders and I were both silent. 'I haven't the slightest doubt that we have a loony in our midst,' said Kroll, and walked off with his camera towards a large boulder which had the Tibetan mantra *Om Mani Padme Hum* inscribed on it.

Is Markovitch really a madman? Or is he just pretending? I have an uneasy feeling in my mind.

Mr Majumder seems to be the least worried person in our group. I have known him for forty years. I never suspected that he had any imagination. He has always pooh-poohed my scientific experiments, and my epoch-making inventions have never produced any admiration or wonder in his mind. But the trips abroad that he made with me—once to Africa and once across the Pacific—seem to have brought about a change in him. There is an English saying that travel broadens the mind. This certainly has been more than true in the case of Mr Majumder. Today he came up to me and whispered in my ears an old poem about Mount Kailash which compares it with a million moons and describes it as the home of heavenly beings. It is clear that Mr Majumder still believes the age-old legends about Kailash. I'm afraid he will be disappointed when he comes face to face with the real thing. Just now he is observing the porters cooking their meal; they're going to have wild goat for dinner.

In the far distance I can see a group of men on horseback coming down the path which we shall take tomorrow. Till a little while ago, the group had seemed like a conglomeration of moving dots. Now I can see them clearly. The sight of them seems to have excited our porters. Who are those people?

The temperature is dropping. We can't stay out much longer.

14 AUGUST, 7 P.M.

A momentous event took place a little while ago.

The group we had seen approaching was a gang of Khampa robbers. We now have proof that this was the very group which waylaid Willard.

Twenty-two men on horseback, everyone with swords and daggers tucked in their belts around their thick tunics, and old-fashioned blunderbusses slung across their shoulders. Besides the men and horses, there were five woolly Tibetan dogs.

When the gang was about a hundred yards away from us, two of our porters, Rabsang and Tundup, rushed up to us and said, 'Please bring out all your weapons, sir.' I asked him if we were supposed to turn them over to the bandits. 'No, no!' said Rabsang, 'They have great respect for foreign weapons. If you don't bring them out, they will just run away with everything we have.'

We had three firearms with us—an Enfield and two Austrian Mannlichers. Besides, I had my own invention—the Stun Gun. This was actually a pistol which produced a 'ping' instead of a 'bang' when the trigger was pressed, and injected a needle which instantly stunned the victim. Saunders and Kroll brought out their guns from the tent. There was no sign of Markovitch. I had to keep my hands free in case the Stun Gun was needed, and yet three guns in the hands of two men seemed odd, so I handed the third to Mr Majumder. He first made a show of protest, then took the gun, turned his back on the bandits and stood facing the river, ramrod straight.

The bandits arrived. The huge shaggy dogs started barking at us as if they were bandits too. These gangs usually raid the encampments of the nomads and make off with all their belongings. To turn against them without proper arms means certain death. It is not easy to run these gangs to ground in the wild, snow-bound country, but when the Tibetan police do get their hands on them, the robbers have their heads and right hands chopped off and sent to Lhasa. I have also heard that the bandits are so afraid of retribution in hell that after each raid they undergo a spell of absolution by either circumambulating Mount Kailash, or climbing a cliff and loudly proclaiming their misdeeds for all the world to hear.

The bandit in front seemed to be the leader. A snub nose, ringed ears, and a deeply lined face belied his youth. His slit eyes now regarded the four of us with deep suspicion. The others held on to their reins, obviously waiting for the word from their chief.

Now the chief dismounted, strode up to Kroll and said in a thick voice: '*Peling*?' Peling is the Tibetan word for a European. I answered for Kroll. 'Yes, I said, '*Peling*.' But how did he guess Kroll was a European?

The deep croak of a rook could be heard from somewhere. Apart from that, the only sound came from the swiftly flowing river. The bandit went up to Mr Majumder. I'm not sure why my friend thought fit to bow in greeting to the robber, but it was obvious that the latter found the gesture highly comic. He gave a sharp prod to the butt of the gun in Mr Majumder's hand and burst into an unseemly guffaw.

I was now alarmed to see Kroll slowly raising his gun towards the bandit, the veins in his forehead standing out in reckless rage. I was forced to restrain him with a sharp gesture. Meanwhile Saunders had moved up to my side. 'They have an Enfield too,' he whispered through clenched teeth.

I turned towards the bandits and found that one of them, a particularly fierce-looking individual, was indeed carrying an Enfield. We know from Willard's diary that he had an Enfield. The gun wasn't among his personal effects when he came to Almora. That and the fact that the chief could recognize a European, made it obvious that this was the gang that had plagued Willard.

But there was nothing that we could do about it. The gang far outnumbered us. I could see that they were just biding their time before getting down to the serious business of plunder.

I was wondering how long this cat-and-mouse game was to go on when a diversion occurred. Markovitch suddenly emerged from his tent, staggered towards the gang and pointing with outstretched arms at the Tibetan dogs, cried out jubilantly, 'Unicorns! Unicorns!'

At this, one of the huge mastiffs suddenly took a menacing stance and with a nasty growl leaped at Markovitch.

But before he could reach his target he had dropped down on the ground senseless. The reason for this was, of course, my pistol. My right hand had for some time been gripped around its butt in my pocket. At the crucial moment the hand had come out and performed the conjuring trick.

Markovitch suddenly seemed to lose grip on himself and collapsed on the ground. Kroll and Saunders lifted him up between them and bore him back into his tent.

And the bandits? There was an incredible transformation in them. Some of them dismounted and were down on their knees, while others who were still on their ponies made repeated gestures of obeisance towards me. The chief too had in the meantime thought it prudent to get back on his mount. That the combined threat of twenty-two bandits would vanish so quickly, I had never imagined.

I approached the man with the Enfield and said, 'Either you hand over that gun or I'll make the whole lot of you suffer the fate of the dog.' He immediately offered the gun to me with shaking hands. I now addressed the whole gang: 'You took this gun from a Peling; I want you to turn over to me whatever else you took from him.'

Within a minute various objects were produced from the bag of the robbers—two tins of sausages, a Gillette safety razor, a mirror, a pair of field glasses, a torn map of Tibet, an Omega watch and a leather bag. I opened the bag and found in it two standard books on Tibet by Morecraft and Tiffenthaler, both bearing Willard's name in his own handwriting.

Having confiscated the objects, I was about to command the bandits to go away when they themselves turned tail and, in the gathering dusk, disappeared the way they came.

I now relieved Mr Majumder of the Mannlicher and went to see how Markovitch was faring.

He was lying on a rug on the ground with his eyes closed. As I flashed my torch on his face, he slowly opened them. One look at his pupils told me that he was under the influence of some potent drug, perhaps the source of his unicorns. Drugs like cocaine, heroin and morphine may well lead to hallucinations. An addict like Markovitch would be a great handicap to our expedition. Either we must get rid of him or of his addiction.

15 AUGUST, 7 A.M.

When last night Markovitch went without dinner even when we urged him to join us, I was even more convinced about his addiction. Drugs tend to deaden one's appetite. When I told Saunders, he blew his top. 'He must be questioned at once,' he insisted. Kroll said, 'You two are too gentlemanly. Let me do the questioning.'

After dinner, Kroll dragged Markovitch out of his tent and taking him by the scruff of his neck, hissed into his ears: 'Come on, out with your drugs, or we'll bury you in the snow and leave you to rot. No one will ever know.'

I could see that, although groggy, Markovitch had turned pale. He wriggled himself free, put his hand in his valise and pulled out a hair brush which he handed to Kroll. At first I thought this was another symptom of the Russian's addiction; but Kroll could, with his German astuteness, immediately make out that Markovitch had given up the real thing. With a little pressure, the wooden back of the brush opened like a lid, revealing a store of white powdered cocaine. In a few moments the powder had become part of the Himalayan atmosphere.

That Markovitch's craving too had disappeared with the cocaine was made clear when this morning at breakfast, the Russian helped himself to four glasses of tea, nearly a pound of goat's meat, and a considerable amount of tsampa.

17 AUGUST
BEYOND SANGCHAN

It is two-thirty in the afternoon now. We are taking rest outside a monastery on the way to Lake Mansarovar. We have passed many monasteries on the way, each of them built on a cliff and each affording a splendid view of the mountains. One must admit that the lamas have a fine sense of atmosphere.

To the north stands the proud peak of Gurla Mandhata, twenty-five thousand feet high. Beside this, many other snow peaks can be seen from here. A little further on are the great lake and Mount Kailash, the goals for which Mr Majumder is gamely striving. Needless to say, no sight of unicorns so far. Animals can be seen frequently, but they consist of wild goats, sheep, donkeys and yaks. Occasionally one can see a hare or a field rat. We know there are deer and bears, but we haven't seen any yet. Last night hyenas were prowling near our camp; I could see their glowing eyes in the light of my torch.

Saunders has almost given up hope. He now believes that Willard too was under the influence of drugs; that flying lamas and unicorns were both drug-induced hallucinations. He seems to forget that we had met Major Horton at Almora, and seen his report concerning Willard. There was no mention of drugs in that.

There is only a single lama living in the monastery outside which we are now resting. We met him a little while ago. A strange experience. We had no intention of going into the monastery; but when Rabsang told us about the solitary lama, and that he hadn't spoken for fifty years, our curiosity was aroused. We climbed the hundred steps from the road and entered the sacred building.

Built of granite, the monastery was dark and clammy inside. In the main hall were seven or eight Buddha statuettes ranged on a shelf at the back. At least three were made of solid gold. A lamp was burning on the shelf. Alongside was a pot with a dollop of butter in it. This, and not oil, was used to light the lamps in the monasteries. Mr Majumder pointed to an object on the shelf and said, 'I'm sure that is used for tantric rites.' It was a human skull.

I said, 'Not only that; lamas are known to drink tea from such skulls.' Mr Majumder gave a slight shiver.

The mute lama was in a small room on the eastern wing of the monastery. He sat cross-legged on the floor beside a small window, slowly and patiently turning his prayer wheel—a lean, shaven-headed man whose arms and legs had grown unusually thin from sitting down for hours at a stretch. One by one, we paid our respects to him. He gave each one of us a red thread as a sign of benediction.

We sat on a low bench facing him while he looked expectantly at us. Since the lama won't speak, we should have to put questions which could be answered in sign language. I went straight to the crucial question.

'Are there any unicorns in Tibet?'

The lama kept smiling at us for a minute or so. Five pairs of eyes were tensely

fixed on him. Now the lama moved his head up and down—once, twice, three times. In other words, there were. But now he moved his head again, this time from side to side, meaning there weren't.

What kind of an answer was that? Could it mean that there were unicorns at one time, but not any more? Kroll turned to me and whispered, 'Ask him where they are.' Markovitch too was all attention.

I put the question Kroll had suggested. In reply, the lama raised his shrivelled left hand and pointed towards north-west. That was the direction we were going—to Chang Thang beyond Mount Kailash. I now felt impelled to put a third question.

'You are a yogi; you can see into the future. Please tell us if we will be able to see this wonderful creature.'

The lama again smiled and moved his head up and down three times.

Kroll was now in the throes of intense excitement. He now said quite loudly in English, 'Ask him if he knows about flying lamas.'

I turned to the lama. 'I have read about your great saint Milarepa,' I said. 'He says he was able to travel from one place to another through the air. Are there any Tibetan saints still living who are capable of such a feat?'

I noticed a hardening of the look of the silent lama. He shook his head sideways quite emphatically, meaning there were none.

Before leaving the monastery, we left some tea and tsampa for the mute lama. Among travellers and nomads in these parts, whoever knows about the mute lama leaves some provisions for him when they pass the monastery.

Coming outside, Kroll and Saunders fell into an argument. Saunders was not prepared to give any credence to the lama's statements. He said, 'One moment he says yes, the next moment no. When you're contradicting yourself like that, you're making no statement at all. I think we have only wasted our time.'

Kroll, by the way, had a totally different interpretation of the lama's answers. He said, 'To me the meaning is crystal clear: "Yes" means that the unicorn exists, and "No" means that he is asking us not to look for it because of the danger involved. But naturally we shall ignore his warning.'

For the first time Markovitch joined in our conversation. He said, 'Suppose we do come across a unicorn; have we decided what we're going to do with it?'

Kroll said, 'We haven't thought of that yet. The first thing is to track down the creature.'

Markovitch lapsed into silence. It seemed that he has some plans of his own. Now that he is rid of the cocaine habit, he seems much more energetic. I have also been observing in him a great interest in lamaseries. When we left the monastery after our talk with the mute lama, Markovitch stayed back to explore the place a little more thoroughly. Is the drug addict turning religious? I wonder.

18 AUGUST, 10 A.M.

Just now we crossed the Chusung-la pass and had a glimpse of the Lake Ravana and the white dome of Mount Kailash behind it. Lake Ravana is called Rakshasa Tal in Tibetan, and Mount Kailash is Kang Rimpoche. The lake isn't a particularly holy one, but the first sight of Kailash made our porters prostrate themselves. Mr Majumder was a little perplexed at first, but the moment he realized what the dome was, he reeled off a dozen names of Lord Shiva, fell on his knees and touched the ground again and again with his head. The holy Mansarovar is to the east of Lake Ravana. We expect to be there by tomorrow.

20 AUGUST, 2.30 P.M.

We have halted by a hot spring to the north-west of Mansarovar. We shall reach the lake as soon as we are over the hump to our left.

Today for the first time in over a week we all had a bath. A pall of vapour hangs over the spring which contains sulphur, and is very warm. One feels remarkably refreshed after a bath in it.

I wouldn't have opened my diary now but for an incident which took place a little while ago.

Mr Majumder and I were using the west side of the spring while the others bathed in the north side. I had finished my bath and Kroll walked over and, as if he had come for a casual tête-à-tête, said in a low voice, 'A messy affair.'

I said, 'Why, what's the matter?'

'Markovitch.'

'Markovitch?'

'A snake in the grass.'

'What has he done now?' I knew Kroll had a particular dislike for Markovitch.

Kroll kept up that smiling, chatty tone and said, 'We had taken off our coats and kept them behind a boulder before we got into the water. I was up after a dip or two. Markovitch's coat was lying next to mine. I could see the inside pocket, and couldn't resist the temptation of looking what was in it. There were three letters. All with British postage stamps, and all addressed to a Mr John Markham.'

'Markham?'

'Markham—Markovitch, John—Ivan, don't you see?'

'Where were the letters sent?' I asked.

'To an address in New Delhi.'

John Markham . . . John Markham . . . the name seemed to ring a bell. Where had I heard it before? Yes. It was in the papers some three years back. A man caught smuggling gold. John Markham. He got a prison sentence too, but had managed to escape by killing a guard. The man was British, but had been living in India for a long time. Used to run a hotel in Nainital. An escaped convict. Now he has teamed up with us and is trying to pass himself off as a Russian living in Poland. He wants Tibet to be his hideout. A swindler all right, and perhaps with more villainy up his sleeve. I had to praise Kroll's sleuthing. I told him of Markham and his dark deeds.

Kroll has kept up his toothy smile simply because Markovitch can see us from where he is. He mustn't suspect that we are talking about him.

Kroll laughed out loudly at nothing, dropped his voice, kept smiling and said, 'I suggest that we leave him behind. Let him freeze to death in the blizzard. That would be his punishment.'

I didn't like the idea. I said, 'No. Let him come with us. We will hand him over quietly to the police when we return.'

In the end Kroll agreed to my proposal. Must find an opportunity to tell Saunders, and must keep a sharp watch over Markovitch.

20 AUGUST, 5.30 P.M.

In the famous Sanskrit poem *Meghdoot* of Kalidasa, there is a description of swans and lotuses in the Mansarovar. We have seen flocks of wild geese but no swans or lotuses as yet. Apart from that I can say that the descriptions of the lake one reads in travel books come nowhere near the real thing. I cannot ever begin to describe how one feels at the sudden sight of the vast expanse of vivid and transparent blue in a terrain of sand and rocks. To the north of the lake stands the twenty-two thousand feet Mount Kailash, and to the south, rising almost straight out of the water, stands Gurla Mandhata. All around are mountains dotted with monasteries, their golden domes glistening in the sun.

We have pitched our tents about thirty feet from the edge of the lake. There are many pilgrims around. Some of them are doing their circumambulation of the lake by crawling, while others are doing it on foot with prayer wheels in their hands. Mansarovar is sacred to both Hindus and Buddhists. Geographically, the place is important because the sources of four great rivers lie close by. They are Brahmaputra, Sutlej, Indus and Karnali.

Apart from doing obeisance by lying prone on the ground, Mr Majumder made our foreign friends get down on their knees by repeatedly saying, 'Sacred, sacred—more sacred than cow!' But what he did after that was far from prudent. He went to the edge of the lake, threw away his overcoat, put his palms together and plunged straight into the water. The icy water numbed him instantly. However, Kroll managed to drag him out and force some brandy down his throat, thus bringing some warmth back into his body.

Mr Majumder is up and about again. He says he has had arthritis in his left thumb for the last twenty-six years which the water of the lake has completely cured. He has filled three empty Horlicks bottles with the holy water which he says he will sprinkle on us from time to time to keep us from trouble. Nearby in Gianima there is a large market from which we have bought dried fruits, cakes of frozen yak milk and woollen tents.

Kroll has bought an assortment of bones, one of which—a human thigh bone—can be played like a flute. He says they will be useful for his research on witchcraft. Markovitch had strayed from the group in the bazaar for a while. He got back only ten minutes ago. We haven't found out what he brought back in his bag. Saunders has managed to get rid of some of his pessimism. He has realized that even if he cannot find a unicorn, the unearthly beauty of Mansarovar and the extraordinarily clear and invigorating atmosphere of the place make the trip more than worthwhile.

We shall set off for the dreaded Chang Thang tomorrow. Our destination will be Lat. 33°3' N and Long. 84° E.

Mr Majumder is now sitting on the sand with the sun on his back, his face turned towards Mount Kailash and the pocket Gita open in his hand. We shall now find out how far his faith is able to tide us over travails.

22 AUGUST
CHANG THANG, LAT. 30°5' N AND LONG. 81°8' E

It is eight-thirty in the morning now. We have set up camp beside a small lake.

A strange occurrence last night. At midnight, with the temperature well below freezing point, Kroll came into my tent, woke me up and announced that he had found highly suspicious objects among Markovitch's belongings. I was amazed. 'But didn't he find out that you were rummaging amongst his things?' I asked.

'How could he? I had mixed some barbiturate in his tea last night. It's not for nothing that I learned sleight of hand. He's now fast asleep.'

'What did you find?'

'Come and have a look.'

I wrapped myself in a thick blanket, left my tent and crawled into Kroll's. The moment I entered, a strong, vaguely familiar odour assailed my nostrils. 'What's this smell?' I asked.

Kroll said, 'Well, this is just one of the things I found. It is in this tin.'

I took the tin and took off the cap. My mouth fell open.

'But this is musk!' I exclaimed in a shocked voice.

'No question about it,' said Kroll.

I knew there were musk deer in Tibet—a species which was fast becoming extinct from the rest of the world. A deer the size of an average dog which carried the extraordinary substance in its stomach. Musk is used in perfumery. A gram of musk costs nearly thirty rupees. In India, soon after the start of our journey, I met a musk dealer in Askot who alone had exported under government licence nearly four-hundred thousand rupees worth of musk. I said, 'Is this something which Markovitch bought from the bazaar at Gianima?'

'Bought it?' The question was put by Saunders, his voice oozing sarcasm. 'You think these were all bought by Markovitch?'

Saunders opened a bag and brought out from its depths a mass of black yak wool, five gold statuettes of Buddha, a gold vajra set with precious stones, and some twenty or thirty loose gems.

'We have a real robber in our midst,' said Saunders. 'I'm absolutely sure that he filched the musk from some shop in Gianima just as he filched the other objects from the monastery.'

Now I realized why Markovitch stayed back in the monastery. What a daredevil the man is!

This morning, Markovitch's behaviour suggested that he hadn't yet found out about last night's raid. Everything was put back in place before we left. We had also discovered that Markovitch was carrying a weapon with him a .45 Colt automatic. Markovitch hadn't mentioned this to us. Not that the weapon is going to serve him any purpose now, because Kroll has made off with all the bullets.

25 AUGUST, 4.30 P.M.
CHANG THANG, LAT. 32°5' N, LONG. 82° E

The terrifying aspect of Chang Thang is gradually revealing itself to us. The elevation here is sixteen-thousand and five hundred feet. We are now in an uneven terrain. Sometimes we have to climb four or five hundred feet to negotiate a pass, and then descend again.

We haven't seen a single tree or shrub since yesterday morning. All around us are sand, rock and snow. Even here the Tibetans have carved their mantra *Om Mani Padme Hum* on rock faces. There are no monasteries here, although we do come across an occasional chorten. Of human habitation there is no sign at all.

The day before yesterday we suddenly found ourselves in a nomad encampment. Nearly five hundred men, women, children, goats, sheep, donkeys, dogs and yaks occupying a large territory with woollen tents pitched everywhere. The people were jolly, with a smile on everyone's face, obviously happy in their rootless, wandering state. We asked one or two about unicorns but got no satisfactory answer.

When they heard that we were going further north, they vehemently advised us against it. 'In the north there is Dung-lung-do,' they said. 'Beyond that you cannot go.' From their description it sounded as if Dung-lung-do was a place surrounded by a high wall which is impossible to scale. Nobody knows what lies beyond the wall. These people have never seen it, but Tibetans have always known about it. In earlier times, some lamas are said to have gone there, but no one in the last three or four hundred years.

When the mute lama's warnings hadn't discouraged us, why should we listen to these nomads? We have Charles Willard's diary with us. We must follow in his footsteps.

28 AUGUST
CHANG THANG, LAT. 32°8' N, LONG. 82°2' E

I am writing my diary sitting in my camp beside a lake. A strange experience today. We were crossing a valley with dark clouds in the sky threatening a storm when Saunders suddenly cried out, 'What are those?'

Further up, where the valley ascended, we could discern a dozen or so dark forms. They did seem like a herd of animals. We asked Rabsang, but he couldn't say what they were. The strange thing is that whatever they were, they all stood rooted to the same spot.

At Kroll's instigation I looked through the omniscope. 'Do you see horns?' Kroll asked breathlessly. I had to admit I didn't.

In another ten minutes the mystery was solved. They were wild donkeys, nearly twenty in number, all standing stiff and lifeless in the snow. Rabsang explained what had happened. They got buried in the snow in the blizzard and died. Summer has since melted the snow and exposed them again.

Our stock of foodstuff is dwindling. We had bought some tea and butter from the nomads with Indian money; they will last for a while. We are all heartily sick of eating meat. But vegetables are in short supply too. Everyone has had to take my food-and-drink pills from time to time. Soon there will be nothing left but these pills. Kroll has been using spells and incantations learnt all over the world from Mexico to Borneo to find out whether we will have the luck to stumble upon a herd of unicorns. Five spells said 'Yes', six said 'No'.

Thirty or forty miles to the north of where we have camped in the direction we are heading, the land seems to rise abruptly. It has the appearance of a table mountain through binoculars. Is that Dung-lung-do? We are actually near the location mentioned by Willard in his diary.

But where is Willard's monastery—Thokchum Gompa? Where is the two-hundred-year-old flying lama?

And where is the herd of unicorns?

29 AUGUST

An electrifying experience in a wonderful monastery.

There is no doubt that this is the Thokchum Gompa of Willard's diary. And we have proof of that too. Three minutes before reaching the monastery we found carved on a rock face by the roadside the letters CRW, which obviously stood for Charles Roxton

Willard. I must mention that all our porters except Rabsang and Tundup have absconded. I doubt if Rabsang will ever desert us. He is not only trustworthy, but there's not a trace of superstition in him. He is a rare exception among Tibetans. The others have taken away with them all our ponies and four yaks. Only two yaks are left. Our tents and some of our heavy baggage can go on their backs. The rest we will have to carry ourselves. And since our ponies are gone, we will have to do the rest of the journey on foot. The high plateau is getting closer by the hour, which is why excitement is running high among the group. We all believe that must be Dung-lung-do, although we still don't know what it is. Saunders believes it is the wall of a fortress, while my feeling is that behind the wall is a lake which is not shown on any map of Tibet.

The monastery I am about to describe was hidden from view till the last moment. It was situated behind a granite hillock. As soon as we crossed the hillock, it came into view, evoking expressions of surprise from all of us. Although the sun was behind the clouds, the splendour of the monastery made it appear paved in gold from base to spire.

As we approached it, we had the impression that there were very few occupants in it. The whole place seemed wrapped in silence. We climbed the slope and made our way through the main entrance. A huge bronze bell hung overhead across the threshold. As Kroll pulled the rope, it rang with a solemn sonority, the reverberations persisting for nearly three minutes.

It was quite clear from the moment of entry that no one had been here for a very long time. There was everything one would expect in a monastery except human beings. When Saunders' loud 'Helios' produced no replies, we decided to explore. Kroll's behaviour made it clear that he was not going to leave Markovitch alone. There were too many gold objects about. Saunders went over to the door to the left of the hall, while Mr Majumder and I went to the door on the right. There was a thick layer of dust on the floor and abundant proof that rats lived here. We had just entered a room when a sudden scream stopped us in our tracks and froze our blood.

It was Saunders' voice. We ran to investigate and were joined by Kroll and Markovitch, the four of us arriving simultaneously at the door of a room on the right of the central hall. Our way was blocked by Saunders who had stopped at the threshold, apparently riveted by something at the back of the low, dank room.

Now I realized the reason for the scream.

An ancient, shaven-headed lama sat cross-legged at a desk on the far side of the room, his body bent forward, his eyes open but unseeing, his shrivelled hands placed on the withered pages of an open manuscript.

The lama was dead. When and how he died there was no way of knowing, nor how his corpse had escaped decay.

We were all inside the room now, Saunders was back to his normal self. He had been suffering from nerves for some time, which explains his extreme fright. I know if our expedition is crowned with success, he will surely regain his health.

Now we turned to the other objects in the room. On one side was an assortment of brass and copper vessels which almost gave the impression that we were in a kitchen. On inspecting the vessels, we found that they contained powdered, liquid and viscous substances of various kinds and hues. I couldn't recognize any of them.

The opposite wall had shelves overflowing with ancient manuscripts. Below the shelves, on the floor, stood eight pairs of Tibetan high boots, all intricately embroidered and set with gems. Besides these, the floor was strewn with bones, skulls and animal skins. Kroll cried excitedly, 'This is the first monastery where I feel I am in the presence of ancient magic!'

I had no feeling of fright, so I approached the dead lama. I wanted to find out what he was studying when he died. I had already noticed that the manuscript was in Sanskrit, not Tibetan.

I gently tugged at the manuscript and it slipped out from under the corpse's fingers and came into my hands. The lama's hand stayed suspended in the air three inches above the desk. A quick glance told me that the subject of the manuscript was scientific. I took it with me and the five of us left the gloom of the monastery and came out into the open.

It is two in the afternoon now, I am sitting on a flat rock outside the monastery. I have gone through a considerable portion of the manuscript in the last couple of hours. That the Tibetans had not confined their studies only to religion is now clear. The manuscript is called *Uddayansutram* or A Treatise on Flying. It describes how a person can be airborne by purely chemical means. I had heard of the treatise. In Buddhist times there was a great scholar in Taxila in India known as Vidyut Dhamani. He was the one who composed the treatise and left for Tibet shortly thereafter. He never came back to India, and no one in India ever learnt about his scientific researches.

The manuscript describes a substance called *ngmung*. With the help of ngmung the weight of a person can be reduced to such an extent that a breath of wind can make him soar 'like a feather plucked from the back of a swan'. There is a description of how ngmung can be prepared, but the ingredients mentioned are totally unfamiliar to me. The dead lama must have known about these ingredients and must have succeeded in preparing ngmung. Doubtless this is the two-hundred-year-old lama with whom Willard flew. That the lama should have died within the last six months is our misfortune, or we too might have flown like Willard.

Everybody is preparing to leave, so I must close now.

30 AUGUST
LAT. 33°3' N, LONG. 84° E

Willard's diary mentions camping on this location. We have done the same thing. We are now reduced to five members including Rabsang. Markham alias Markovitch has disappeared, and he must have persuaded Tundup to go with him. Not only that, they have made off with our two last yaks. I had noticed Markham chatting with Tundup several times. I had paid no attention then; now I realize they had been conspiring. It happened yesterday afternoon. Within two hours of leaving the monastery we were caught in a blinding storm. We didn't know who was going which way. When after half an hour the storm subsided, we found that we were two members and two yaks short. On top of that, when we found that there was a gun missing, we realized that it was not an accident. Markham had deliberately run away and had no intention of returning. One way to look at it is that it is good riddance, but the regret remains that he has escaped punishment. Kroll is greatly upset. He says this is the result of mollycoddling him. However, there's no use crying over spilt milk; we shall proceed to Dung-lung-do without him.

The wall of Dung-lung-do is now constantly in our sight. There are still another four or five miles to go, but even from this distance, the great height of the wall is apparent. In width it seems at least twenty-five miles. The depth, of course, cannot be guessed from here.

The wind is rising again. Must hurry back into the tent.

1.30 P.M.

The sky is overcast, and a blizzard is blowing with the sound of a million shrill flutes. It is a good thing we bought those woollen tents in Gianima.

It looks as if we will have to spend the whole day in the tent.

5 P.M.

One of the highlights of our expedition took place a little while ago.

At three the storm let up a little, and Rabsang brought butter tea for the four of us. Although the fury of the storm had abated, occasional gusts of wind caused the tents to flap.

Mr Majumder had just sipped his tea and said 'Aaahh!' in appreciation when we heard a yelling from somewhere. We couldn't make out the words, but the tone of panic was clear. We put down our pots and rushed out of the tent.

'Help! Help! Save me! . . . Help!'

Now it was clear. And we could recognize the voice too. Till now Markham had been speaking English with a Russian accent; now, for the first time, he sounded thoroughly British. But where was he? Rabsang too looked around in a bewildered way, because one moment the voice seemed to be coming from the south, and the next moment from the north.

Suddenly Kroll shouted, 'There he is!'

He wasn't looking north or south, but up in the sky, directly above us.

I looked up and was astounded to see Markovitch come floating towards us. One moment he plummeted down, and the next a gust of wind sent him soaring up. It was in such a state that he waved his arms about and screamed to draw our attention.

There was no time to think how he had arrived at such a predicament; the question was how to bring him down, because the wind kept blowing him this way and that.

'Let him stay there,' Saunders suddenly bawled out. Kroll promptly dittoed the suggestion. They both thought it was an excellent way to punish the miscreant. And yet the scientist in me said that unless he was brought down, we wouldn't be able to find out how he got airborne in the first place. Rabsang, meanwhile, had used his native intelligence and got down to business. He had tied a stone at the end of a long rope and was ready to fling it at Markham. Kroll stopped him. Markham was now directly above us. Kroll shouted at him, 'Drop that gun first.' I hadn't noticed that Markham was carrying a gun. Like an obedient boy, Markham released his hold on the weapon which dropped with a loud thud on the ground, sending up a spray of snow ten feet away from us.

Now Rabsang sent the stone flying up to Markham with unerring aim. Markham grabbed it, and Rabsang brought him down by vigorous pulls at the rope.

Now I noticed that Markham was wearing the ornate boots of which we saw eight pairs in the dead lama's room. Besides this, the bag he was carrying on his shoulder turned out to contain valuable gold objects pilfered from the monastery. There was no

doubt that the robber had been caught red-handed. But, at the same time, he had brought to light something so exciting that we forgot all about reprimanding him.

Markham had run away from us all right, and the first thing he had done was to go to the Thokchum monastery and load himself up with some of the precious objects kept in the central hall. Having done that he had gone to the dead lama's room and helped himself to a pair of the gem-studded boots. Walking in them had made him realize that he was feeling lighter. When he had gone a couple of miles with Tundup, a storm had come up from the south and wrecked all his plans by hoisting him up and blowing him back in our direction.

Kroll and Saunders were naturally astonished to hear the story. It was then that I told them about the manuscript and the substance ngmung. 'But what is the connection between the substance and the boots?' asked Kroll.

I said, 'The manuscript mentions a connection between the substance and the sole, or underside of the foot. I'm sure the lining of the boot has a coating of ngmung.'

This might have led to an argument, but having seen Markham aloft with their own eyes, Kroll and Saunders accepted my explanation. Of course, all three of us were now anxious to possess such boots. Rabsang said he would bring them for us from the monastery.

Markham is now completely tamed. We have taken away from him everything he had stolen. We shall put them all back in place on our way back. I do hope Markham will behave himself from now on, although at the back of my mind runs the Sanskrit proverb which says that coal will never shed its blackness however much you may wash it.

31 AUGUST

We have pitched our tents about two hundred yards away from the wall of Dung-lung-do. We are going about in our boots, waiting for a strong wind to take us across the wall to the unknown region beyond. The wall rises steeply up to a height of about one hundred and fifty feet. Even the geologist Saunders couldn't tell what kind of stone it was made of. It is remarkably smooth and hard, bluish in colour, and resembles no known variety of stone. Kroll has made a few attempts to scale the wall by leaping with the boots on, but in the absence of a strong wind he couldn't rise beyond twenty or thirty feet. I am consumed with curiosity about what lies beyond the wall. Saunders still insists that it must be a fortress. I have stopped guessing.

8 SEPTEMBER

In the far distance, I can see a large group of people approaching. If this turns out to be a bandit gang, then there is no hope for us. It was the magical climate of Dung-lung-do that gave us the energy to walk ten miles on foot and arrive at this spot. But now that energy is ebbing. The wind is blowing from a direction opposite to the way we are going; so the boots are of no help at all. Our stock of food is dangerously depleted, and there are few of my tablets left. In this state, in spite of being armed, a bandit gang could cause no end of trouble. As it is, we have lost one of our members, although he was himself responsible for what happened. It was his excessive greed that spelled his doom.

A little while ago, Mr Majumder said, 'I don't know what your omniscope reveals; Kailash, Mansarovar and Dung-lung-do have endowed me with supernatural vision. I can already see those people are nomads. So they will do us no harm.'

Well, if they do turn out to be nomads, they would not only do us no harm, but might actually provide us with ponies, yaks and provisions—in fact, everything we need for our return journey.

After waiting for thirty-seven hours, on the first of September, at one-forty in the afternoon, the state of the sky and a rumble of thunder told us that the kind of wind that we had been waiting for was in fact on its way. Mr Majumder had dozed off, and I woke him up. Then we five booted men stood with our backs to the approaching storm and our faces to the wall. In three minutes the storm hit us. Being the lightest of the group, I was the first to get aloft.

It is difficult for me to describe the extraordinary experience. The storm carried us streaking through the air both forwards and upwards, while the wall ahead plunged forward and downward at the same time, revealing more and more of the view beyond.

First we could see snow-capped peaks in the far distance beyond the wall on the far side; then came into view a wonderful green world—not a fort, nor a lake—which the wall had kept hidden from us. We were about to enter this world over the top. From behind me I could hear Kroll, Saunders, and Markham expressing their child like wonder in English and German, while Mr Majumder exclaimed, 'Why, this must be the garden of Eden— yes, the garden of Eden!'

As soon as we crossed the wall, the storm magically abated. We landed gently on the green grass, very much like a 'feather plucked from a swan's back'. I said green because of the green colour, but never before have I seen such grass. Saunders shouted, 'Do you know, Shonku, not a single tree here is familiar to me. This is a completely new environment.'

Saunders proceeded immediately to collect specimens of flora, while Kroll got busy with his camera. Mr Majumder rolled on the grass saying, 'Let us stay here. Why go back to Giridih? The soil here is wonderful. We can grow anything we want. Markham took off his boots and made his way through the tall grass.

Dung-lung-do seemed to be at least as large as Mansarovar. It was a concave valley surrounded by the wall. Although the wall on the outer side dropped steeply, the inner side came down in a gentle slope. Saunders was right; not a single specimen of flora here was known to us. The trees abounded in varicoloured flowers and fruits which we now recognized as the source of the exquisite, heady smell which had drifted across the wall to reach our camp.

The four of us were exploring the place in our boots, advancing by gentle leaps, when we suddenly heard a swishing sound. The next moment something passed across the sun casting a giant shadow. And now we saw it: a colossal bird as large as five hundred eagles put together, with feathers as resplendent as that of a South American macaw.

'Mein Gott' cried Kroll in a hoarse whisper. The next moment he was about to raise his gun when I restrained him by raising my hand. Not only was the gun useless against the bird, but my mind told me that the bird would do us no harm.

The bird circled above us three times and then, with a long cry like a foghorn, flew back the way it came. I found myself involuntarily saying, 'Roc'

'What?' Kroll asked in bewilderment.

I said, 'Roc, or Rukh. The giant bird in Sindbad's tale.'

'But we're not in the land of Arabian Nights, Shonku,' said Kroll impatiently. 'This is a real world. There is the ground under our feet, we can touch the leaves with our fingers, smell the flowers with our noses.'

Saunders shook off his wonder and said, 'There isn't a single insect around—which is most surprising.'

The four of us were advancing when we suddenly found ourselves up against an obstacle. For the first time we were faced with an object on the ground which was not a species of flora. A twelve-foot-high boulder, bluish green in colour, obstructed our path. How far it stretched on either side was hard to tell. Kroll suddenly gave a mighty leap which took him soaring and landed him gently on top of the boulder. And then something wholly unexpected happened; the boulder heaved, and then started to move to our left. Kroll too was being borne along with it when he suddenly yelled out, 'My God, it's a dragon!'

Yes, it was a dragon. One of its legs was now passing in front of us. Meanwhile Kroll had jumped off the back of the beast and had joined us. We stared in amazement at what was visible to us of the giant beast. It took it nearly three minutes to pass by us swishing its huge scaly tail, and disappear behind the dense foliage. The smoke which now hung over the forest must have come from the nostrils of the beast.

Saunders had sat down on the grass and was holding his head in his hands. He said, 'I feel like an uneducated boor up against these strange creatures in these unfamiliar surroundings, Shonku.'

I said, 'But I like it. I'm glad to discover that there are still surprises left even for learned men like us in this planet of ours.'

I have lost count of the wonderful things we saw in the next hour of our expedition. We have watched a Phoenix consumed by flames, and a new Phoenix rising from its ashes and flying off towards the sun. We have seen the Gryphon, the Simurgh of Persian legends, the Anka of the Arabs, the Nork of the Russians, and the Feng and the Kirne of the Japanese. Among lizards we have seen the Basilisk whose unblinking stare can reduce anything to ashes, and we have seen the Salamander which is proof against fire and which, as if to prove the truth of the legend, was again and again passing through flames and emerging unscathed. We have also seen a four-tusked elephant which could only be Oiravat, the mount of the Indian god Indra. The stately pachyderm stood eating the leaves of a tree whose dazzling brilliance could only mean that it was the celestial tree Parijat of our mythology.

But Dung-lung-do is not just a forest of gorgeous trees. We had proceeded a mile or so along the northern wall when we were suddenly confronted with an open country bereft of vegetation. Before us were enormous boulders with caves in them from which emerged blood-curdling roars and snarls. We realized we had come to the region of legendary demons and rakshasas, a common feature of fairy tales of all nations. Emboldened by the fact that none of the creatures paid the slightest attention to us, I was debating whether to enter the caves or not when a frenzied, high-pitched cry made us all turn to our left.

'Unicorns! Unicorns! Unicorns!'

It was Markham, and his voice was coming from behind a large boulder.

'Has he been taking cocaine again?' asked Kroll.

'I don't think so,' I said, advancing towards the boulder. As I crossed it, a unique sight nearly stopped my heartbeat.

A big herd of animals, both adult and young, was passing in front of us. Each looked like a cross between a cow and a horse, was pinkish grey in colour, and had a single spiral horn on its forehead. I realized that they were what launched us on our expedition. They were unquestionably unicorns, Pliny's unicorns, the unicorn of western mythology, the unicorn on the seals of Mohenjo Daro.

Not all the animals were on the move. Some stood chewing grass, some frisked about, while others playfully butted each other with their horns. Like Willard, we too were watching the scene in full possession of our senses.

But where was Markham?

The question had just crossed my mind when we saw a strange sight. Markham had emerged from the herd of unicorns and was running towards the wall behind us. But he

was not alone; he was grasping with both hands a unicorn cub.

Saunders cried out, 'Stop that scoundrel! Stop him!'

'Put your boots on! Put your boots on!' screamed Kroll. He had started running after Markham. We too followed him leaping.

If the warning had reached Markham in time, perhaps he wouldn't have acted the way he did. Running up the grass slope Markham gave a leap as he reached the wall and dropped out of sight behind it.

Later we learnt from Rabsang that as soon as he saw Markham jump over the wall, he had run towards him. But there was nothing for him to do. The two-hundred-foot fall had crushed all the bones in his body. When we asked about the unicorn, he shook his head and said he had only found Markham's body; there was no unicorn cub with him.

My conclusions about Dung-lung-do have found favour with both Kroll and Saunders. My feeling is that if a great many people believe in an imaginary creature over a great length of time, the sheer force of that belief may bring to life that creature with all the characteristics human imagination has endowed it with. Dung-lung-do was a repository of such imaginary creatures. Perhaps it was the only place of its kind on earth. To try to bring anything from Dung-lung-do into the world of reality was futile, which is why the unicorn vanished as soon as Markham crossed the limits of the world of fantasy.

The mute lama's saying yes and no almost in the same breath now bears a clear meaning; the unicorn exists, though not in reality. But the lama was wrong when he said no to the question of flight. Perhaps he didn't know about the manuscript.

Mr Majumder said at the end of our discussion. 'So there is nothing for us to show when we get back home?'

I said, 'I'm afraid not. Because I doubt if Kroll's photographs will come out, and our boots won't help us to fly, because the manuscript says that ngmung melts in the heat of the plains.'

Mr Majumder sighed. Now I played my trump card. 'Have you realized that we are going back younger by about twenty years?'

'How's that?'

I wiped the snowflakes off my beard and moustache.

'Why, they're black again!' exclaimed Mr Majumder.

'So is your moustache,' I said. 'Look in the mirror.'

At this point Saunders came in. He looked younger too and a weak tooth of his had become stronger again. He heaved a deep sigh of relief.

'Nomads, not robbers,' he said. 'Thank God!'

I can hear the sound of horses' hooves, and the barking of dogs, and the shouting of men, women and children. The cloud has lifted and the sun shines again.

Om Mani Padme Hum!

TELLUS

Originally published in *Anandamela* (Puja Annual 1978) as *Compu*. It was translated by the author himself to be part of the compilation titled *Stories* (Secker & Warburg, 1987). The illustrations in the story are by Satyajit Ray.

12 MARCH
Osaka

There was a demonstration of Tellus today in the presence of more than three hundred scientists and a hundred journalists from all over the world. Tellus was placed on a three-foot-high pedestal of transparent pellucidite on the stage of the hall of the Namura Technological Institute. When two of the workers of the Institute came in carrying the smooth, elegant platinum sphere, the hall echoed with spontaneous applause. That an apparatus which can answer a million questions should be only as large as a football, weigh forty-two kilos and bear no resemblance to a machine, came as a complete surprise to the audience. The fact is, in this age of microminiaturisation, no instrument, however complicated, need be very large. Fifty years ago, in the age of cabinet radios, could anyone have imagined that one would one day be watching television programmes on one's wrist watch?

There is no doubt that Tellus is a triumph of modern technology. But it is also true that in the making of intricate instruments, man comes nowhere near nature yet.

The machine we have constructed contains ten million circuits. The human brain is one fourth the size of Tellus, and contains about one hundred million neurons. This alone indicates how intricate is its construction.

Let me make it clear that our computer is incapable of mathematical calculations. Its job is to answer questions which would normally require a person to consult an encyclopedia. Another unique feature of the computer is that it gives its answers orally in English, in a clear, bell-like tone. The first question has to be preceded with the words 'Tell us', which activate the instrument and which gives it its name. At the end the words 'Thank you' turn it off. The battery, whose life is one hundred and twenty hours is of a special kind, and is housed in a chamber inside the sphere. There are two hundred minute holes on the surface of the sphere covering an area of one square inch; these allow the questions to enter and the answers to come out. The questions have to be of a nature which call for short answers. For instance, although the delegates were briefed before today's demonstration, a journalist from the Philippines asked the instrument to talk about ancient Chinese civilization. Naturally no answer came out. And yet when the same journalist asked about certain specific aspects of specific Chinese civilizations, the instrument astonished everyone by answering instantly and precisely.

Tellus can not only supply information, but is also capable of reasoning logically. The biologist Doctor Solomon from Nigeria asked the instrument whether it would be safer to keep a young baboon before a hungry deer or a hungry chimpanzee. Tellus answered in a flash! 'A hungry deer'. 'Why?' asked Doctor Solomon. Came the answer in a sharp, ringing voice: 'Because the chimpanzee is carnivorous'. This is a fact which has only recently come to light; even ten years ago everyone thought that monkeys and apes of all species were vegetarian.

Besides these, Tellus is able to take part in games of bridge and chess, point out a false note or a false beat in music, identify ragas, name a painter from a verbal description of one of his paintings, prescribe medicines and diets for particular kinds of ailments, and even indicate the chances of survival from the description of a patient's condition.

What Tellus lacks are abilities to think and feel, and supernatural powers. When Professor Maxwell of Sydney University asked it if a man would still be reading books a hundred years from now, Tellus was silent because prognostication is beyond it. In spite of these deficiencies, Tellus surpasses human beings in one respect: the information fed into its brain suffers no decay. The most brilliant of men often suffer from a loss of faculties with age. Even I, only the other day in Giridih, found myself addressing my servant Prahlad as Prayag. This is the kind of mistake which Tellus will never make. So, in a way, although it is a creation of human beings, it is more dependable than man.

The original idea for the instrument came from the famous Japanese scientist Matsue, one of the great names in electronics. The Japanese Government approved of his scheme and agreed to bear the expenses of constructing it. The technicians of the Namura Institute put in seven years of hard labour to construct Tellus. In the fourth year, just before the preliminary work was over, Matsue invited seven scientists from five continents to help feed information into the computer. Needless to say, I was one of the seven. The other six were: Doctor John Kensley of Britain, Doctor Stephen Merrivale of the Massachusetts Institute of Technology, Doctor Stassof of USSR, Professor Stratton of Melbourne, Doctor Ugati of West Africa, and Professor Kuttna of Hungary. Of these, Merrivale died of a heart attack three days before leaving for Japan. He was replaced by Professor Marcus Wingfield from the same MIT. Some of these scientists have stayed the full stretch of three years as guests of the Japanese Government. Others, such as myself, have come for short stretches at regular intervals. I have been here eleven times in the last three years.

I should like to mention an extraordinary event. The day before yesterday, on March the tenth, there was a solar eclipse. Japan fell in the zone of totality. Because it was a special day, we had already decided to finish our work before the tenth. We thought we had done so on the eighth of March when we discovered that no speech was coming out of the machine. The sphere was built so that it could be taken apart down the middle. We did that. Now we had to find out which of the ten million circuits was at fault.

We searched for two days and two nights. On the tenth, just as the eclipse was about to begin—at 1.37 p.m. in the afternoon—a high-pitched whistle issued from Tellus' speaker. This indicated that the fault had been repaired. We heaved a sigh of relief and went out to watch the eclipse. I wondered if there was any significance in the fact that the beginning of the eclipse coincided exactly with the coming to life of the instrument.

Tellus has been kept in the Institute. A special room has been built for it to keep it under controlled temperature. The room is a most elegant one. Tellus rests on the concave surface of the pellucidite pedestal in the middle of one side of the room against the wall. On the ceiling is a hole through which a concealed light sends a powerful beam to illuminate the sphere. The light is kept on all the time. Because Tellus is a national treasure, the room is guarded by watchmen. One mustn't forget that even nations can be jealous of one another; I have already heard Wingfield grumble twice about the USA losing the race to Japan in computer technology. A word about Wingfield here. There is no question that he is a qualified man; but nobody likes him very much. One probable reason is that Wingfield is among the most glum-faced of individuals. Nobody in Osaka remembers seeing him laugh in the last three years.

Three of the scientists from abroad are going back home today. Those who are staying behind are Wingfield, Kensley, Kuttna and myself. Wingfield suffers from gout and is getting himself treated by a specialist in Osaka. I hope to travel around a bit. I'm going to Kyoto with Kensley tomorrow. A physicist by profession Kensley's interests range wide. He is something of an authority on Japanese art. He is most anxious to go to Kyoto if only to see the Buddhist temples and the Zen gardens.

The Hungarian biologist, Krzystoff Kuttna, does not much care for art, but there is one thing that interests him which only I know of, because I am the only person he discusses it with. The subject does not come strictly under the province of science. An example will make it clear.

We were having breakfast together this morning. Kuttna took a sip of coffee and said quite unexpectedly, 'I didn't watch the eclipse the other day.'

I wasn't aware of this. For me the total solar eclipse is a phenomenon of such outstanding importance. The corona around the sun at the time of totality is for me such an extraordinary sight, that I never notice who else is watching besides me. I was amazed that Kuttna could deprive himself of such an opportunity. I said, 'Do you have any superstition about watching an eclipse?'

Instead of answering, Kuttna put a question to me: 'Does a solar eclipse exert any influence on platinum?'

'Not that I know of,' I said. 'Why do you ask?'

'Why then did the sphere lose its lustre during those two and a half minutes of totality? I clearly noticed a pall descending on the sphere as soon as totality began. It lifted the moment totality ended.'

I didn't know what to say. 'What do you think?' I asked at last, wondering how old Kuttna was and whether it was a symptom of senility.

'I have no thoughts,' he said, 'because the experience is completely new to me. All I can say is that if it turns out to be an optical illusion, I would be happy. I am not superstitious about an eclipse, but I am about mechanical brains. When Matsue asked me to come, I told him about it. I said, if man continues to use machines to serve human functions, there may come a time when machines will take over.'

The discussion couldn't go on because of the arrival of Kensley and Wingfield. What Kuttna felt about machines was nothing new. That man may one day be dominated by machines has been a possibility for quite some time. As a simple example, consider man's dependence on vehicles. Even city dwellers, before the days of mechanical transport, used to walk seven or eight miles a day with ease, now they feel helpless without transport. But this doesn't mean that one should call a halt to scientific progress. Machines will be made to lighten the work of man. There is no going back to primitive times.

14 MARCH
KYOTO

Whatever I have read or heard in praise of Kyoto is no exaggeration. I wouldn't have believed that the aesthetic sense of a people could permeate a whole city in such a way. This afternoon we had been to see a famous Zen temple and the garden adjoining it. It is hard to imagine a more peaceful atmosphere. We met the famous scholar Tanaka in the temple. A saintly character, his placidity harmonizes perfectly with his surroundings. When he heard about our computer, he smiled gently and said, 'Can your machine tell us whose will works behind the sun and the moon coinciding so perfectly for a solar eclipse?'

A true philosopher's question. The moon is so much smaller than the sun, and yet

its distance from the earth is such that it appears to be exactly the same size as the sun.

I had realized the magnitude of the coincidence as a small boy. Ever since then I have had a feeling of profound wonder at the phenomenon of total eclipse. How can Tellus know the answer to the question when we don't know it ourselves?

We will spend another day here and then go to Kamakura. I have benefitted a lot from Kensley's company. Good things seem even better when you are with someone who appreciates them.

15 MARCH

I am writing this in the compartment of our train in the Kyoto station. There was a severe earthquake here last night at 2.30 a.m. Tremors are common in Japan, but this one was of a great magnitude and lasted for nine seconds. But this is not the only reason we are returning. The earthquake has precipitated an incident which calls for our immediate return to Osaka. Matsue phoned at five this morning and gave me the news.

Tellus has disappeared.

It wasn't possible to talk at length over the telephone. Matsue speaks in broken English anyway. In his agitation he could barely make himself understood. This much he told us: immediately after the earthquake it was seen that the pellucidite pedestal was lying on the floor and Tellus was missing. Both the guards were found lying unconscious and both had their legs broken. They are in the hospital now, and haven't yet regained consciousness. So it is not yet known what brought them to this state.

In Kyoto, ninety people were killed by houses collapsing. In the station everybody is talking of the earthquake. To be honest, when the tremor started last night, I too felt helpless and uneasy. I had run out of the hotel along with Kensley, and we could make out from the vast crowd outside that everybody had come out.

What a calamity! So much money, labour and experience gone into the making of the world's most sophisticated apparatus, and in three days it disappears.

15 MARCH, 11 P.M.
Osaka

I am sitting in my room in the International Guest House which faces the Namura Institute across a public park. From the window could be seen the tower of the Institute. It is no longer there; it came down during yesterday's earthquake.

Matsue came to the station with his car to receive us. The car took us straight to the Institute. One of the guards has regained consciousness. His story goes like this: his friend and he had both considered running out into the open when the earthquake started, but hearing a sound from Tellus' room they had unlocked the door and gone in to investigate.

The guard's version of what happened thereafter is wholly unbelievable. He says, what they saw upon entering the room was that the pedestal was lying on the floor while Tellus was rolling from one end of the room to the other. By then the tremor had abated in intensity. Both the guards had advanced towards the sphere to capture it. At this the sphere had come charging towards them and hit them in their legs with force enough to break their bones and render them unconscious.

If the story of the ball rolling by itself is not true, then the other possibility is theft. That both the guards were a little drunk has been admitted by Konoye, the one who has regained consciousness. In that state it was not unnatural that they would both dash out of the building; there were people working in the Institute laboratory that night, and everybody had run out into the compound. This means that most of the doors were open. There was nothing to prevent outsiders from entering the Institute. A clever thief could easily have taken advantage of the panic and made off with a forty-two-kilogram sphere without anybody noticing.

Theft or no theft, Tellus was no longer in its place. Who has taken it, where it is at the moment, whether there is any possibility of retrieving it—are questions which remain unanswered. The Government has already announced that whoever finds Tellus will get a reward of five hundred thousand yen. The police have started their investigations. Meanwhile the second guard has regained consciousness and vehemently asserts that the sphere was not stolen but, guided by some mysterious force, had assaulted its protector and made its escape.

Only Kuttna amongst us has believed the guards' story, although unable to support it by any rational explanation. Kensley and Wingfield both believe that theft is the only possible explanation. Platinum is a most precious metal. These days the younger generation of Japanese are quite capable of doing reckless things under the influence of drugs. Some of the more radical amongst them would be quite prepared to undertake such a robbery if only to embarrass the Government. If such a group has made off with Tellus, they will surely extract a high price before giving it up.

The search will not be easy, for the agitation over the earthquake hasn't subsided yet. More than a hundred and fifty people have been killed in Osaka, while the number of those injured exceeds two thousand. And there is no guarantee that there will be no more tremors.

Kuttna was here till a little while ago. Although he believes that Tellus escaped on its own, he cannot find a reason for its doing so. He believes that crashing on the floor during the tremor has done something to its innards. In other words, Tellus has lost its mind.

I myself feel wholly at a loss. This is an unprecedented experience for me.

16 MARCH, 11.30 P.M.

Let me set down the nerve-racking experiences of today.

Of the four of us, only Kuttna is able to hold his head high because his guess has turned out to be largely correct. I doubt if anyone will have the temerity to work on artificial intelligence after this.

Last night, after I had finished writing my diary, I found it difficult to go to sleep. Finally, I decided to take one of my Somnolin pills. As I left my bed to get the phial, my eye was drawn to the north window. This is the window which looks out over the park and faces the Namura Institute. What had caught my eye was the light from a torch in the park. The torch was being turned off and on and roved over a fairly large area.

This went on for about fifteen minutes. It was clear that the owner of the torch was searching for something. Whether he succeeded or not I do not know, but I saw him picking out his way with the help of the torch as he finally left the park.

This morning I described the incident to my three colleagues. We all decided to take a look in the park after breakfast.

At about eight the four of us set off. Like most other cities of Japan, Osaka is not flat, and one has to climb up a slope before reaching the park. The path in the park winds through flowering trees and bushes. Maple, birch, oak and chestnut abound. The Japanese had started a long time ago to uproot their own trees and plant English ones instead.

After walking for about fifteen minutes, we met our first stranger: a Japanese schoolboy, about ten years old, with pink cheeks, close-cropped hair, and his satchel around his shoulder. The boy halted in his tracks, and was now looking at us with an expression of alarm. Kuttna knew Japanese. 'What is your name?' he asked the boy.

'Seiji.'

'What are you doing here?'

'I'm going to school.'

'What were you looking for in the bush?'

The boy said nothing.

Meanwhile Kensley had moved over to the right. 'Come here, Shonku,' he called out.

Kensley was looking down at the grass. Wingfield and I joined him and found that a patch of grass and a sprig of wild flower had been flattened by something rolling over them. A few feet away we saw a flattened lizard.

This time the boy had to answer. He said he had seen a metal ball behind a bush on his way back from school yesterday. As he had approached it, the ball had rolled away. He had kept chasing the ball for a long time but had failed to catch it. Coming back home he had heard on the television about the reward. So he had looked for the ball with a torch the night before but had not found it.

We told the boy that if we found the ball in the park, we would see that he got his prize. The boy looked relieved, left his address and ran off to school. The four of us split up and went off in four directions to look for the sphere. Anybody finding it would call out to the others.

I left the beaten track and started looking behind bushes. If Tellus had really become mobile, it was doubtful whether it would surrender. On top of that, if it has developed an antipathy to human beings, it would be hard to predict what it might do.

Casting wary looks around, I walked on for another five minutes when I found a couple of butterflies lying on the grass. One of them was dead, while the other's wings still flapped weakly. It was clear that something heavy had passed over them only a little while ago.

I now proceeded slowly and with great caution when I was pulled up short by a sudden sharp sound. If one were to describe it in words, it would be—'Coo-ee!'

I was trying to locate the source of the sound when I heard again—'Coo-ee!'

This was unmistakably Tellus, and the sound could only mean one thing: it was playing hide-and-seek with us.

I didn't have to go far. Tellus was behind a geranium tree, glistening in the sunlight. It didn't move at my approach. It must have been the 'Coo-ee' which had told the others of Tellus' proximity. All three converged on the same spot. The smooth metal sphere made a strange contrast with the surrounding vegetation. Was there a slight change in Tellus' appearance? That we can tell only if we removed the dust and grass from the surface.

'Tell us—tell us—tell us . . .'

Kensley knelt on the grass and called out the two words to activate Tellus. We were all anxious to find out if it still functioned.

'In which battles was Napoleon victorious?'

The question came from Wingfield. The same question had been asked by one of the journalists on the day of the demonstration, and Tellus had answered instantly.

But no answer came today. We exchanged glances. My heart filled with a deep foreboding. Wingfield moved up closer to the sphere and repeated the question.

'Tell us what battles Napoleon won.'

This time there was an answer. No, not an answer, but a counter-question.

'Don't you know?'

Wingfield was flabbergasted. Kuttna's mouth had fallen open. The fear that was mixed with his look of surprise was characteristic of someone confronted by a supernatural event.

Whatever the cause, Tellus was no longer the same. By some unknown means it had surpassed the skill human beings had endowed it with. I was sure that one could converse with it now. I asked it:

'Did someone bring you here or did you come by yourself?'

'I came by myself.'

Kuttna put the next question. He was excited to the point where his hands trembled and beads of perspiration showed on his forehead.

'Why did you come?'

The answer came like a flash.

'To play.'

'To play?' I asked in great surprise.

Wingfield and Kensley were now squatting on the grass.

'A child must play,' said Tellus.

What kind of talk was this? The four of us now spoke almost in unison.

'A child? You are a child?'

'I am a child because you are all children.'

I don't know how the others felt, but I could see what Tellus was trying to say. Even towards the end of the twentieth century man has to admit that what he knows is very little compared with what he doesn't know. Gravity, which pervades the universe and whose presence we feel every moment of our existence, is to this day a mystery to us; we are indeed children if we take such things into account.

The question now was: what to do with Tellus. Now that it had a mind of its own, it would be best to ask it. I said, 'Have you finished playing?'

'Yes, I am growing older.'

'What will you do now?'

'Think.'

'Will you stay here, or come with us?'

'Go with you.'

'Thank you.'

We picked up Tellus and started on our way back.

On reaching the guest house, we sent for Matsue. We explained to him that it wouldn't do to keep Tellus in the Institute any longer because one would have to keep an eye on him all the time. At the same time, it wouldn't be wise to make any public statement about his present state.

In the end, it was Matsue who decided on the course of action. There were two trial spheres made before the one that was actually used. One of them would be kept in the Institute and an announcement made to the effect that the sphere had been retrieved. The real Tellus could be kept in the guest house where there were no other residents apart from the four of us. It was a two-storey building with sixteen rooms. The four of us were occupying four rooms on the first floor. We could communicate with each other by phone.

Within a few hours a glass case arrived in my room from Matsue. Tellus has been placed in it in a bed of cotton. While wiping the dust from the sphere I noticed that its surface was not as smooth as before. Platinum is a metal of great hardness, so that in spite of all the rolling the sphere had done, there was no reason for it to lose its smoothness. In the end I asked Tellus. After a few moments' pause it answered: 'I do not know. I am thinking.'

In the afternoon, Matsue arrived with a tape recorder. The speciality of this particular model is that it starts recording the moment a sound is produced, and stops as the sound stops. The recorder has been kept in front of Tellus. It'll work by itself.

Matsue is overcome by a feeling of helplessness. All his mastery over electronics is of no use in the present situation. He wanted to take apart the sphere and examine the circuit but I dissuaded him. I said, 'Whatever may have gone wrong inside it is important that we shouldn't interfere with what is happening now. Man is able to build a machine, and will do so in future too, but no human skill can produce an object like Tellus as it is now. So all we do now is keep observing it and communicating with it.'

In the evening the four of us were sitting in our room having coffee when we heard a sound from the glass cage. A well-known, high-pitched, flutey sound. And yet nobody had said the two words to switch it on. Tellus was obviously able to activate itself. I went over to the cage and asked: 'Did you say anything?'

The reply came: 'I know now. It is age.'

Tellus had found the answer to the question I had asked in the morning. The roughness of the sphere was a sign of ageing.

'Are you old now?' I asked.

'No,' said Tellus. 'I am in my youth.'

Among the four of us, only Wingfield's behaviour seems a little odd to me. When Matsue suggested taking Tellus apart, it was only Wingfield who supported him. He regrets that Tellus is no longer serving the purpose for which it was built. Whenever Tellus starts to talk on its own, Wingfield appears to feel ill at ease. I agree Tellus' behaviour has something of the supernatural about it, but why should a scientist react like that? In fact, today it gave rise to a most unpleasant incident. Within a minute of Tellus' talking to me, Wingfield left his chair, strode up to the glass cage and said, 'What battles did Napoleon win?'

The answer came like a whiplash.

'To want to know what you already know is a sign of an imbecile.'

I can't describe the effect the answer had on Wingfield. The words that came out of his mouth were of a nature one would scarcely associate with an aged scientist. Yet the fault was Wingfield's. That he could not accept Tellus' transformation was only an indication of his stubbornness.

The most extraordinary thing, however, was Tellus' reaction to Wingfield's boorishness. 'Wingfield, I warn you!' I heard it say in a clear voice.

It was not possible for Wingfield to stay in the room any longer. He strode out, shutting the door behind him with a bang.

Kensley and Kuttna stayed on for quite a while. Kensley feels Wingfield is a psychopathic case who shouldn't have accepted to come to Japan. As a matter of fact, Wingfield has made the least contribution among the seven of us. Had Merrivale been alive things might have been different.

We had dinner in my room. None of us spoke, nor did Tellus. All of us noticed that the sphere was getting rougher by the hour.

After my two colleagues left, I shut the door and sat down on the bed. Just then,

Tellus' voice set the tape recorder in motion again. I moved up to the glass cage. Tellus' voice was no longer high-pitched; a new solemnity had come into it.

'Are you going to sleep?' asked Tellus.

'Why do you ask?'

'Do you dream?' came the second question.

'I do sometimes. All human beings do.'

'Why sleep? Why dream?'

Difficult questions to answer. I said, 'The reasons are not clear yet. There is a theory about sleep. Primitive man used to hunt for food all day and then sit in the darkness of his cave and fall asleep. Daylight would wake him up. Perhaps we still retain that primal habit.'

'And dreaming?'

'I don't know. Nobody knows.'

'I know.'

'Do you?'

'I know more. I know how memory works. I know the mystery of gravity. I know when man first appeared on earth. I know about the birth of the universe.'

I was watching Tellus tensely. The recorder was turning. Was Tellus about to explain all the mysteries of science?

No, not so.

After a pause, Tellus said, 'Man has found the answer to many questions. These too he will find. It will take time. There is no easy way.'

Then, after another pause: 'But one thing man will never know. I too do not know it yet, but I will. I am not a man; I am a machine.'

'What are you talking about?'

But Tellus was silent. The recorder had stopped. After about a minute it turned again, only to record two words: 'Good night'.

18 MARCH

I am writing my diary in the hospital. I feel much better now. They say they will release me this afternoon. I had no idea such an experience awaited me. I realize what a mistake

I had made in not taking Tellus' advice.

The day before yesterday, I went straight to bed after saying goodnight to Tellus. I fell asleep within a few minutes. Normally I sleep very lightly and wake up at every sound. So when the phone rang I was up at once. The time on my travelling clock with the luminous dial was 2.33 a.m. It was Wingfield calling.

'Shonku, I've run out of sleeping pills. Can you help me?' I said I'd be over in a minute with the pill. Wingfield said he would come himself.

I had brought out the phial from my suitcase when the doorbell rang. Almost at once came the voice from the glass cage: 'Don't open the door.'

I was startled. 'Why not?' I asked.

'Wingfield is evil.'

'What kind of talk is that, Tellus?'

The doorbell rang again, and was followed by Wingfield's anxious voice.

'Have you fallen asleep, Shonku? I've come for the sleeping pills.'

Tellus had given its warning and fallen silent. I was in a dilemma. How could I not open the door? How could I explain my action? What if Tellus' warning was baseless?

I opened the door. Something descended with force on my head and I lost consciousness.

When I came to, I was in a hospital. Three scientists stood at my bedside — Kensley, Kuttna and Matsue. It was they who provided me with the details.

Having knocked me out, Wingfield had taken Tellus apart and taken the hemispheres into his room. He had put them in his suitcase, waited until dawn, and then gone down and asked the manager to arrange a car for him to take him to the airport. Meanwhile the porter who had brought Wingfield's luggage down had been suspicious about the great weight of the suitcase, and had informed the policeman on duty at the gate. The policeman had challenged Wingfield, and the latter had desperately pulled out his revolver. But he wasn't quick enough. He was now in custody. It is suspected that he may be responsible for his colleague Merrivale's death in Massachusetts. He was afraid that Tellus, with his supernatural abilities, would reveal unpleasant facts about him. This is why he was anxious to run away with the sphere, hoping to dispose of it somewhere on the way to the airport.

'Where is Tellus now?' I asked after I had listened to the extraordinary story.

'It is back in the Institute,' replied Matsue. 'You see, it was no longer safe to keep it in the guest house. It is back in its place on the pedestal. I put it together again.'

'Has it said anything since?'

'It has asked to see you,' said Matsue.

I couldn't contain myself any more. To hell with the pain in my head — I had to go to the Institute.

'Can you make it?' asked Kuttna.

'I'm sure I can.'

Within half an hour we were in the elegant room once again. Tellus was seated on its throne on the pedestal, bathed in the shaft of light from the ceiling. I could see there were cracks all over the sphere. There was no question that these four days have aged Tellus considerably.

I went over and stood near it. Before I said anything, I heard its calm, grave voice.

'You have come at the right time. There will be an earthquake in three and a half minutes. A mild tremor. You will feel it, but it will do no damage. As the tremor ends, I will know the answer to my last question.'

There was nothing to do except wait with bated breath. A few feet above Tellus was the electric clock whose second hand moved steadily along.

One minute . . . two minutes . . . three minutes . . . We watched with amazement a glow beginning to pervade Tellus as the cracks widened. The colour of the sphere was changing. Yes, it was turning into gold!

Fifteen seconds . . . twenty seconds . . . twenty-five seconds.

Just at the stroke of the half hour, the floor under our feet shook, and in that very instant, the sphere exploded into a thousand bits and scattered on the floor. Then, from the ruins was heard an eerie, disembodied voice declaiming—

'I know what comes after death!'

ASHAMANJABABU'S DOG

Originally published in *Sandesh* (Puja Annual 1978) as *Asamanjababur Kukur*. The English translation by Ray was published in *Target*, September 1985. The illustrations in the story, including the Bengali calligraphy in the headpiece, are by Satyajit Ray.

On a visit to a friend in Hashimara, Ashamanjababu had one of his long-cherished wishes fulfilled. Ashamanjababu lives in a room and a half, in a flat on Mohini Mohan Road in Bhowanipore. As a clerk in the registry department of Lajpat Rai Post Office, Ashamanjababu is able to avoid the hassle of riding in trams and buses, because it takes him only seven minutes to walk to work. Not being one to sit and brood about what might have been or done had Fate been kinder to him, Ashamanjababu is quite content with his lot. Two Hindi films, a dozen packets of cigarettes a month, and fish twice a week—these are enough to keep him happy. But being a bachelor and lacking friends, he has often wished to possess a pet dog. Not a large dog like the Talukdar's Alsatian, two houses away to the east, but a medium-sized dog which would keep him company, wag its tail when he came home from work and show love and devotion by obeying his orders. One of Ashamanjababu's pet conceits was that he would speak to his dog in English. 'Stand up', 'Sit down', 'Shake hands'—how nice it would be if his dog obeyed such commands! Ashamanjababu liked to believe that dogs belonged to the English race. Yes, an English dog, and he would be its master. That would make him really happy.

On a cloudy day marked by a steady drizzle, Ashamanjababu had gone to the market in Hashimara to buy some oranges. At one end of the market sat a Bhutanese by a stunted kul tree holding a cigarette between his thumb and forefinger. As their eyes met, the man smiled. Was he a beggar? His clothes made him seem like one, for there were five patches on his jacket and trousers. But the man didn't have a begging bowl. Instead, by his side was a shoe box with a little pup sticking its head out from it.

'Good morning!' said the Bhutanese in English, his eyes reduced to slits in a smile. Ashamanjababu was obliged to return the greeting.

'Buy dog? Dog buy? Very good dog.' The man had taken the pup out of the box and put it down on the ground. 'Very cheap. Very good. Happy dog.'

The pup shook itself free of the raindrops, looked at Ashamanjababu and wagged its two-inch tail. Nice pup.

Ashamanjababu moved closer to the pup, crouched on the ground and put his hand towards it. The pup gave his ring finger a lick with his pink tongue. Nice, friendly pup.

'How much? What price?'

'Ten rupees.'

A little haggling, and the price came down to seven-fifty. Ashamanjababu paid the money, put the pup back in the shoe box, closed the lid to save it from the drizzle, and turned homewards, forgetting all about the oranges.

Birenbabu, who worked in the Hashimara State Bank, didn't know of his friend's wish to own a dog. He was naturally surprised and a bit alarmed to see what the shoe box contained. But when he heard the price, he heaved a sigh of relief. He said in a tone of mild reprimand, 'Why come all the way to Hashimara to buy a mongrel? You could easily have bought one in Bhowanipore.'

That was not true. Ashamanjababu knew it. He had often seen mongrel pups in the streets in his neighbourhood. None of them had ever wagged their tail at him or licked his fingers. Whatever Biren might say, this dog was something special. But the fact that the pup was a mongrel was something of a disappointment to Ashamanjababu, and he said so. But Birenbabu's retort came sharp and quick. 'But do you know what it means to keep a pedigree dog as a pet? The vet's fees alone would cost you half a month's salary. With this dog you have no worries. You don't even need a special diet for him. He'll eat what you eat. But don't give him fish. Fish is for cats; dogs have trouble with the bones.'

Back in Calcutta, it occurred to Ashamanjababu that he had to think of a name for the pup. He wanted to give it an English name, but the only one he could think of was Tom. Then, looking at the pup one day, it struck him that since it was brown in colour, Brownie would be a good name for it. A cousin of his had a camera of an English make called Brownie, so the name must be an English one. The moment he decided on the name and tried it on the pup, it jumped off a wicker stool and padded up to him wagging its tail. Ashamanjababu said, 'Sit down.' Right away the pup sat on its haunches and opened its mouth in a tiny yawn. Ashamanjababu had a fleeting vision of Brownie winning the first prize for cleverness in a dog show.

It was lucky that his servant Bipin had also taken a fancy to the dog. While Ashamanjababu was away at work, Bipin gladly took it upon himself to look after Brownie. Ashamanjababu had warned Bipin against feeding the dog rubbish. 'And see that he doesn't go out into the street. The car drivers these days seem to wear blinkers.' But however much he might instruct his servant, his worry would linger until, after returning from work, he would be greeted by Brownie with his wagging tail.

The incident took place three months after returning from Hashimara. It was a Saturday, and the date was November the twenty-third. Ashamanjababu had just got back from work and sat down on the old wooden chair—the only piece of furniture in the room apart from the bed and the wicker stool—when it suddenly gave under him and sent him sprawling on the floor. He was naturally hurt and, in fact, was led to wonder if, like the rickety leg of the chair, his right elbow was also out of commission, when an unexpected sound made him forget all about his pain.

The sound had come from the bed. It was the sound of laughter or, more accurately, a giggle, the source of which was undoubtedly Brownie, who sat on the bed and whose lips were still curled up.

If Ashamanjababu's general knowledge had been wider, he would surely have known that dogs never laughed. And if he had a modicum of imagination, the incident would have robbed him of his sleep. In the absence of either, what Ashamanjababu did was to sit down with the book *All About Dogs* which he had bought for two rupees from a second-hand book shop in Free School Street. He searched for an hour but found no mention in the book about laughing dogs.

And yet there wasn't the slightest doubt that Brownie had laughed. Not only that, he had laughed because there had been cause for laughter. Ashamanjababu could clearly recall an incident from his own childhood. A doctor had come on a visit to their house in Chandernagore and had sat on a chair which had collapsed under him. Ashamanjababu had burst out laughing, and had his ears twisted by his father for doing so. Ashamanja babu shut the book and looked at Brownie. As their eyes met, Brownie put his front paws on the pillow and wagged his tail, which had grown an inch and a half longer in three months. There was no trace of a smile on his face now. Why should there be? To laugh without reason was a sign of madness. Ashamanjababu felt relieved that Brownie was not a mad dog.

On two more occasions within a week of this incident, Brownie had occasion to laugh. The first took place at night, at nine-thirty. Ashamanjababu had just spread a white sheet on the floor for Brownie to sleep on when a cockroach came fluttering into the room and settled on the wall. Ashamanjababu picked up a slipper and flung it at the insect. But it missed its target, landed on a hanging mirror, and sent it crashing to the floor. This time Brownie's laughter more than compensated for the loss of his mirror.

The second time it was not laughter, but a brief snicker. Ashamanjababu was puzzled, because nothing had really happened. So why the snicker? The servant Bipin provided the answer. He came into the room, glanced at his master and said, smiling, 'There's shaving soap right by your ears, sir.' With his mirror broken, Ashamanjababu had to use one of the window panes for shaving. He now felt with his fingers and found that Bipin was right.

That Brownie should laugh even when the reason was so trifling surprised Ashamanjababu a great deal. Sitting at his desk in the post office he found his thoughts turning again and again to the smile on Brownie's face and the sound of the snicker. *All About Dogs* may say nothing about a dog's laughter, but if he could get hold of something like an encyclopedia of dogs, there was sure to be a mention of laughter in it.

When four book shops in Bhowanipore—and all the ones in the New Market—failed to produce such an encyclopedia, Ashamanjababu wondered whether he should call on Mr Rajani Chatterji. The retired professor lived not far from his house on the same street. Ashamanjababu didn't know what subject Rajanibabu had taught, but he had seen through the window of his house many fat books in a bookcase in what appeared to be the professor's study.

On a Sunday morning, Ashamanjababu invoked the name of the goddess Durga for good luck and turned up at Professor Chatterji's. He had seen him several times from a distance, and had no idea he had such thick eyebrows and a voice so grating. But since the professor hadn't turned him away, Ashamanjababu took courage in occupying a seat on a sofa across the room from him. Then he gave a short cough and waited. Professor Chatterji put aside the newspaper and turned his attention to the visitor.

'Your face seems familiar.'

'I live close by.'

'I see. Well?'

'I have seen a dog in your house; that is why . . .'

'So what? We have two dogs, not one.'

'I see, I have one too.'

'Are you employed to count the number of dogs in the city?'

Being a simple man, Ashamanjababu missed the sarcasm in the question. He said, 'I have come to ask if you have something I've been looking for.'

'What is it?'

'I wonder if you have a dog encyclopedia.'

'No, I don't. Why do you need one?'

'You see, my dog laughs. So I wanted to find out if it was natural for dogs to laugh. Do your dogs laugh?'

Throughout the time it took the wall clock in the room to strike eight, Professor

Chatterji kept looking at Ashamanjababu. Then he asked, 'Does your dog laugh at night?'

'Well, yes—even at night.'

'And what are your preferences in drugs? Only ganja can't produce such symptoms. Perhaps you take charas and hashish as well?'

Ashamanjababu meekly answered that his only vice was smoking—and even that he had had to reduce from four packets a week to three ever since the arrival of his dog.

'And yet you say your dog laughs?'

'I have seen and heard him laugh, with my own eyes and ears.'

'Listen.' Professor Chatterji took off his spectacles, cleaned them with his handkerchief, put them on again and fixed Ashamanjababu with a hard stare. Then he declaimed in the tones of a classroom lecture. 'I am amazed at your ignorance concerning a fundamental fact of nature. Of all the creatures created by God, only the human species is capable of laughter. This is one of the prime differences between homo sapiens and other creatures. Don't ask me why it should be so, because I do not know. I have heard that a marine species called the dolphin has a sense of humour. Dolphins may be the single exception. Apart from them there are none. It is not clearly understood why human beings should laugh. Great philosophers have racked their brains to find out why; but have not succeeded. Do you understand?'

Ashamanjababu understood, and he also understood that it was time for him to take his leave because the professor had once again taken up his newspaper.

Doctor Sukhomoy Bhowmick—some called him Doctor Bhow-wowmick—was a well-known vet. In the belief that if ordinary people didn't listen to him a vet might, Ashamanjababu made an appointment with him on the phone and turned up at his residence on Gokhale Road. Brownie had laughed seventeen times during the last four months. One thing Ashamanjababu had noticed is that Brownie didn't laugh at funny remarks; only at funny incidents. Ashamanjababu had recited the 'King of Bombardia' to Brownie, and it had produced no effect on him. And yet when a potato from a curry slipped from Ashamanjababu's fingers and landed on a plate of curd, Brownie had almost choked with laughter. Professor Chatterji had said that none of God's creatures laughed except human beings, and yet here was proof that the learned gentleman was wrong.

So Ashamanjababu went to the vet in spite of knowing that the latter charged twenty rupees per visit.

Even before he had heard of the dog's unique trait, its very appearance had the vet's eyebrows shooting up. 'I've seen mongrels, but never one like this.'

The vet lifted the dog and placed him on the table. Brownie sniffed at the brass paperweight at his feet. 'What do you feed him?'

'He eats what I eat, sir. He has no pedigree, you see . . .' Doctor Bhowmick frowned. He was observing the dog with great interest. 'We can tell a pedigree dog when we see one. But sometimes we are not so sure. This one, for instance. I should hesitate to call him a mongrel. I suggest that you stop feeding him rice and dal. I'll make a diet chart for him.'

Ashamanjababu now made an attempt to come out with the real reason for his visit. 'I—er, my dog has a speciality—which is why I have brought him to you.'

'Speciality?'

'The dog laughs.'

'Laughs—?'

'Yes. Laughs, like you and me.'

'You don't say! Well, can you make him laugh now so I can see?'

And now Ashamanjababu was in a quandary. As it is he was a very shy person, so he was quite unable to make faces at Brownie to make him laugh, nor was it likely that something funny should happen here at this very moment. So Ashamanjababu had to tell the doctor that Brownie didn't laugh when asked to, but only when he saw something funny happening.

After this Doctor Bhowmick didn't have much time left for Ashamanjababu. He said, 'Your dog looks distinctive enough; don't try to make him more so by claiming that he laughs. I can tell you from my twenty-two years' experience that dogs cry, dogs feel afraid, dogs show anger, hatred, distrust and jealousy. Dogs even dream, but dogs don't laugh.'

After this encounter, Ashamanjababu decided that he would never tell anyone about Brownie's laughter. When immediate proof was not forthcoming, to talk about it was to court embarrassment. What did it matter if others never knew? He himself knew, Brownie was his own dog, his own property. Why drag outsiders into their own private world?

But man proposes, God disposes. Even Brownie's laughter was one day revealed to an outsider.

For some time now, Ashamanjababu had developed the habit of taking Brownie for a walk in the afternoon near the Victoria Memorial. One April day, in the middle of their walk, a big storm came up suddenly. Ashamanjababu glanced at the sky and decided that it wasn't safe to try and get back home as it might start raining any moment. So he ran with Brownie and took shelter below the marble arch with the black equestrian statue on it.

Meanwhile, huge drops of rain had started to fall and people were running this way and that for shelter. A stout man in white bush shirt and trousers, twenty paces away from the arch, opened his umbrella and held it over his head when a sudden strong gust of wind turned the umbrella inside out with a loud snap.

To tell the truth, Ashamanjababu was himself about to burst out laughing, but Brownie beat him by a neck with a canine guffaw which rose above the sound of the storm and reached the ear of the hapless gentleman. He stopped trying to bring the umbrella back to its original shape and stared at Brownie in utter amazement. Brownie was now quite helpless with laughter. Ashamanjababu had given up trying to suppress it by clapping his hand over the dog's mouth.

The dumbfounded gentleman now walked over to Ashamanjababu as if he had seen a ghost. Brownie's paroxysm was now subsiding, but it was still enough to make the gentleman's eyes pop out of his head.

'A laughing dog!'

'Yes, a laughing dog,' said Ashamanjababu.

'But how extraordinary!'

Ashamanjababu could make out that the man was not a Bengali. Perhaps he was a Gujarati or a Parsi. Ashamanjababu braced himself to answer in English the questions he knew he would soon be bombarded with.

The rain had turned into a heavy shower. The gentleman took shelter alongside Ashamanjababu, and in ten minutes had found out all there was to know about Brownie. He also took Ashamanjababu's address. He said his name was Piloo Pochkanwalla, that he knew a lot about dogs and wrote about them occasionally, and that his experience today had surpassed everything that had ever happened to him, or was likely to happen in the future. He felt something had to be done about it, since Ashamanjababu himself was obviously unaware of what a priceless treasure he owned.

It wouldn't be wrong to say that Brownie was responsible for Mr Pochkanwalla being knocked down by a minibus while crossing Chowringhee Road soon after the rain had stopped—it was the thought of the laughing dog running through his head which made him a little unmindful of the traffic. After spending two and a half months in hospital, Pochkanwalla had gone off to Nainital for a change. He had come back to Calcutta after a month in the hills, and the same evening had described the incident of the laughing dog to his friends Mr Balaporia and Mr Biswas at the Bengal Club. Within half an hour, the story had reached the ears of twenty-seven other members and three bearers of the Club. By next morning, the incident was known to at least a thousand citizens of Calcutta.

Brownie hadn't laughed once during these three and a half months. One good reason was that he had seen no funny incidents. Ashamanjababu didn't see it as cause for alarm; it had never crossed his mind to cash in on Brownie's unique gift. He was happy with the way Brownie had filled a yawning gap in his life, and felt more drawn to him than he had to any human being.

Among those who got the news of the laughing dog was an executive in the office of *The Statesman*. He sent for the reporter Rajat Chowdhury and suggested that he should interview Ashamanjababu.

Ashamanjababu was greatly surprised that a reporter should think of calling on him. It was when Rajat Chowdhury mentioned Pochkanwalla that the reason for the visit became clear. Ashamanjababu asked the reporter into his bedroom. The wooden chair had been fitted with a new leg, and Ashamanjababu offered it to the reporter while he himself sat on the bed. Brownie had been observing a line of ants crawling up the wall; he now jumped up on the bed and sat beside Ashamanjababu.

Rajat Chowdhury was about to press the switch on his recorder when it suddenly occurred to Ashamanjababu that a word of warning was needed. 'By the way, sir, my dog used to laugh quite frequently, but in the last few months he hasn't laughed at all. So you may be disappointed if you are expecting to see him laugh.'

Like many a young, energetic reporter, Rajat Chowdhury exuded a cheerful confidence in the presence of a good story. Although he was slightly disappointed he was careful not to show it. He said, 'That's all right. I just want to get some details from you. To start with, his name. What do you call your dog?'

Ashamanjababu bent down to reach closer to the mike. 'Brownie.'

'Brownie . . .' The watchful eye of the reporter had noted that the dog had wagged his tail at the mention of his name. 'How old is he?'

'A year and a month.'

'Where did you f-f-find the dog?'

This had happened before. The impediment Rajat Chowdhury suffered often showed itself in the middle of interviews, causing him no end of embarrassment. Here too the same thing might have happened but for the fact that the stammer was unexpectedly helpful in drawing out Brownie's unique trait. Thus Rajat Chowdhury was the second outsider after Pochkanwalla to see with his own eyes a dog laughing like a human being.

The morning of the following Sunday, sitting in his air-conditioned room in the Grand Hotel, Mr William P. Moody of Cincinnati, USA, read in the papers about the laughing dog and at once asked the hotel operator to put him through to Mr Nandy of the Indian Tourist Bureau. That Mr Nandy knew his way about the city had been made abundantly clear in the last couple of days when Mr Moody had occasion to use his services. *The Statesman* had printed the name and address of the owner of the laughing dog. Mr Moody was very anxious to meet this character.

Ashamanjababu didn't read *The Statesman*. Besides, Rajat Chowdhury hadn't told him when the interview would come out, or he might have bought a copy. It was in the fish market that his neighbour Kalikrishna Dutt told him about it.

'You're a fine man,' said Mr Dutt. 'You've been guarding such a treasure in your house for over a year, and you haven't breathed a word to anybody about it? I must drop in at your place sometime this evening and say hello to your dog.'

Ashamanjababu's heart sank. He could see there was trouble ahead. There were many more like Mr Dutt in and around his neighbourhood who read the Statesman and who would want 'to drop in and say hello' to his dog. A most unnerving prospect.

Ashamanjababu made up his mind. He decided to spend the day away from home. Taking Brownie with him, he took a taxi for the first time, went straight to the Ballygunge station and boarded a train to Port Canning. Halfway through, the train pulled up at a station called Palsit. Ashamanjababu liked the look of the place and got off. He spent the whole day in quiet bamboo groves and mango orchards and felt greatly refreshed.

Brownie, too, seemed to enjoy himself. The gentle smile that played around his lips was something Ashamanjababu had never noticed before. This was a benign smile, a smile of peace and contentment, a smile of inner happiness. Ashamanjababu had read somewhere that a year in the life of a dog equalled seven years in the life of a human being. And yet he could scarcely imagine such tranquil behaviour in such sylvan surroundings from a seven-year-old human child.

It was past seven in the evening when Ashamanjababu got back home. He asked Bipin if anyone had called. Bipin said he had to open the door to callers at least forty times. Ashamanjababu couldn't help congratulating himself on his foresight. He had just taken off his shoes and asked Bipin for a cup of tea when there was a knock on the front door. 'Oh, hell!' swore Ashamanjababu. He went to the door and opened it, and found himself facing a foreigner. 'Wrong number' he was at the point of saying, when he caught sight of a young Bengali standing behind the foreigner. 'Whom do you want?'

'You,' said Shyamol Nandy of the Indian Tourist Bureau, 'in case the dog standing behind you belongs to you. He certainly looks like the one described in the papers today. May we come in?'

Ashamanjababu was obliged to ask them into his bedroom. The foreigner sat in the chair, Mr Nandy on the wicker stool, and Ashamanjababu on his bed. Brownie, who seemed a bit ill at ease, chose to stay outside the threshold; probably because he had never seen two strangers in the room before.

'Brownie! Brownie! Brownie!' The foreigner had leaned forward towards the dog and called him repeatedly by name to entice him into the room. Brownie, who didn't move, had his eyes fixed on the stranger.

Who were these people? The question had naturally occurred to Ashamanjababu when Mr Nandy provided the answer. The foreigner was a wealthy and distinguished citizen of the United States whose main purpose in coming to India was to look for old Rolls-Royce cars.

The American had now got off the chair and, sitting on his haunches, was making faces at the dog. After three minutes of abortive clowning, the man gave up, turned to Ashamanjababu and said, 'Is he sick?'

Ashamanjababu shook his head.

'Does he really laugh?' asked the American.

In case Ashamanjababu was unable to follow the American's speech, Mr Nandy translated it for him.

'Brownie laughs,' said Ashamanjababu, 'but only when he feels amused.'

A tinge of red spread over the American's face when Nandy translated Ashamanjababu's answer to him. Next, he let it be known that he wasn't willing to squander any money on the dog unless he had proof that the dog really laughed. He refused to be saddled with something which might later cause embarrassment. He further let it be known that in his house he had precious objects from China to Peru, and that he had a parrot which spoke only Latin. 'I have brought my chequebook with me to pay for the laughing dog, but only if it laughed.'

The American now pulled out a blue cheque book from his pocket to prove his statement. Ashamanjababu glanced at it out of the corner of his eyes. Citi Bank of New York—it said on the cover.

'You would be walking on air,' said Mr Nandy temptingly. 'If you know a way to make the dog laugh, then out with it. This gentleman is ready to pay up to twenty thousand dollars. That's two lakhs of rupees.'

The Bible says that God created the universe in six days. A human being, using his imagination, can do the same thing in six seconds. The image that Mr Nandy's words conjured up in Ashamanjababu's mind was of himself in a spacious air-conditioned office, sitting in a swivel chair with his legs up on the table, with the heady smell of hasu-no-hana wafting in through the window. But the image vanished like a pricked balloon at a sudden sound.

Brownie was laughing,

This was like no laugh he had ever laughed before.

'But he is laughing!'

Mr Moody had gone down on his knees, tense with excitement, watching the extraordinary spectacle. The cheque book came out again and, along with that, his gold Parker pen.

Brownie was still laughing. Ashamanjababu was puzzled because he couldn't make out the reason for the laughter. Nobody had stammered, nobody had stumbled, nobody's umbrella had turned inside out, and no mirror on the wall had been hit with a slipper. Why then was Brownie laughing?

'You're very lucky,' commented Mr Nandy. 'I think I ought to get a percentage on the sale—wouldn't you say so?'

Mr Moody had now risen from the floor and sat down on the chair. He said, 'Ask him how he spells his name.'

Although Mr Nandy had relayed the question in Bengali, Ashamanjababu didn't answer, because he had just seen the light, and the light filled his heart with a great sense of wonder. Instead of spelling his name, he said, 'Please tell the foreign gentleman that if he only knew why the dog was laughing, he wouldn't have opened his cheque book,'

'Why don't you tell me?' Mr Nandy snapped in a dry voice. He certainly didn't like the way events were shaping. If the mission failed, he knew the American's wrath would fall on him.

Brownie had at last stopped laughing. Ashamanjababu lifted him up on his lap, wiped his tears and said, 'My dog's laughing because the gentleman thinks money can buy everything.'

'I see,' said Mr Nandy. 'So your dog's a philosopher, is he?'

'Yes, sir.'

'That means you won't sell him?'

'No, sir.'

To Mr Moody, Shyamol Nandy only said that the owner had no intention of selling the dog. Mr Moody put the cheque book back in his pocket, slapped the dust off his knees and, on his way out of the room, said with a shake of his head, 'The guy must be crazy!'

When the sound of the American's car had faded away, Ashamanjababu looked into Brownie's eyes and said, 'I was right about why you laughed, wasn't I?'

Brownie chuckled in assent.

BIG BILL

Originally published in *Sandesh* (March 1980) as *Brihachchanchu*. It was translated by the
author himself to be part of the compilation titled *Stories* (Secker & Warburg, 1987).
The illustrations in the story, including the Bengali calligraphy in the headpiece,
are by Satyajit Ray.

By Tulsibabu's desk in his office on the ninth floor of a building in Old Court House Street there is a window which opens on to a vast expanse of the western sky. Tulsibabu's neighbour Jaganmoy Dutta had just gone to spit betel juice out of the window one morning in the rainy season when he noticed a double rainbow in the sky. He uttered an exclamation of surprise and turned to Tulsibabu. 'Come here, sir. You won't see the like of it every day.'

Tulsibabu left his desk, went to the window, and looked out.

'What are you referring to?' he asked.

'Why, the double rainbow!' said Jaganmoy Dutta. 'Are you colour-blind?'

Tulsibabu went back to his desk. 'I can't see what is so special about a double rainbow. Even if there were twenty rainbows in the sky, there would be nothing surprising about that. Why, one can just as well go and stare at the double-spired church in Lower Circular Road!'

Not everyone is endowed with the same sense of wonder, but there is good reason to doubt whether Tulsibabu possesses any at all. There is only one thing that never ceases to surprise him, and that is the excellence of the mutton kebab at Mansur's. The only person who is aware of this is Tulsibabu's friend and colleague, Prodyot Chanda.

Being of such a sceptical temperament, Tulsibabu was not particularly surprised to find an unusually large egg while looking for medicinal plants in the forests of Dandakaranya.

Tulsibabu had been dabbling in herbal medicine for the last fifteen years; his father was a well-known herbalist. Tulsibabu's main source of income is as an upper division clerk in Arbuthnot & Co. but he has not been able to discard the family profession altogether. Of late he has been devoting a little more time to it because two fairly distinguished citizens of Calcutta have benefitted from his prescriptions, thus giving a boost to his reputation as a part-time herbalist.

It was herbs again which had brought him to Dandakaranya. He had heard that thirty miles to the north of Jagdalpur there lived a holy man in a mountain cave who had access to some medicinal plants including one for high blood pressure which was even more efficacious than rauwolfia serpentina. Tulsibabu suffered from hypertension; serpentina hadn't worked too well in his case, and he had no faith in homeopathy or allopathy.

Tulsibabu had taken his friend Prodyotbabu with him on this trip to Jagdalpur. Tulsibabu's inability to feel surprise had often bothered Prodyotbabu. One day he was forced to comment, 'All one needs to feel a sense of wonder is a little imagination. You are so devoid of it that even if a full-fledged ghost were to appear before you, you wouldn't be surprised.' Tulsibabu had replied calmly, 'To feign surprise when one doesn't actually feel it, is an affectation. I do not approve of it.' But this didn't get in the way of their friendship. The two checked into a hotel in Jagdalpur during the autumn vacation. On the way, in the Madras Mail, two foreign youngsters had got into their compartment. They turned out to be Swedes. One of them was so tall that his head nearly touched the ceiling. Prodyotbabu had asked him how tall he was and the young man had replied, 'Two metres and seven centimetres.' Which is nearly seven feet. Prodyotbabu couldn't take his eyes away from this young giant during the rest of the journey; and yet Tulsibabu was not surprised. He said such extraordinary height was simply the result of the diet of the Swedish people, and therefore nothing to be surprised at.

They reached the cave of the holy man Dhumai Baba after walking through the forest for a mile or so then climbing up about five hundred feet. The cave was a large one, but since no sun ever reached it, they only had to take ten steps to be engulfed in darkness, thickened by the ever-present smoke from the Baba's brazier. Prodyotbabu was absorbed in watching, by the light of his torch, the profusion of stalactites and stalagmites while Tulsibabu enquired after his herbal medicine. The tree that Dhumai Baba referred to was known as *chakrapama*, which is the Sanskrit for 'round leaves'. Tulsibabu had never heard of it, nor was it mentioned in any of the half-dozen books he had read on herbal medicine. It was not a tree, but a shrub. It was found only in one part of the forest of Dandakaranya, and nowhere else. Baba gave adequate directions which Tulsibabu noted down carefully.

Coming out of the cave, Tulsibabu lost no time in setting off in quest of the herb. Prodyotbabu was happy to keep his friend company; he had hunted big game at one time—conservation had put an end to that, but the lure of the jungle persisted.

The holy man's directions proved accurate. Half an hour's walk brought them to a ravine which they crossed and in three minutes they found the shrub seven steps to the south of a neem tree scorched by lightning—a waist-high shrub with round green leaves, each with a pink dot in the centre.

'What kind of a place is this?' asked Prodyotbabu, looking around.

'Why, what's wrong with it?'

'But for the neem, there isn't a single tree here that I know. And see how damp it is. Quite unlike the places we've passed through.'

It was moist underfoot, but Tulsibabu saw nothing strange in that. Why, in Calcutta itself, the temperature varied between one neighbourhood and another. Tollygunge in the south was much cooler than Shambazar in the north. What was so strange about one part of a forest being different from another? It was nothing but a quirk of nature.

Tulsibabu had just put the bag down on the ground and stooped towards the shrub when a sharp query from Prodyotbabu interrupted him. 'What on earth is that?'

Tulsibabu had seen the thing too, but was not bothered by it. 'Must be some sort of egg,' he said.

Prodyotbabu had thought it was a piece of egg-shaped rock, but on getting closer he realized that it was a genuine egg, yellow, with brown stripes flecked with blue. What could such a large egg belong to? A python?

Meanwhile, Tulsibabu had already plucked some leafy branches off the shrub and put them in his bag. He wanted to take some more but something happened then which made him stop.

The egg chose this very moment to hatch. Prodyotbabu had jumped back at the sound of the cracking shell, but now he took courage to take a few steps towards it.

The head was already out of the shell. Not a snake, nor a croc or a turtle, but a bird.

Soon the whole creature was out. It stood on its spindly legs and looked around. It was quite large; about the size of a hen. Prodyotbabu was very fond of birds and kept a mynah and a bulbul as pets; but he had never seen a chick as large as this, with such a large beak and long legs. Its purple plumes were unique, as was its alert behaviour so soon after birth.

Tulsibabu, however, was not the least interested in the chick. He had been intent on stuffing his bag with as much of the herb as would go into it.

Prodyotbabu looked around and commented, 'Very surprising; there seems to be no sign of its parents, at least not in the vicinity.'

'I think that's enough surprise for a day,' said Tulsibabu, hoisting his bag on his shoulder. 'It's almost four. We must be out of the forest before it gets dark.'

Somewhat against his wish, Prodyotbabu turned away from the chick and started walking with Tulsibabu. It would take at least half an hour to reach the waiting taxi.

A patter of feet made Prodyotbabu stop and turn round.

The chick was following them.

'I say—' called out Prodyotbabu.

Tulsibabu now stopped and turned. The chick was looking straight at him.

Then it padded across and stopped in front of Tulsibabu where it opened its unusually large beak and gripped the edge of Tulsibabu's dhoti.

Prodyotbabu was so surprised that he didn't know what to say, until he saw Tulsibabu pick up the chick and shove it into his bag. 'What d'you think you're doing?' he cried in consternation. 'You put that nameless chick in your bag?'

'I've always wanted to keep a pet,' said Tulsibabu, resuming his walk. 'Even mongrels are kept as pets. What's wrong with a nameless chick?'

Prodyotbabu saw the chick sticking its neck out of the swinging bag and glancing around with wide-open eyes.

Tulsibabu lived in a flat on the second floor of a building in Masjidbari Street. Besides Tulsibabu, who was a bachelor, there was his servant Natobar and his cook Joykesto. There was another flat on the same floor, and this was occupied by Tarit Sanyal, the proprietor of the Nabarun Press. Mr Sanyal was a short-tempered man made even more so by repeated power failures in the city which seriously affected the working of his press.

Two months had passed since Tulsibabu's return from Dandakaranya. He had put the chick in a cage which he had specially ordered immediately upon his return. The cage was kept in a corner of the inner verandah. He had found a Sanskrit name for the chick: *Brihat-Chanchu*, or Big Bill; soon the Big was dropped and now it was just Bill.

The very first day he had acquired the chick in Jagdalpur, Tulsibabu had tried to feed it grain. The chick had refused.

Tulsibabu had guessed, and rightly, that it was probably a meat eater; ever since he has been feeding it insects. Of late the bird's appetite seems to have grown, and Tulsibabu has been obliged to feed it meat; Natobar buys meat from the market regularly, which may explain the bird's rapid growth in size.

Tulsibabu had been far-sighted enough to buy a cage which was several sizes too large for the bird. His instinct had told him that the bird belonged to a large species. The roof of the cage was two and a half feet from the ground, but only yesterday Tulsibabu had noticed that when Bill stood straight its head nearly touched the roof; even though the bird was only two months old, it would soon need a larger cage.

Nothing has so far been said about the cry of the bird, which made Mr Sanyal choke on his tea one morning while he stood on the verandah. Normally the two neighbours hardly spoke to each other; today, after he had got over his fit of coughing, Mr Sanyal demanded to know what kind of an animal Tulsibabu kept in his cage that yelled like that. It was true that the cry was more beast-like than bird-like.

Tulsibabu was getting dressed to go to work. He appeared at the bedroom door and said, 'Not an animal, but a bird. And whatever its cry, it certainly doesn't keep one awake at night the way your cat does.'

Tulsibabu's retort put an end to the argument, but Mr Sanyal kept grumbling. It was a good thing the cage couldn't be seen from his flat; a sight of the bird might have given rise to even more serious consequences.

Although its looks didn't bother Tulsibabu, they certainly worried Prodyotbabu. The two met rarely outside office hours, except once a week for a meal of kebab and paratha at Mansur's. Prodyotbabu had a large family and many responsibilities. But since the visit to Dandakaranya, Tulsibabu's pet was often on his mind. As a result he had started to drop in at Tulsibabu's from time to time in the evenings. The bird's astonishing rate of growth and the change in its appearance were a constant source of surprise to Prodyotbabu. He was at a loss to see why Tulsibabu should show no concern about it. Prodyotbabu had never imagined that the look in a bird's eye could be so malevolent. The black pupils in the amber irises would fix Prodyotbabu with such an unwavering look that he would feel most uneasy. The bird's beak naturally grew as well as its body; shiny black in colour, it resembled an eagle's beak but was much larger in relation to the rest of the body. It was clear, from its rudimentary wings and its long sturdy legs and sharp talons, that the bird couldn't fly. Prodyotbabu had described the bird to many acquaintances, but no one had been able to identify it.

One Sunday Prodyotbabu came to Tulsibabu with a camera borrowed from a nephew. There wasn't enough light in the cage, so he had come armed with a flash gun. Photography had been a hobby with him once, and he was able to summon up enough courage to point the camera at the bird in the cage and press the shutter. The scream of protest from the bird as the flash went offsent Prodyotbabu reeling back a full yard, and it struck him that the bird's cry should be recorded; showing the photograph and playing back the cry might help in the identification of the species. Something rankled in Prodyotbabu's mind; he hadn't yet mentioned it to Tulsibabu but somewhere in a book or a magazine he had seen a picture of a bird which greatly resembled this pet of Tulsibabu's. If he came across the picture again, he would compare it with the photograph.

When the two friends were having tea, Tulsibabu came out with a new piece of information. Ever since Bill had arrived, crows and sparrows had stopped coming to the flat. This was a blessing because the sparrows would build nests in the most unlikely places, while the crows would make off with food from the kitchen. All that had stopped.

'Is that so?' asked Prodyotbabu, surprised as usual.

'Well, you've been here all this time; have you seen any other birds?'

Prodyotbabu realized that he hadn't. 'But what about your two servants? Have they got used to Bill?'

'The cook never goes near the cage, but Natobar feeds it meat with pincers. Even if he does have any objection, he hasn't come out with it. And when the bird turns nasty, one sight of me calms it down. By the way, what was the idea behind taking the photograph?'

Prodyotbabu didn't mention the real reason. He said, 'When it's no more, it'll remind you of it.'

Prodyotbabu had the photograph developed and printed the following day. He also had two enlargements made. One he gave to Tulsi Babu and the other he took to the ornithologist Ranajoy Shome. Only the other day an article by Mr Shome on the birds of Sikkim had appeared in the weekly magazine *Desk*. But Mr Shome failed to identify the bird from the photograph. He asked where the bird could be seen, and Prodyotbabu answered with a barefaced lie. 'A friend of mine has sent this photograph from Osaka. He wanted me to identify the bird for him.'

Tulsibabu noted the date in his diary: February the fourteenth, 1980. Big Bill, who had been transferred from a three-and-a-half foot cage to a four-and-a-half-foot one only last month, had been guilty of a misdeed last night.

Tulsibabu had been awakened by a suspicious sound in the middle of the night. A series of hard, metallic twangs. But the sound had soon stopped and had been followed by total silence. Still, the suspicion that something was up lingered in Tulsibabu's mind.

He came out of the mosquito net. Moonlight fell on the floor through the grilled window. Tulsibabu put on his slippers, took the electric torch from the table, and came out on to the verandah.

In the beam of the torch he saw that the meshing on the cage had been ripped apart and a hole large enough for the bird to escape from had been made. The cage was now empty.

Tulsibabu's torch revealed nothing on this side of the verandah. At the opposite end, the verandah turned right towards Mr Sanyal's flat.

Tulsibabu reached the corner in a flash and swung his torch to the right.

It was just as he had feared.

Mr Sanyal's cat was now a helpless captive in Bill's beak. The shiny spots on the floor were obviously drops of blood. But the cat was still alive and thrashing its legs about.

Tulsibabu now cried out 'Bill' and the bird promptly dropped the cat from its beak.

Then it advanced with long strides, turned the corner, and went quietly back to its cage.

Even in this moment of crisis, Tulsibabu couldn't help heaving a sigh of relief.

A padlock hung on the door of Mr Sanyal's room; Mr Sanyal had left three days ago for a holiday, after the busy months of December and January when school books were printed in his press.

The best thing to do with the cat would be to toss it out of the window on to the street. Stray cats and dogs were run over every day on the streets of Calcutta; this would be just one more of them.

The rest of the night Tulsibabu couldn't sleep.

The next day Tulsibabu had to absent himself from work for an hour or so while he went to the railway booking office; he happened to know one of the booking clerks which made his task easier. Prodyotbabu had asked after the bird and Tulsibabu had replied he was fine. Then he had added after a brief reflection—'I'm thinking of framing the photo you took of it.'

On the twenty-fourth of February, Tulsibabu arrived in Jagdalpur for the second time. A packing case with Bill in it arrived in the luggage van in the same train. The case was provided with a hole for ventilation.

From Jagdalpur, Tulsibabu set off in a luggage caravan with two coolies and the case, for the precise spot in the forest where he had found the bird.

At a certain milepost on the main road, Tulsibabu got off the vehicle and, with the coolies carrying the packing case, set off for the scorched neem tree. It took nearly an hour to reach the spot. The coolies put the case down. They had already been generously tipped and told that they would have to open the packing case. This was done, and Tulsibabu was relieved to see that Bill was in fine fettle. The coolies, of course, bolted screaming at the sight of the bird, but that didn't worry Tulsibabu. His purpose had been served. Bill was looking at him with a fixed stare. Its head already touched the four and a half foot high roof of the cage. 'Goodbye, Bill.'

The sooner the parting took place the better. Tulsibabu started on his journey back to the Tempo. Tulsibabu hadn't told anybody in the office about his trip, not even Prodyotbabu, who naturally asked where he had been when he appeared at his desk on Monday. Tulsibabu replied briefly that he had been to a niece's wedding in Naihati. About a fortnight later, on a visit to Tulsibabu's place, Prodyotbabu was surprised to see the cage empty. He asked about the bird. 'It's gone,' said Tulsibabu.

Prodyotbabu naturally assumed that the bird was dead. He felt a twinge of remorse. He hadn't meant it seriously when he had said that the photo would remind Tulsibabu of his pet when it was no more; he had no idea the bird would die so soon. The photograph he had taken had been framed and was hanging on the wall of the bedroom. Tulsibabu seemed out of sorts; altogether the atmosphere was gloomy. To relieve the gloom, Prodyotbabu made a suggestion. 'We haven't been to Mansur's in a long while. What about going tonight for a meal of kebab and paratha?'

'I'm afraid I have quite lost my taste for them.' Prodyotbabu couldn't believe his ears. 'Lost your taste for kebabs? What's the matter? Aren't you well? Have you tried the herb the holy man prescribed?'

Tulsibabu said that his blood pressure had come down to normal since he tried the juice of the chakrapama. What he didn't bother to mention was that he had forgotten all about herbal medicines as long as Bill had been with him, and that he had gone back to them only a week ago.

'By the way,' remarked Prodyotbabu, 'the mention of the herb reminds me — did you read in the papers today about the forest of Dandakaranya?'

'What did the papers say?'

Tulsibabu bought a daily newspaper all right, but rarely got beyond the first page. The paper was near at hand. Prodyotbabu pointed out the news to him. The headline said 'The Terror of Dandakaranya'.

The news described a sudden and unexpected threat to the domestic animals and poultry in the village around the forests of Dandakaranya. Some unknown species of animal had started to devour them. No tigers are known to exist in that area, and proof has been found that something other than a feline species has been causing the havoc. Tigers usually drag their prey to their lairs; this particular beast doesn't. The shikaris engaged by the Madhya Pradesh government had searched for a week but failed to locate any beasts capable of such carnage. As a result, panic has spread amongst the villagers. One particular villager claims that he had seen a two-legged creature running away from his cowshed. He had gone to investigate, and found his buffalo lying dead with a sizeable portion of his lower abdomen eaten away.

Tulsibabu read the news, folded the paper, and put it back on the table.

'Don't tell me you don't find anything exceptional in the story!' said Prodyotbabu.

Tulsibabu shook his head. In other words, he didn't.

Three days later a strange thing happened to Prodyotbabu.

At breakfast, his wife opened a tin of Digestive biscuits and served them to her husband with his tea.

The next moment Prodyotbabu had left the dining table and rushed out of the house.

By the time he reached his friend Animesh's flat in Ekdalia Road, he was trembling with excitement.

He snatched the newspaper away from his friend's hands, threw it aside and said panting: 'Where d'you keep your copies of *Readers' Digest*? Quick—it's most important!'

Animesh shared with millions of others a taste for *Readers' Digest*. He was greatly surprised by his friend's behaviour but scarcely had the opportunity to show it. He went to a bookcase and dragged out some dozen issues of the magazine from the bottom shelf.

'Which number are you looking for?'

Prodyotbabu took the whole bunch, flipped through the pages of issue after issue, and finally found what he was looking for.

'Yes—this is the bird. No doubt about it.' His fingers rested on a picture of a conjectural model of a bird kept in the Chicago Museum of Natural History. It showed an attendant cleaning the model with a brush.

'Andalgalornis', said Prodyotbabu, reading out the name. The name meant terror-bird. A huge prehistoric species, carnivorous, faster than a horse, and extremely ferocious.

The doubt which had crept into Prodyotbabu's mind was proved right when in the office next morning Tulsibabu came to him and said that he had to go to Dandakaranya once again, and that he would be delighted if Prodyotbabu would join him and bring his gun with him. There was too little time to obtain sleeping accommodation in the train, but that couldn't be helped as the matter was very urgent. Prodyotbabu agreed at once.

In the excitement of the pursuit, the two friends didn't mind the discomfort of the journey. Prodyotbabu said nothing about the bird in the *Readers' Digest*. He could do so later; there was plenty of time for that. Tulsibabu had in the meantime told everything to Prodyotbabu. He had also mentioned that he didn't really believe the gun would be needed; he had suggested taking it only as a precaution. Prodyotbabu, on the other hand, couldn't share his friend's optimism. He believed the gun was essential, and he was fully prepared for any eventuality. Today's paper had mentioned that the Madhya Pradesh government had announced a reward of five thousand rupees to anyone who succeeded in killing or capturing the creature, which had been declared a man-eater ever since a woodcutter's son had fallen victim to it.

In Jagdalpur, permission to shoot the creature was obtained from the conservator of forests, Mr Tirumalai. But he warned that Tulsibabu and Prodyotbabu would have to go on their own as nobody could be persuaded to go into the forest any more.

Prodyotbabu asked if any information had been received from the shikaris who had preceded them. Tirumalai turned grave. 'So far four shikaris have attempted to kill the beast. Three of them had no success. The fourth never returned.'

'Never returned?'

'No. Ever since then shikaris have been refusing to go. So you had better think twice before undertaking the trip.'

Prodyotbabu was shaken, but his friend's nonchalance brought back his courage. 'I think we will go,' he said.

This time they had to walk a little further because the taxi refused to take the dirt road which went part of the way into the forest. Tulsibabu was confident that the job would be over in two hours, and the taxi agreed to wait that long upon being given a tip of fifty rupees. The two friends set off on their quest.

It being springtime now, the forest wore a different look from the previous trips. Nature was following its course, and yet there was an unnatural silence. There were no bird calls; not even the cries of cuckoos.

As usual, Tulsibabu was carrying his shoulder bag. Prodyotbabu knew there was a packet in it, but he didn't know what it contained. Prodyotbabu himself was carrying his rifle and bullets.

As the undergrowth was thinner they could see farther into the forest. That is why the two friends were able to see from a distance the body of a man lying spreadeagled on the ground behind a jackfruit tree. Tulsibabu hadn't noticed it, and stopped only when Prodyotbabu pointed it out to him. Prodyotbabu took a firm grip on the gun and walked towards the body. Tulsibabu seemed only vaguely interested in the matter.

Prodyotbabu went halfway, and then turned back.

'You look as if you've seen a ghost,' said Tulsibabu when his friend rejoined him. 'Isn't that the missing shikari?'

'It must be,' said Prodyotbabu hoarsely. 'But it won't be easy to identify the corpse. The head's missing.'

The rest of the way they didn't speak at all.

It took one hour to reach the neem tree, which meant they must have walked at least three miles. Prodyotbabu noticed that the medicinal shrub had grown fresh leaves and was back to its old shape.

'Bill! Billie!'

There was something faintly comic about the call, and Prodyotbabu couldn't help smiling. But the next moment he realized that for Tulsibabu the call was quite natural. That he had succeeded in taming the monster bird, Prodyotbabu had seen with his own eyes.

Tulsibabu's call resounded in the forest.

'Bill! Bill! Billie!'

Now Prodyotbabu saw something stirring in the depths of the forest. It was coming towards them, and at such a speed that it seemed to grow bigger and bigger every second.

It was the monster bird.

The gun in Prodyotbabu's hand suddenly felt very heavy. He wondered if he would be able to use it at all.

The bird slowed down and approached them stealthily through the vegetation.

Andalgalornis. Prodyotbabu would never forget the name. A bird as tall as a man. Ostriches were tall too; but that was largely because of their neck. This bird's back itself was as high as an average man. In other words, the bird had grown a foot and a half in just about a month. The colour of its plumes had changed too. There were blotches of black on the purple. And the malevolent look in its amber eyes which Prodyotbabu found he could confront when the bird was in captivity, was now for him unbearably terrifying. The look was directed at its ex-master.

There was no knowing what the bird would do. Thinking its stillness to be a prelude to an attack, Prodyotbabu had made an attempt to raise the gun with his shaking hands. But the moment he did so, the bird turned its gaze at him, its feathers puffing out to give it an even more terrifying appearance.

'Lower the gun,' hissed Tulsibabu in a tone of admonition.

Prodyotbabu obeyed. Now the bird lowered its feathers too and transferred its gaze to its master.

'I don't know if you are still hungry,' said Tulsibabu, 'but I hope you will eat this because I am giving it to you.'

Tulsibabu had already brought out the packet from the bag. He now unwrapped it and tossed the contents towards the bird. It was a large chunk of meat.

'You've been the cause of my shame. I hope you will behave yourself from now on.'

Prodyotbabu saw that the bird picked up the chunk with its huge beak, and proceeded to masticate it.

'This time it really is goodbye.'

Tulsibabu turned. Prodyotbabu was afraid to turn his back on the bird, and for a while walked backwards with his eyes on the bird. When he found that the bird was making no attempt to follow him or attack him, he too turned round and joined his friend.

A week later the news came out in the papers of the end of the terror in Dandakaranya. Prodyotbabu had not mentioned anything to Tulsibabu about Andalgalornis, and the fact that the bird had been extinct for three million years. But the news in the papers today obliged him to come to his friend. 'I'm at a loss to know how it happened,' he said. 'Perhaps you may throw some light on it.'

'There's no mystery at all,' said Tulsibabu. 'I only mixed some of my medicine with the meat I gave him.'

'Medicine?'

'An extract of chakrapama. It turns one into a vegetarian. Just as it has done me.'

TIPU, THE MATHS TEACHER AND THE PINK MAN

Originally published in *Sandesh* (Puja Annual 1982) as *Anka Sir, Golapibabu aar Tipu*. The English translation by Ray was published in *Target* (August 1984). The illustrations in the story, including the Bengali calligraphy in the headpiece, are by Satyajit Ray.

অঙ্ক স্যার, গোলাপী বাবু আর টিপু

Tipu shut the geography book and glanced at the clock. He had been reading for forty-seven minutes at a stretch. Now it was thirteen minutes past three. What if he took a stroll now? It was around this time that the man had turned up the other day. He said he'd come again if Tipu had a reason to feel unhappy. Well, there was a reason now. A very good reason. What if he quietly sneaked out and took a look?

No. Mother had come out on the verandah for some reason. He heard her shooing off a crow. And then a soft, creaking noise which told him that she had set down on the arm chair. Perhaps to bask in the afternoon sun. Tipu would have to wait.

He recalled the man he had met. Tipu had never seen anyone like him before. A very small man with no hair on his face, though not a child. No child ever spoke in such a deep voice. Was he an old man then? Even that Tipu hadn't been able to make out. There

were no wrinkles on his skin, which was pink with a touch of sandalwood yellow in it. Tipu thought of him as the Pink Man. Ha hadn't known the man's name. He had asked, but the man had said, 'What's the point? You'll never be able to pronounce it without twisting your tongue.'

Tipu had felt slighted and said, 'Why should I twist my tongue when I can say "indefatigability" and "ambidextrousness" and even "floccinacinihilipilification"?'

The man had said, 'You need more than one tongue to pronounce my name.'

'You mean you have more than one tongue?'

'You don't need more than one to speak Bengali.'

The man was standing below the leafless shirish tree behind the house. There was an open meadow behind the shirish tree, and beyond it the paddy fields, and even further beyond was a range of low hills. A few days back Tipu had seen a mongoose frisking around a bush close by. Today he had come with some bits of bread to scatter by the bush to tempt back the mongoose. And then he had caught sight of the strange man below the tree. Their eyes had met and the man smiled and said, 'Hallo.'

Was he an Englishman? Tipu was afraid the conversation wouldn't go very far if he was, so for a while he just stood saying nothing. Then the man had walked up to him and said in Bengali, 'Is there anything you feel unhappy about?'

'Unhappy?'

'Unhappy.'

Tipu was greatly taken aback. No one had ever asked him such a question. He had said, 'Why, no, there's nothing I feel unhappy about.'

'Are you sure?'

'Of course I am sure.'

'But you're supposed to feel unhappy. It showed that way in the calculations.'

'What kind of calculations do you mean? I thought I'd find the mongoose, but I haven't. That makes me sorry. Is that what you mean?'

'Oh no. I mean the kind of sorrow that turns the backs of your ears green and dries up your palms.'

'You mean great sorrow?'

'Yes.'

'No. I have no great sorrow.' The man shook his head.

'Then there's no freedom for me yet.'

'Freedom? You mean you will be free only when I have great sorrow?'

The man stared at Tipu for a while and said, 'You're ten and a half years old?'

'Yes,' said Tipu.

'And your name is Tarpan Chowdhury?'

'Yes.'

'Then everything tallies.'

Tipu couldn't think where the man had all the information about him. He said, 'It's only when I'm unhappy that you'll be free?'

'Not when you're unhappy but when I've made you happy again.'

'But so many people aren't happy,' said Tipu. 'Nikunja, who comes to beg and sings with his *ektara* says there's no one in the world to care for him. He's a very sorrowful man.'

'He won't do,' said the man. 'Is there anyone else here who has the same name and is of the same age as you?'

'Most probably not. Tarpan is not a common name.'

'Then it's you I was looking for.'

Tipu was puzzled by one thing and he asked, 'What is this freedom you're talking about? You seem to be free enough to roam about.'

'But this is not the world where I belong. I have been banished here.'

'Why?'

'Why so inquisitive?'

'But I've just met you. Naturally I want to know more about you. Where you live, what you do, what your name is . . .'

'To know so much will cause you *jinjiria*.'

Actually the man hadn't said 'jinjiria', but something infinitely more difficult for Tipu to pronounce. But greatly simplified, it sounded like jinjiria. Not being sure what kind of a disease jinjiria was, Tipu didn't question the man any more. Who did the man remind him of? Rumpelstiltskin? Or the little man in Ghanghasur whom Manik had met?

Or one of the seven dwarfs in Snow White? Tipu adored fairy stories. His grandpa would bring three or four books of fairy stories every time he came from Calcutta during the Pujas. His mind would soar across the seven seas and the thirteen rivers and the thirty-six mountains as he read them. He would be a turbaned prince, with a diamond-studded sword riding forth in quest of the string of the elephant pearls, or the fearful, firebreathing dragon he had sworn to kill.

'Goodbye.'

But the Pink Man had disappeared, having broken the world record for high jump by clearing a ten-foot-high kul tree with a leap.

All this happened a month and a half ago. The man hadn't shown up in all these days. But now he should, because Tipu was truly unhappy. And the reason for this was the new maths teacher in his school, Naraharibabu.

Tipu hadn't taken to the new teacher from the very beginning. When he came into the class the very first day, the way he stood glowering at the boys made it seem as if he wanted to turn them into ashes before he began his lesson. Tipu had never seen such a bristling moustache except on a monster in a picture book he remembered. And then the booming voice. Nobody in the class was deaf, so why bellow?

But the real trouble came two days later, on Thursday. It had been a cloudy day, which added a chill to an already cold December morning. During tiffin, Tipu stayed in the class to finish reading the story of Dalimkumar. Who would have guessed that the maths teacher would pass by the class just then?

'What's that you're reading, Tarpan?'

Tipu had to admit that the maths teacher had an excellent memory. It had taken him only two days to learn the names of all the boys in their class. Although he was a bit shaken, Tipu knew it wasn't wrong to read story books during recess. So he said, 'It's *Grandma's Bag of Tales*, sir.'

'Let me see.'

Tipu handed the book to the teacher. The latter leafed through it for a minute or so and said, 'Ogres eating human flesh, emerald birds on diamond trees, princes hidden in sea shells—what's all this you're reading? It's nothing but fiddle-faddle. How's it going to help you in your maths?'

'But these are stories, sir,' Tipu managed to say.

'Stories? Stories must make sense. You can't write poppycock and call them stories.'

Tipu was determined not to give up so easily. He said, 'But you have Hanuman and Jambuban in the Ramayana, sir, and Baka the demon and Hirimba the ogress in the Mahabharata, and so much else.'

'Don't be impertinent,' snarled the maths teacher. 'Those were written by sages two thousand years ago. Ganesh has an elephant's head on man's body, and Durga has ten arms—so what? They're not the same as your cock-and-bull stories. You should read the lives of great men, stories of travel and great discoveries, how humble men have gone up in the world through their own efforts. At your age, you should be reading real stories, true stories. These stories are for boys who walked barefoot to school, wrote on palm leaves with quill pens, and learnt everything by rote. Can you do all that?'

Tipu said nothing. He had no idea he'd be ticked off in such a way for reading a fairy story.

'Who else reads such books in the class?'

As a matter of fact, no one else did. Sital had once borrowed The Folk Tales of Hindustan from Tipu and returned it the next day saying, 'Lousy stuff. Not a patch on The Phantom.'

'Nobody else,' said Tipu.

'H'm . . . what's your father's name?'

'Taranath Chowdhury.'

'Where do you live?'

'Station Road. Number 5.'

'I see.'

Tipu didn't go back home directly from school. Instead, he went eastwards, beyond the mango grove to Bishnuram Das's house. Here he stood leaning against a jamrul tree observing Mr Das's white horse tethered outside the house. Bishnurambabu was the owner of a bidi factory, and rode to his office every day. He was a sprightly man, although past middle age.

Tipu was in the habit of watching the horse, and enjoyed doing so. But today he felt gloomy. He had a feeling the maths teacher was out to stop him from reading fairy stories for good. And yet he couldn't think of life without such stories. In a whole year, not a day has passed without his reading at least one of those stories which Naraharibabu called fiddle-faddle. And he never did badly in maths because he read such stories. Why, in the last exam he got forty-four out of fifty. And the last maths teacher Bhudebbabu never said he was not well up in maths.

The days being shorter in winter, Tipu was about to make for home when something made him hide quickly behind the jamrul tree.

Naraharibabu was approaching with his books and his umbrella under his arm.

'Was this the neighbourhood where he lived?' Tipu wondered. There were four or five houses after Bishnurambabu's house before the wide open stretch of Hamlatuni's field. Way back in the past, the silk factory stood in the field. The manager for a long time was one Mr Hamilton. He was something of a tyrant. After working for twenty years, he died in his bungalow by the factory. The local people had turned into Hamlatuni.

In the quickly failing light of this December afternoon, Tipu watched the maths teacher from behind the tree. What he saw surprised him a great deal. The maths teacher was stroking the horse's back while making soft endearing noises.

The front door of the house now opened with a screech, and Bishnurambabu came out with a lighted cigar in his hand.

'Namaskar!'

The maths teacher had taken his hands off the horse to put his palms together and turned to Bishnurambabu. The latter returned his greeting and said, 'What about a quick game?'

'That's why I've come,' said Naraharibabu. So he played chess too. Tipu knew that Bishnurambabu did. The maths teacher now said, 'What a splendid horse you have. Where did you get it?'

'In Calcutta. It belonged to Mr Mitter of Sovabazar. I bought it from him. Used to be a race horse. It's called Pegasus.'

Pegasus? It rang a bell in Tipu's mind, but he couldn't recall where he'd heard it.

'Pegasus?' said the maths teacher. 'What an odd name!'

'But race horses do have funny names. Happy Birthday, Shobhan Allah, Forget-me-not . . .'

'Do you ride?'

'Oh yes. It's a fine animal. Never given me any trouble.'

The maths teacher was gazing at the horse. 'I used to ride regularly at one time.'

'Really?'

'We lived in Sherpur then. Father was a doctor. He used to go on rounds on horseback and I would ride whenever I had a chance. But that was ages ago.'

'Would you like to ride?'

'You wouldn't mind?'

'Go ahead.'

Tipu watched in amazement as the maths teacher put down his books and umbrella, untied the rope and swung himself up on the back of the horse. Then with a couple of prods on the flank with his shoes, he set the beast trotting.

'Don't go too far.'

'You get the chessmen ready. I'll be back in no time.'

Tipu set off homewards. It had been quite a day.

But there were more surprises in store for him . . .

It was a little after seven when Tipu finished his homework. He was just about to open a story book when his father called him from downstairs.

Tipu went down to the drawing room and found the maths teacher sitting with his father. His heart stopped beating. 'The books that your grandpa gave you,' said his father, 'Naraharibabu would like to see them.'

Tipu brought the books down. Twenty-seven in all. He had to make three trips. For ten minutes or so the maths teacher glanced through the books. He would shake his head now and then and click his tongue. Then he put aside the books, turned to Tipu's father and said, 'Listen Mr Chowdhury—what I'm going to say is the outcome of a great deal of thought on the subject. Folk tales, fairy tales and myths all do the same thing; they sow the seeds of superstition in a child's mind. Children will believe whatever they are told. Just think what a responsibility it puts on us elders. Do we tell them that the life of a human being is contained in the stomach of a boal fish when the fact is that the real place is his heart and nowhere but his heart?'

Tipu wasn't sure if his father believed all that the maths teacher was telling him, but he knew he believed in boys obeying their teachers. 'When one is your age, one must learn to obey,'—his father had told him many times—'especially one's elders. There is also a time when one does as one feels, but that comes when one has finished one's studies and stands on one's own legs. Then no one will tell you do this, do that. Or even if they did, you'd be free to do as you thought best. But the time for that is not now.'

'Aren't there any books here suitable for one of his age?' asked the maths teacher.

'Oh yes,' said Tipu's father. 'Books which I won as prizes in school. Haven't you seen them, Tipu?'

'I've read them all, Father.'

'All of them?'

'All of them. *The Life of Vidyasagar, The Life of Colonel Suresh Biswas, Captain Scott's Polar Expedition, Mungo Park's African Expedition, The Story of Steel, The Conquest of Air* . . . there aren't that many prizes you won, Father.'

'Very well,' said Father. 'I'll get you some new books.'

'If you place an order with Tirthankar Book Stall,' said the maths teacher, 'they'll get them for you from Calcutta. And those are the books you will read, Tarpan. Not these.'

Not these. The two words sounded the note of doom for Tipu. *Not these.*

And to ensure that Tipu had no more access to them, Father locked them up in his bookcase.

Mother wasn't too pleased about it, though. She kept grumbling for a while and, finally, at dinner time, she said straightaway, 'What kind of a teacher is he who carries such silly notions in his head?'

Father said 'No' three times in quick succession and added, 'You don't understand. What he said was for Tipu's own good.'

'Nonsense.'

Then she put her hand on Tipu's head and said, 'Don't worry; I'll tell you stories. I heard many from my grandma when I was your age. There are quite a few I remember.'

Tipu said nothing. The trouble was, Tipu had already heard many stories from his mother. It was unlikely that she knew any besides the ones she'd already told. And in any case, it was much more fun reading a story from a book than listening to one. It was so wonderful to get lost in a book. How could he make Mother understand?

It took Tipu two more days to realize that he was now truly unhappy. This was the sorrow that the Pink Man was talking about. He was the only one who could do something about it.

Today was Sunday. Father was having his afternoon siesta. Ma had left the verandah and was at the sewing machine in the bedroom. It was half past three. Now was the time to go out by the back door. The man should have told him where he lived. Tipu could have gone straight to him if he didn't show up.

Tipu tiptoed down the stairs and came out by the back door.

In spite of the bright sunlight, the air was cool. The paddy fields stretched like a carpet of gold right up to the hills. A dove kept calling mournfully, and chirping must be coming from the squirrel that lived on the shirish tree.

'Hallo.'

How strange! Tipu had no idea when the man had appeared below the tree.

'You're green behind the ears and your palms are dry, so it's clear you have cause to be unhappy.'

'I certainly have.'

The Pink Man moved up. He wore the same clothes as last time, and like last time the tuft of hair on his head fluttered in the breeze.

'You must tell me the cause of your sorrow, or I'd be ambifatigable.'

Tipu was ticked, but he didn't bother to correct the man. He described briefly what had happened between him and the maths teacher. He was on the verge of tears as he spoke, but he checked himself with an effort.

'H'mmm . . .' said the Pink Man and nodded sixteen times. Tipu thought he'd never stop, and it struck him that the man was probably stumped. Tears welled up in his eyes just to think what would happen if the man let him down. But the man stopped nodding and said 'H'm' again and Tipu felt relieved.

'Do you think you could help?' Tipu asked hesitantly.

'I'll have to think. I must use my stomach.'

'Stomach? Don't you use your head?'

Instead of answering, the man said, 'Didn't I see your maths teacher on horseback today?'

'Where? Near the Hamlatuni field?'

'Near the old broken-down factory.'

'Yes, yes. Is that where you live?'

'My Tridingpiditi is just behind the ruins.'

That's what the strange word sounded like, although it must have been far more complicated.

The man was still there, and he had started to nod again. This time he nodded thirty-one times. Then he stopped and said, 'It's full moon tonight. If you want to see what happens you must be there when the moon reaches the top of the date palm tree in the middle of the field. Take cover behind a bush so you're not spotted.'

Tipu had a sudden frightening thought.

'I hope you're not going to kill the maths teacher?'

For the first time the man broke into loud laughter, and Tipu saw he had two tongues in his mouth, one above the other.

'Kill him!' The man had to make a real effort to stop laughing. 'No, we don't kill anybody. It was because I had the wish to pinch someone that I was banished. They decided on Earth after some calculations, and then they calculated some more and the name of the town came up. And then your name. Now I have to make you happy again so I can go home.'

'Well, then—'

But the imp had once again leaped over the kul tree and vanished.

The tingling which Tipu felt in his nerves lasted till evening. What luck!—Ma and Pa had both been invited to dinner to Sushilbabu's for his grandson's birthday. Tipu was asked too, but the annual exams were coming up in a few days and Ma said, 'You'd better stay at home and study.'

They went out at seven-thirty. Tipu waited for five minutes and then, making sure that the eastern sky was touched with yellow, he sallied forth.

He took the short cut behind the school and reached Bishnurambabu's house in ten minutes. The horse was not there. Tipu guessed it was in the stable at the back of the house. A rectangle of light from the sitting room window fell on the road. Inside the room, cigar smoke was curling up towards the ceiling.

'Check!'

That was the maths teacher playing chess with Bishnurambabu. Wasn't he going out riding tonight? There was no way of knowing. The Pink Man had asked him to go to Hamlatuni's field. Tipu made off without a second thought.

Here was the full moon, now a disc of gold which will soon turn silver. It would take at least another ten minutes for it to reach the top of the date palm tree. The moonlight was soft but Tipu could make out the trees and the bushes. And the huddled ruins of the factory too. He wondered where behind it the Pink Man lived.

Tipu took cover behind a bush and prepared for the wait. He had brought a sweetmeat wrapped in a piece of newspaper in his pocket. He brought it out, took a bite off it, and chewed. The chorus of jackals sounded from the thickets in the far distance. Something dark whizzed by overhead. Must be an owl. Tipu had a deep brown shawl wrapped over his woollen jacket that would keep off the cold while keeping him hidden in the shadows.

He heard the faint sound of a clock chiming eight. Must be from Bishnurambabu's house.

And the next moment Tipu heard the clop-clop.

The horse was approaching. Cautiously, Tipu put out his head from behind the bush and looked intently towards the curve in the road.

Yes, there it was—the white horse with the maths teacher on its back.

But something terrible happened just then.

A mosquito had been buzzing around Tipu's head for some time, and Tipu had been trying to keep it at bay by waving his arms, but all of a sudden it found its way into his nostrils.

Tipu knew that one could keep from sneezing by pressing one's nose with one's fingers, but the thought it would trap the mosquito in his nose kept him from doing so. As a result the inevitable sneeze came and shattered the stillness of the cold December night.

The horse stopped, and the next moment the powerful beam from a torch struck Tipu full in the face.

'Tarpan!'

Tipu felt numb. He could hardly keep on his feet. What a shame! What would the Pink Man think now that he was letting him down so badly?

The horse was trotting up towards him with the maths teacher on its back when, suddenly, it reared up, almost throwing the rider off its back, let out an ear-splitting neigh, and leaped off the road on to the field.

The next moment Tipu's eyes nearly fell out of their sockets to see that the horse was no longer on the ground. It had grown wings which it waved to lift it skywards while the maths teacher crouched down with his arms clasped tightly around its neck, the lighted torch rolling on the road where it fell from his hand.

The lower rim of the full moon now touched the tip of the date palm tree, the moonlight flooded the countryside, and Bishnuram Das's flying horse fast dwindled in size as it took its rider higher and higher in the star-filled sky.

Pegasus!

It all came back to Tipu in a flash. A Greek story. The fearsome Medusa who had venomous snakes growing on her head instead of hair, turning everyone who set eyes on her into stone, until the brave Perseus chopped her head with his sword and from her blood was born the flying horse Pegasus.

'Go home now, Tarpan.' The Pink Man stood beside him, the moonlight playing on his tuft of hair. 'Everything is all right.'

The maths teacher was in the hospital for three days. There were no signs of injury on his person, but he shivered from time to time and said not a word in answer to all the questions he was asked.

On the fourth day, the maths teacher came to Tipu's house. He had a talk with Tipu's father, but Tipu never found out what was said. After he left, Father called Tipu.

'You can take your books out of my bookcase,' said Father. 'He said he had no objection to your reading them.'

Tipu never saw the Pink Man again. He had gone looking for him behind the tumbledown factory. On the way he had found Bishnuram Das's horse standing as it had always done. But he found nothing behind the ruins.

Except for a small lizard, pink in colour, darting about in the rubble.

THE DUEL

Originally published in *Sandesh* (May 1984) as *Lucknower Duel*. It was translated by
the author himself to be part of the compilation titled *Stories* (Secker & Warburg, 1987).
The illustrations in the story are by Satyajit Ray.

'Do you know what the word "duel" means?' asked Uncle Tarini.
'Oh yes,' said Napla. 'Dual means double. Some actors play dual roles in films.'
'Not that kind of dual,' Uncle Tarini said, laughing. 'D-U-E-L, not D-U-A-L.
Duel means a fight between two persons.'

'Yes, yes, of course,' we all shouted together.

'I once read up on duels out of curiosity,' went on Uncle Tarini. 'The practice of duelling spread from Italy to the rest of Europe in the sixteenth century. Swords were then part of a gentleman's dress, and sword-play or fencing was part of their education. If a person was insulted by someone, he would immediately challenge the other to a duel in order to save his own honour. Whether the honour was saved or not depended on the challenger's skill as a swordsman. But even when the skill was lacking, the duel took place because to swallow an insult was looked upon in those days as the height of cowardice.

'In the eighteenth century the pistol replaced the sword as the duelling weapon. This led to so many deaths that there was a move to pass a law against duelling. But if one ruler banned it, the next one would relax the law and duelling would rear its head again.'

Uncle Tarini took a sip of milkless tea, cleared his throat and continued.

'A duel was fought according to a set of strict rules. Such as identical weapons to be used by both parties, each to have his "second" or referee to see that no rules were broken: the obligatory gap of twenty yards between the two opponents, and both pistols to be fired the moment the challenger's second gave the command.'

As usual we were impressed with Uncle Tarini's fund of knowledge, which was little short of his fund of experience. We knew that all this rigmarole — or 'instructive information', as Uncle Tarini called it—was a prelude to yet another episode from his colourful life. All we had to do was bide our time before we would be regaled with what Uncle Tarini called fact but which struck us as being more fiction-like than fiction.

'I don't know if you are aware,' resumed Uncle Tarini, 'that a famous duel took place in our country—in fact, in Calcutta itself—two hundred years ago.'

Even Napla didn't know, so we all shook our heads.

'One of the two who fought was a world-famous person: the Governor General Warren Hastings. His adversary was Philip Francis, a member of the Viceroy's Council. Hastings had written an acrimonious letter to Francis which made the latter challenge him to a duel. You know the National Library in Alipur—the duel took place in an open spot not far from it. Since Francis was the challenger, a friend of his procured the pistols and served as his second. The pistols were both fired at the same time, but only one of the two men was felled by a bullet: Philip Francis. Luckily the wound was not fatal.'

'That's history,' said Napla. 'It's time we had a story, Uncle Tarini. Of course, living in the twentieth century, you couldn't possibly have taken part in a duel.'

'No,' said Uncle Tarini, 'but I watched one.'

'Really?'

Uncle Tarini took another sip of milkless tea, lighted an export-quality bidi and began his story.

I was then living in Lucknow. I had no regular job and no need for one because a couple of years earlier I had won a lakh and a half rupees in the Rangers Lottery. The interest on it was enough to keep me in clover. This was in 1951. Everything cost less then and, being a bachelor, one could live in comfort on six or seven hundred rupees a month.

I lived in a small bungalow on La Touche Road, wrote occasional pieces for the *Pioneer*, and paid regular visits to an auction house in Hazratgunj. In those days one could still pick up objects belonging to the time of the great Nawabs. One made a sizeable profit by buying them cheap and selling them at a good price to American tourists. I was both a dealer and a collector. Although my sitting room was small, it was crowded with objects bought at this auction house.

Going to the auction house one Sunday morning, I saw a brown mahogany box lying amongst the items to be sold. It was a foot and a half long, about eight inches wide and three inches high. I couldn't guess what it contained, and this made me very curious indeed. There were other things being auctioned, but I had my eyes only on the mahogany box.

After an hour of disposing of other objects, the auctioneer picked up the box. I sat up expectantly. The usual praises were sung. 'May I now present to you something most attractive and unique. Here you are, ladies and gentlemen, as good as new although more than a hundred years old, a pair of duelling pistols made by the famous firm of Joseph Manton. A pair without compare!'

I was immediately hooked. I had to possess those pistols. My imagination had started working. I could see the duellists facing each other, the bullets flying, and the bloody conclusion.

As my mind worked and the bidding went on, I suddenly heard a Gujarati gentleman cry out 'Seven hundred and fifty!' I at once topped it with a bid of a thousand rupees. This ended the bidding and I found myself the owner of the pistols.

Back home, I opened the box and found that the pistols were even more attractive than I thought they were in the auction house. They were truly splendid specimens of the gunsmith's art. The name of the maker was carved on the butt of each pistol. From the little I had read about weapons, I knew that Joseph Manton was a most distinguished name among the gunsmiths of eighteenth-century Britain.

I had arrived in Lucknow three months earlier. I knew there were many Bengalis living there, but I hadn't met any so far. In the evenings, I usually stayed at home writing or listening to music on the gramophone. I had just sat down at my desk to write a piece

on the Hastings—Francis encounter when the doorbell rang. Perhaps a customer? I had already built up a small reputation as a supplier of antiques.

I opened the door and found a sahib standing outside. He was in his mid-forties and looked clearly like someone who had spent a long time in India. Indeed, he could well have been an Anglo-Indian.

'Good evening.'

I returned his greeting, and he said, 'Do you have a minute? There's something I wanted to discuss with you.'

'Please come in.'

There was no trace of an Indian accent in the man's speech. He came in, and I could see him more clearly in the light of the lamp. He was a good-looking man with blue eyes, reddish-brown hair and a stout moustache. I apologized for not being able to offer him any liquor, but perhaps he would care for a cup of tea or coffee? The sahib refused saying that he had just had dinner. Then he went straight to the reason for his visit.

'I saw you at the auction house in Hazratgunj this morning.'

'Were you there too?'

'Yes, but you were probably too preoccupied to see me.'

'The fact is, my mind was on something which had caught my eye.'

'And you succeeded in acquiring it. A pair of duelling pistols made by Joseph Manton. You were very lucky.'

'Did they belong to someone you know?'

'Yes, but he has been dead for a long time. I don't know where the pistols went after his death. D'you mind if I take a look at them? I happen to know an interesting story about them . . .'

I handed him the mahogany box. He opened the lid, took out one of the pistols and held it in the light of the lamp. I could see that his eyebrows had gone up and a faraway look had come into his eyes. 'Do you know,' he said, 'that these pistols were used in a duel which was fought in this very city?'

'A duel in Lucknow!'

'Yes. It took place a hundred years ago. In fact, it will be exactly a hundred years three days from now—on October the sixteenth!'

'How extraordinary! But who fought the duel?' The sahib returned the pistols and sat down on the sofa. 'The whole thing was so vividly described to me that I can almost see it before my eyes. There was a very beautiful woman in Lucknow in those days. She was called Annabella, the daughter of Doctor Jeremiah Hudson. She was not only beautiful but also formidable in that she could ride a horse and wield a gun as well as any man. Besides this she was an accomplished singer and dancer. A young portrait painter, John Illingworth by name, had just arrived in Lucknow hoping for a commission from the Nawab himself. When he heard of Annabella's beauty, he turned up at the house of Doctor Hudson with an offer to paint her portrait. Illingworth got the commission, but before the portrait was finished he had fallen deeply in love with the sitter.

'Some time earlier, Annabella had been to a party where she had met Charles Bruce, a captain in the Bengal Regiment. Bruce too had lost his heart to Annabella at first sight.

'Soon after the party, Bruce called on Annabella at her residence. He found her seated on the verandah posing for her portrait to a stranger. Illingworth was an attractive young man and it took little time for Bruce to realize that he had a rival in the painter.'

'Now, Bruce regarded painters with scant respect. On this occasion he chose to make a remark to Illingworth in the presence of Annabella which clearly showed his attitude of disdain.'

'As befits the practitioner of a gentle art, Illingworth was of a mild disposition. Nevertheless, the insult in the presence of the woman he loved was something he couldn't swallow. He challenged Bruce to a duel forthwith. Bruce took up the challenge, and the date and time of the duel were settled on the spot. Now, I suppose you know that each participant in a duel has to have a second?'

I nodded.

'Usually the second is a friend of the challenger,' said the sahib. 'Illingworth's circle of acquaintances in Lucknow was not very large, but there was one whom he could call a friend. This was a government employee by the name of George Drummond. Drummond agreed to be his second and to procure a pair of identical pistols. On the opposite side, Charles Bruce asked his friend Philip Moxon to be his second.'

'The day of the duel drew near. Everyone knew what the outcome would be, because Charles Bruce was a superb marksman while Illingworth was not nearly as adept with the gun as with the paint brush.'

The sahib stopped. I asked him eagerly, 'Well, what was the outcome?'

The sahib smiled and said, 'You can find that out for yourself.'

'How?'

'Every year on October the sixteenth the duel is re-enacted.'

'Where?'

'In the same spot where it took place. To the east of Dilkhusha, below a tamarind tree by the river Gumti.'

'What do you mean by re-enacted?'

'Just what I say. If you were to come at six in the morning the day after tomorrow, you will see the whole incident before your eyes.'

'But that is impossible! Do you mean to say—'

'You don't have to take my word for it. All you have to do is go and see for yourself.'

'I would very much like to, but I don't think I could find my way there. I haven't been here long, you know.'

'Do you know Dilkhusha?'

'Yes, I do.'

'I will wait outside the gate of Dilkhusha at a quarter to six in the morning of October the sixteenth.'

'Very well.'

The sahib bade goodnight and left. It was then that it struck me that I hadn't asked his name. But then he didn't ask mine either. Anyway, the name wasn't important; it was what he had said that mattered. It was hard to believe that Lucknow had been the scene of such chivalry and romance, and that I was in possession of a pair of pistols which had played such an important part in it. But who really won the hand of Annabella in the end? And which of the two did she really love?

The alarm clock woke me up at five on the morning of the sixteenth. I had a cup of tea, wrapped a muffler around my neck and set off for Dilkhusha in a tonga. Dilkhusha had been at one time Nawab Sadat Ali's country house. There used to be a spacious park around it where deer roamed and into which an occasional leopard strayed from the forests nearby. Now only the shell of the house remained and a garden which was tended and open to the public.

At twenty to six I reached my destination. In my best Urdu, I told the tongawallah to wait as I would be going back home in half an hour's time.

I had to walk only a few steps from the tonga to find the sahib waiting for me below an arjun tree. He said he had arrived only five minutes ago. We started to walk.

In a few minutes we found ourselves in an open field. The view ahead was shrouded in mist. Perhaps it had been misty on the morning of the duel too.

Another minute's walk brought us to a dilapidated cottage which must have belonged to some sahib in the last century.

We stood with our backs to the ruins and faced east. In spite of the mist I could clearly make out the huge tamarind tree at some distance from us. To our right, about twenty yards away, stood a large bush. Beyond the tree and the bush I could dimly discern the river; its water reflecting the eastern sky just beginning to turn pink. The surroundings were eerily quiet.

'Can you hear it?' asked my companion suddenly.

Yes, I could. The sound of horses' hooves. I can't deny that I felt a chill in my bones. At the same time, I was gripped by the keen anticipation of a unique experience.

Now I saw the two riders. They rode down our left, pulled up below the tamarind tree and dismounted.

'Are those the two duellists?' I asked in a whisper.

'Only one of them,' said my companion. 'The taller of the two is John Illingworth, the challenger. The other is his friend and second, George Drummond. You can see Drummond is carrying the mahogany box.'

Indeed he was. I couldn't make out the faces in the mist, but I could clearly see the box. It gave me a very strange feeling to see it in the hands of someone when I knew the same box was at this very moment lying in my house locked up in my trunk.

Presently two more riders arrived and dismounted.

'The blond one is Bruce,' whispered my companion.

Drummond now consulted a pocket watch and nodded to the two protagonists. The two took their positions face to face. Then they turned right about and each took fourteen paces in the opposite direction from the other. Then they stopped, swung round and faced each other again.

The protagonists now raised their pistols and took aim. The next moment the silence was broken by Drummond's command: 'FIRE!'

The shots rang out, and I was astonished to see both Bruce and Illingworth fall to the ground.

But there was something else that caught my eye now. It was the hazy figure of a woman running out from behind the bush and disappearing into the mist away from the group around the tamarind tree.

'Well, you saw what happened,' said my companion. 'Both men were killed in the duel.'

I said, 'Very well, but who was the woman I saw running away?'

'That was Annabella.'

'Annabella?'

'Annabella had realized that Illingworth's bullet wouldn't kill Bruce, and yet she wanted both of them out of the way. So she hid behind the bush with a gun which she fired at Bruce the moment the command was given. Illingworth's bullet went wide of the mark.'

'But why did Annabella behave like that?'

'Because she loved neither of the two men. She realized that Illingworth would be killed in the duel leaving Bruce free to court her against her will. She didn't want that because she loved someone else—someone she went on to marry and find happiness with.'

I could see the scene of a hundred years ago swiftly fading before my eyes. The mist was growing thicker by the minute. I was thinking of the extraordinary Annabella when a woman's voice startled me.

'George! Georgie!'

'That's Annabella,' I heard my companion saying.

I turned to him and froze. Why was he suddenly dressed in the clothes of a hundred years ago?

'I haven't had a chance to introduce myself,' he said in a voice which seemed to come floating across a vast chasm. 'My name is George Drummond. It was me, Illingworth's friend, that Annabella really loved. Good-bye . . .'

On getting back home, I opened the mahogany box and took out the pistols once more. Their muzzles were warm to the touch, and an unmistakable smell of gunpowder assailed my nostrils.

Satyajit Ray during his art-school days at Shantiniketan
Photograph by Shambhu Shaha

SATYAJIT'S
ORIGINAL
STORIES *in English*

Illustration by Saila Chakravortty

ABSTRACTION

Original English story by Satyajit Ray published in the *Sunday Amrita Bazar Patrika*,
18 May 1941.

He was twenty-four, tall and lean. He had lean limbs, a lean face and a leaner purse. He was an artist.

The story starts at a moment when a casual observer could see him sitting on a three-legged chair in an attitude of utmost inertia. A half-consumed cigarette hung precariously from his lips, and his hands held a book which seemed to absorb all his attention.

The same observer would see nothing unusual in the scene. But a closer inspection by one not so casual would reveal the one inexplicable touch in the picture. The book in his hand was held, upside down.

This startlingly unusual way of perusing a novel is explained by the fact that he was not reading at all. He was not even looking at the book. He was merely gazing at what is called the 'middle distance'. His eyes had that particular, wide-open stare which reveals that a person is preoccupied. He was, in fact, thinking of the Exhibition.

It was an insertion in the morning papers which told him about it. The Fine Arts Exhibition, 'on a scale infinitely bigger than has hitherto been possible', was to open its doors to the public on the fifteenth of January. A wide range of subjects and an unlimited choice of medium were two conspicuous features of the Exhibition. This gave the artists considerable scope for displaying their talents.

It was this announcement about the Exhibition which occupied his mind now. So cold and matter-of-fact in print, it had proved to be an unusually exciting bit of news for him. He had waited long and patiently for an opportunity like this. It was the one and only chance of his gaining a certain amount of public recognition as a fairly adept wielder of the brush. Not that he had any illusions about his talents. Far from it. He knew that he could barely hope for an official commendation of his work, far less for one of the substantial cash prizes which were being offered. But he must see his picture hung all the same, and let the public see it.

And, of course, there is always the possibility that the critics would just happen to mention your name in the review columns. You never can tell! 'Of no little interest,' they might perhaps write, 'is Mr _____'s canvas, entitled "A Family Group". An attractive composition, executed with a judicious choice of colours . . .' and so on.

In that attitude of languid relaxation, with the inverted book in his hand, he gave himself up to meditation. He had to think out a subject for his painting.

If he had any leaning in his personal views on Art, it was towards Realism. Like a strip of adhesive tape, he stuck to it faithfully and tenaciously. Those horrible distortions of Nature which seemed to be the essence of Modern Art enraged his aesthetic sense. He dreaded that thing called Surrealism. And 'Abstractions', a term used for those fantastic combinations of lines and forms drawn with a lunatic incoherence, left him utterly cold and unmoved. Among his friends who dabbled in Art either in the capacity of amateur critics or as painters, those who were modern in their viewpoints reproached him for his narrow outlook. 'It's ridiculous, old man!' They would say, 'You can't carry on with those outmoded notions of yours! You must study and appreciate the Moderns, you have to. How can you ignore geniuses like . . .' and here an avalanche of metallic sounding names would descend upon him, which left his ears ringing but his opinion unchanged.

More than once in the past, he had made attempts to read books on Modern Art, but each time he found the pictures in them so ridiculous that it speedily rendered such attempts null and void. He remembered once having seen such an illustration. It seemed to him a rather amateurish attempt at drawing a Neanderthal woman with elephantiasis and a giraffe's neck. The title put the finishing touch to it: 'Le Beau Ideal,' it was called. He considered it the funniest joke he had ever come across.

The following day he set to work on his picture. It would be a water colour, that particular medium being his forte. He had decided about the subject during the previous evening's meditation. It was to be a pictorial representation of one of his favourite scenes from Shakespeare. He would draw Lady Macbeth walking in her sleep, and call it 'The Somnambulist.'

Never before had he felt so much enthusiasm in commencing work on a picture as he felt now. He whistled softly as he tried various colour combinations on a sheet of paper. After he had hit upon a satisfactory scheme, the actual work on the contemplated masterpiece began.

* * *

For the ten days that his picture took, he was rarely seen outside the gloomy, depressing little room which served as his studio. For the first time he was putting all his heart and soul into a picture. The patience and energy which he put into his work now was most unusual in a man so sluggish and slovenly in his ways.

The last touches were put on the fifth of January. It was approaching darkness when he finally put down his brushes and stretched his arms to relieve the tension of his muscles.

Then he went a few steps backwards and gazed at the easel from a distance, appraising the finished work.

He kept looking at it for full five minutes—his eyes half closed and his head hanging sideways. The longer he looked, the more it grew in his estimation. The colour, the expression, the composition, they all seemed to bear testimony to his inspiration.

With a sudden thrill he realized that he had excelled himself. It was a far finer thing that met his eye now than he had ever imagined himself to be capable of. It gave him a keen sense of satisfaction to know that ten days of concentrated labour had not been in vain.

But he could not afford to waste time in idle appreciation of his own work. It was the last day for sending the entries, and he must post the thing that very night. After all it was more important that the critics should see all that he saw.

Going over to the easel, he unmounted the picture and went in search of a piece of string and brown paper . . .

* * *

When he came out of the Post Office, his eyes were aching, and his temples throbbing. It was a natural reaction.

With slow, heavy steps he proceeded towards the more-secluded part of the city. He needed fresh air very badly.

The cool evening breeze did him good, and he returned home, after an hour, feeling considerably refreshed.

* * *

The following morning found him minus the last traces of fatigue. He felt like a thoroughly invigorated man. While breakfasting he had a casual glance at the newspaper. There was a small announcement by the Society of Fine Arts to the effect that they were gratified to see the unusually large number of entries they received. The Exhibition, they assured, was going to prove an unqualified success.

He had half a mind to go up and arrange his studio a bit. He knew it was in a hopeless mess, but at the same time he felt too lazy to do it. After a bit of mental argument he decided in favour of relaxation, feeling that the arrangement might come later.

It was late in the evening when he went up to his studio. Groping in the darkness for a moment, he switched on the light. The room presented a sad spectacle, with tubes thrown here and there, brushes flung far and wide in moments of haste, and little bits of rag and paper strewn all over the place.

He was surveying this chaotic confusion of objects when a sheet of paper caught his eye. It was lying on the ground just below the easel. Somehow it seemed alarmingly familiar. Stooping down, he picked it up.

For a moment the world seemed to grow dark around him, and he clutched at the easel to support himself. For his hand held his beloved masterpiece — 'The Somnambulist'; it was Lady Macbeth—his very own creation—who was staring at him now with those glassy, unseeing eyes which he had himself given her!

When the first numbing shock of surprise passed away, a mist of black, brooding despair enveloped him. It did not take him long to realize what had happened. Once more he was a victim of absent-mindedness. It was not a new thing with him. He had been guilty of it more than once in the past. But those occasional fits of preoccupation, and the consequences thereof, had always had a touch of the ludicrous in them. They never brought any serious consequences in their wake.

No, this time it was different. It was tragic and mercilessly so.

He felt sick and feverish. How the Committee must have laughed when they received a parcel which contained a stiff cardboard, and a small piece of paper with his name and the title of a picture—without the picture itself!

The cruel humour of it made him grind his teeth, and he solemnly cursed himself and his fate.

The Picture he tore to pieces and threw the bits into the wastepaper basket—

* * *

During the week that followed he made every effort to forget about the 'disaster'. To this end he resorted to all sorts of diversions which he had never tried his hand at before. He had all but succeeded when, on the morning of the fifteenth of January, the opening day of the Exhibition, he received a letter. He was breakfasting when a blue oblong envelope was handed to him. The neat crest on it revealed its source. It was a communication from the Society of Fine Arts.

He speculated momentarily on its contents before tearing open the envelope. It was most likely, he felt, that the Society was making an enquiry about the mysterious parcel. It was perhaps a mere routine with them.

Very carefully, with fingers as steady as he could manage to make them, he took the note out.

'Dear Sir,' he read, 'We feel pleasure in congratulating you . . .' It was incredible! He could hardly believe his own eyes. Briefly, in a semi-formal manner, the Society informed him that his production, 'The Somnambulist', was the proud winner of a first prize. The note concluded with an invitation to the opening ceremony of the Exhibition. His brain was in a whirl now. He felt more perplexed than pleased. The first ecstatic thrill passed away, giving way to a realization of the utter improbability of the whole thing . . .

He reached the Town Hall half an hour later, breathless and gasping with a suppressed excitement.

The imposing gates were now open to the public, and people had started coming in. He jostled past two substantial Art connoisseurs who seemed to be unnecessarily blocking the traffic.

The Exhibition was on the first floor. He raced up the magnificent carpeted staircase, taking three steps at a time.

The hall presented a truly 'colourful' spectacle. All the four walls of it were teeming with pictures—pictures of varying sizes, from the smallest miniatures to the most colossal canvases.

With a heart beating wildly with excitement he started scanning the pictures. Each of the prize-winning works had a neat label attached to its bottom, announcing the name of the artist and the title of the picture. He decided to concentrate on those little bits of paper.

After an hour's scrutiny he had exhausted the North, the East and the South walls. Landscapes, Figures, Still Life studies, Sketches in various media—nothing had escaped him. The thing was proving an ordeal for his eyes, which were now red and aching. Only his determination to solve the mystery helped him to carry on.

But it was with an ebbing enthusiasm that he faced the West wall. His heart sank lower still when he saw what confronted him. They were those dreadful, nightmarish paintings—those Abstractions!

Reluctantly—somewhat mechanically—he glanced at the label below the first picture, which was the first prize winner.

The name seemed familiar—why, it was his own name! And the title?—'The Somnambulist.'

But what was this bizarre-looking thing—this weird conglomeration of multi-coloured brush strokes? Surely, he had never drawn anything—but a sudden flash of recognition told him.

It was the paper he had tried his colour scheme on.

SHADES OF GREY

Original English story by Satyajit Ray published in the *Sunday Amrita Bazar Patrik*a, 22 March 1942.

I emerged from the musty obscurity of the second-hand bookshop and came out on the street, carrying my 'acquisition' under my arm. It was one of those gloomy, oppressive August evenings which weigh down on a person like a heavy load. But there was an unmistakable jauntiness in my steps as I walked homewards. I noticed, too, that the slight touch of the doldrums I had the day before had vanished. And why not? It was one of my luckier evenings, and my frantic search in the dusty shelves of the bookshop was rewarded with a 'find' which would make any connoisseur's mouth water. It was a rare French treatise on Chinese Ceramics—a magnificent tome . . . superbly illustrated. And the ridiculous price I paid for it! It made me wonder whether those booksellers ever care to know just what they are selling.

Musing on the prospects of a fortnight's interesting study, I took the usual turning near the Post Office. I was preoccupied, and walked, as preoccupied people are prone to do, with my eyes on the pavement. It was a sixth sense perhaps, which prompted me to look up. I looked up, and a few yards ahead of me, a strange man was walking with the pace of a crippled tortoise. On looking more carefully I had the feeling that he might not be so strange, after all. In fact, he had a slouch which vividly recalled a very close friend of mine whom I had lost touch with since a decade. I strode up close enough to have a glance at his features and verify my suspicions.

Yes, it was my long-lost friend—strangely, pathetically transformed, but still recognisable. I touched him on his shoulder, and he turned to me, startled. My God, what a change! He looked a shadow, a mere spectre of his old self. He was apparently too moved for words—and so was I. There was a cafe nearby and I dragged him into it. We chose a table in one of the dimmer and quieter corners and seated ourselves in silence.

Over a cup of tea, I threw my mind back to the past . . .

We were at school together, and at college. It was our mutual interest in, art which brought us so close together. Even while at college he had a remarkable flair for daubing paints on canvases and turning out masterpieces, one after another. I was the critic, keen, fearless and impartial, weighing every picture of his with all the precision I could command, and setting forth my frank views on them. He was a colourist par excellence—a wizard with pigments. It was wonderful the way he smeared paints on a canvas, seemingly with an utter disregard for final effects. It always made the finished thing look like a phenomenon.

But, and it is a significant 'but', like all progressive young, intellectuals of the modern age, he was a 'Leftist'. A 'Leftist', that is, in his paintings—a fact which made him an outcast from the circle of those cosy conservatives in his line. It was only natural that it should have been so, and he ignored the fact altogether. And it was only known to me how he loathed anything which smacked of the Academy.

His views on art, progressive as they were, found an echo in me. For I was a down-and-out 'Modern' myself. I could see and appreciate the vital mind that was behind all his paintings. I remembered that he had once held a public exhibition of his paintings which had ended up in a miserable fiasco, disillusioning him forever as to the heights to which the level of public intelligence was capable of rising. Thenceforth the venue of his exhibitions had been his own studio. And they were essentially a one-spectator-one-critic affair. I myself working in both the capacities.

It was not such a bad life the two of us led with our respective artistic métiers complementing each other. In his case, the question of earning money hardly arose. For his father had been a businessman of repute and had left him a considerable amount of money, which gave him enough rope to carry on. Art for Art's sake, without having to bother about how best to use it for money-making purposes. For my own part, I managed, shortly after graduation, to get the post of librarian in my own alma mater—an unfamed occupation which, nevertheless, did not stand in the way of my pursuit of art.

During the years which I had spent in close touch with him I had watched him mature with an astonishing rapidity. He had revealed such unmistakable signs of consummate genius that I was only waiting for the time when he would suddenly, inevitably leap into fame as one of the most versatile minds in the world of Modern Art. I could clearly see that it was not far off.

But I was wrong. I was very wrong. Some unforeseen thing happened which caused us to drift apart, taking him to some remote region which was far, far away from fame, from his art, from humanity.

It started in mere pleasantry. On a very cold January evening, ten years ago, I had gone over to his flat for our usual evening causerie. It was not customary for him to work in the evenings: his myopia stood in the way. But that evening he seemed to be particularly absorbed in splashing colours on a fairly big canvas—so absorbed, in fact, that he was quite unaware of my arrival. I was intrigued, and approached the easel from his back. What I saw on the canvas roused my curiosity to a degree. A magnificent figure of a woman—one of those spacious, exotic type—was being painted with the exuberance of a Renoir. He was evidently putting all his passion into the work. I hemmed significantly, and asked him who that sinuous senorita was supposed to be. Was it a creature of own imagination, or did she exist in reality? He turned to me and smiled a slow, enigmatic smile, which revealed a lot more than spoken words would have done.

With a little more sounding I got the story out of him. I had never imagined that my friend was susceptible to the softer emotions. But I was evidently wrong. It seemed that the very first sight he had of this woman had caused him to totter dangerously. But as he had made no efforts at recovering himself he was now completely out of depth. I had found it rather funny at first, and told him so. I could not bring myself to believe that he could fall for a woman who was little more than an obvious man trap. But there it was.

And it was far more serious than I thought. A week later I received a hurriedly written note which said that they were married the previous day and were heading for one of those obscure tropic isles. He would, he promised, write from there.

But the promised letter never came. Instead of it came a shocking bit of news in the form of an obituary notice in the newspaper. It recorded the death of my friend's wife—'drowned while swimming'.

I wondered what might have happened to my friend. I had a conviction that he would come back home—and to his senses. But with the passage of years it dwindled into nothingness and once more, I gave myself up to the study of Art, this time alone.

And here he was back to his old place, a sad, sombre, emaciated ghost of his former self. I had never known that he had loved his wife so much that her death could bring such a tragic transformation.

I watched him as he sipped his tea. All the vivacity, vitality of his former self seemed to have been squeezed forcibly out of him. He really looked no better than a middle-aged physical wreck, although he was hardly more than thirty-five.

It was hard to start a conversation under the circumstances. But I spoke first, asking him when he had arrived.

'This morning,' he replied, in a soulless voice. Was he putting up at his former place?

'No'—the same cold, mechanical tone.

His condition, it seemed, was anything but satisfactory. He had no money. What little he had was spent in his journey back. He had been starving the whole day, had no home, and no idea where he was going to spend the night.

So I brought him along with me to my flat. As if I could do any less for one who had once been my closest friend! Even, while staying with me he continued to be the same brooding, lifeless man as I found him. He slept little, ate even less and spoke on rare occasions. With one object in view, that of bringing him back to his old, his normal self, I placed all my art treasures at his complete disposal. But the very mention of art brought an expression of such intense resentment on his face that I had soon to give up hope, leaving it to time to heal things . . .

The great temptation for a final effort at revitalising my friend came to me one evening. Art had been pushed to the background for some time past. Owing to an unusual pressure of work in the library, it was a chance glance at a poster which brought it forcibly back to my mind. The Gallery, true to its tradition, was holding an exhibition of French paintings from Cézanne onwards.

The past came back rushing to me—the time when the two of us would spend hours in the Gallery, feasting on the glorious masterpieces which adorned their walls annually. Even after he had left me, I had gone to their exhibition every year; but somehow, I was never able to enjoy it quite as thoroughly as I did when I used to have him with me, adding his voice to my excited eulogies.

I found him sitting on an easy chair, staring vacantly at the ceiling, his legs stretched out in front of him and his arms dangling limply by his sides.

I blurted out the news without unnecessary overtures.

'The Gallery has done it again,' I announced, hoping to see some signs of enlightenment.

'Eh?' he said, looking at me, still vacantly.

I made myself a little more explicit.

'There's an exhibition on at the Gallery. Late nineteenth and twentieth century French stuff, if you want to see the details . . . It's the usual annual affair, don't you remember?'

'Exhibition?' he questioned dubiously. There was a faraway look in his eyes, as if he was trying to collect scattered memories.

It was incredible that he should forget about it all. I told him so.

'Don't tell me you've managed to forget all about those exciting hours we spent in the Gallery? Don't you remember that Matisse's 'Odalisque' you went into raptures over?'

'In any case,' I added, with an air of finality, 'you are coming with me tomorrow in the afternoon. It will be the least crowded then . . .'

We were standing in front of a masterly Seurat. The subtle, almost scientific

Illustration by Saila Chakravortty

precision of his colour harmonies reminded me of the intricate harmonies of music. I was so absorbed in the galaxy of great paintings around me that I hardly paid any attention to my friend. I was literally struck dumb by the extravagance of masterpieces.

But a glorious Cézanne loosened my tongue, and I burst into rapturous praise of it.

I wonder how long I dwelled on its merits. It struck me suddenly that my friend had not spoken a single word since we entered the hall. I turned towards him, and the expression on his face froze the eulogistic torrent in my mouth.

I had never seen a man look more a picture of stark tragedy than he did now. I feared that he might collapse any moment, so pale and ghastly did he look.

Holding him by the hand, I gently led him to the gate, and out into the street. It was approaching evening, and the vast masses of cumuli in the sky were bathed in an unearthly orange glow. I had no idea we were inside the hall so long.

'Are you ill?' I asked him. 'You're not looking well after all.'

He faced me, looking straight into my eyes for the first time since he came back.

And then he spoke:

'I must tell you all,' he said, and his voice was grave and ominous. 'I had no wish to, but I can't stand the strain any longer.'

He paused, and drew in a deep breath.

'It is not my wife's death, as you may imagine, that has brought the change in me . . . Oh! She was a wretched woman! No, it is not her death at all, for that was good riddance! It was the thing which came after it . . .'

He paused again and seemed to be making a violent effort.

'One fine morning,' he went on, 'not long after her death, I woke up from sleep and found myself looking at a strange world. Everything around me had a strangely monotonous and mouldy appearance. I jumped up from bed and looked at the mirror. My face was looking pale and bleached. I had the terrible fear that I was losing my eyesight. Trembling in mortal terror, I ran to the physician. He saw me, saw my eyes, and asked me questions. And do you know what he told me, do you know? He said I was not going blind—no, no; it was not so bad as all that—but I was going colour-blind! Imagine I—I, whose language was colour, was going colour-blind! Do you think I was too weak because I crumpled down under my own fate? Myself, I am amazed that I didn't take my own life. Perhaps I love it too dearly or I may be a coward. For what is life to me? What is art? What are Cézanne and Matisse and Renoir to a man who sees no other hue than grey—dull, drab, appalling shades of grey?'

ACKNOWLEDGEMENTS

Lolita Ray

Souradeep Ray

Indrani Majumdar

Arup K. De

Debajyoti Guha

Sourit Dey

Parimal Roy

Amitava Chakraborty

Satyaki Ghosh

Samudra Basu

Sayantan Dasgupta

Kaushik Ghosh

Shiny Das

Neeraj Nath

Rachita Raj

Aslesha Kadian

Nazaqat Ahamed

Kafeel Ahmad

Sandesh

Anandamela

Ekshan

Prostuti Parbo

Target

Now

Ananda Publishers

Secker & Warburg

Amrita Bazar Patrika

Times of India

Writers Workshop, Kolkata

CrossAsia-Repository, Heidelberg University

www.bengalichildrensbooks.in

SOCIETY FOR THE PRESERVATION OF SATYAJIT RAY ARCHIVES

PRESERVING A PRICELESS LEGACY

Sometime after the demise of Satyajit Ray, a number of actors and public personalities—Amitabh Bachchan and the late Ismail Merchant being among them—teamed up to form what is today Society for the Preservation of Satyajit Ray Archives. Popularly known as the Satyajit Ray Society, it was founded in 1994 with the objective of restoring and preserving the priceless legacies left by the master director as also disseminating his work worldwide.

RAY RESTORATION

When Ray breathed his last in 1992, negatives and prints of many of his films, especially those of his early classics, were in a precarious state. David H. Shepard, a noted film preservationist in California, came to India to examine the original negatives of the Ray films. He found the negatives of eighteen of his films in 'tatters'. Restoration of Ray films was the society's primary concern at the time. It went into a tie-up with the Los Angeles based Academy of Motion Picture Arts and Sciences, the hallowed institution which had conferred the Oscar for Lifetime Achievement on Ray. So far, a large number of the maestro's thirty-six film-oeuvre have been restored at the Academy Archive.

RAY ARCHIVES

Apart from his films, Ray left behind an astonishingly wide artistic universe comprising scripts, storyboards, posters, set, costume and book jacket designs, literary manuscripts, illustrations, music notations, advertisement artworks and so on. The society has arguably the largest and most authentic archive on Ray in its custody. A veritable treasure trove, the Ray paper archive contains almost the entire creative output of his many-faceted genius. A large part of Ray's paper legacy was restored under the supervision of Mike Wheeler, senior conservator (Paper Preservation) at the Victoria-Albert Museum, London, and is housed in his family home in Kolkata. The large personal library that Ray left and his personal effects are also being carefully preserved.

PUBLISHING RAY BOOKS

As part of the dissemination campaign, the society has begun to publish books by Ray. It brought out *Deep Focus: Reflection on Cinema*, a collection of long-lost essays by Ray, in December 2011 in collaboration with HarperCollins India. The society published, jointly with HarperCollins India, *Satyajit Ray's Ravi Shankar*, a facsimile edition of the visual script that the master director drew for his intended film on the sitar maestro. The society also brought out *Probandho Sangroho*, a collection of Bengali essays by Ray, jointly with Ananda Publishers Pvt. Ltd. on 1 May 2015. Next, the society brought out yet another book in collaboration with HarperCollins India—*The Pather Panchali Sketchbook*, which is a facsimile of the visual storyboard that Ray created for his maiden film. The last publication, which too is the outcome of the joint collaboration between the society and HarperCollins India, is *Travails with the Alien*. The book includes Ray's script for *The Alien*, a film which he wanted to make in Hollywood but failed to do so. The book was launched by Sharmila Tagore at a ceremony that the society organized on 28 April 2018 to mark the ninety-seventh birth anniversary of Satyajit Ray. Now the

Ray Society has tied up with Penguin Random House India to create the 'Penguin Ray Library' which will strive to bring out the entire oeuvre of writings created by the master. Satyajit Ray has a long association with Penguin India, and the coming together of the society with Penguin Random House India is a homecoming of sorts.

RAY MEMORIAL LECTURES

The society has been organizing lectures dedicated to Ray's memory by distinguished film personalities for quite a few years. Javed Akhtar gave the first lecture in 2009, followed by Shyam Benegal (2012) and Naseeruddin Shah (2014). Soumitra Chatterjee delivered the next lecture on the eve of Ray's ninety-fourth birth anniversary on 1 May 2015, and Aparna Sen on 1 May 2017. Sharmila Tagore delivered the lecture on 28 April 2018. In 2019, Penguin Random House India collaborated with the society to create the Annual Penguin Ray Lecture Series. On that occasion, Tarun Majumdar gave a lecture on 27 April 2019.

EXHIBITIONS, SEMINARS AND FILM SHOWS

The society has arranged quite a number of exhibitions of Ray's artworks, as also festivals of his films and seminars on his work, at home and abroad. Some of the places where such shows and film retrospectives have taken place are Kolkata, Mumbai, Delhi, Hyderabad, Bangalore, Toronto, Valladolid, San Francisco, London and Amsterdam. The Society organized its largest seminar (on *Pather Panchali*) in August 2015 in Kolkata. The participants were Sharmila Tagore, Aparna Sen, Dibakar Banerjee, Shoojit Sircar, Nandita Das, Sujoy Ghosh, Suman Mukhopadhyay and Dileep Padgaonkar. The seminar was moderated by Dhritiman Chaterji. In 2019, the society organized an exhibition to commemorate fifty years of *Goopy Gyne Bagha Byne* at Kolkata.